THE UNIVERSITY OF WINCHESTER

OXFORD HISTORICAL MONOGRAPHS

Aristocratic Women and Political Society in Victorian Britain

K. D. REYNOLDS

CLARENDON PRESS · OXFORD

1998

Oxford University Press, Great Clarendon Street, Oxford OX2 6DP

Oxford New York

Athens Auckland Bangkok Bogota Bombay Buenos Aires
Calcutta Cape Town Dar es Salaam Delhi Florence Hong Kong Istanbul
Karachi Kuala Lumpur Madras Madrid Melbourne Mexico City
Nairobi Paris Singapore Taipei Tokyo Toronto Warsaw

and associated companies in
Berlin Ibadan

Oxford is a registered trade mark of Oxford University Press

Published in the United States
by Oxford University Press Inc., New York

British Library Cataloguing in Publication Data
Data available

Library of Congress Cataloging in Publication Data
Data applied for

ISBN 0–19–820727–1

1 3 5 7 9 10 8 6 4 2

Typeset by Jayvee, Trivandrum, India
Printed in Great Britain
on acid-free paper by
Biddles Ltd., Guildford & King's Lynn

Acknowledgements

I have incurred many obligations during the preparation of this book. The Economic and Social Research Council funded the initial years of research; I am also grateful to Balliol College, Oxford, for further support.

To the owners of the manuscript collections who generously gave permission for their use, I owe many thanks: to Her Majesty the Queen for gracious permission to use the Royal Archives, Windsor; to the late duke of Atholl, the marquess of Hertford, the marquess of Londonderry, the marquess of Tweeddale, the earl of Jersey, the earl of Portsmouth, the earl of Sandwich, the countess of Sutherland, the earl of Wharncliffe, Lord Ramsay, Mr Ben Drummond Moray, the hon. Mrs Crispin Gascoigne; Olive, countess Fitzwilliam's Wentworth Settlement Trustees, and the Trustees of the Broadlands Archives. I have attempted to trace the owners of copyright; any corrections will be made in future editions.

I am also grateful to the following individuals and institutions who have made this work possible: the Master and Fellows of Balliol College, Oxford; Mrs Jane Anderson, Blair Castle Archives; the Trustees of the British Library; Buckinghamshire Record Office; Cambridgeshire County Record Office, Huntingdon; the Corporation of London: London Metropolitan Archives; the Master and Fellows, Corpus Christi College, Cambridge; the County Archivist, Durham Record Office; Hampshire Record Office; the Clerk of the Records, House of Lords; the Trustees of the National Library of Scotland; the Oriental and India Office Collections, British Library; Rhodes House Library, Oxford; the Royal Archives, Windsor; the Scottish Record Office; the Director, Sheffield City Libraries; Somerset Archive and Record Service; Dr C. M. Woolgar, the Hartley Library, University of Southampton; Staffordshire Record Office; the Master and Fellows, Trinity College, Cambridge; West Devon Record Office; the Dean and Chapter of Westminster Abbey; and the librarians and archivists of Balliol College, and of the Bodleian Library, Oxford.

A version of parts of Chapter 5 appeared as 'Politics without Feminism: The Victorian Political Hostess', in Clarissa Campbell Orr (ed.), *Wollstonecraft's Daughters: Womanhood in England and France, 1780–1920* (Manchester: Manchester University Press, 1996).

The idea for this project was originally developed at the State University of New York at Stony Brook; to the faculty there, especially Ruth Schwartz

Cowan, Fred Weinstein, and William R. Taylor, I offer belated thanks. In Oxford, Colin Matthew has supported, encouraged, and challenged me for the last eight years, and I am more than grateful. Various people have read, commented on, or listened to different stages of this project over the years; in particular I would like to record my thanks to Jane Garnett and Michael Thompson, who examined the thesis on which this book is based; Lady de Bellaigue, Elaine Chalus, Matthew Cragoe, Mary Heimann, Janet Howarth, Rosemary Mitchell, and Clarissa Campbell Orr, who have read and commented on various stages of the work. The usual caveats apply.

Friends, family, and colleagues have lived with this project, thesis and book, for a long time; for their patience, tolerance, moral support, intellectual stimulation, tea, and sympathy I thank them, especially David Bowes, Michelle Cale, John Wells, Tim Barringer, and my colleagues at the *New DNB*. My greatest debt is to my parents, who have had faith.

Contents

A Note on Names

Aristocratic names present considerable complexities for the reader, particularly those of women. For example, despite being married only once, the duchess of Sutherland was known successively as Lady Harriet Howard, Lady Gower, Lady Stafford, and the duchess of Sutherland. In most cases, I have used the woman's superior title in combination with her forename (hence, Harriet Sutherland) to identify her, even if she had not yet attained that rank. In those instances where I have used an inferior title, it has been to avoid confusion with another holder of the superior title, as, for instance, where I have used 'Frances Milton' to identify that lady as the daughter-in-law rather than the wife of the fifth earl Fitzwilliam. Male holders of titles I have identified by those titles: as there can only be one duke of Rutland at a time, there can be no confusion as to their identity.

Political Society: Gender and Power in Victorian Britain

In 1912 Lady Dorothy Nevill looked back nostalgically to her mid-Victorian youth, bemoaning the declining standards of social behaviour, the rise of the 'plutocrat', dissatisfaction among the working classes, and the excesses of the suffragettes. Unrelentingly hostile to the reduction of any form of exclusive aristocratic power and equivocal about publicly defined women's rights, she commented:

> Whilst aristocracy all over Europe, I fear, is suffering an eclipse, woman, in spite of plaints and protests, remains an aristocrat, whom no one really wishes to depose. Say what she will, she is the only being who elects without voting, governs without law, and decides without appeal.[1]

This book is an examination of the women of Lady Dorothy's own class and heyday, the aristocratic women of the first two-thirds of Victoria's reign, and the ways in which they exercised power and authority within the constraints of a patriarchal society.

Despite changes to the political system, social habits, and the economic infrastructure of society, the British aristocracy maintained a distinctive, cohesive culture during the first three-quarters of the nineteenth century, a culture which was in its very essence political. Whether Whig or Tory, English, Scottish, Welsh, or Irish, Catholic or Protestant, fabulously wealthy or merely 'comfortable', British aristocrats shared the belief that it was both their destiny and their duty to govern. The attempt to fulfil this mission dominated every facet of aristocratic life, from the design of their houses to holding office at the royal court, from their relations with tenants and dependants to their conversations over dinner. Women in these families played an important part in maintaining this political culture, not only at a local level, but also on the metropolitan and national stage.

Historians of the upper classes and of nineteenth-century politics have in recent years recognized that there are much stronger ties of continuity with the eighteenth century, at least until the 1880s, than has previously been allowed. Rather than viewing the Reform Act of 1832 as an irrevocable break with the past, ushering in an age of political modernization, bureaucracy,

---

[1] Lady Dorothy Nevill, *My Own Times* (Methuen, 1912), 129.

and, ultimately and inexorably, democracy, cogent arguments have been made for viewing the first forty years of Victoria's reign as belonging to a tradition with its roots in the Glorious Revolution of 1688, rather than as a precursor of the twentieth century.[2] Similar trends are evident in social history, and indeed in women's history, which tend to see a natural dividing point in the nineteenth century between around 1870 and 1880.[3] This study has its chronological centre in the mid-nineteenth century, between 1830 and 1880, with occasional excursions beyond both limits. The modes of operation of the aristocratic women of this period had more in common with the salons and political friendships of their mothers and grandmothers in the eighteenth century than with their granddaughters who were caught up in the age of public campaigning, suffrage, and the mass destruction of the First World War. The gradual decline of the aristocracy from the last quarter of the nineteenth century has been widely documented. After 1880, new generations of aristocrats came to abandon the view that it was their destiny and their duty to govern, and the political culture which had both justified and maintained their existence at the heart of the political nation gradually crumbled away.[4] This book is not, therefore, a study of adaptation to change, but a study of women living in accordance with a set of precepts and understandings of their world which would have been familiar, in broad outline at least, to aristocratic women for many centuries.

Histories of the British aristocracy have tended to push women to the sidelines, while political historians only infrequently see any place for women at all. This book demonstrates that the belief that 'wealth, status, power, and class consciousness' were 'masculine assets and attributes' is mistaken, but the belief is widely held.[5] Historians of landed estates have considered women predominantly as transmitters of property, whose significance consisted in marriage settlements, the production of heirs, and the

---

[2] See e.g. Jonathan Parry, *The Rise and Fall of Liberal Government in Victorian Britain* (New Haven: Yale University Press, 1993); the debate is summarized in Richard Price, 'Historiography, Narrative and the Nineteenth Century', *Journal of British Studies*, 35(Apr. 1996), 220–56.

[3] e.g. Jose Harris, *Private Lives, Public Spirit: Britain 1870–1914* (Oxford: Oxford University Press, 1993); Jane Lewis, *Women in England, 1870–1950: Sexual Divisions and Social Change* (Brighton: Wheatsheaf Books, 1984); Carol Dyhouse, *Feminism and the Family in England 1880–1939* (Oxford: Blackwell, 1989).

[4] David Cannadine, *The Decline and Fall of the British Aristocracy* (New Haven: Yale University Press, 1990), is devoted to this theme, which is also developed by F. M. L. Thompson, *English Landed Society in the Nineteenth Century* (Routledge & Kegan Paul, 1971; 1st pub. 1963), chs. 10–12; J. V. Beckett, *The Aristocracy in England, 1660–1914* (Oxford: Blackwell, 1989; 1st pub. 1986), chs. 13 and 14; and, in an Irish context, Mark Bence-Jones, *The Twilight of the Ascendancy* (Constable, 1987).

[5] Cannadine, *Decline and Fall*, 7.

drain on estate finances occasioned by lengthy widowhoods.[6] At the same time, British women's history, born out of socialist and feminist movements of the 1960s and 1970s, has concentrated on the experiences of middle- and working-class women, to the exclusion of the aristocracy. This book, then, is an attempt to put women into the history of the British aristocracy, and the aristocracy into the history of British women.

The central paradigm of the historiography of British women has been the notion of 'separate spheres'—the analysis of gender roles in society through a series of binary oppositions, such as public/private, active/passive, political/domestic. Sustained criticism of this construction has come from a number of historians, prominent among them Leonore Davidoff and Catherine Hall in their influential work *Family Fortunes: Men and Women of the English Middle Class, 1780–1850* (1987), and the position of the ideology of separate spheres within historical discourse has become more equivocal, with few historians accepting it as a reflection of any kind of historical reality. Forays into postmodern theoretical approaches have offered an attractive (to some) escape from the problems of working with recalcitrant empirical data; but by positing the necessity for a constant redefinition of terms and categories, by asserting the continual flux of individual identities, and by denying the possibility of knowledge of any historical reality, they restrict the field of enquiry to one of constant linguistic critique. There is undeniable value in attempting to understand the meanings attributed by contemporaries to particular terms and categories; but attempting to limit understanding of the experiences of women in the past to linguistic analysis leaves the subject impoverished and its practitioners marginalized.[7] In the absence of a satisfactory method for categorizing social relations which does not depend on geographical and territorial tropes, I have chosen to work within an empirical tradition, to look at what aristocratic women said and did, rather than at the silences and absences in their records, and to make use of the framework of 'separate spheres'—fractured, dislocated, and

---

[6] A notable exception to this trend is Jessica Gerard, *Country House Life: Family and Servants 1815–1914* (Oxford: Blackwell, 1994).

[7] The classic statements of the postmodernist approach are Joan Wallach Scott, *Gender and the Politics of History* (New York: Columbia University Press, 1988); Denise Riley, *'Am I that Name?': Feminism and the Category of 'Women' in History* (Basingstoke: Macmillan, 1988). The opposite case is forcefully made by Joan Hoff, 'Gender: A Postmodern Category of Paralysis?', *Women's History Review*, 3 (1994), 149–68, and by June Purvis in her introduction to *idem* (ed.), *Women's History: Britain 1850–1945* (UCL Press, 1995). For the debate on separate spheres, see Linda K. Kerber, 'Separate Spheres, Female Worlds, Woman's Place: The Rhetoric of Women's History', *Journal of American History*, 75 (1988–9), 9–39; Amanda Vickery, 'Golden Age to Separate Spheres? A Review of the Categories and Chronology of English Women's History', *Historical Journal*, 36 (1993), 383–414.

inadequate as that framework is—in order to understand the activities of one small, privileged group of Victorian women, whose lives were not lived in accordance with any model yet advanced.

It has been all too frequently assumed—by feminists, as well as by their opponents—that women are predicated in all their actions by their gender, and that their identity is primarily constructed in terms of their sex. Men, by contrast, are free to construct themselves in line with (or to acquire their identities from) class, religion, race, or any other organizing concept of their choice.[8] The identity of woman as woman has been a major preoccupation of gender historians, an emphasis which, ironically, has been strengthened by the concentration of the postmodern feminist historians on challenging the stability of the notion of womanhood and the idea of the cohesive individual identity. This study attempts to reverse the emphasis, taking gendered identity for granted, at least up to a point, and looking beyond it to the ways in which women operated in the external world as members of a privileged social and political élite. The assumption of 'sisterhood', of an identity of interest based on gender rather than class, race, region, or other organizing concept, which was much employed by early feminist historians, must be modified, if not abandoned entirely, when the analysis of class and gender is extended above the middle classes. Women's experiences were—and are— by no means identical as a result of their gender, as modern feminists, particularly in the United States, have discovered both historiographically and politically. The experience of white, middle-class, heterosexual women can no longer be posited as normative in the face of research into the lives of women of different races, classes, sexual orientations, and cultures. A duchess had only as much in common with the wife of a factory worker as their respective husbands had with each other. In relation to their own families and, to an extent, their own class, aristocratic women were first and foremost women. In relation to the rest of the world, they were aristocrats first and last.

FAMILY AND FEMININE IDEALS

The degree to which early and mid-Victorian aristocratic women were influenced by the emergence of a more vigorously prescriptive feminine

---

[8] Edward Shorter, *A History of Women's Bodies* (New York: Basic Books, 1982); Carol Dyhouse, *Girls Growing Up in Late Victorian and Edwardian England* (Routledge & Kegan Paul, 1981); Deborah Gorham, *The Victorian Girl and the Feminine Ideal* (Croom Helm, 1982). The argument of Leonore Davidoff and Catherine Hall in *Family Fortunes: Men and Women of the English Middle Class, 1780–1850* (Hutchinson, 1987) that the role of women was an essential defining characteristic in the creation of the middle classes does not affect this case: class is an incidental by-product of the gendering of industrializing labour. Hence it is something that through women is attributed to men, and then reflected back on women.

ideal varied, between families, between generations, according to religious beliefs, and (an often neglected factor) according to their stage in the life cycle: a woman who had completed her childbearing was in a position to respond to situations and expectations in completely different ways to an unmarried girl or a young woman with many small children. It will become apparent that for many of the women in this study, the end of childbearing marked an opening up of horizons, and a greater importance at home and in public affairs. In their relationships with their husbands, aristocratic women were not exempt from the prescriptions offered to middle-class women: this seems to have been particularly true in religious households, where the subjugation of wife to husband apparently received divine sanction. The advice offered to Lady Cecil Talbot by her father when she married Lord Lothian could be a blueprint for a middle-class evangelical:

After the Almighty, let your husband reign in your heart. You have now no duty but to obey him. Watch his looks and fulfil all his wishes, conform yourself to his habits and inclinations. Have but one mind, have no secrets from him. Be open, unreserved with him, reserved and cautious with all other men. . . . The married life is either one of happiness or of misery, and much depends on the tact and conduct of the wife.[9]

The difference remained that aristocratic women were neither expected to, nor did they in fact, confine their entire life's activities to the care of their husbands and children. Lady Lothian might have considered it her domestic duty to obey her husband; but as the mistress of an estate, she had in addition social, spiritual, and economic obligations to tenants and dependants to fulfil, which could only indirectly or partially be construed as obedience to her husband. As a member of the governing class, her obligations could also extend to the national arena. A culture of female dependency was most pronounced in the Lothian household, and the early death of Lord Lothian in 1841 left his widow with seven children, and a sense of loss exacerbated by her previous self-subordination. The despair and sense of personal inadequacy engendered by the loss of a husband, which was later to be eloquently—and frequently—expressed by the century's most famous widow, Queen Victoria, was prefigured in Cecil Lothian's lament: 'During the ten years of my happy married life I was so entirely in the habit of relying on my dearest husband's strong and honourable mind for everything, that I hourly feel my own weakness.'[10]

[9] Charles, 2nd earl Talbot to Lady Cecil Talbot, July 1831, quoted in Cecil Kerr, *Cecil Marchioness of Lothian: A Memoir* (Sands & Co., 1922), 11–12.
[10] Cecil Lothian's journal, 12 Dec. 1841, quoted in Kerr, *Cecil . . . Lothian*, 34.

Undoubtedly, there were unhappy aristocratic marriages in which the husband tyrannized or neglected his wife. For example, the marriage of the second duke of Wellington (then Lord Douro) with Lady Elizabeth Hay was marked by his expectations of subservience, and by his anger when they were not fulfilled. When she contradicted her husband, Lady Douro was 'reproached for *self* sufficiency' for not conforming to the model of feminine obedience.[11] Other marriages failed from incompatibility, from sexual infidelity, from all the usual reasons; the habits of aristocratic society, however, made it possible for incompatible partners seldom to meet, for sexual intrigues to be carried on without publicity; in effect, for spouses to live separate lives within marriage. But, although the failed relationships should not be ignored, a great many marriages were successful, according to their own criteria: it is significant that the archives of the majority of those women examined here reveal a sense of partnership in marriage, not subjection, supporting the argument that marriages, including aristocratic ones, had become companionate by this time.[12] Reciprocal affection shines through the letters of the Palmerstons, whose marriage represented one of the great partnerships of the nineteenth century, an aspect of the prime minister's career wholly ignored even in the most recent analysis of Palmerston's political life.[13] The aristocratic practice of spouses spending long periods apart did not meet with Palmerston's approval; he remarked: 'What is the use of People being Married if they are to pass their Lives away from Each other?'[14] Sir Robert Peel's correspondence with his wife, whom he consistently addressed as 'My own dearest Love', likewise demonstrates his unhappiness at their separations.[15]

It is useful to consider these marriages in the light of the work of social anthropologists such as Shirley Ardener, who have used the term 'incorporated wives' to describe women who, with no official, professional status, nevertheless played an important part in the success (or otherwise) of their

---

[11] Elizabeth Douro to James, 10th earl of Dalhousie, 21 Dec. 1841, Dalhousie Muniments, Scottish Record Office (hereafter Dalhousie MSS), GD45/14/582, emphasis original, and *passim*.

[12] Judith Schneid Lewis, *In the Family Way: Childbearing in the British Aristocracy, 1760–1860* (New Brunswick, NJ: Rutgers University Press, 1986); Lawrence Stone, *The Family, Sex and Marriage in England 1500–1800* (Weidenfeld & Nicolson, 1977). M. Jeanne Peterson, *Family, Love and Work in the Lives of Victorian Gentlewomen* (Bloomington, Ind.: Indiana University Press, 1989), has much to say about the nature of marriage among the Victorian upper middle classes.

[13] E. D. Steele, *Palmerston and Liberalism, 1855–1865* (Cambridge: Cambridge University Press, 1991).

[14] Henry, 3rd viscount Palmerston, to Emily Palmerston, 5 Sept. 1840, Broadlands Papers, Southampton University Library (hereafter Broadlands MSS), BR23 AA/1.

[15] Sir Robert Peel to Lady Peel, 14 Dec. 1841, quoted in George Peel (ed.), *The Private Letters of Sir Robert Peel* (John Murray, 1920), 188.

husbands' careers.[16] This idea is more useful than one of simple partnership or of companionate marriage in a discussion of mid-Victorian aristocratic women. Partnership acknowledges nothing beyond the relationship between two individuals, while the debates about companionate marriage tend to produce polarized views, in which marriages are perceived as being based either on companionship and family affection, or on dynastic, family ambitions and projects. Incorporation implies a whole social structure (in this case a political culture) to which both partners must accommodate themselves, and does not exclude the possibility of a couple forming a loving family, while maintaining dynastic ambition and pride. Aristocratic women in this period did not normally seek careers in their own right or on their own behalf, but saw a natural role for themselves as promoters of the interests of their husbands and families. This book will examine the female half of such relationships, and attempt to assess the contributions which wives made; it should not be forgotten that they did not operate in isolation from their husbands. Nor yet should it be assumed that husbands were always the dominant partners in marriages. Martin Pugh has indicated a number of cases at the turn of the century where the wife was the guiding partner (notably Theresa, marchioness of Londonderry, and Margaret, countess of Jersey), and there are many similar examples in the period under consideration here.[17] Such dominance was not necessarily strident or openly displayed. Harriet, duchess of Sutherland's description of her marriage before the illness of her husband reveals a method of management which vested a considerable degree of authority in the duchess, while leaving the nominal headship of the household with the duke:

To ease as much business from him as I could—to tell him nothing disagreeable that was not useful—to take charge of all details—of all the trivial worries which are notwithstanding wearing,—to bear the greater [illeg.] a burden—to let all be ready to his hand—to prevent his even asking—to be cheery tho so much that was harrowing had occurred—These were light Duties of past life.[18]

Similarly, Anne, duchess of Athole,[19] was from the first the dominant partner in her marriage: she reported to her father that she had been '*trying*

---

[16] Shirley Ardener and Hilary Callan (eds.), *The Incorporated Wife* (Croom Helm, 1984), and Shirley Ardener (ed.), *Perceiving Women* (Croom Helm, 1975). Laurel Thatcher Ulrich, *Good Wives: Image and Reality in the Lives of Women in Northern New England 1650–1750* (New York: Knopf, 1980) prefers the term 'deputy husband'.

[17] Martin Pugh, *The Tories and the People 1880–1935* (Oxford: Blackwell, 1985), 47.

[18] Harriet Sutherland to W. E. Gladstone, 13 Feb. 1861, British Library Additional Manuscript (hereafter BL Add. MS) 44,325, fos. 80–3.

[19] The 6th and 7th dukes and their families chose to spell their name in this way, and I have retained their usage; all previous and subsequent dukes have used the spelling 'Atholl'.

at least to act in my new station according to what I thought was *right*, and what I hoped would eventually effect the purposes I had in mind', and saw in her husband a man 'more likely to be *led* than *driven*'. She went on to assess her future prospects, concluding that

few have married with so little cause for uneasiness as to the future, I mean as far as *that* future depends upon the habits and disposition of one's husband. *His* temper may be quick, but no one could be more *truly kind & considerate* in *every* way, & when you add to that the most perfect *candour & fairness of dealing*, surely *my* ticket in the *marriage lottery* may be considered a *prize!*[20]

As sexual partners and mothers, and as wives and daughters, gender was the defining characteristic of aristocratic women. In this domain, their biologically female functions dominated their lives, but it was not their only domain. Beyond it, they frequently used their gender as a means of self-deprecation, as a preface to the expression of opinion, as, for example, when Lady De Grey wrote to Sir Robert Peel coupling disapproval of Russell's appointment as prime minister in 1845 with the caveat that 'It is presumptuous in a foolish Woman to have an Opinion on such subjects.'[21] Charlotte Buccleuch's use of her husband's name as a reinforcement to her own opinion was in a similar vein: 'The Duke confirms my report of Mr Kennedy having constantly heard him spoken of as a most impracticable man to deal with—he has just read my letter to you & has given me permission to add this statement from him.'[22] Such language, on one level, betrays a sense of the inferiority of female opinion, which it would be rash to understate. But it acted only as a preamble to the text which followed. The aristocratic woman made a show of deference to men of her own class, but proceeded to offer her opinion, give her advice, or make her request just the same. Any real sense of incapacity on the part of the woman was thereby completely undermined. Such deference undoubtedly operated on a rhetorical level: whether it represented anything more is difficult to assess.[23]

---

[20] Anne Athole to Henry Home Drummond, 26 Nov. 1839, Abercairny Papers, Scottish Record Office (hereafter Abercairny MSS), GD24/1/532, fos. 36–40.

[21] Lady De Grey to Sir Robert Peel, 18 Dec. [1845], BL Add. MS 40,581, fos. 15–18.

[22] Charlotte Buccleuch to George, 4th earl of Aberdeen, 9 Dec. 1853, BL Add. MS 43,201, fos. 106–9.

[23] It is perhaps significant that this rhetorical device was most widely used by aristocratic women when they wanted to achieve an end (in Charlotte Buccleuch's case, the appointment of a relative), or when they were addressing men on the fringes of their social world—in both these examples, the cotton-manufacturer's son Sir Robert Peel was being addressed. See also Harriet Sutherland to Lord John Russell, 18 Mar. 1849, Russell Papers, Public Record Office, Kew (hereafter Russell MSS, PRO) 30/22/7F, and Elizabeth Argyll to W. E. Gladstone, [2 May 1870], BL Add. MS 44,426, fos. 192–3.

A culture riddled with recollections and reinventions of a chivalric tradition necessarily had a tendency to treat women, and especially women of rank, as objects of courtly admiration. Some aristocratic men succumbed to this fantasy, given ceremonial form in the Eglinton Tournament in 1839, presided over by the 'Queen of Beauty', Lady Seymour (later duchess of Somerset).[24] But the archives contain surprisingly little of the language of chivalry, or of the supposedly universal admiration for womanly women that accompanied it, particularly from the pens of aristocratic men. Benjamin Disraeli (predictably), as a non-aristocrat dependent upon the aristocracy, made most use of the trivializing language of chivalry. To the queen he made extravagant professions of subservience and obedience to her will (while actually wielding power himself, of course)[25]; Lady Londonderry he flattered with an inflated vision of her social and political authority: 'What are you going to do with Ireland?', he asked her in 1846. 'They ought to make you Queen. It is the only chance left.'[26] He regularly declared his fondness for women and expounded their virtues as patrons: 'There is nothing like female friendship—the only thing worth having,' he told Frances Anne Londonderry.[27] But even he was unable to persuade himself of the incapacity of his correspondents, particularly Lady Londonderry and Queen Victoria herself, with both of whom he had extensive correspondences on political matters, although he constantly reminded himself and the recipients of his letters of their femininity. This tactic worked extremely well with Victoria, who felt herself overburdened and in danger of losing her femininity as a result of her public duties; how the formidable Frances Anne, marchioness of Londonderry, felt is not evident.

Sexuality was at the root of gender identities, and the need to guarantee legitimate sons for the inheritance of property—of greater importance to the landowning classes than to any other—meant that sexual activity had to be controlled. This control came not in the form of directly stated restrictions, but in the codes of aristocratic propriety which governed social intercourse, codes which were to be adopted and adapted by the middle classes

---

[24] See Mark Girouard, *The Return to Camelot: Chivalry and the English Gentleman* (New Haven: Yale University Press, 1981); Philip Mason, *The English Gentleman: The Rise and Fall of an Ideal* (Deutsch, 1982); and Ian Anstruther, *The Knight and the Umbrella: An Account of the Eglinton Tournament, 1839* (Geoffrey Bles, 1963).

[25] See e.g. Elizabeth Longford, *Victoria R. I.* (Weidenfeld & Nicolson, 1987; 1st pub. 1964), 355–7.

[26] Disraeli to Frances Anne Londonderry, 26 Dec. 1846, in Lady Londonderry (Edith Vane-Tempest-Stewart) (ed.), *Letters from Benjamin Disraeli to Frances Anne, Marchioness of Londonderry, 1837–1861* (Macmillan, 1938), 22.

[27] Disraeli to Frances Anne Londonderry, 7 Jan. 1858, in ibid. 172.

during the nineteenth century.[28] The cardinal rule was that the legitimacy of the first son (and preferably the second as well) must not be in doubt. This required female virginity on marriage and fidelity in marriage until the heirs were provided. After that, fidelity was no longer a primary *social* requirement: instead discretion became the watchword. This was the code of propriety that governed the sexual licence among the Devonshire House set in the late eighteenth century, that part of Society (loosely defined, the 'upper ten thousand' who were received at court and participated in the London season) which gathered around Albert Edward, prince of Wales, in the 1870s, and of the articulate, artistic, and aristocratic group of friends known as 'the Souls' at the turn of the century.[29] Although liaisons such as those of the duchess of Manchester and Lord Hartington (and indeed those of the prince of Wales himself) were widely known in Society, they remained discreet, and were therefore accepted. The boundaries of acceptable behaviour were demonstrated when the third duke of Sutherland overstepped them in his affair with Mrs Mary Blair, earning the rebuke of the philandering prince of Wales: 'Stafford seems to have lost all sense of propriety & decency by taking his Mistress to his Wife's & Children's home.'[30] Adeline de Horsey was even less discreet in her affair with the married Lord Cardigan, riding with him in the London parks, and being widely rumoured to have had his child. Even their marriage, following the death of the first Lady Cardigan, could not restore her to social acceptability.[31]

The suggestion, however, that all, or even many, aristocratic women took advantage of this sexual licence is misleading. Most appear to have

---

[28] Leonore Davidoff, *The Best Circles: Society, Etiquette and the Season* (The Cresset Library, 1986, 1st pub. 1973).

[29] Iris Leveson Gower, *The Face without a Frown: Georgiana, Duchess of Devonshire* (Frederick Muller, 1944); Betty Askwith, *Piety and Wit: A Biography of Harriet, Countess Granville 1785–1862* (Collins, 1982); countess of Airlie (Mabell Ogilvie), *In Whig Society 1775–1818: The Correspondence of Elizabeth, Viscountess Melbourne, and Emily Lamb, Countess Cowper and afterwards Viscountess Palmerston* (Hodder & Stoughton, 1921); Christopher Hibbert, *Edward VII: A Portrait* (Allen Lane, 1976), ch. 11; Anita Leslie, *Edwardians in Love* (Hutchinson, 1972); Angela Lambert, *Unquiet Souls: The Indian Summer of the British Aristocracy 1880–1918* (Macmillan, 1984). I have followed Leonore Davidoff's usage of 'Society' to denote the participants in the London season, and 'society' for all other purposes.

[30] Albert Edward, prince of Wales, to Anne Sutherland, n.d., Sutherland Papers, Staffordshire County Record Office (hereafter Sutherland MSS (Staffs.)), D593 P/28/2, Bundle 3. See also Denis Stuart, *Dear Duchess: Millicent, Duchess of Sutherland, 1867–1955* (Victor Gollancz, 1982), 43–5.

[31] She had her revenge in the publication in 1909 of a scandalous volume of memoirs: Cardigan and Lancastre, *My Recollections* (Eveleigh Nash, 1909); see esp. 91–112. Rumours also flew about Lady Dorothy Walpole, who was hastily married off to a middle-aged cousin, Reginald Nevill. See Guy Nevill, *Exotic Groves: A Portrait of Lady Dorothy Nevill* (Salisbury: Michael Russell, 1984), ch. 2.

remained faithful to their partners, and most were concerned with maintaining the formalities of propriety, although few went as far as Charlotte, countess Canning (herself plagued with an unfaithful husband), as described by the duke of Athole in a letter to his wife: '*Wonderful to say* I had an *invite* to dine on Saturday with Lady Canning. She is the *most proper person* I ever met with. She sent me a few lines, asking me to come and dine, but her note was *sent open*!!! Ha!!! Haw!!! She <u>is</u> a *model of correctness*.'[32] (An open letter implied that the contents were blameless, as they could be read by anybody.) Indeed, the Atholes' correspondence shows little of the sexual prudery associated with the Victorians, the duke describing to his wife the view of the chorus girls' legs from the duke of Wellington's box,[33] as well as describing for her benefit a Mrs Capel, who was '*got up* after the Old Pictures you see, & always wears a low gown in the Morning, a *very low* one, & two wonderful orbs appearing, I could not take my eyes off them'.[34] But this was not for public consumption. More typically, Harriet Sutherland, inviting W. E. Gladstone to escort her to an art exhibition, had scruples as to the lateness of the hour and the publicity of the venue; and Georgiana, Lady Bloomfield, was brought up on the French dictum, 'Un homme peut braver les préjugés du monde, une femme doit s'y soumettre' (A man may fly in the face of Society's rules, a woman must submit to them).[35]

As with so much of aristocratic life, the standards for feminine behaviour were not stated until they had been breached. Judith Schneid Lewis and Pat Jalland have both discussed in detail the internal family relationships of aristocratic women between 1760 and 1914, placing their emphases on the specifically gendered identities of their subjects. The emphasis in this book is on their external relationships, those which reached beyond family and kinship networks. In these relationships, there is little discussion of proper feminine behaviour: in the mid-Victorian years, action, not analysis, sufficed.

RANK AND DUTY

Like gender, class was not a subject much discussed by aristocratic women themselves. It is a truism that it is only when challenged or insecure that thoughts turn to definitions and delineations of membership of groups, be it

---

[32] George, 6th duke of Athole, to Anne Athole, [8 July 1846], Atholl Papers, Blair Castle, Blair Atholl, Perthshire (hereafter Atholl MSS), Box 61.

[33] Athole to Anne Athole, n.d. [1846], Atholl MSS, Box 61.

[34] Athole to Anne Athole, 23 Jan. 1846, Atholl MSS, Box 61.

[35] Harriet Sutherland to Gladstone, 8 July 1861, BL Add. MS 44,325, fos. 172–3. Georgiana, Lady Bloomfield, *Reminiscences of Court and Diplomatic Life* (2 vols., Kegan Paul, Trench & Co., 1883), i. 12.

as members of a class, a profession, or a moral category.[36] The great eras of aristocratic anxiety and alarm occurred in the aftermath of the French Revolution and from the 1880s to the First World War, when aristocratic authority and status were most effectively challenged; during these periods, the upper classes were assailed by the self-doubt which led to public analysis of their roles. The intervening years, however, saw a resurgence of aristocratic confidence; women shared in this security of identity, which consequently remains, for the most part, a subtext to aristocratic life. Most discussion of the nature of aristocracy in the papers of the women studied here comes from one of two sources: either from non-aristocratic persons offering advice or flattery, or from women whose social status was not assured. The central theme which can be extracted, not just from the documents, but also from the actions of aristocratic men and women, is the sense that duty and responsibility were owed in return for privilege and power.[37] Duties of care were owed to tenants and dependants, for their physical and spiritual well-being, and for their advancement through patronage. The bishop of Durham, in thanking Frances Anne Londonderry for her gift of a church for New Seaham, pointed out that 'if Property has its duties and its responsibilities, so it has its Privileges and its pure Pleasures. For it is indeed a Privilege to be entrusted by a gracious Providence with that which may, when rightly used, be the instrument of such Blessings to others both for time and Eternity.'[38]

This comment serves not only as congratulations and thanks, but also as a reminder that the gift (which included paying the clergyman's stipend) was not more than should be expected from one in her position. A similar sentiment was expressed by Louisa, duchess of Northumberland: ' "Large Possessions" surely only make one feel that there as the cistern is larger, more ought to flow out of it, *for all*.'[39] Duties towards so many dependants could seem an enormous burden to the conscientious, and the responsibilities of rank could appear to outweigh the benefits of position to a young woman recently married into the aristocracy. Mary, countess of Minto, who had

---

[36] Davidoff, Best Circles, 37–40.

[37] David Roberts, *Paternalism in Early Victorian England* (New Brunswick, NJ: Rutgers University Press, 1979); D. C. B. Lieven, *The Aristocracy in Europe 1815–1914* (Basingstoke: Macmillan, 1992) offers a comparative perspective, useful for the reminder that the failure of the French and Russian aristocracies to recognize their reciprocal duties and obligations contributed to the violent end of their privileges and power.

[38] Bishop Longley of Durham to Frances Anne Londonderry, 2 Mar. 1859, Londonderry Estate Archives, Durham Record Office (hereafter Londonderry MSS), D/Lo/C 176 (3).

[39] Louisa Northumberland to Mary Salisbury, n.d. [1868], quoted in Lady Burghclere (Winifred Gardner) (ed.), *A Great Lady's Friendships: Letters to Mary, Marchioness of Salisbury, Countess of Derby, 1862–1890* (Macmillan, 1933), 204.

been born into the Berwickshire gentry, confided her feelings of inadequacy to her journal in 1851, forty-five years after her marriage:

All or most women are the victims of circumstance, but in no case is it marked more thoughly [sic] than in mine; the accident of a pretty face has placed me where I am, and I have always painfully felt that tho' to that account I owe all happiness of my life, yet that it was productive of the only feelings of real misery I ever experienced, & which for many years weighed so heavily on me. I mean the conviction of my utter unfitness for the position I was called on to fill.[40]

Of course, this elevated expectation of the role of the aristocracy was not always realized. Plenty of aristocrats paid only lip-service to their duties to their tenants, and many lived frivolous and exploitative lives. The land-owning classes were often criticized for absenteeism from their estates—periodically in England, but perennially in Ireland—and condemned for failing in their duties to their localities.[41] The picture of the aristocratic woman which has the greatest currency is that of the frivolous, selfish, 'social butterfly', without a serious thought or concern for anyone beyond her social circle, who might divert herself by playing the part of the 'Lady Bountiful', but who could never understand lives so unlike her own. Although there is some truth in this image, it is essentially the product of propaganda on the part of the middle classes, who were asserting their own claims to moral, social, and political leadership, on grounds very different from those of inherited land, rank, and tradition. The vision of the aristocratic woman as a childlike, unreflective, decorative appendage to a corrupt power structure represents a superimposition of the idea of femininity on to a political system by people with a vested interest in reading aristocratic lives in a negative light. The feeling of disdain was mutual, the aristocracy retaining a deep suspicion of the middle classes, despite their incorporation into the political system in 1832, and sometimes regarding them as a greater threat to the social order than the labouring masses. 'I have a leaning amongst our classes for the aristocratic element and the democratic one, the gentry and the masses,' Sir Henry Bulwer explained to Mary, countess of Derby. 'My sympathy is not bourgeois . . . [the middle class] has neither the energy nor the elevation which can carry on a Government.' These

---

[40] Mary Minto's journal (transcripts), Mar. 1851, Minto Papers, National Library of Scotland (hereafter Minto MSS), MS12011, fo. 4.

[41] Isaac Tomkins's *Thoughts upon the Aristocracy of England* (no pub., 1835), made this point, as did Lady Rose Weigall, 'Our Friends in the Village', *Macmillan's Magazine*, 20 (Oct. 1869), 519–27. See also the social protest novels of the 1840s, particularly Benjamin Disraeli, *Sybil; or, The Two Nations* (1845).

sentiments found political expression in the Tory radicalism of Disraeli's 'Young England' movement, and in the paternalism of Whig landowners.[42]

Such opinions about the nature of government and the constitution both informed and were enhanced by the social exclusivity of the aristocracy, an exclusivity which not infrequently took the form of petty snobberies and care for marks of distinction. Much historical debate has centred on the question of how far the aristocracy (and hence the political system) was open to newcomers, and the criteria for admittance.[43] Less attention has been given to the responses of the aristocracy to those persons who succeeded in gaining admission. In certain groups, hostility to newcomers remained strong, as the wailings of Lady Dorothy Nevill at the turn of the century about the declining standards in Society make plain. Anxiety about the preservation of the dignity of rank and fear of newcomers is clear in Susan Dalhousie's interrogation of her husband on his joining Peel's administration in 1845: 'I am longing to hear how Mr Gladstone treats you, it is the only point I am not satisfied about, not because he is your age and above you but because I am always afraid of these people that are not born in good rank.'[44] Those 'not born in good rank' were all very well in their place, which was not in the drawing-rooms of the aristocracy. The bourgeoise Lady Shelley drew the contempt of her hostess, Lady William Powlett, who displayed all the arrogance of which the class was capable: 'Ly Laura so justly says she is like a very disagreeable instructed [sic] Governess, whose vulgarity annihilates one.'[45] Emily, Lady Palmerston, exhibited unease when thrown into close proximity with the middle classes: 'My journey yesterday was very safe but not agreable [sic]. Dawson [her maid] and I had to get into a Carriage with four Shopkeepers, who had got excursion tickets to return Monday—but they were not acquainted with each other and none of us spoke.'[46]

Although the British aristocracy enjoyed virtually no formal privileges beyond membership of the House of Lords, such as those enjoyed at various periods by their continental counterparts,[47] small distinctions had been avail-

---

[42] Sir Henry Bulwer to Mary Derby, 5 Oct. 1866, in Burghclere (ed.), *A Great Lady's Friendships*, 88–9. See D. C. Moore, *The Politics of Deference: A Study of the Mid-Nineteenth-Century English Political System* (Hassocks: Harvester, 1976), and Peter Mandler, *Aristocratic Government in the Age of Reform: Whigs and Liberals 1830–1852* (Oxford: Clarendon Press, 1990).

[43] Beginning with Lawrence Stone and Jeanne C. Fawtier Stone, *An Open Elite? England 1540–1880* (Oxford: Clarendon Press, 1984).

[44] Susan Dalhousie to Dalhousie, [25 May 1845], Dalhousie MSS, GD45/14/591.

[45] Lady William Powlett to Sarah Jersey, 15 Nov. [?1835], Jersey Papers, Corporation of London: London Metropolitan Archives (hereafter Jersey MSS), Acc 510/482.

[46] Emily Palmerston to Palmerston, 15 Apr. 1849, Broadlands MSS, BR30.

[47] Lieven, *Aristocracy in Europe*; M. L. Bush, *The English Aristocracy: A Comparative Synthesis*

able to them, on account not of rank but of wealth or access to the channels of political power, and because of the 'sneaking kindness for a lord' which Gladstone is said to have observed as a British national characteristic.[48] It is notable that the women most interested in defending the privileges of the aristocracy and in marking out the social boundaries were often those whose status as aristocrats was least secure. For example, Lady Mary Fox, who had married out of the peerage (her title marks her as the daughter, not the wife, of a peer), bemoaned even such an apparently beneficial innovation as the penny post ('It goes so to my heart to see disappear all the little priviledges [sic], the *prestige* that we enjoyed—but low Vulgar penny wise and pound foolish ideas are the order of the day'[49]), while Lady Jane Hay, an unmarried, elderly woman, living in her brother's house, had no time for equality before the law, objecting to the sentence meted out to an aristocratic officer for striking a policeman ('I wish they had fined him 500£ instead. It is so degrading for an officer to be sent to the House of Correction, and hard labour').[50] This tendency can be seen most clearly in the case of Lady Charlotte Guest, daughter of the earl of Lindsay and wife of the Welsh ironmaster John Josiah Guest. Lady Charlotte's mother had remarried, her children's tutor, and had had more children by her second marriage. This alliance effectively excluded the earl's children from appearing in Society, and Lady Charlotte's marriage to one deemed socially inferior seemed to confirm the trend. Lady Charlotte, however, had a strong sense of the rank into which she was born, and to which she felt herself entitled, and engaged in a long campaign to gain admittance to the highest Society, in which she was ultimately successful:

> Though my husband is peculiarly formed to shine and rise, and is infinitely more eloquent than half the lordlings that I meet, and though I have my own rank which is high enough to assist me, the consciousness frequently obtrudes itself that in this aristocratic nation the word Trade conveys a taint. I am determined to overcome the prejudice, I will force them, whether or no to disguise, if they do not forget its existence in my case.[51]

It is of no small interest that it was Lady Charlotte, unsure of her position in Society, who alone among the aristocratic women examined here devoted

(Manchester: Manchester University Press, 1984); Jonathan Powis, *Aristocracy* (Oxford: Blackwell, 1984).

[48] Quoted in G. M. Young, *Portrait of an Age: Victorian Britain*, ed. and annotated by George Kitson Clark (Oxford: Oxford University Press, 1936; repr. 1977), 94.

[49] Lady Mary Fox to Sarah Jersey, 6 Feb. [1840], Jersey MSS, Acc 510/520.

[50] "Aunt Jane" [Lady Jane Hay] to Lord Charles Hay, 15 May 1851, Yester Papers, National Library of Scotland (hereafter Yester MSS), MS14446, fos. 266–9.

[51] Quoted in Revel Guest and Angela V. John, *Lady Charlotte: A Biography of the Nineteenth Century* (Weidenfeld & Nicolson, 1989), 27–8.

much explicit thought to her identity as a woman, to the compromised femininity of her role as helpmate to an industrialist husband, and as manager of the ironworks after her husband's early death.

PATRONAGE AND INFLUENCE

Aristocratic females were hardly exempt from gender roles; nor should the idea that they shared power equally with men be entertained for a moment. But there were ways in which aristocratic women could participate legitimately in affairs which fell into the 'public' domain. Furthermore, they could do so without imperilling either their gender identity or their class status. In this respect they differed greatly from most women of lesser rank. Middle-class women were not debarred from 'public' activity (particularly those activities which stemmed from charity), but engaging in work, however genteel, endangered their social position, and political or campaigning activity threatened their identity as womanly women.

If the family, rather than the individual, is given a central position in an examination of the Victorian aristocracy, the importance of women's roles in that unit becomes clear. It has been pointed out that although historians of the Victorian middle and working classes have concentrated on the family, studies of the nineteenth-century aristocracy have lagged behind in this respect.[52] Medieval and early modern historians have had no difficulty with the idea that the needs of the family could take legitimate precedence over the needs or wishes of individuals within the family.[53] Marriage, viewed in this context, was not the union of two individuals, but of two families, and the furthering of the claims of those families was the object of its members. Because of the tendency to view the nineteenth century as the era of the triumph of the individual, it is easy to disregard the continuation of a long tradition based on entirely different values in the most powerful sector of society. In these 'family projects', women, incorporated into new families by marriage, could and did play active parts, far beyond the question of alliances and the production of a suitable number of heirs (although the importance of these tasks should not be underestimated), particularly in the realm of patronage.[54]

[52] J. S. Lewis, *In the Family Way*, 4–8.

[53] See e.g. Jennifer C. Ward, *English Noblewomen in the Later Middle Ages* (Harlow: Longman, 1992); Stone and Stone, *Open Elite*; Roger Mettam, *Power and Faction in Louis XIV's France* (Oxford: Blackwell, 1988), esp. 59–65.

[54] By the nineteenth century, aristocratic women had a definite, if not a dominant, voice in determining the family alliances of their children: Davidoff, *Best Circles*, 49–50; Pat Jalland, *Women, Marriage and Politics, 1860–1914* (Oxford: Oxford University Press, 1988; 1st pub. 1986), 47–54.

The operation of patronage in Victorian Britain has received little attention from historians, except in the very limited area of electoral politics.[55]
The language of 'Old Corruption' which prevailed in the first decades of the
nineteenth century coupled with notions of progress and changing ideas of
legitimate influence led contemporaries to look for a decline in the power of
patronage, and historians have followed their lead in seeing an end to the
politics of the patron in the nineteenth century.[56] This book will not attempt
to explore the theme of the continued use of patronage fully; nor does it
aspire to analyse in depth the patron–client relationships which have been so
admirably treated for other periods and other cultures.[57] But a sense of the
prevalence of such relationships will lie beneath much of the argument. In
Victorian Britain, as in other periods and places, clients sought the assistance
of patrons in furthering their careers or those of their families, and looked to
them for employment or charity. Aristocratic women were expected to lend
glamour and prestige to social events and to charitable endeavours, in the
same way that aristocratic men were increasingly in demand to lend
respectability and financial security as figure-head directors of companies
and fiscal schemes. It is less easy to ascertain the benefits of these relationships for aristocrats in an age when a large string of retainers and clients had
little apparent function. But just as aristocrats continued to build and inhabit
vast houses as an expression of their dominance of the countryside, in com-
petition with the wealth of the *arrivistes*, and just as the exercise of hospitality continued to demonstrate their social standing, so too the ability to
advance clients, to offer them employment or the means of subsistence,
remained an index of the power of a noble family.

The perpetuation of a system in which patronage played an important part
also structured the methods of advancement for aristocratic families. The

---

[55] The exception is J. M. Bourne, *Patronage and Society in Nineteenth-Century England* (Edward
Arnold, 1986). Even he is concerned primarily with 'official' patronage. See also Mandler, *Aris-
tocratic Government*; Roberts, *Paternalism in Early Victorian England*; Alan Heesom, ' "Legitim-
ate" *versus* "Illegitimate" Influences: Aristocratic Electioneering in Mid-Victorian Britain',
Parliamentary History, 7 (1988), 283–305. On the pre-reform period, see Frank O'Gorman,
Voters, Patrons and Parties: The Unreformed Electorate of Hanoverian England, 1734–1832 (Oxford:
Clarendon Press, 1989).

[56] W. D. Rubinstein, 'The End of "Old Corruption" in Britain, 1780–1860', *Past and Present*,
101 (Nov. 1983), 55–86. Of course, eighteenth-century studies have moved a great distance
from Namier's vision of graft-inspired politics, but the new interpretations have yet to filter
much into Victorian history.

[57] Linda Levy Peck, *Court Patronage and Corruption in Early Stuart England* (Unwin Hyman,
1990); Mettam, *Power and Faction*; William Beik, *Absolutism and Society in Seventeenth-Century
France: State Power and Provincial Aristocracy in Languedoc* (Cambridge: Cambridge University
Press, 1985); Sharon Kettering, 'The Patronage Power of Early Modern French Noblewomen',
Historical Journal, 32 (Dec. 1989), 817–41.

patronage of the Crown or of a political party was necessary for advancement in the peerage and for the acquisition of lucrative and desirable appointments for individuals. Aristocratic women frequently engaged in the manipulation of patronage in the names of their families. In 1842, Charlotte Buccleuch took advantage of her connections with Peel's government (her husband was in the cabinet, and she herself served as mistress of the robes throughout the administration) to request a peerage for her brother:

> I make the request independent of the Duke, in my own name, & for my own fam-ily, there being no-one now to take any charge of the interests of our generation. This being the case, I have consented to come forward in a manner which no other con-sideration would have induced me to do.[58]

Rank, not gender, clearly marked out the duchess as the head of her genera-tion's interest in the Thynne family: at the time of the request, four brothers (one of them the third marquess of Bath) and two older sisters were still living. Concern over rank was seldom expressed in terms of personal inter-est; it was more commonly seen as a benefit acquired for future generations, in the same way as the improvement of estates and fortunes was generally viewed, at least rhetorically, as improvement held in trust for the future. In 1822, Lady Stewart petitioned the government for a peerage for herself. Her husband was heir presumptive to his brother's marquessate of Londonderry (which he in fact inherited later that year), but as he had a son by a previous marriage, her own son was not her husband's heir. As she had brought huge wealth and extensive estates into the Stewart family by her marriage, she felt herself entitled to ensure both that her own son's status would be assured and that her family property would descend to her own blood. At the same time, her distaste for the procedure was evident.

> Rank as Countess to me has been distinctly refused; but that I don't care about as, provided Henry [her son] is to be a peer, it little signifies about my being a peeress, and whether he inherits a title from his father or his mother *revient au même*. We shall see in time whether they will do anything for us, but that old beast Lord Liverpool is not an agreeable person to deal with.[59]

This request came before the 'end of Old Corruption', but the process and the sentiments are echoed throughout the Victorian period. Lady Charlotte Guest claimed that her attempts to have her place in Society recognized were not on her own account, but for her children:

---

[58] Charlotte Buccleuch to Sir Robert Peel, 12 Oct. 1842, BL Add. MS 40,516, fos. 336–9.

[59] Frances Anne Stewart to her mother, 26 Dec. 1822, quoted in Lady Londonderry (Edith Vane-Tempest-Stewart), *Frances Anne: The Life and Times of Frances Anne, Marchioness of London-derry and her Husband Charles, Third Marquess of Londonderry* (Macmillan, 1958), 115–16.

I have striven hard to place myself in the situation in life in which I was born and from which my mother's unfortunate marriage so long excluded me—and now I really believe I have accomplished it and need not henceforth toil through pleasure for the sake of Society. My children now I hope and believe will have none of those struggles to make which I have felt so humiliated by.[60]

The indices of Lady Charlotte's success were the marriages of her children, one of whom married a daughter of the duke of Marlborough, and another the daughter of the marquess of Westminster. (Her eldest son was himself created a peer as Baron Wimborne in 1880.) Placing the interests of children above their own should not, then, in this context be viewed simply as another manifestation of the practice of female self-sacrifice: rather, it was a facet of aristocratic behaviour which aimed at the furtherance of the interests of the family as a whole.

ARISTOCRATIC IDENTITY

The aristocracy is a notoriously difficult group to define. Neither rank nor economic status nor cultural attributes are sufficient to encompass and exclude in a satisfactory fashion.[61] Persons of inferior rank could be raised to the peerage; many extremely wealthy persons did not hold titles (even among landowners); and cultural criteria—attendance at public schools and Oxbridge, patronage of the arts, 'life-style'—and political influence could all be emulated by any person with enough imagination to recognize their significance, and enough money to put their ideas into effect: aristocratic political culture, although exclusive, was not impermeable. There is also the problem of the hereditary nature of the aristocracy: did it follow primogeniture, vesting only in the eldest son? And if not, through how many generations did it persist, without renewal? Defining a pool of aristocrats is thus no simple task, and the difficulties are multiplied in the case of women. Women took the status of their fathers and then, if they married, their husbands (but not vice versa). In so far as they had financial, cultural, or social status in their own right, it was generally overridden on marriage.[62] Thus, when the

---

[60] Guest and John, *Lady Charlotte*, 85.

[61] Historians seldom use the same definitions. See Beckett, *Aristocracy in England*, 16–42; Thompson, *English Landed Society*, ch. 1; John Cannon, *Aristocratic Century: The Peerage of Eighteenth-Century England* (Cambridge: Cambridge University Press, 1984), ch. 1; Cannadine, *Decline and Fall*, 8–25; Bush, *English Aristocracy*, 2–8; Powis, *Aristocracy*, 6–8; Lieven, *Aristocracy in Europe*, ch. 1; Stone and Stone, *Open Elite*, 6–9.

[62] For the property laws, see Lee Holcombe, *Wives and Property: Reform of the Married Women's Property Law in Nineteenth-Century England* (Oxford: Martin Robertson, 1983). Courtesy rank, such as that granted to the daughters of peers, could not be removed by marriage. The main exception to the rule of the wife's identity being subsumed in that of her husband was in the case of a queen regnant, whose legal identity remained separate from and superior to that

actress, widow, and former mistress of banker Thomas Coutts, Harriet Mellon, married the duke of St Albans in 1827, she became an indisputable duchess, and she was always received at court, despite the reluctance of some sections of Society to acknowledge her. (Thomas Creevey, for example, remarked of her that 'a more disgusting, frowsy, hairy old B could not have been found in the Seven Dials'.[63]) Likewise, the marriage in 1852 of Lady Adelaide Vane to her father's chaplain, Frederick Law, could not take away her rank as the daughter of the marquess of Londonderry, but the offending marriage resulted in her being cast off by her family, and excluded from aristocratic society.[64]

The most important factor in defining the aristocracy of a woman was thus the position of her male relatives. Various accounts point to the emergence of the non-working feminine ideal as an imitation of aristocratic feminine precept and practice.[65] Thus, in acquiring leisure, a woman of the middling ranks believed herself to be acquiring both social status and an enhanced femininity. It is significant that proponents of this kind of feminine ideal allied in their perfect women both femininity and social status—as, for instance, in Tennyson's 'The Princess', Ruskin's 'Queen's Gardens', and (in a heavenly parallel) Coventry Patmore's 'Angel in the House'. Such an account of the emergence of the feminine ideal fails to take into account the fact that a defining characteristic of the aristocratic male was that he did not work either. Leisure defined the aristocratic as well as the feminine.

This leads to several interesting reflections. Hostile observers picked up on the identity between aristocracy and this new version of femininity, ascribing to the class the least desirable qualities of the gender—frivolity and lack of application, corruptibility, frailty, interest in the trivial, especially clothes, and sexual weakness. In particular, they detected an increasing effeminacy in the aristocratic male, an inability or lack of will to engage in the kinds of activities—principally work—which defined the manly man.[66] Just as women were defined and restricted by their sexual personae, the aristocracy could be described in sexual terms. A second observation arising from this association of ideas is the notion that, in whatever fashion an

---

of her husband. It is one of the great ironies that Victoria never ceased to regret that she was obliged to remain legally distinct from her husband.

   [63] Quoted in Edna Healey, *Lady Unknown: The Life of Angela Burdett-Coutts* (Sidgwick & Jackson, 1978), 46.

   [64] Londonderry, *Frances Anne*, 227.

   [65] Davidoff and Hall, *Family Fortunes*, 397–401; Roszika Parker, *The Subversive Stitch: Embroidery and the Making of the Feminine* (Women's Press, 1984), ch. 6.

   [66] Thomas Carlyle promoted the idea of the nobility of work in *Past and Present* (1843), which also offers an extended critique of the aristocracy.

aristocrat spent his time, that occupation did not constitute work. Governing the country or the colonies, entertaining the county, running an estate, managing industrial enterprises based on aristocratically owned land, could not be accounted work, because they were performed by aristocrats, who by definition did not work. Moreover, the same reflection applied to those tasks carried out by women who were described as ladies. Ladies did not work, because work removed title to be called a lady. Therefore such occupations as filled their days, whether productive of money, domestic comfort, charitable benevolence, or mere decoration, could not be construed as work.

Thus, while the middle-class woman sought to abandon her labours in the family business or in the farmhouse, and to take up motherhood as a full-time occupation in accordance with evangelical advice and social aspiration,[67] a misconceived idea as to the nature of the aristocratic woman's leisure developed, leaving a wide gap between middle- and upper-class perceptions of feminine obligation and behaviour. Whatever the realities of the separation of the spheres, it was difficult for a middle-class woman to live without reference to, conflict with, obedience to, or aspiration for conformity with its doctrine. Aristocratic women were not defined in strict contrast to the men of their own class (the home / work, public / private dichotomies could not easily be drawn where neither gender went 'out' to work), and in consequence the binary oppositions had less impact on their lives. Barbara J. Harris has made this point with reference to women in the early sixteenth century:

[Aristocratic women] conflated concerns that we would label as either personal or political and virtually ignored the distinction between the public and the private. Thus women moved unselfconsciously into the world of politics as they fulfilled their responsibilities as wives, mothers and widows.[68]

Their roles were, of course, gendered, but not within the context of the oppositional and mutually exclusive categories which are widely believed to have defined the lives of middle-class women.

In order to avert some of the difficulties of definition, and in order to limit the scope of this study to those women who were recognizably aristocratic—and hence to be able to test the thesis against as consistent a group as possible, whilst recognizing the heterogeneity of the aristocracy—I will here

---

[67] The extent of their success, and indeed the extent to which they actually sought to conform to the models they were offered, are discussed at length in Davidoff and Hall, *Family Fortunes*, ch. 6, and Catherine Hall, *White, Male and Middle Class: Explorations in Feminism and History* (Cambridge: Polity Press, 1992), esp. chs. 3 and 4.

[68] Barbara J. Harris, 'Women and Politics in Early Tudor England', *Historical Journal*, 33 (June 1992), 260.

adopt the definition used by Queen Victoria in determining eligibility for service in her household. Maids of honour had to be within two degrees of the peerage (i.e. at least one grandfather had to be a peer), while ladies of the bedchamber had to be wives of peers. Although this is a somewhat arbitrary delimitation, it has the virtues of being contemporary and of being readily verifiable. Moreover, it clearly defines how far aristocracy was transmitted between generations, marking a cut-off between the aristocracy and the merely well-born. A further benefit of this definition is that it allows women who were not British by birth, but who married into the British aristocracy, and often played a significant part in Society, to be included. For example, Countess Louise von Alten of Hanover married successively the dukes of Manchester and Devonshire, and was a leader of the conservative social world from the 1860s until the turn of the century. While the period of this study pre-dates the great influx of American heiresses of the end of the century,[69] the aristocracy was cosmopolitan throughout the nineteenth century. Similarly, this book will not focus exclusively on the English aristocracy: the internal boundaries of the British Isles bore little relation to the lives of aristocrats, many of whom owned land in several of the four nations,[70] and still less to aristocratic women, whose lives were frequently trans-national.[71]

Royal women are, by and large, excluded from this study. With the exception of the queen, who saw her own position as very much opposed to current aristocratic values and *mores* (Lord Beauvale commented to his sister, Lady Palmerston, in 1846, 'There is a great wish [at court] to undervalue the Aristocracy and (I doubt not) a great willingness to see them lowered'[72]), they participated in the aristocratic culture of the period, and constituted the highest rank of the social world. At the same time, they stood apart from that world. Partly this was a matter of policy, due to the need to register a difference between sovereign and subjects, monarchy and aristocracy, and partly it was a result of differences in how the world was experienced by members of the royal family. Victoria, and by extension, her family, was at the head of Society: that position necessarily altered her relationship to it. Although the

[69] For whom see Maureen E. Montgomery, *'Gilded Prostitution': Status, Money, and Trans-atlantic Marriages, 1870–1914* (Routledge, 1989).

[70] As, for example, the marquesses of Bute, who owned land in Glamorgan, the Isle of Bute, and Ayrshire, in addition to a town house in London, while the Londonderrys owned land in England, Wales, and Ireland.

[71] As in the case of Louisa, marchioness of Waterford. Born in Paris to a branch of the (Scottish) Bute family, she grew up in Hampshire, married an Irish peer, and resided in Ireland until his death, whereupon she retired to Northumberland.

[72] Lord Beauvale to Emily Palmerston, 5 Jan. 1846, quoted in countess of Airlie (Mabell Ogilvie), *Lady Palmerston and her Times* (2 vols., Hodder & Stoughton, 1922), ii. 10.

aristocracy rigorously maintained distinctions of rank and precedence, once friendly or polite relationships were established, it operated as a society of equals. No matter how polite or friendly relationships with members of the royal family might become, there was never, on either side, any question of equality, or forgetfulness of rank. Victoria's comment that Lady Ely, one of the ladies-in-waiting with whom she enjoyed a long and close association, was 'almost one of us',[73] indicates adequately the distance which Victoria at least sought to maintain between herself and non-royal persons. Other royal females, particularly the princess of Wales and Princess Mary of Cambridge, were more inclined to go into Society than the queen, but distance was always maintained. It is therefore difficult to include royal women fully in a study of this nature, as the contradictions and exceptions outweigh the similarities. Royal women present a backdrop, a reminder that the aristocracy did not constitute the apex of the social pyramid: in a society marked by deferential behaviour, it was to the royal family that the aristocracy deferred.

At the other end of the social spectrum of the aristocracy were those women who, themselves of aristocratic birth, married out of the land-owning aristocracy, men obliged to earn their livings in the professions, in trade, or in industry. Few such women are discussed in this work (the principal exceptions being Lady Charlotte Guest and those women who married 'professional' courtiers, such as Mary Bulteel), because, like royal women, they present too many anomalies, too great a divergence from the experience of the landed aristocratic family which is my predominant concern here. An examination of the families of younger sons of the peerage, and of the patterns of their social mobility, would be a valuable exercise, but has not been undertaken here. The 'incorporation' of the women in this study was into the non-salaried, landed, and political aristocracy, rather than into any professional structure or hierarchy such as the Church, the Army or the law.

SOURCES

The irregular survival of collections of the papers of aristocratic women, and the unsystematic cataloguing of such papers where they do exist (they are usually subsumed within the papers of their husbands and sons, and are hence often difficult to trace), meant that the construction of a statistically sound sample of women with existing, accessible papers proved too problematical. Tables could be produced, but their qualifications would be longer than their contents. Concentrating chiefly, but not exclusively, on those women active in the years 1830 to 1880 whose papers are held in

---

[73] Quoted in Elizabeth Longford (ed.), *Louisa, Lady in Waiting: The Personal Diaries and Albums of Louisa, Lady in Waiting to Queen Victoria and Queen Alexandra* (Jonathan Cape, 1979), 7.

public repositories rather than private houses, I focus as far as possible on collections of women's papers (which often contain more letters to, and between, women than letters from the woman herself, along with other kinds of materials), rather than on their letters to men which are to be found scattered throughout the main (male) archives of Victorian manuscripts; the sample is thus kept wide, and women are kept at the centre of the analysis. The perspective reverses the usual pattern of placing men at the centre and women at the margins of aristocratic life, but seeks to emphasize that these women were not acting in an isolated, gender-specific sphere, but in association and co-operation with the men of their class.

It will be observed that women from Whig and Liberal families tend to predominate in this work. This was far from a deliberate choice. The initial list of women to be investigated included all those who held office at court, those who had a clear public profile as political hostesses, and wives of cabinet ministers, who were active in the period 1837–80. In addition, they had to meet the definition of aristocracy outlined above, and to have papers that were both open and accessible. In the course of the process of selection of subjects and tracking down relevant papers, it became clear that proportionally fewer Tory families met the criteria. While later in the century the court was dominated by Tories, very few of them left traceable papers (it proved impossible, for example, to find significant deposits of papers for Louise, duchess of Manchester and Devonshire, for Jane, Lady Ely, and for Jane, Lady Churchill); political hostesses were predominantly Whig and Liberal (the Tory hierarchy was perennially worried by its lack of successful hostesses, as Chapter 5 shows); and a perusal of the lists of Tory cabinet ministers between 1835 and 1880 reveals the surprising fact that only a small minority of such men had wives who met the definition of aristocracy, and that many more were either unmarried or widowed. Add to this the fact that several potentially important collections (notably those of the Rutland family and the family papers of the dukes of Wellington) remain closed to research, and the emphasis on the Whig aristocracy, while regrettable, becomes explicable.

Examination of the letters, diaries, and other papers of aristocratic women revealed a great diversity of interests which were shared to a greater or lesser extent by all the women. Beyond the preoccupation with family, friends, and social affairs common to all the women—which most men also shared, a fact that is frequently neglected—these broke down into two general levels, the local and the national, or provincial and metropolitan. The first three chapters (on household and estate management, on religion and education, and on charity) concentrate on the local level; the last two (on political hostesses and on the court) on the national level; Chapter 4, which examines the roles of aristocratic women in parliamentary elections, provides a bridge between the two. This structure enables us to begin by considering those activities, on the estates and in relation to their dependants, in which all aristocratic women participated, before discussing the more specialized roles, at court and as political hostesses, which some of them undertook additionally. The chapters also show aristocratic women in their relationships with different sections of the social hierarchy, from the very poor to the respectable labourers, from their social equals to their social superiors at court. The middle classes do not figure prominently in this study: excluded from the paternalist ethos by their financial independence, they would have had little contact with aristocratic women in the country, while in town their commercial and industrial interests were an effective barrier from the drawing-rooms of the upper classes.

The material has been treated thematically, rather than chronologically or biographically, which has the benefits of demonstrating continuity of interest across generations and drawing attention to the essential similarities of aristocratic concerns. Some themes of potential interest have not been pursued: manners and fashion, for example, and the patronage of artistic and literary production, or influence in matters of architectural taste. The areas examined here illustrate the central concerns of aristocratic life—the enhancement of family prestige, influence, and economic strength; the maintenance of a hierarchical, paternalist society; the exercise of patronage; and the government of the country. In all these interests, it has been my intention to demonstrate that aristocratic women participated, not on terms of equality with men, but in active partnership with them. The nature of the aristocratic world was such that it defies a simple division into male and female, public and private spheres; in fulfilling their roles as aristocrats, women did not attempt to meet the requirements of a dichotomized 'feminine ideal'. Trollope admirably summarized the unease with which aristocratic women could be regarded, in an assessment of his most flamboyant creation, the political hostess Lady Glencora Palliser:

There were many things about this woman that were not altogether what a husband might wish. She was not softly delicate in all her ways; but in disposition and temper she was altogether generous. I do not know that she was at all points a lady, but had Fate so willed it she would have been a thorough gentleman.[74]

---

[74] Anthony Trollope, *Can You Forgive Her?* (Penguin Classics, 1986; 1st pub. 1864–5), 523–4. See John Halperin, *Trollope and Politics: A Study of the Pallisers and Others* (Macmillan, 1977) for Trollope as a social and political observer.

1

'The Lady at their Head': Women and the Landed Estates

The construction of the home as the dominant, legitimate sphere for women by middle-class commentators from the 1790s to the 1880s has been well documented by historians both in Britain and in the United States.[1] While John Ruskin's classic exposition of the 'true nature of home' in his 1864 lecture 'Of Queens' Gardens'[2] can no longer be accepted as either definitive or descriptive, his romantic vision of the home as 'a sacred place, a vestal temple', guarded and inspired by representatives of 'pure woman-hood', continues to colour our understanding of the lives of Victorian women. The home in Ruskin's conception was not a physical location but a state of mind, of withdrawal from 'the inconsistently-minded, unknown, unloved, or hostile society of the outer world', to the 'place of peace'. It was a place of Pooter-esque values, of keeping oneself to oneself, where guests were a rarity and an unwelcome intrusion into the family circle. This ideal home had no purpose beyond the servicing of its immediate members, the nuclear family unit; in turn, the constant reproduction of home and family for its own sake—the creation of a 'haven in a heartless world', in Christopher Lasch's evocative phrase—became the normative function for women.[3] While superficially similar, aristocratic homes and families were constructed in relation to an entirely different ideological model. For aristocratic women, the meanings of home and family anteceded and were radically different from the middle-class ideal.

Historians of the family have seen the dominance of the companionate marriage and the nuclear family as the leading characteristics of nineteenth-century family life, trends which have also been noted in changing architec-

---

[1] Catherine Hall, 'The Early Formation of Victorian Domestic Ideology', in her *White, Male and Middle Class*, 75–93; Davidoff and Hall, *Family Fortunes*; Patricia Branca, *Silent Sisterhood: Middle-Class Women in the Victorian Home* (Croom Helm, 1975); Barbara Welter, 'The Cult of True Womanhood', *American Quarterly*, 18 (1966), 151–74; Kathryn Kish Sklar, *Catherine Beecher: A Study in American Domesticity* (New Haven: Yale University Press, 1973).

[2] John Ruskin, *Sesame and Lilies* (Everyman edn., 1907; first published 1864), 59–60.

[3] Christopher Lasch, *Haven in a Heartless World: The Family Besieged* (New York: Basic Books, 1977).

tural styles.[4] It would be misleading to suggest that these trends had no effect on the aristocracy—Judith Schneid Lewis has conclusively demonstrated their impact on aristocratic childbearing, for example.[5] But an older understanding of the family, as a dynastic, kinship network persisted in aristocratic circles throughout the nineteenth century. Their families did not merely consist of parents and children, tended by physically and socially distanced servants, but in large networks of relationships, bound together by kinship, patronage, and dependence (what in Scotland was, and is, aptly termed 'the connexion'). The 'Whig Cousinhood' of the first half of the century was only the most prominent (and, arguably, most successful) of these continuing networks.[6] Marriage remained a matter of dynastic alliances, with transmission of property high on the list of priorities in the selection of a mate, as the novels of the period, notably those of Anthony Trollope, amply demonstrate. The increasingly romantic ideas of marriage which young aristocratic women shared with women of the middle class could be allowed to flourish in perfect safety as the increasingly rigid mechanisms of Society and the season permitted them to meet only their social equals.[7] Even archetypally private experiences, such as pregnancy and childbirth, carried public significance among the aristocracy, where the birth of an heir, preferably male, was of paramount importance for the perpetuation of the family tradition and the transmission of its property.[8] Moreover, when an heir was satisfactorily produced, the occasion would be marked with a public celebration, involving not only the extended family, but also tenants, servants, and labourers.[9] As the significance of the family extended beyond its immediate members, so the roles of women within it had enhanced meanings. The metaphor of separate spheres can only be made to apply to aristocratic women by ignoring the ways in which public and private life converged in their experience.

[4] Stone, Family, Sex and Marriage; Randolph Trumbach, The Rise of the Egalitarian Family: Aristocratic Kinship and Domestic Relations (New York: Academic Press, 1978); Davidoff and Hall, Family Fortunes, ch. 7; Mark Girouard, Life in the English Country House: A Social and Architectural History (New Haven: Yale University Press, 1980; 1st pub. 1978).

[5] J. S. Lewis, In the Family Way, esp. ch. 1.

[6] Marjorie Villiers, The Grand Whiggery (John Murray, 1939); Mandler, Aristocratic Government, demonstrates the political consequences of such networks.

[7] Davidoff, Best Circles, 49–52. Although marriages across class lines took place, unless sweetened with great wealth, they usually ended the association of the transgressor with his or, more usually, her family. See e.g. H. V. Bayley to Sarah Jersey, n.d., Jersey MSS, Acc 510/539.

[8] J. S. Lewis, In the Family Way, 60–1. See also Consuelo Vanderbilt Balsan, The Glitter and the Gold (Maidstone, Kent: George Mann, 1973; 1st pub. 1953), 55–7.

[9] Thompson, English Landed Society, 76–7.

More importantly, the aristocratic household had functions, meaning, and consequence beyond the servicing of the immediate family, which involved aristocratic women in a variety of activities inconceivable in the introverted middle-class home. Far removed from Ruskin's 'vestal temple', where only the beloved could enter, the aristocratic household in the nineteenth century exhibited a continuity of tradition with the country houses and London palaces of previous generations. Far from being places of retreat, they were the public arena in which the aristocracy reinforced and reinvented its power, maintained their dominance over rural communities, engaged in the political life of the nation, and sought to fulfil their dynastic ambitions.[10] Not 'homes' in Ruskin's sense, the houses and households of the aristocracy, modelled on the political courts of monarchs, were sophisticated tools, used to uphold and enhance the status of the family. Aristocratic households were political structures; their relationship with the estates from which they drew their wealth also gave them an extensive economic role which had no counterpart in the bourgeois home. The country house was a 'centre of a considerable complex of social and business responsibilities':[11] in contributing to the maintenance of these households, aristocratic women simultaneously fulfilled and undermined the expectations of their gendered roles.

There is a great contrast between the actual experiences of aristocratic women in the field of domestic and estate management and the model of ideal womanhood so vigorously promoted around ideas of the home. In this they differed from women of other classes (about whom considerable scholarly energy has been expended in demonstrating the hollowness of the 'feminine ideal') less than widely held images of aristocratic females (as pampered, leisured parasites, social butterflies, or do-gooding ladies bountiful) suggest. To draw this contrast, we must establish what exactly it was that aristocratic women did in their households, on their estates, and in their families' economic enterprises. By accumulating evidence of their involvement in such activities and analysing the nature of their participation, a modified image emerges, of women active in promoting the interests and in asserting the local authority of their families.

THE HOUSEHOLD

The scale of the aristocratic household, and the commensurate size of the task of running it, differentiated it sharply from the middle-class home. Few

---

[10] See Ward, *English Noblewomen*, ch. 3; Norbert Elias, *The Court Society*, trans. Edmund Jephcott (Oxford: Blackwell, 1983; 1st pub. 1969), ch. 3; Kate Mertes, *The English Noble Household, 1250–1600: Good Governance and Politic Rule* (Oxford: Blackwell, 1988).

[11] Beckett, *Aristocracy in England*, 337.

aristocratic families restricted themselves to a single house. Most would expect to spend the social and parliamentary season in London, if not annually, then at least when they had daughters to marry or when significant activity was taking place in the House of Lords. Many owned town houses—the Jerseys lived in Berkeley Square, the Salisburys in Arlington Street, while Stafford, Devonshire, and Montagu Houses were the London residences of the dukes of Sutherland, Devonshire, and Buccleuch respectively. Less wealthy, and less regular, participants in the London season either rented houses in the fashionable districts, or put up in private hotels, such as St George's Hotel in Albemarle Street, where the duchess of Athole stayed in 1856.[12] In addition to a London base, many aristocratic families acquired, through purchase, marriage, and inheritance, a variety of country houses in different parts of the kingdom. The fashion for shooting deer and grouse and the royal patronage of Scotland made a shooting lodge in 'North Britain' a *sine qua non* of the later Victorian period. The duke of Somerset regularly lived in his houses at Maiden Bradley near Bath, Stover Lodge in Devon, and Bulstrode Park near Gerrards Cross in Buckinghamshire. The Wharncliffes' houses were Wortley Hall, near Sheffield; Belmont Castle in Perthshire, and Simonston, York. Even relatively impoverished aristocratic families, such as that of the fifth earl of Portsmouth (burdened with twelve children) maintained two country houses, Hurstbourne Park in Hampshire and Eggesford House in Devon. The aristocratic household in the nineteenth century persisted in the medieval tradition of peregrination between houses and estates, partly for reasons of fashion and variety, but more importantly as a method of reinforcing their authority and social dominance over their widespread estates.[13]

The degree to which aristocratic women were directly involved in, and responsible for, the maintenance of the household varied considerably, as did the extent to which households were subjected to a division of managerial labour along gendered lines. In larger households, such as that of the duchesses of Sutherland, daily superintendence was placed in the hands of an upper servant or agent (usually male); in such cases, the role of the aristocratic woman can be likened to that of a company director, whose competence and expectations stimulate the efficient functioning of the firm, without her becoming directly involved in the functioning of any specific department. As Harriet Sutherland's obituarist remarked: 'The ordering of a very large establishment in-door and out of doors must always be a true

---

[12] Anne Athole to Athole, n.d. [1856], Atholl MSS, Box 58.
[13] See Ward, *English Noblewomen*, ch. 3.

test of the right understanding of her duties towards her household by the Lady at their head.'[14] The importance of having a female at the head of the domestic establishment is highlighted by the practice of unmarried men and widowers calling on the services of unmarried sisters or other female relatives to oversee their establishments: Alice Balfour's supervision of the household of A. J. Balfour is one of the best-known examples.[15] In *Castle Richmond*, Trollope observed the necessity of a female at the head of the domestic arrangements of a household, for the steadying and moralizing influence of 'tea and small talk', and for the correct management of both servants and guests. In an authorial aside, he remarked: 'When I hear of a young man sitting down by himself as the master of a household, without a wife, or even without a mother or sister to guide him, I always anticipate danger.'[16]

Aristocratic women were not, either through choice or necessity, domestic figure-heads, and all involved themselves to a greater or lesser degree with the management of their households. Some personally supervised the minute details of the daily regulation of the household. Mary Minto was one such, as her correspondence with two former servants in 1847 reveals. James Garner, clearly a butler, wrote that he was 'sorry that the Spoons seem not to be right, but I think the mistake is in the 6 Egg Spoons being counted with the Tea Spoons. I understood that they had always been counted so as to make 50 altogether . . . I counted the Housekeepers Room Plate over to Mrs Smart before leaving Minto.'[17] And Martha Willis, probably a house-keeper, who had moved on to the household of the earl of Stair in Wigtownshire, was also called to account for missing property. She was 'sorry to hear that so much has been missed but there must be some mistake I am quite sure the d'oylies were right also the soap cloths dresser cloths and kitchen rubbers . . . I can truthfully say that I did not miss the linen or I should have mentioned it before leaving your Ladyship.'[18] It is hard to envisage great ladies like Harriet Sutherland worrying over the whereabouts of a few spoons and old dishcloths, but as we shall see, she too involved herself closely in the general supervision of her household and staff.

The scope for corruption in aristocratic households was immense: servants and other employees could profit from their employers' absence by purchasing additional goods and then selling them, or by appropriating materials, for example. It was for this purpose that detailed accounting

[14] *In Memoriam: Harriet, Duchess of Sutherland* (Newcastle, Staffs.: no publisher, 1872).
[15] See Jalland, *Women, Marriage and Politics*, 268–72. See also Jane Ridley and Clayre Percy (eds.), *The Letters of Arthur Balfour and Lady Elcho 1885–1917* (Hamish Hamilton, 1992), 291.
[16] Anthony Trollope, *Castle Richmond* (Oxford: World's Classics, 1989; 1st pub. 1860), 7.
[17] James Garner to Lady Minto, 21 July [1847], Minto MSS, MS11908, fos. 63–4.
[18] Martha Willis to Lady Minto, 28 July [1847], Minto MSS, MS11908, fos. 75–6.

procedures were set up in these households, which applied to purchases made outside the estate and to the transfer of goods inside the estate, from the gardens to the house, from the farms to the house and stables, and from the game preserves. When Beatrix Cadogan made enquiries about the system of board wages for servants at Gorhambury (by which the servants were paid a weekly allowance for their food, rather than being allowed to eat at the expense of the family), Elizabeth, countess of Verulam, replied that they found the system to be economical, to create less waste, and that the servants liked it, except the cook, 'and I believe the plain English of that is that she cannot get so large a profit out of the dripping and other perquisites'.[19]

In 1840, the Sutherlands' agent James Loch drew up a detailed set of regulations for the household at their Scottish seat, Dunrobin Castle, in the duke's name, with intent to control the expenditure of the establishment.[20] This example serves as a reminder that although the aristocratic woman was often depicted as the principal agent in the management of the household, the household was by no means an exclusively female domain. Not only was the direct supervision of the household in the hands of a male agent (and it is worth remembering that in the hierarchies of servants, the butler took precedence over the female establishment), but it is also clear that the duke had regular responsibilities in authorizing the expenditure of the household; the regulations of the household were given not in the name of the duchess, but of the duke.[21] Some years later, the next duchess of Sutherland produced a memorandum for the duke of Newcastle about the management of a large household, demonstrating the grasp of the system which was necessary, even for women who could delegate their authority to agents.[22] She described the finances of the household in some detail, mirroring the practice of the previous generation and pointing out by implication the dangers

[19] Elizabeth Verulam to Beatrix Cadogan, 12 Feb. [1867?], Cadogan Papers, House of Lords Record Office (hereafter Cadogan MSS), CAD/79. Henrietta Stanley of Alderley told her husband that 'Mme. de Flahault's cook might do if she has been in the country—we give 30 gns. *no perquisites* & I pay my own bills': Nancy Mitford (ed.), *The Ladies of Alderley* (Chapman and Hall, 1938), 304.

[20] 'Directions for the Regulation of the Duke of Sutherland's Household while at Dunrobin Castle', 28 July 1840, Sutherland MSS (Staffs.), D593 P/20.

[21] The exclusively female character of household management has, of course, been widely overstated. See John Tosh, 'Domesticity and Manliness in the Victorian Middle Class: The Family of Edward White Benson', in Michael Roper and John Tosh (eds.), *Manful Assertions: Masculinities in Britain since 1800* (Routledge, 1991), 44–73. See also Mertes, *English Noble Household*, 57–9, who demonstrates that the household in the medieval period was almost exclusively male, and suggests that it was only as the aristocratic household diminished in significance that it became feminized.

[22] This section is based on 'Rough Draft of Memoranda for Duke of Newcastle', [n.d.], Sutherland MS (Staffs.), D593 P/24/9/6.

of a more lax accounting procedure. Once or twice a week, order-books were submitted to the duke or his secretary, whose authority was needed for new purchases. When the bills were payable, they were sent to the secretary, who compared them with the order-books. Anne Sutherland explained the sanctions procedure against erring servants and uncooperative tradesmen which came into effect if the accounting process was abused or ignored:

If the bill contains items which do not appear in the order book strike them out of the bill & direct the tradesman to send the bill to the person who gave the irregular order & who is responsible. Tradespeople very soon fall in with this plan—and if an old one does not a new one will gladly for the sake of the custom.[23]

Despite the necessity of the duke's authority for financial transactions, Anne Sutherland had a clear grasp of the value of money and the operation of the market. The household accounts from Blair Castle (Table 1.1) give a good indication of the scale of expenditure that might be expected in a ducal household; the Atholes' self-perceived poverty meant that control over expenditure was rigorous, and from the duchess's frequent reminders to the duke about their financial situation, we can infer that she had a clear grasp of the accounts. (By contrast, Frances Anne Londonderry's Ascot week expenses in 1859 amounted to £189. 2s. 8d.—more than it cost to light Blair Castle for a whole year—which included the rent of a house and carriages, and food and drink for around forty guests and the servants.[24]) Anne Athole evidently took a direct hand in organizing the household, and demonstrated little faith in her husband's ability to take her place in her absence, as, for instance, when she was in waiting at Balmoral in 1862, wondering aloud 'if you will remember to give Seammen a *cheque* for the *Servants wages* today'.[25]

One of the most important respects in which the tasks of household management can be interpreted as having a public aspect lies in the fact that through it the aristocratic woman became a direct employer of labour on a considerable scale.[26] Census returns provide an indication of the numbers and kinds of servants employed, and also reflect the shifting patterns of employment. The Sutherlands were at Stafford House in London for the 1841 census, with five of their children. In attendance were forty-one other persons, most of whom appear to have been servants.[27] Ten years later, also

[23] 'Rough Draft of Memoranda for Duke of Newcastle'.

[24] 'Ascot Expenses 1859', Londonderry MS, D/Lo/F 468.

[25] Anne Athole to Athole, 15 May 1862, Atholl MSS, Box 58.

[26] Jill Franklin, 'Troops of Servants': Labour and Planning in the Country House 1840–1914', *Victorian Studies*, 19 (Dec. 1975), 211–39. Gerard, *Country House Life*, examines country house service in detail.

[27] Census Records, PRO HO107/739 (1841). This return does not specify occupations.

Table 1.1. Household expenses at Blair Castle

Year	Food	Lights	Coals	Liveries	Repairs	Refitting	Annual Extras	Stables	Wages	Totals
1850	1374. 13. 0	118. 0. 1	163. 6. 1. 5	297. 4. 6	180. 18. 7. 5	312. 9. 7	214. 13. 7	692. 15. 9	743. 17. 5	£4097. 18. 8
1853	1111. 19. 6	85. 13. 7. 5	130. 11. 1. 5	165. 3. 8	171. 14. 8. 5	205. 13. 6	161. 2. 9. 5	759. 17. 8. 25	773. 13. 7	£3565. 9. 8. 25
1856	1678. 9. 8. 5	157. 19. 10	119. 19. 5. 5	234. 4. 10	155. 3. 4. 5	199. 9. 8	257. 17. 11	972. 18. 6. 5	762. 8. 7	£4538. 11. 11
1859	1705. 11. 9. 5	170. 4. 6	262. 18. 3	189. 11. 3	205. 14. 2. 5	541. 10. 1	275. 15. 4	807. 13. 4	852. 4. 8. 75	£5011. 3. 2. 75
1862	1707. 16. 4. 5	175. 4. 1. 5	289. 9. 2. 25	207. 19. 6	82. 18. 4	284. 2. 3	347. 15. 8. 5	793. 14. 10	788. 8. 11	£4677. 8. 4

Source: 'Abstract of Household Expenses', Atholl MSS, Bundle 38.

at Stafford House, with three (different) children, the duke and duchess were served by thirty-six members of staff, including a tutor, a governess, the duke's secretary, a confectioner, a cook, eight housemaids, and three kitchen-maids.[28] The business of maintaining a full complement of servants was a time-consuming one, despite having the pick of the market: unlike the ubiquitous images drawn from costume dramas, few households retained the same personnel over long periods of time, although it was hoped that key personnel, such as the butler, steward, housekeeper, and cook would stay for some time. There were many reasons for this fluctuating employment market, not least of which was the practice of taking on new staff at each place of residence and dismissing them when the employer moved on. In this they differed from the gentry families who constitute the focus of Jessica Gerard's work, who were more likely to have only one residence and to retain their staff over many years.[29] Changing needs in the household also accounted for altering household composition. The Portsmouths and their ten children, aged between 1 and 15 years old, were looked after by twenty-three servants at Eggesford House in 1871, of whom five—two governesses, the nurse, the nursery maid, and the schoolroom maid—were directly concerned with the children.[30] It is also worth recording that parents and children frequently resided in different houses, requiring the maintenance of more than one household at a time. Thus in 1861, the recently widowed Harriet Sutherland was at Cliveden with some of her children and grandchildren and thirty-one servants; Trentham was in the hands of ten servants, and at Stafford House, her 9-year-old grandson, now marquess of Stafford, and two of his sisters were in the charge of a tutor and a governess and sixteen other servants. Likewise, when the childless Frances Waldegrave became the guardian of her second husband's two nieces, she set up separate establishments for them at Dudbrook House in Essex and in London.[31]

Most aristocratic households maintained a minimal permanent staff at all their houses, even when the owners were absent. At Hurstbourne Park, the Portsmouth's Hampshire property, the census of 1861 reveals a staff of four—a housekeeper, two housemaids, and a male servant—while in 1871, the pattern is repeated, with a housekeeper, three housemaids, a cellarman, and an 88-year-old woman, described as a servant, but almost certainly a pensioner rather than an active employee.[32] Some crucial servants—the

---

[28] PRO HO107/1481 (1851).　　[29] Gerard, Country House Life, esp. ch. 7.
[30] PRO RG10/2158 (1871).
[31] PRO RG9/56 (1861). Frances Waldegrave to Chichester Fortescue, [28 Aug. 1858], Strachey Papers, Somerset Archive and Record Service (hereafter Strachey MSS), DD/SH C1189 G336.　　[32] PRO RG9/712 (1861) and RG10/1238 (1871).

lady's maid and the valet—would travel with the family on most occasions, but other servants would be moved as and when required: for example, in September 1853 Lady Palmerston summoned her butler, Singleton, and a kitchen maid to come to London from Broadlands to receive Lord Palmerston and herself.[33]

Other households would employ staff only on a temporary basis, when their residence on an estate required a full complement of staff; this undoubtedly contributed to the temporary nature of much domestic service, and the constant activity of aristocratic women in the business of employing servants and seeking employment for former servants. Typically, Lady Lyttelton sent a lady's maid to Mary Minto, who was looking for such a person for her soon-to-be-married daughter. The servant 'lived with me last year for several months, & was dismissed because I was going abroad'.[34] A study from 1899 showed that the average length of time that a domestic servant stayed in one position was less than two years.[35] The implication of this for the employers—usually, but not always, women—was a constant search for reliable and, for some positions, long-term service. Susan, Lady Wharncliffe's generally uninformative diary records, without comment, the hiring and firing of servants on a regular basis.[36] After interviewing a Mr Lewis for the post of butler, Anne Athole wrote to her husband (interestingly describing the contents of her letter as 'business') thus:

Several people came to see me as I passed thro' London, wishing for the situation, but I would not see any of them, as I had heard from Mr Benham of this superior man, & I determined to wait & see if he would like us upon investigation, (as somebody *probably Mr Mabe* [a previous applicant] had been giving us a bad character which of course has come to *naught*) and as he has come here to see me I presume he means to like us very much, as he told me he was not fond of change, & if he suited, he would like to remain with us—I said *that* was just what we would like, & that I was so satisfied with him, that I would be willing to write for his character immediately.[37]

The production of references was vital for employment, and the refusal to give a 'character' would effectively end a servant's hopes of getting another position. Giving references in the aristocratic world was a serious business,

[33] Emily Palmerston to Palmerston, 23 [Sept. 1853], Broadlands MSS, BR30.
[34] Sarah Lyttelton to Mary Minto, [June 1841?], Minto MSS, MS11907, fos.195–7.
[35] *Parliamentary Papers* (1899), xcii. 25–6, 'Money Wages of Indoor Domestic Servants', quoted in Theresa M. McBride, *The Domestic Revolution: The Modernization of Household Service in England and France, 1820–1920* (Croom Helm, 1976), 76.
[36] Susan Wharncliffe's diary, 20 and 27 Mar. 1876, Wharncliffe Muniments, Sheffield City Library (hereafter Wharncliffe Muniments), WhM 485. See also Anne Athole to Athole, 16 and 22 May 1859, Atholl MSS, Box 58.
[37] Anne Athole to Athole, 7 Nov. 1855, Atholl MSS, Box 58.

as any inaccuracies could be brought home to the referee by an enraged employer, as Emily Cowper found when she recommended a maid to Mary Minto:

I am quite concerned to think Mellor should not have suited you. . . . perhaps her manner on first acquaintance may lead one to think her fine, but I never found her so, & the recommendations I had with her said quite the contrary . . . I never found her make any difficulty about any thing—otherwise I should certainly not have praised her as much as I did. I only mention this to clear myself—for I would on no account give a character lightly—as I know the trouble of trying different people & finding they don't suit.[38]

The system of personal recommendation could require a long memory. Lord Clanricarde sought references from Frances Waldegrave for Henry May, who was applying for a position as hall porter, who claimed to have been in her service ten years previously, prior to going into business for himself.[39]

Presentation counted for a great deal among aristocratic servants, as they represented their families, rather as receptionists do today. Thus for Anne Athole it was of no small importance that the appearance of the applicant to be her butler met with her approval: 'His age is 42,' she wrote, '& his appearance is quite in his favor, a good height, tho' not so tall as Mr Baker, & stouter; extremely respectable looking, & a very pleasant address. In short to my mind he looks like what our upper servant ought to look like.'[40] Lady Palmerston also had a clear sense of the importance of appearances, and of the hierarchy among servants which reflected the social status of their employers. Staying in Brighton with her daughter, the countess of Shaftesbury, she sent for her butler to provide appropriate service for a dinner for the duke of Devonshire, because 'I felt ashamed of my set out, and thought it better to have Singleton to put everything straight. . . . Minny's Footman who takes precedence of mine is such a Vulgar little fellow. I think he would shock the Duke's delicacy and tact.'[41]

It will be surmised that the relationship between the aristocratic woman and her servants was an important part of a continuing tradition of patronage, which in many ways set the aristocratic household apart from the inward-looking middle-class home. In what was perhaps a remnant of the medieval understanding of the household, in which for servants, 'the

[38] Emily Cowper to Mary Minto, 24 Sept. [1838], Minto MSS, MS11907, fos. 122–3.
[39] Clanricarde to Frances Waldegrave, 15 Feb. 1862, Strachey MSS, DD/SH C1189 G248.
[40] Anne Athole to Athole, 7 Nov. 1855, Atholl MSS, Box 58.
[41] Emily Palmerston to Palmerston, [22 Jan. 1851], Broadlands MSS, BR30.

household was not just a place of work or trade, but a field for political, social and economic advancement',[42] aristocratic employers frequently solicited their friends and relations for new jobs for their departing servants, and were often called upon to exercise their patronage in favour of former servants, in either promotion, finding employment, or charity.[43] The relationship between aristocrat and domestic servant was thus often seen and exploited as one conferring obligation on the aristocrat to continue to maintain the interests of her clients, even after the supposed basis for the relationship, the employment, had terminated.

The patronage relationship did not benefit the servant exclusively. The existence of this aristocratic network assisted both those seeking employment and the employers themselves, providing the employers with a reliable source of suitable candidates for the available positions, guaranteed by the personal knowledge of friends and relations.[44] Harriet Sutherland told Gladstone that she had 'engaged the attendant of your old Aunt & feel much pleased to have done so & very thankful to you for having thought of her for me'.[45] Similarly, succinctly expressing the patronage nature of the relationship between ex-servant and mistress, Anne Sutherland refused with regret a solicitation for re-employment (the position had already been filled), saying 'I shall always be very glad to be of any use to you that I can.'[46]

The prospect of long-term patronage was one of the great attractions of aristocratic employment for servants, which partially accounts for the relative lack of difficulty which such households found in attracting good servants. This patronage could be particularly valuable to tutors and governesses, who perhaps came closest to the clients of pre-modern households, in that their social status was superior to that of the domestic staff, but below that of the family and its guests.[47] Moreover, their employment span in any given household was naturally limited. Employers could go to considerable lengths to find work for their protégées, perhaps reflecting the fact that governesses were generally of a social class closer to that of their employers than other servants. Thus the baroness de Clifford sought assistance for her children's governess:

[42] Mertes, *English Noble Household*, 1.   [43] See Ch. 3.

[44] Anne Athole to Louisa Athole, 27 July 1887, Atholl MSS, Bundle 1657; Harriet Sutherland to Henry D. Erskine, 4 Apr. [n.y.], Bodleian Library, Oxford (hereafter Bod.), MS. Eng. lett. b. 24, fo. 216.

[45] Harriet Sutherland to Gladstone, [1 July 1867], BL Add. MS 44,329, fos. 231–2.

[46] Anne Sutherland to Mrs Blinks, [n.d.], Sutherland MSS (Staffs.), D593 P/28/12.

[47] See M. Jeanne Peterson, 'The Victorian Governess: Status Incongruence in Family and Society', in Martha Vicinus (ed.), *Suffer and be Still: Women in the Victorian Age* (Methuen, 1980; 1st pub. 1972), 3–19.

I have also lately engaged a most excellent French Governess, as though the last was one of the most indefatigable pleasing young women I ever met with, she did not teach French well. I am very desirous of promising her another situation, and should you happen to know any body who wants an English woman, who *thoroughly grounds* in History, Geography, writing and arithmetic, and the rudiments of Latin, I should be so much obliged to you.[48]

Similarly, Mrs Robert Arkwright wrote to Lady Jersey offering the services of a *very superior Governess* with 'unexceptionable' references.[49]

The uses of patronage to support aged, ill, or otherwise distressed servants will be examined in greater detail in Chapter 3. The retention of an extremely old servant by the Portsmouths has already been noted; on similar lines, the patronage function of aristocratic families towards their retainers manifested itself in Harriet Sutherland's concern about one of her gardeners, John Mathieson, who had been suffering from ill health. He had been employed at Trentham, and it was suggested that he return to Dunrobin; but, it was reported, he

seemed to fear that he would not be as well 'cared' for if he left Trentham. I told him that he must dispell [sic] all such thoughts, as wherever he should be Your Grace's wishes would be carried out. He then decidedly said he would return if he got a cottage to live in. His thoughts seem to be about his wife in case anything happens to him. His wife very truly says that she would be better at Dunrobin if her husband was taken from her.[50]

Mathieson returned to Scotland, and the duchess received the information that 'He certainly seems this year in better health, but says he is not capable of any exertion. He helps at the flower garden a [illeg.] in tying up things & much light work as Macdonald can give him.'[51] It was, however, understood by the duchess and her agents that as he was no longer able-bodied and was unable to perform heavy labour, his wages would be reduced, about which Jackson (the secretary) anticipated 'some difficulty'.

Not all servants viewed their relationship with their masters as one of patron and dependant. An undated petition was signed by eleven under-gardeners at Strawberry Hill requesting 'an Advance of Wages as most of us have to pay 5 shillings per Week for Rent. We have heretofore been Satisfied with our money but provisions and fuel being so dear we can hardly live on the money should this meet with your Approbation we should be most

[48] Sophia de Clifford to Sarah Jersey, [6 Nov. 1835], Jersey MSS, Acc 510/480.

[49] Mrs Robert Arkwright to Sarah Jersey, [n.d.], Jersey MSS, Acc 510/537.

[50] G. Fleming to Harriet Sutherland, 20 Sept. 1854, Sutherland MSS (Staffs.), D593 P/22/1/32.

[51] T. Jackson to Harriet Sutherland, [n.d.], Sutherland MSS (Staffs.), D593 P/20.

thankful.'[52] This document reveals as clearly as possible that Frances Waldegrave's gardeners viewed their relationship as being fundamentally one of employer and employee. The aristocratic woman might have perceived the relationship as one of patronage and service, in which she had paternal duties towards her dependants; but the under-gardeners at Strawberry Hill clearly viewed it as an economic relationship, in which they provided labour in return for the means of subsistence. Unfortunately, we do not have Frances Waldegrave's response to this petition.

Once the servants were employed, aristocratic women were by no means free from the difficulties with servants which plagued their middle-class counterparts. The scale of their potential retribution against servants who were adjudged unsatisfactory, particularly in small communities, and their ability to blight a future career, however, meant that an erring servant had few alternatives but to beg forgiveness. Such surely is the subtext of the letter from Thomas Christie to Anne Athole in 1889, in which he wished to

sincerely acknowledge my foolish and blameworthy conduct in Dunkeld House four years ago, . . . It is the wish of my Father that I should now write Your Grace at Abercairny; and I would therefore humbly approach Your Grace earnestly desiring forgiveness for my past misconduct, and for the trouble and annoyance caused thereby.[53]

It is not incidental that the father referred to was Anne Athole's agent and factor. The duchess's reply, offering a haughty absolution, also reveals the cause of Christie's offence: 'I am very willing to forgive the Past, with the hope that you will by God's help be able [to] retrieve your character in the future & entirely give up drink which led you so far astray.'[54] The consequences of dismissal could be tragic: revealing the few options available to the unsatisfactory servant, Lady Ashburton recorded:

We are very much upset at the dreadful suicide of B. [Lord Ashburton]'s old Valet, Mason—B. had to give him warning on account of drunkenness . . . & on Saty. morning the door was locked, & the police entered by the Window, to find him hung up by the Bed post.[55]

Aristocratic employers tended to be interventionist in the private lives of their servants, setting conditions as to marital status, and attempting to

[52] 'Petition from the Under Gardeners, Strawberry Hill', [n.d.], Strachey MSS, DD/SH C1189 G216.
[53] Thomas Christie to Anne Athole, 30 Jan. 1889, Atholl MSS, Bundle 1664.
[54] Anne Athole to Thomas Christie, 31 Jan. 1889, MSS, Atholl Bundle 1664.
[55] Louisa Ashburton to Richard Monckton Milnes, 29 July [1860?], Houghton Papers, Trinity College Library, Cambridge (hereafter Houghton MSS), 1/226.

forestall any potentially disruptive relationships within their households. Looking for a servant, Harriet Sutherland thought 'a married person would be quite an objection'[56]—marriage gave the employee interests beyond those of the household in which he or she served, and limited the amount of time available to be devoted to the employers' interests. Queen Victoria's notorious aversion to the marriages of any of her household, which, along with those of the rest of the royal family, comprised the only household in which persons of rank served in addition to domestic servants, has often been commented on unfavourably;[57] it merely reflected the widespread prejudices of aristocratic employers. Setting up house in England after many years abroad in the diplomatic service, Lord Westmorland reported to his wife that 'The cook has asked for a woman to attend him, which I have agreed to; but the housekeeper is to choose for him, which he has consented to—it would otherwise be too dangerous.'[58] The consequences of failure to observe the moral and sexual codes were the same in aristocratic households as elsewhere, but because of the nature of the communities in which most aristocratic estates were situated, where social codes could still enforce marriages, the fate of the pregnant servant could be less harsh. The duke of Athole told his wife that 'I had to expel yesterday from the House *your* Mary Robertson. She is to swear her child to Dond. McBeath; it occurred about April last, so will be born next month.'[59] Supervision of the morals and behaviour of servants was thus part of the code of paternalist behaviour which aristocrats sought, with varying degrees of success, to perpetuate not just in their houses, but on their estates and in the wider communities which they affected, a theme which will be pursued in later chapters.[60]

The country house was the preferred habitat of the aristocrat throughout the nineteenth century; aristocratic women were in large measure responsible for the creation and perpetuation of that province. Many were closely engaged in designing and redesigning their physical surroundings; furnishing, decorating, and building their houses in a manner which would facilitate their comfort, display their wealth, status, and taste, and enhance the position of their families occupied women no less than their husbands. Harriet Sutherland took great interest in the furnishings and decoration of her houses, down to such details as the commissioning of a clock for

[56] Harriet Sutherland to Gladstone, 9 Aug. [1867?], BL Add. MS 44,329, fos. 242–3.
[57] See Ch. 6, p. 199.
[58] Lord Westmorland to Priscilla Westmorland, 7 Jan. 1856, quoted in Lady Rose Weigall (ed.), *The Correspondence of Priscilla, Countess of Westmorland* (1909), 278.
[59] Athole to Anne Athole, [10 Dec. 1857], Atholl MSS, Box 58.
[60] Roberts, *Paternalism in Early Victorian England*, esp. 2–9.

Dunrobin, and following up on its delayed appearance.[61] On a bigger scale, she took part in the extensive correspondence with Benjamin Wyatt in the 1830s over the plans for, and redecoration of Stafford House, the London palace acquired from the duke of York in 1827.[62] The countess of Abingdon took time off from her stormy family life to redesign parts of their house, Wytham Abbey. Her husband reported to his stepmother-in-law that '[Lavinia] has got a good plan for improving the dining room without any expense & will save a good deal of paint, by knocking down the pillars, which are no support to the room & merely ornament'.[63] Others concerned themselves extensively with their gardens, an important resource for the aristocratic family, as they provided the main form of outdoor recreation for visitors, particularly women, who did not participate in the hunting and shooting expeditions which were for many the *raison d'être* for visits to the country. Lady Dorothy Nevill's interest in her exotic gardens at Dangstein in Hampshire, and especially in the cultivation of orchids, brought her into contact with many renowned naturalists, including Darwin, extending the range of guests she entertained.[64] As with other facets of household management, this interest could take the form of involvement in minute details of planting and cropping the flowers and vegetables which were to adorn the houses and feed the guests, alongside the more abstract and intellectual concerns of Lady Dorothy.[65]

The work of maintaining the household thus largely fell to the lot of the aristocratic woman. It might even be termed 'women's work'—although the involvement of men of all ranks in the household requires caution in making such a designation. Indeed, the relationship between a female aristocrat and her male servants provides one of the few examples of a situation in which men could be regularly responsible to women. But the household cannot be said to have existed as a 'separate sphere' of female interest, divorced from the interests of men; nor can it be viewed as a private realm diametrically opposed to a masculine, public culture, despite the development of increasingly gendered areas within the house—drawing-rooms,

---

[61] Charles Barry to Harriet Sutherland, 14 Mar. 1849, Sutherland MSS (Staffs.), D593 P/20.

[62] Correspondence of duke and duchess of Sutherland with Benjamin Wyatt, Sutherland MSS (Staffs.), D593 P/22/1/16, *passim*.

[63] Abingdon to Frances Waldegrave, 23 Apr. 1855, Strachey MSS, DD/SH C1189 G240.

[64] G. Nevill, *Exotic Groves*; Ralph Nevill (ed.), *The Life and Letters of Lady Dorothy Nevill* (Methuen, 1919), 56–7.

[65] See e.g. Georgiana Somerset to [unknown], [n.d., *c*.1860?], Bulstrode Papers, Buckinghamshire County Record Office (hereafter Bulstrode MSS), D/RA/5/22A; and Richard Bottom to Frances Waldegrave, 9 Apr. 1858, Strachey MSS, DD/SH C1189 G215.

billiard- and smoking-rooms, for example.[66] In 1855, Benjamin Disraeli, bemoaning the burdens of managing his domestic and estate concerns, wrote to Frances Anne Londonderry:

What you, great personages, do, and how you contrive to manage with so many seats, I am at a loss to conceive. But perhaps you need not know so much as we, little persons, are obliged to become acquainted with. Though, for my part, I think, that in affairs domestic ignorance is bliss, for knowledge seldom benefits you.[67]

Ignorance of domestic affairs was a luxury which no aristocratic woman could afford; far from knowing less of their affairs than the 'little people', they had to have an intimate knowledge of the minutiae of their households, which would enable their smooth functioning as the showcases of aristocratic power and authority. Nor yet did the house comprise the limits of the aristocratic woman's activities.

THE ESTATE

Estate management in the nineteenth century has generally been treated as an exclusively masculine occupation; in the extensive literature on the subject, women seldom feature except as sources of property or as causes of expenditure in the form of dowries for daughters about to be married, maintenance for unmarried daughters, and provision for widows.[68] Yet even the most cursory reading of the papers of aristocratic families shows that women were commonly active partners in the economic enterprises of their families. Of course, the extent of their activity depended on particular circumstances: marital status had a significant effect on women's autonomy, the widow of independent means having the greatest scope, the married woman the least. Again, the enterprise was not divided along rigidly

---

[66] Girouard, *Life in the English Country House*, ch. 10. Girouard's schematic approach, marking a movement from 'formal' to 'moral' design, does not, take into account, however, the extent to which many aristocratic households continued to live in unreconstructed, formal houses.

[67] Benjamin Disraeli to Frances Anne Londonderry, 2 Sept. 1855, Londonderry MSS, D/Lo/C 530 (153).

[68] Cannadine, *Decline and Fall*, 7, is egregiously deliberate in his exclusion of women, but he is far from alone; see also Matthew Cragoe, *An Anglican Aristocracy: The Moral Economy of the Landed Estate in Carmarthenshire* (Oxford: Oxford University Press, 1996), 1; Thompson, *English Landed Society*; David Spring, *The English Landed Estate in the Nineteenth Century: Its Administration* (Baltimore: Johns Hopkins University Press, 1963); Susanna Wade Martins, *A Great Estate at Work: The Holkham Estate and its Inhabitants in the Nineteenth Century* (Cambridge: Cambridge University Press, 1980). The coffee-table and heritage markets have covered aristocratic women more extensively, although they have not necessarily served them better. See Trevor Lummis and Jan Marsh, *The Woman's Domain: Women and the English Country House* (Viking, 1990); Pamela Horn, *Ladies of the Manor: Wives and Daughters in Country-House Society 1830–1918* (Stroud: Alan Sutton, 1991); John Martin Robinson, *The English Country Estate* (Century, 1988).

gendered lines, but, where expediency demanded, could be undertaken by either husband or wife. This joint approach to the management of estates provides a working example of the 'incorporated wife'—one who plays a necessary part in the execution of a job, which is formally her husband's, for which she receives little or no public recognition (except in the breach), but which none the less could provide a woman with meaningful occupation and a source of self-identification.[69] Although the married woman had little formal involvement in the running of estates, and although a discussion of the activities and interests of aristocratic women in the estates can do little to further the complex arguments about the economic aspects of landowner-ship during the period, their activities were often a vital support to the poli-cies of their husbands and agents. It is also worth remembering that for most aristocratic men, as much as for their wives, broad policies and decisions were not the stuff of everyday life: those who engaged regularly with their estates and farms were more usually concerned with the day-to-day issues of the state of the harvest, the weather, the collection of rents, and the condi-tion of the property.

Despite these caveats, the estates played a large part in the lives of many aristocratic women. For most they provided at least a residual concern; if this is insufficient reason for examining their involvement, the position of the widow in possession of her own estates—and indeed the significant numbers of women who were large landowners in their own right for at least a part of their lives—make some consideration of the matter necessary: John Bateman, in his 'modern Domesday' survey of 1883, counted some 412 large estates owned by women (by no means all aristocratic). This certainly understates the number of women who owned estates, as Bateman explains that 'I have given in every case . . . the son's acres to the father, the Dowa-ger's property in every case where it will probably go back to the main estate, to her eldest son, and the wife's property to the husband'.[70] The degree of activity by women on the estates, whether on an occasional or a long-term basis, confirms that aristocratic women were expected by virtue of their social position to play an economic role in the family business. If the role of the aristocratic woman on the estate was essentially one of repre-senting her husband or son to the tenants and labourers in his absence, it was no less important for that, in a hierarchical society where symbols and the

---

[69] Ardener and Callan (eds.), *Incorporated Wife*, esp. Hilary Callan, Introduction, 1–24. It also suggests the persistence of the pre-industrial 'family economy', among the landowning class, for which see Louise A. Tilly and Joan W. Scott, *Women, Work and Family* (New York: Holt, Rinehart & Winston, 1978).

[70] John Bateman, *The Great Landowners of Great Britain and Ireland*, 4th edn. rev. (Harrison, 1883), p. xvii.

forms of behaviour counted for a great deal. Moreover, as Thompson has pointed out, the central aristocratic concept in landownership was one of stewardship: land was always held in trust for future generations, and while it was generally expedient for that trust to be executed by and between men, there was no absolute reason for the trust not to be transmitted through women.[71] Thus the aristocratic woman was not debarred *per se* from involvement in estate business, and many took full advantage of the opportunity, although the laws on women's property ownership and capacity to enter into contracts prior to the 1882 Married Women's Property Act made it extremely difficult for a married woman to execute business on her own behalf.[72]

Representing an absent husband was not merely a symbolic process. It could entail taking on the burdens of daily administration as well, a function for which aristocratic women were not on the whole trained, but which they learned by experience. In 1852, Lord Malmesbury reported that the duchess of Northumberland had turned down the place of mistress of the robes at court, 'on the plea that she would have to manage the Duke's private business, now that he is First Lord of the Admiralty'.[73] The extraordinary Adeline, Lady Cardigan, cannot be regarded as an entirely reliable source, particularly where the affairs of others are concerned, but there is no reason to doubt her statement that 'When Lord Cardigan transacted any business matters connected with his great estates [principally Deene Park, Northamptonshire], he always insisted on my being in the room and listening to all the details. "You will have to do this by yourself one day," he would say to me.'[74] That training was put to early use, as Cardigan died after a decade, leaving Adeline all he possessed. Its success was pointed to by the widow, who took pride in having paid off huge mortgages and spent £200,000 on improvements to the property.[75]

Most of the burden of estate management would, of course, generally fall on the husband, by convention, convenience, or choice. Frances Waldegrave acquired a great deal of land by the wills of her first three husbands; it is interesting that the agent of her Chewton Priory estate in Somerset communicated almost exclusively with her last husband, Lord Carlingford. The exceptions were requests for cheques to pay wages, or thanks for the

[71] Thompson, *English Landed Society*, 6.

[72] Lee Holcombe, 'Victorian Wives and Property: Reform of the Married Women's Property Law, 1857–1882', in Martha Vicinus (ed.), *A Widening Sphere: Changing Roles of Victorian Women* (Bloomington, Ind.: Indiana University Press, 1980; 1st pub. 1977), 6–7.

[73] Lord Malmesbury's journal, 26 Feb. 1852, quoted in earl of Malmesbury, *Memoirs of an Ex-Minister: An Autobiography* (2 vols., Longmans, Green & Co., 1884), i. 308–9.

[74] Cardigan, *My Recollections*, 108.   [75] Ibid. 111.

same, which reveal that if Carlingford was responsible for the day-to-day management decisions, Frances Waldegrave retained her control of the purse-strings, a reversal of the usual pattern that we have seen in relation to household management.[76] In the 1870s, Hannah Rothschild inherited at an early age the vast fortune of her father, the banker Baron Meyer Rothschild. Her cousin, Lady Battersea, commented that although Hannah had 'an excellent head for business', the burden of estate management was lifted by her marriage to Lord Rosebery in 1878, clearly reflecting the assumption that such work was primarily the business of men, where one was available.[77] Of the Sutherlands' agents, the factor at Scoursie directed all his correspondence to the duke.[78] George Loch, the general factor of the estates (who had succeeded his better-known father, James, in the same position), on the other hand, clearly fell in with the duchess's plan of relieving her husband of all unnecessary burdens, and corresponded with her on estate matters. Thus in 1856 he consulted her on improving the accommodation at a cottage rented by Lord Elcho at Alt-na-Lynie, and on the renewal of his lease, despite the reservations expressed about the changes by the duke.[79] Again, it was to memoranda from Harriet that Loch replied discussing forestry, grass, cottage improvements, the overstocking of the Reay forest with deer, and types of agricultural show.[80]

Estate improvements, particularly in housing for tenants and labourers, were an area of interest to many aristocratic women, who sometimes took an active part in planning the changes. Lady Westmorland described the creation of gardens for four improved cottages, concluding that 'You can have no idea how pretty it is. We have also taken away that smithy's shop at the corner near the stables, and which was so ugly, and in its place have built a charming cottage with a garden before and behind.'[81] The impact of this kind of prettification on the lives of the inhabitants, and indeed, how they were to manage without the blacksmith on hand, did not seem to enter into Lady Westmorland's calculations. Harriet Sutherland was also involved in the improvement of the housing stock on her estates; she received letters

---

[76] Correspondence of J. Dart with Carlingford and Frances Waldegrave, Strachey MSS, DD/SH C1189 G217, *passim*.

[77] Lady Battersea (Constance Flower), *Reminiscences* (Macmillan, 1922), 51.

[78] Correspondence of E. M'Ivor and the duke of Sutherland, Sutherland MSS (Staffs.), D593 P/22/1/22, *passim*.

[79] George Loch to Harriet Sutherland, 30 Aug. 1856, Sutherland MSS (Staffs.), D593 P/22/1/25.

[80] George Loch to Harriet Sutherland, 28 Sept. and 9 Oct. 1856, Sutherland MSS (Staffs.), D593 P/22/1/25.

[81] Priscilla Westmorland to Pauline Neale, 30 June 1858, in Weigall (ed.), *Correspondence of Priscilla Westmorland*, 367.

from a Mr Fowler discussing the building of cottages, principally concerned with the siting of the new buildings and the colour of stone to be used,[82] and commented on the designs to George Loch, who was 'delighted to hear that Your Grace likes the pauper Cottages—the windows are very convenient, but certainly not becoming'.[83]

Later in the same month, Loch sent a memorandum to the duchess concerning the replacement of some cottages on the estate, analysing the condition of both the buildings and the inhabitants. With one exception, which was to be retained and repaired, by the duchess's permission, the cottages were 'wretched huts'. Despite this squalor, one, occupied by 'Widow Mackenzie a nice respectable old person' and her son, who was a plasterer, also supported a charity case (an ailing old woman,) of whom Loch wrote 'I never saw a human being in so distressing a state. These people have always struggled to be independent, and have never applied for parochial relief— they would well deserve some little aid at His Grace's hands.'[84] Their home was, none the less, still scheduled for demolition.

The casual disregard for the wishes and interests of the tenants demonstrated in this kind of improvement scheme was nowhere more vividly seen than in the controversial policy of Highland clearance. First put into effect on a massive scale on the Sutherland estates in 1806–20, at the direction of the then owners, the first duke, and Elizabeth, the duchess-countess, who had inherited the estate which included most of the vast county of Sutherland and the earldom of Sutherland in her own right, it was continued under their successors.[85] Under this policy, whole communities of crofters and farmers were removed, sometimes forcibly, from the Highland land which they worked and moved to the coasts, leaving the Highlands depopulated and available for more profitable exploitation by the landowners. Duchess Harriet was implicated in the controversy, being accused in the penny press of hypocrisy for her treatment of her tenants as compared with her championing of the African slave, by no less a person than Karl Marx, in an article called 'Sutherland and Slavery; or, The Duchess at Home'.[86] In 1856, a condemnatory letter from Donald Ross was published, which the duchess sent with her comments to George Loch, who replied that, whatever the

<hr />

[82] Mr Fowler to Harriet Sutherland, 23 and 24 Sept. 1856, Sutherland MSS (Staffs.), D593 P/22/1/25.

[83] George Loch to Harriet Sutherland, 31 Aug. 1856, Sutherland MSS (Staffs.), D593 P/20.

[84] 'Memorandum', [George Loch], 28 Sept. 1856, Sutherland MSS (Staffs.), D593 P/22/1/25.

[85] Eric Richards, *The Leviathan of Wealth: The Sutherland Fortune in the Industrial Revolution* (Routledge & Kegan Paul, 1973), p. 3.

[86] *People's Paper*, 12 Mar. 1853, p. 5 cols. a–b.

merits of the question, 'there is one thing which must be acknowledged emphatically, and that is the responsibility incumbent on us all to strive Earnestly to render the result of the changes as beneficial to the people as possible—that it has been so already in a very great degree I am quite sure, as I am that it will continue'.[87]

Dislike for the policies and attitudes displayed in the duchess's correspondence on the clearances should not blind us to the significance of the correspondence taking place. Aristocratic women could be just as self-interested, authoritarian, and neglectful of their estates as aristocratic men. Lady Palmerston paid the price for neglect when she visited some of hers after an absence of nine years: 'Your letter found me on a tour of hard labour something like the treadmill, and I was so fatigued every day—with talking and walking, Inspecting Farms and fields and mines making the agreable [sic] and listening to all the various Conflicting reports on the same subject that I was quite worn out.'[88] On the death of the third Lord Melbourne in 1853, Emily Palmerston succeeded to the family estates of Melbourne Hall and Brocket. On a visit to the former, she spent the morning admiring the place, and visiting the tenants with Fox, the agent.[89] However, the house was surplus to requirements, so she arranged with the agent to let the property, setting detailed conditions—including the hope that the tenant would 'not want to have a Laundry at home'—for the agreement herself.[90]

As we have seen, the economic needs of the landowning family, and even their aesthetic preferences, took precedence over the needs and wishes of their tenants. Moreover, the conduct of estates could become a politically charged question: in 1850, Sir Robert Peel put his estate concerns before the public, in an attempt to lessen the hostility of the protectionist party to the repeal of the Corn Laws. The protectionist duke of Rutland was disgusted, and told Lady Londonderry, who probably shared his gloomy prognostications: 'I am in continual C[onflict?] with my Tenants, but I should think myself full of Presumption if I were to imagine that the Publick could feel an interest in the Transactions of my Steward's Office here. I think we shall before 12 months have passed, be obliged to lower our Rents by one half and to shut up our House.'[91] In times of economic hardship and social tension, the fear of encouraging other tenants to demand rent reductions must surely

---

[87] George Loch to Harriet Sutherland, 31 Oct. 1856, Sutherland MSS (Staffs.), D593 P/22/1/25.

[88] Emily Palmerston to Richard Monckton Milnes, 7–8 Sept. [n.y.], Houghton MSS, 19/163.

[89] Tresham Lever, *The Letters of Lady Palmerston* (John Murray, 1957), 333.

[90] Emily Palmerston to Mr Fox, 18 Apr. 1858, quoted in ibid. 353.

[91] Rutland to Frances Anne Londonderry, 10 Feb. 1850, Londonderry MSS, D/Lo Acc 451 (D) File 33.

have been the duke's motivation for inhibiting press discussion of estate business, rather than any fear of fatiguing the delicate sensibilities of the reading public. The Londonderrys' tenants entered into the fray, demanding rent reductions, but were withstood by their landlords, who received Rutland's congratulations on the 'Triumphant Pleasure to you & L.—that your Tenantry have seen and acknowledged the Errors of their ways'.[92] Rutland's violent conservatism caused him to be deeply unpopular on his own estates in the early 1850s; he was unable to rent the farms immediately surrounding Belvoir Castle, and could not leave its walls 'without being assail'd and importuned'.[93] The prevailing image of the aristocratic woman as 'lady bountiful', dispensing charity and goodwill about her husband's estates, tends to obscure the fact that she shared her husband's economic interests and attitudes; it would be a mistake to assume that the involvement of women in estate management entailed any weakening of aristocratic interests, or soft-heartedness towards tenants.

Irish landownership had its peculiar difficulties for aristocratic women who had been brought up on the British mainland, involving residence in an alien country, among an often hostile and intensely suffering people. A great many aristocrats held lands in Ireland, contributing by their infrequent residence to all the problems of absenteeism which fuelled Irish resistance to British rule. The Palmerstons took the opportunity of the fall of the Whig ministry in 1841 to make a rare tour of inspection of their Irish property in County Sligo;[94] the Londonderrys had lands in Counties Down, Derry, Donegal, and Antrim, most of which they visited infrequently, Mount Stewart in Derry being the exception, until Lady Londonderry built her retreat, Garron Tower, on the Antrim coast.[95] Indeed, the Londonderrys were positively discouraged from paying their first visit (in 1846, twenty-four years after succeeding to the estates) by their Irish agent, who was afraid that such a visit would raise the hopes of the Irish tenants as to the abandoning of their rents during the Famine, which the agent was resisting strongly.[96] The visit

---

[92] Rutland to Frances Anne Londonderry, 7 Nov. 1850, Londonderry MSS, D/Lo Acc 451 (D) File 34.

[93] Lady William Powlett to Frances Anne Londonderry, 30 Mar. 1851, Londonderry MSS, D/Lo Acc 451 (D) File 35.

[94] Lever, *Letters of Lady Palmerston*, 259. See too Airlie, *Lady Palmerston and her Times*, ii. 69, which also describes improvements made to the estate at Cliffoney, Co. Sligo, on Palmerston's behalf.

[95] Frances Anne Londonderry to Benjamin Disraeli, 9 Nov. 1847, Londonderry MSS, D/Lo/C 530 (33). On Lady Londonderry's visits to Garron Tower, see e.g. Frances Anne Londonderry to Benjamin Disraeli, 18 Sept. [1850], Londonderry MSS, D/Lo/ C 530 (92).

[96] John Andrews to Frances Anne Londonderry, 15 Nov. 1846, Londonderry MSS, D/Lo (Add), Correspondence File 28.

was paid the following year, and Lady Londonderry was congratulated by the duke of Rutland, who considered that 'Such an Excursion as you have made, if followed up by all the Owners of Irish Property, would soon solve the Riddle of Irish *ungovernableness*, on which so many volumes have been written.'[97] (Neglect of estates was not confined to Ireland; in 1856 the duke of Somerset visited some of his estates in Cambridgeshire for the first time, and showed a considerable disdain for them to his wife: 'My property here seems to be much scattered and in every respect as uninteresting, and except for its rental, as undesirable as possible.'[98])

Some women, such as Louisa, marchioness of Waterford, took to life in Ireland with enthusiasm. After her marriage, she lived there virtually permanently, despite the nightmare of the Great Famine, throughout which she and Lord Waterford worked to relieve some of the worst consequences on their estates by employing their tenants in improvement works. Lady Canning, her sister, remarked that 'she is such a real Irish woman now that she willingly consents to spend her whole life in Ireland if she thinks she can be of the least use'.[99] Louisa Waterford left Ireland only after the early death of her husband in 1852. Less happy was the sister of the duchess of St Albans, who married a Mr Blake, the duke of Marlborough's Irish agent. Unlike the aristocratic woman married to a landowner, Edith Blake was subject to the will of her husband's employer, who did not make their lives comfortable:

They have got such a nice house, & had just had all to rights, when orders came from the Duke of Marlborough they were to move to *Thane*, a *filthy* place in the wilds of Galway, scarcely a soul to speak to, & a most desolate spot in a very disturbed district. . . . [Edith] is in *despair* at this uprooting.[100]

The employment of a good factor or agent was crucial to the well-being of an estate, and women were often involved in their selection. When a good factor was found, he was looked after as a treasure: the duchess of Sutherland's offer to send round the doctor to attend to George Loch when he was unwell was not necessarily an entirely disinterested one.[101] The

[97] Rutland to Frances Anne Londonderry, 8 Dec. 1847, Londonderry MSS, D/Lo (Add) Correspondence File 29.

[98] Somerset to Georgiana Somerset, 27 Aug. 1856, Bulstrode MSS, D/RA/A/2B/2/6.

[99] Charlotte Canning to Catherine Gladstone, 20 Aug. 1847, BL Add. MS 46,226, fos. 280–1. See also Augustus J. C. Hare, *The Story of Two Noble Lives: Being Memorials of Charlotte, Countess Canning, and Louisa, Marchioness of Waterford* (3 vols., George Allen, 1893), i and ii, *passim*. For an account of the kind of public works carried out on Irish estates in the 1840s, see Lady Dover to Harriet Sutherland, 20 Oct. [n.y.], Sutherland Papers, National Library of Scotland (hereafter Sutherland MSS (NLS)), Dep. 313/905.

[100] Grace St Albans to Frances Waldegrave, 10 Dec. [n.y.], Strachey MSS, DD/SH C1189 G281.

[101] George Loch to Harriet Sutherland, 30 Aug. 1856, Sutherland MSS (Staffs.), D593 P/22/1/25.

marquess of Hertford, in weighing up the pros and cons of a removal from one rented estate to another, considered the fact that his wife 'would have no head man like Brebuer to apply to in difficulty when I am absent' to be one of the major considerations against the proposal.[102] The reliance that was placed on a factor or agent was great, and not only in matters directly connected to the management of farms and tenants. In 1896, the widowed duchess of Athole was irritated to find herself with the returns for the registration of county voters to complete, and no factor on hand to perform the task. She wrote in indignation to her companion, cousin, and secretary, Emily Murray MacGregor,

There!—The Factor has gone to France! What do *you* think should be done about the Papers? *I* cannot fill them up you know, & unless you were at Dunkeld to refer to the *last* batch, I doubt if *you* could. It strikes me, that wretched 'hard working' Factor forgot all about them, otherwise perhaps Gillespie could have been left with the means of filling them up, & returning them—and *now*, can *he* not do something? 14 days from 29th May will be 12th June,—& I gave the Factor leave of absence till the 20th!—It is dreadful how *every body* expects to have holidays!—'six days shalt thou labour' you know, Sundays are the *only* exceptions!!!![103]

When Lady Londonderry's agent died in 1854, she received the heartfelt condolences of her friends, who sympathized with the difficulties she would have in finding a suitable replacement.[104] In 1858, Lady Londonderry was again looking for a new agent. The reference given for Percy Brakenbury was sufficient to ensure that he was not taken on, for although his referee wrote that 'these farms he has put into such a good state of cultivation, that last year I had no difficulty in finding Tenants . . . and they were let at a great increase of rent', he also said that Brakenbury had 'no control over the Tenants who had known him as a boy, and paid no attention to what he said to them', and that he was personally 'a very tiresome person to transact business with, as he will talk by the hour'.[105]

The duchess of Somerset's letter to her husband in 1863 about Mr Witham who became bailiff of the Bulstrode estate in that year sums up the requirements for the job of agent, and also shows the involvement of a woman in such a significant appointment. 'I have now *seen* the man,' she

---

[102] 'Pro's and Con's for moving from Bagshot to Holly Grove', [Marquess of Hertford], [n.d.], Seymour of Ragley Papers, Warwickshire County Record Office (hereafter Seymour of Ragley MSS), CR114A/650.

[103] Anne Athole to Emily Murray MacGregor, 4 June 1896, Atholl MSS, Bundle 1649.

[104] Rutland to Frances Anne Londonderry, 22 Jan. 1854, Londonderry MSS, D/Lo Acc 451 (D) File 18.

[105] Captain Henry Savile to Frances Anne Londonderry, 16 Jan. 1858, Londonderry MSS, D/Lo/C 182 (4).

wrote; 'I like his appearance and manner *very* much—a tidy dapper un-
affected well educated gentlemanlike little man, in conversation.—He
seems *very* intelligent and *very straightforward.*' That the duchess was also
concerned in the terms of his employment, and that she was accustomed to
having her opinion canvassed is clear from the postscript, in which she said:
'I think if you let him have the cottage near the reservoir with the garden as
you intended for the other man you need *not* give him [£]100 per annum but
much less.'[106] In this last, the duchess's advice clearly prevailed, for a document outlining the duties of the bailiff (including the requirement that 'The
whole of the Bailiffs time is to be devoted to the Duke's business',)
concluded with the terms of the appointment: 'The Salary of the Bailiff will
be 80£ per ann. with a cottage and garden rent free.'[107] However, in her other
assessments, especially that of Witham's character, the duchess's confidence
proved to be misplaced, as an episode in 1866 made clear. The incident,
trivial in itself, is worth relating in detail for the light it sheds on the role
the duchess took in the daily business of overseeing the family estates and
farms.

Witham bought a number of farm implements at a farm sale, and
informed the duchess of the purchases after the event, offering to sell them
to the Bulstrode estate, which he claimed had need of them. The duchess
wrote back very formally, declining the purchases, and adding that 'Mr
Witham should not have placed them in her barn without permission. The
duchess does not understand concerning the chaff box & cart. The cart the
bull has drawn have [sic] been some time here also the chaff box.'[108] The
duchess copied the correspondence to her husband, adding her analysis of
the occurrence:

There is some shuffling lie about the whole—for he enclosed the Moat Farm sale
papers also—dated & printed *January 26th 1866.* The Coachman *found in the stables* the
only chaff box he uses . . . and that was for the cart horses when they were up and he
has used it more than *two years*—he knows of no other. Osborne tells me that the
only cart he knows of for the bull is one Witham asked him to buy *when he came* as
bailiff and for which I believe you have paid him.—The bull has worked in [it] all last
year!! I expect myself that the tenant at Moat farm is going to throw it up—& I begin
to believe W. has been in partnership all the time.—He has also *bought* of Moat Farm
Grinsdale tells me *scotch firs* and planted them in my marigold sq. & in the most
foolish way close to wall.[109]

---

[106] Georgiana Somerset to Somerset, [Apr. 1863], Bulstrode MSS, D/RA/4/91/3.
[107] 'The Duties of Bailiff of Bulstrode Estate', [1863], Bulstrode MSS, D/RA/4/91/4.
[108] H. Witham to Georgiana Somerset, 17 Feb. 1866, and Georgiana Somerset to H. Witham,
18 Feb. 1866, Bulstrode MSS, D/RA/4/94.
[109] Georgiana Somerset to Somerset, Monday [18 Feb. 1866], Bulstrode MSS, D/RA/4/95.

Georgiana Somerset clearly had a very firm grasp of what was going on on her estates, and exercised direct personal authority in matters concerning the farms. Indeed, it is significant that she refers to 'her barn' and not 'the duke's barn' when dealing with her employees. The letter to her husband is not a request for permission to act, nor does it ask what action is to be taken; rather, it is a letter of information, and as such implies an equality of authority and confidence in the discretion of both partners to act. It is likely that the duchess took on much of the management of the estates whilst her husband was engaged in parliamentary business—he regularly held political office between 1835 and 1866. The co-operative nature of the Somersets' managerial strategy is reflected throughout their correspondence. A cottage was in need of repair; the duke suggested that the work be done by men already engaged in plastering the house, 'if you can arrange with Philcox that it should be a separate account (as you are to pay for it). I can then pay you, but this will keep it separate from the building-accounts.'[110]

Witham remained in the Somersets' employment until 1879—perhaps an indication of the shortage of suitable candidates. His successor, J. C. King, was informed by the duchess on taking up the appointment that 'we have not been content with the conduct of your predecessor, so that he will not be so useful in recommending workmen to you or giving information of all things'.[111] The Somersets had been unlucky in their choice of staff, for the duchess revealed in the same letter that the man who had been in charge of the park and cattle had been 'sent away for gross dishonesty, and of course he made those under him dishonest also'. With King's appointment, the administrative structure of the estate was reorganized, King acting as bailiff, but also having direct charge of the park and cattle, with a new under-bailiff as his assistant. In the same letter, the duchess also gave brief character résumés of the other important staff, showing her personal knowledge of her employees:

There is also *Wilmot* the Cowman we have had a long time, and I should be sorry to have to turn him away for anything but he is rather shuffling about his work. . . . The under-gardener at the Mansion Lodge, the little garden attached & the Shrubbery are under the management of the Head Gardener who lives at the Slough Lodge. The Carters and Carthorses are down near what will be your cottage. I believe them to be respectable men.

The duchess also kept a sharp eye out for any infringement of the rules affecting the labourers and tenants, although in 1879 she commented that since she had been ill, and since there had been no bailiff for a period, she had

[110] Somerset to Georgiana Somerset, 7 Apr. 1863, Bulstrode MSS, D/RA/A/2B/2/79.
[111] Georgiana Somerset to J. C. King, 16 June 1879, Bulstrode MSS, D/RA/4/97.

been less able to control what had gone on. For example, she sent word to one, Godbeer, who had charge of the sheep, that 'I thought I saw a pig-sty being put up at the end of your Garden. I therefore warn you in time . . . that the men in charge of the animals, and occupying the Lodges, are not allowed to keep pigs or poultry of any kind. That is the reason the Duke gives such high wages.' The reason for the ban was not a dislike for pigs, but to avert the temptation for petty theft among the men who had access to the estate oats and other animal supplies, should they have their own livestock to care for as well.[112] The duchess had a great interest in her own pigs, and the duke suggested that when next she went to their Maiden Bradley estate, 'you might with profit buy another pig, there is plenty of food for a second. I am giving cabbages to the cows; because they will not keep.'[113]

Georgiana Somerset was not alone in her interest in livestock. Augusta, countess of Dartmouth, raised poultry, taking pride in her cross-bred bantams;[114] and Anne Athole kept cows, recording their condition in her diary alongside her appointment as mistress of the robes.[115] The cattle were an interest shared with her husband, whose prize herd was a great consolation to him after illness drove him from public life. The year 1862 was a busy one for the Blair herd, the duchess commenting in April that 'you have *really* been *very* unlucky with the Cows this year'; by May, she had told the queen about his bovine difficulties, 'but I did *not* mention that you lived *both day & night* in the Byre, lest you should appear quite *cracked!*'[116] The difficulties were clearly overcome, as she wrote to her mother in July 1862 that her husband 'is now at Dunkeld again, having *refused £400* for his *prize Cow* in London. He did not even sell *one* of the others! *Well a day!!*'[117] The duke's eccentric passion was recorded by Lord Malmesbury, who noted in his diary that Athole

has a beautiful cow exhibited at the Battersea Agricultural Show. The dairymaid who has the care of the cow appears in a sort of costume, very becoming, and is of course much admired by gentlemen. The Duke attended upon her and the cow, bringing hay and water for the latter. One day he and the dairymaid sat together on a bundle of straw, eating sandwiches, and she and the cow were the admiration of society.[118]

[112] Georgiana Somerset to Godbeer, 23 June 1879, and to J. C. King, 23 June 1879, Bulstrode MSS, D/RA/4/97.

[113] Somerset to Georgiana Somerset, 23 Sept. 1858, Bulstrode MSS, D/RA/A/2B/2/59.

[114] F. D. How, *Noble Women of our Time* (Ibister & Co., 1903).

[115] Anne Athole's diary, 8 Mar. 1852 and 13 Mar. 1854, Atholl MSS, Bundle 639.

[116] Anne Athole to Athole, 26 Apr. and 15 May 1862, Atholl MSS, Box 61.

[117] Anne Athole to Mrs Home Drummond, 7 July 1862, Abercairny MSS, GD24/1/532, fos. 118–22.

[118] Malmesbury's journal, 2 July 1862, in Malmesbury, *Memoirs of an Ex-Minister*, i. 275.

Fortunately, Anne Athole managed to retain her sense of humour about the place of the cows in her husband's affections, writing to him on this occasion, 'I congratulate you on the safe return of your Cows—The Queen has heard by telegraph this morning of the safe arrival of Prince & Princess Louis at Antwerp.'[119]

From very early in her marriage, the duchess of Athole had played an active part in running the estates, transacting business and keeping her husband informed of developments. Thus in 1844 it was Anne who arranged for the letting of the shooting on much of the estate, as her husband was then in London. Among other offers, the agent Mr Loudie had received one from 'some charming young man, a cousin of the Hopes, but I told him I thought you would not let it. If I am mistaken pray let him know.'[120] The duke (then Lord Glenlyon) approved of his wife's actions in 1842, saying 'you acted quite right in desiring the Laundry field to be ploughed. I had always forgot to order it to be done.'[121] Her husband showed no reluctance in admitting his own inadequacies and his wife's business sense, commenting that 'You have acted with your usual discretion & good sense when left alone, & I approve of all you have done; I really think I must give up the management of my affairs to you I think you would act so much better than I can myself.'[122] In the same way as the duchess kept watch over the general household expenditure, so she also argued for prudence in estate matters, querying the £400 for a new pair of gates, especially at a time when there was so much hardship among the peasantry. However, she was prepared to relieve her conscience 'by remembering they are not our own people [starving], if I was *quite sure* the Gates were *exactly* the things we want'.[123] The want of capital which plagued the Atholes' estates in the nineteenth century was forcefully brought home to the duchess in 1853. '[W]e went on to the farm,' she declared, 'where every thing *would* be perfect if *I* could become possessed of somebody's bank stock—I should not care who's—I could spend it *so* judiciously!'[124]

As dowager duchess, Anne Athole moved from Blair Castle to Dunkeld House, some twelve miles away. There she remained in command of her estates, although her son, the seventh duke, to whom her real estate would revert on her death, carried out many of the administrative duties. Thus she

[119] Anne Athole to Athole, 9 July 1862, Atholl MSS, Box 61.
[120] Anne Athole to Athole, 22 July 1844, Atholl MSS, Box 61.
[121] Glenlyon to Anne Glenlyon, [24 Dec. 1842], Atholl MSS, Box 61.
[122] Glenlyon to Anne Glenlyon, [14 Dec. 1842], Atholl MSS, Box 61.
[123] Anne Athole to Athole, 18 July 1847, Atholl MSS, Box 61.
[124] Anne Athole to Athole, 12 July 1853, Atholl MSS, Box 61.

heard from him in 1881 that he had been arranging new leases for three of her farms; they were to be for fifteen years, or terminable with her life, in order to avoid conflict with the authorities as to the value of the unexpired portion 'should you not live out the fifteen years which I need hardly say I heartily trust you may'.[125] (She did.) The duchess's interest in the details of her estate did not wane. She required details of damage done to the woods at Dunkeld by a hurricane in 1880,[126] and in 1887 she reported to Miss Murray MacGregor that

I heard from Gillespie 2 days ago in a more cheerful tone, than when we saw him last—Wool is up 1/6d a stone since last year; & *mine* is sold to Conacher at Pitlochrie at 15/-. The Young Horse is sold for £50 to North British Railway—rather less than he expected—but too late in the Season—why did he not sell it sooner I wonder— Perhaps he *couldn't*—Turnips good crop generally,—& country not so scorched as in July.[127]

As a widow, Lady Palmerston had very decided views on the kinds of property she wished to own, and issued instructions to her agent accordingly. She disliked 'House property' because of the expenses entailed in repairs. 'I much prefer buying land,' she said, concluding that in the instance of some specific houses, 'as they are so close to the House it may be well to have them, but don't buy any thing more.'[128] The dowager Lady Morley also maintained an active interest in the management of her affairs: in October 1880, she noted in her diary that 'Morley so busy going over farms etc with Hornerman & with me in the afternoon'; as the new year opened, she commented gloomily that her prospects were not 'very bright' with regard to 'money matters as at present no sound of much rents'.[129] (Too ready a concurrence with aristocratic cries of poverty should be tempered by the valuation of Harriet Morley's freehold estates on her death in 1897 for estate duty: they were worth more than £55,000.[130])

Lady Londonderry is undoubtedly the best example of a widow who took the management of her property into her own hands on the death of her husband. Her interests were, however, principally in industry (see below), and

---

[125] John, 7th duke of Athole, to Anne Athole, [1 Dec. 1881], Atholl MSS, Bundle 1656.

[126] John McGregor to Anne Athole, 1 Jan. 1880, Atholl MSS, Bundle 1664.

[127] Anne Athole to Emily Murray MacGregor, 6 Aug. 1887, Atholl MSS, Bundle 1659.

[128] Emily Palmerston to Mr Fox, 25 Aug. [1869], quoted in Lever, *Letters of Lady Palmerston*, 367.

[129] Harriet Morley's diary, 23 Oct. 1880 and 1 Jan. 1881, Parker of Saltram Papers, West Devon Record Office (hereafter Parker of Saltram MSS), Box 31.

[130] 'Valuation of Freehold Estates of Dowager Countess of Morley', Parker of Saltram MSS, Box 31.

she placed the management of her Irish estates in the hands of her stepson, the fourth marquess, and his agents.[131] This sort of division of labour was far from uncommon: in addition to providing an independent residence, sending the heir to take charge of one of the subsidiary estates had the dual benefit of giving him and his wife experience of their future role while bringing another of the estates under the direct supervision of the landowner.[132] Earl Fitzwilliam sent his heir Lord Milton to live on his Irish estate, Coollattin, in County Wicklow, during the 1840s and 1850s; the regime which was implemented, on an English model, was widely regarded as one of the best in Ireland, and the Fitzwilliam estates were spared the worst excesses of the Land War.[133]

Women were central to the organization of the social life of the estate, which revolved around the dual functions of field sports and maintaining the social ties of the community. While hunting and shooting were predominantly male preserves, some women, such as Lady Seymour (later duchess of Somerset), also indulged in the sport.[134] Lady Wharncliffe's otherwise laconic diary for the autumn of 1864 becomes its most animated on the subject of the quality of the shooting at the various hunting-lodges she visited, although it is not clear whether she was taking part or merely recording the experiences of others: for instance on 17 November, she pronounced Cheveley 'a nice little place', where the shooting was 'good', whilst that at Brome Hall on the 22nd was 'wonderful'.[135] The passion for shooting, and for Scotland in particular, was not universally shared. Despite Queen Victoria's unbounded enthusiasm for Scotland, Sarah Lyttelton felt herself able to listen to the queen's raptures on Scottish subjects with equanimity only by the reflection that she would never have to experience the delights herself.[136] Palmerston's disgust with the place was probably shared by his wife,

---

[131] Frederick, 4th marquess of Londonderry, to Frances Anne Londonderry, 12 May 1854, Londonderry MSS, D/Lo/C 543 (1).

[132] The need for a separate residence was enhanced when the heir had a large family of his own and the father showed no signs of decline. Family tensions could also exacerbate the need for separate homes, and in the case of the quarrelsome Stanleys of Alderley, led to Edward and Henrietta Stanley preferring a house at some distance from the older generation at Alderley to a more proximate home. See Mitford (ed.), *Ladies of Alderley*, 24–5.

[133] R. F. Foster, *Paddy and Mr Punch: Connections in Irish and English History* (Allen Lane, 1993), 50. See also George Thomas Watson to Milton, 5 Aug. 1854, Wentworth Woodhouse Muniments, Sheffield City Library (hereafter Wentworth Woodhouse Muniments), WWM T28/4.

[134] Lord Malmesbury's journal, 8 Aug. 1845, in Malmesbury, *Memoirs of an Ex-Minister*, i. 160. See also Georgiana Somerset [Lady Seymour]'s letters to her children, Bulstrode MSS, D/RA/A/2A/284.

[135] Susan Wharncliffe's diary, 17 and 22 Nov. 1864, Wharncliffe Muniments, WhM 485.

[136] Sarah Lyttelton to Caroline Lyttelton, 5 Oct. 1849, in Hon. Mrs Hugh Wyndham (ed.), *The Correspondence of Sarah Spencer, Lady Lyttelton, 1787–1870* (John Murray, 1912), 393.

to whom he wrote the following account of the deer forests created by the policy of Highland Clearance:

It takes from ten to fifteen years to people it with these Quadrupeds, after it has been dispeopled of all Bipeds, and then one finds oneself very like Robinson Crusoe on his Desert Island . . . For my Part I would not accept Ten Square Miles of such Country on the condition of being obliged to pass Ten days of each year upon them.[137]

He continued to express his amazement at the popularity of such country, with sympathy for the women who were obliged to spend time there without the entertainment of killing deer: 'How poor Lady Abercorn contrives to amuse herself I know not, except that I conclude they generally have their House & wigwams full.' The duchess of Athole also contrived to have a full wigwam for the hunting season in 1851, reporting to the queen, with whom she compared notes on the shooting successes of their respective husbands, that 'Next week we shall have a hunt on the low grounds for the smaller game, when we expect about 20 guests.'[138]

The celebration of major family events by the whole of an estate, such as the coming of age of the heir, or his marriage, and their implications for the maintenance of community ties have been plentifully charted by Thompson and others.[139] Less consideration has been given to the much more regular festivals which performed the same functions of drawing an estate together, such as rent-days, the marking of the birthday of the landowner or his wife, and the annual celebrations at Christmas and New Year. For instance, in 1848, Palmerston wrote to thank his wife for 'your rural Festival to the Labourers on my Birth Day',[140] while the duke of Athole regularly commemorated his wife's birthday with treats for the servants, tenants, and schoolchildren on the estate: in 1860, for example, he booked a train to take 300 people to the seaside.[141] In a similar vein, demonstrations of approval from tenants and servants, whether or not they were spontaneous expressions of goodwill, were de rigeur on the reappearance of an aristocratic family on an estate. After an absence abroad (which in complex ways was intended to validate her second marriage), Frances Waldegrave and her husband, the seventh earl Waldegrave, returned to their Somerset estate,

---

[137] Palmerston to Emily Palmerston, 10 Sept. 1847, Broadlands MSS, BR23 AA/1.

[138] Anne Athole to Victoria, 21 Oct. 1851, Atholl MSS, Box 61.

[139] Thompson, *English Landed Society*, 76–81; Beckett, *Aristocracy in England*, 344–5. Such celebrations at Blair Atholl in the nineteenth century are recorded by John, duke of Athole, *Chronicles of the Atholl and Tullibardine families*, iv, (1908), 433–4, 435, 468–9, 478, and 486, while Lady Cardigan provides an amusing reminiscence of her reception on her re-marriage in *My Recollections*, 163.

[140] Palmerston to Emily Palmerston, 21 Oct. 1848, Broadlands MSS, BR23 AA/1.

[141] e.g. Athole to Anne Athole, 18 June 1846 and 16 June 1860, Atholl MSS, Box 61.

Harptree Court, to find 'all the tenants turned out, triumphal arches appeared overnight, Waldegrave's yeomanry were there in force'.[142] During her fourth marriage, a correspondent wrote to Lady Waldegrave of his regret that 'the bells were not ringing when you arrived [in Chewton] yesterday', an omission occasioned by the ringers watching the wrong road for their approach.[143] Even in Ireland, visits by aristocratic families were used as the occasion for communal festivities, as the duchess of St Albans on a visit to Kilree in County Clare found: 'This is the wildest little Sea place *imaginable*, & primitive to a degree. The inhabitants improvised a little welcome for us the other night, in the shape of tar barrels & Band &c.'[144] Also in Ireland, some years earlier, Lady Dover had visited her husband's Irish estate at Gowran with less ceremony. They 'were allowed to arrive very quietly, but we had an illumination, which we walked down the town to look at . . . yesterday they had the "long dance" in which the children joined . . . the dancers were very respectable, but the spectators a most grotesque assemblage'.[145]

If the estates served to fuse together rural society, they did so in a highly hierarchical and class-conscious fashion. Neighbours, tenants (often divided by the size of their holdings), labourers, and servants were all feted at different times and in different ways by the aristocratic household. Even the paying of rent was done by rank: at Apethorpe, Lady Westmorland returned home to find a gathering of farmers 'dining in the arcade, to-day being the first of three *rent-days* when the tenants come to pay their first half-year rent. They begin with the large farmers, to-morrow the little ones will come, and the day after the tenants of the cottages.'[146] Only on the predominantly masculine hunting field did landowners, neighbours, and tenants join together in any kind of social activity. Events presided over by women, on the other hand, tended to be highly stratified by rank. In 1856, Frances Waldegrave revived the tenants' ball at the Green Man in Navestock, Essex,[147] while Lady Morley noted that 1880 ended with 'The Labourers dinner, wh. they enjoyed very much. Morley arrived unexpectedly at 9 & went & wished them a happy new year wh. pleased them much.' The class-segregated celebrations continued into 1881, when in early January the tenants went to

[142] Quoted in Osbert Wyndham Hewett, *Strawberry Fair: A Biography of Frances, Countess Waldegrave 1821–1879* (John Murray, 1956), 46.

[143] Theo Mayo to Frances Waldegrave, 20 Aug. [n.y.], Strachey MSS, DD/SH C1189 G217.

[144] Grace St Albans to Frances Waldegrave, 14 Sept. [n.y.], Strachey MSS, DD/SH C1189 G281.

[145] Lady Dover to Harriet Sutherland, 4–5 Sept. 1838, Sutherland MSS (NLS), Dep. 313/903.

[146] Priscilla Westmorland to Pauline Neale, 16 Dec. 1856, in Weigall (ed.), *Correspondence of Priscilla Westmorland*, 303.

[147] Hewett, *Strawberry Fair*, 123.

Saltram for their dance, which lasted until four o'clock the following morning. Servants would generally be treated to a separate ball.[148] Lady Westmorland's commentary on a tenants' ball demonstrates the social distance which remained between landowner and tenant farmer:

We ended the year here by the ball for the farmers and their families, which every year more nearly approaches a *society* ball; for not only do the wives and daughters of the good people wear hoops, big sleeves, and are fashionably coiffée, but they dance the polka, schottische, and quadrilles, instead of country dances and reels. It makes one die of laughter to see them, for you know the English nature is not graceful in dancing.[149]

Invitations to events in country houses to neighbours (rather than to tenants and employees) were much coveted, and provided one of the great links between 'county society', the resident gentry, and the aristocracy who spent only part of each year on the estates. In the early part of the century there was much criticism of the aristocracy for neglecting their duties to their county neighbours, complaints which were reiterated towards the end of the century, when enhanced mobility and decreasing aristocratic dependence on the estates for their income and position again weakened the ties in rural society.[150] But the Victorian heyday witnessed many such events, and attempts on the part of the aristocracy to reinforce their domination of the local societies in which their principal seats were located. For example, on 5 January 1852, the *Morning Post* published an account of a ball given at Hatfield House by the Salisburys to some 300 guests 'of the nobility and gentry of the county'.[151] Not that such events were without their difficulties. Disputes with neighbours, such as that between the duke of Athole and a Perthshire neighbour, Mr McInroy, could make holding such an event exceedingly awkward, as Louisa Athole wrote to her mother-in-law in 1888: 'We *always* ask the few neighbours to our balls . . . & the other older people think *so* much of the compliment of being asked, . . . [but] McInroy *cannot* be left out *if* the others are asked.'[152]

---

[148] Harriet Morley's diary, 31 Jan. 1880 and 3 Jan. 1881, Parker of Saltram MSS, Box 31. See also e.g. Grace St Albans to Frances Waldegrave, [n.d.], Strachey MSS, DD/SH C1189 G281.

[149] Priscilla Westmorland to Pauline Neale, 5 Jan. 1858, in Weigall (ed.), *Correspondence of Priscilla Westmorland*, 352.

[150] For criticisms of the aristocracy, see e.g. Tomkins, *Thoughts on the Aristocracy of England*, and reviews of that work in *Blackwood's Magazine*, 38 (July 1835), 98–111; *Edinburgh Review*, 61 (Apr. 1835), 64–70; and *Quarterly Review*, 53 (1835), 540–8. See also 'Hints to the Aristocracy', *Blackwoods Magazine*, 35 (Jan. 1834), 68–80, which warns that the decline of social intercourse between aristocracy and gentry 'opened the door to the Demon of Revolution'.

[151] *Morning Post*, 5 Jan. 1852, p. 7 col. c.

[152] Louisa Athole to Anne Athole, [24 Oct. 1888], Atholl MSS, Bundle 1657.

To write aristocratic women out of an account of the functioning of rural society, then, would be a mistake; they were often vital partners in the management of these economic enterprises, with considerable command of the daily round of labour. Disraeli's query to Lady Londonderry, about how the 'great personages' managed their vast empires, can thus be answered in part by the consideration of the dual nature of the management structure of many estates. While the husband generally dealt with most of the business, some, like the Somersets, saw their enterprises as a partnership; some aristocratic women like Harriet Sutherland saw a responsibility for estate affairs as part of their social and wifely duties; other women, such as Ladies Palmerston and Londonderry were accustomed to considerable autonomy in business as in other spheres of their lives, and acted accordingly when their legal status as widows formally enabled such freedom of action.

INDUSTRY

Whereas the management of estates was generally viewed as an occupation suitable for a gentleman rather than as 'work', it was more difficult to put the same interpretation on industrial and commercial enterprises.[153] The number of aristocratic men who engaged directly in business in this period was small, although many had indirect industrial interests, particularly in mineral exploitation and transport networks.[154] To be too closely involved in manufacturing and commerce was to endanger caste and class, as the very definition of the aristocracy involved separation from the toiling and business classes. The discovery of an admittedly small number of aristocratic women actively engaged in the industrial and commercial business of their properties prompts speculation that the aristocratic woman could take advantage of her gender to overturn the dictates of her class, and of her class to transcend the limitations imposed by her gender.[155]

Lady Charlotte Guest, mindful of the merits of her industrialist husband, recognized that 'in this aristocratic nation the word Trade conveys a Taint. I am determined to overcome the prejudice, I will force them, whether or no to disguise, if they do not forget its existence in my case.'[156] The duke of

---

[153] Martin J. Wiener, *English Culture and the Decline of the Industrial Spirit, 1850–1980* (Cambridge: Cambridge University Press, 1981), esp. 30–9.

[154] See for exceptions John Davies, *Cardiff and the Marquesses of Bute* (Cardiff: University of Wales Press, 1981); Hugh Malet, *Bridgewater, the Canal Duke, 1736–1803* (Manchester: Manchester University Press, 1977); Richards, *Leviathan of Wealth*.

[155] For women and work, see e.g. Davidoff and Hall, *Family Fortunes*, ch. 6; Tilly and Scott, *Women, Work, and Family, passim*; Nancy F. Cott, *The Bonds of Womanhood: 'Woman's Sphere' in New England, 1780–1835* (New Haven: Yale University Press, 1977), ch. 1; Catherine Clinton, *The Other Civil War: American Women in the Nineteenth Century* (New York: Hill & Wang, 1984), ch. 2.

[156] Guest and John, *Lady Charlotte*, 27–8.

Rutland's comment to another woman who directly managed a vast business concern, Frances Anne Londonderry, was a typical aristocratic response: 'I was surprised at your Preference of the Commercial over the Agricultural work which you have to go through.' Land management was the province of the gentleman, commerce of the bourgeois. The implied criticism was tempered by a show of humility, however, as the duke went on to say: 'The former is so much intricate [sic] and complicated that I am sure I for one should give it up in Despair.'[157]

Much as some members of the aristocracy might try to distance themselves from the processes of industrialization which were transforming British society during this period, it was from that industry that the aristocracy derived an increasing part of its income.[158] Either by directly exploiting the resources available to them by virtue of the ownership of land, or by reaping the rewards of the labour and investment of others through rentals, the aristocracy, both male and female, was indubitably implicated in the 'industrial revolution', and profited from it in many ways. There were occasional prices to be paid by way of inconvenience, such as the blackening of the landscape by soot around the Fitzwilliams' house at Wentworth, but these were slight in comparison with the enormous rewards.[159] The railways, greeted initially with suspicion by many aristocrats who did not want their land carved up by the lines or their peace disturbed by the noise, were to prove one of the greatest boons of the century. (Lord Wharncliffe was surprised to find that, when he went out in 1843 to inspect the new line that ran through his estate, 'so far from being an eyesore, . . . it has the effect upon you of increasing the idea of the Vastness of the wood'.[160]) Other aristocrats enthusiastically took on directorships of the new companies. One rent-day in Devonshire in the 1850s the earl of Portsmouth informed his wife that 'I have had a *glorious* receipt here taking it altogether £4500 & odd & about

---

[157] Rutland to Frances Anne Londonderry, 10 Dec. 1855, Londonderry MSS, D/Lo Acc 451 (D) File 18.

[158] Thompson, *English Landed Society*, 316–17; Beckett, *Aristocracy in England*, ch. 6, esp. 230–7. Of course, this account does not fully consider those industrialists who were raised to the peerage or the debate about their divestment of industrial interests. See W. D. Rubinstein, *Elites and the Wealthy in Modern British History: Essays in Social and Economic History* (Brighton: Harvester Press, 1987), chs. 6 and 8.

[159] Lady Westmorland considered that the 'proximity of the coal-mines, which blacken everything', made the Fitzwilliams 'pay dearly . . . for the enormous income they produce': Priscilla Westmorland to Pauline Neale, 20 Sept. 1861, in Weigall (ed.), *Correspondence of Priscilla Westmorland*, 423.

[160] Wharncliffe to Elizabeth Wharncliffe [n.d., 1843], in Caroline Grosvenor and Charles Beilby, Lord Stuart of Wortley (eds.), *The First Lady Wharncliffe and Her family, 1779–1856* (2 vols., Heinemann, 1927), ii. 331–2.

£100 or so more to be paid in. The effect of the Railway is beginning to tell.'[161] Portsmouth was less keen, however, on the benefits of the railway intruding on his Hampshire property, and opposed the building of a new line, occasioning considerable annoyance to his brother-in-law, Lord Carnarvon, for whom the line, passing through his property, was of 'great importance'. Eveline Portsmouth was called on to intercede between her brother and husband.[162] Railways were a predominantly masculine business, but even here the redoubtable Frances Anne Londonderry was active, and her energy in such matters exhausted her friends: 'I cannot understand where & how you find the means to carry out such mighty works as you have in Hand,' the duke of Rutland wrote. 'You make nothing of adding 2 Miles more to a Railway already constructed of 3 Miles—*I* could very much increase my Revenue in Coal & Iron in Derbyshire if I could have a Railway of 5 Miles—But I could as soon [illeg.] to the Sky as execute it with my own hands!'[163] Frances Anne Londonderry's example suggests that it was not his class that prevented Rutland from the exertion.

The average aristocrat had little more to do with his or her industrial concerns than the receipt of the rents. Lady Waldegrave's mining interests, acquired from her first two husbands, were principally managed by her third husband, George Granville Vernon Harcourt, and her lawyer; it is significant that after their deaths in 1861 and 1862, the receipts of the mining enterprise dropped considerably.[164] The agent at the Radstock collieries, John Parfitt, appears to have communicated with his employer infrequently; the letters which remain are generally to inform the countess of the amount of her income from the mines and to comment on the state of the industry in such terms as make clear the infrequency of her involvement, as, for example:

Our Trade I am sorry to say is in a most depressed state, the demand for coal being very little indeed. . . . We have had two or three narrow escapes from accident on account of the unsafe state of the Sudlow pit: I have therefore commenced putting the shaft in proper order, but do not intend making any alteration in the Machinery until times improve.[165]

---

[161] Isaac, 15th earl of Portsmouth, to Eveline Portsmouth, [n.d. 1856?], Wallop MSS, Hampshire Record Office (hereafter Wallop MSS), 15M84, Box 30.

[162] Henry, 4th earl of Carnarvon, to Eveline Portsmouth, 15 Jan. 1862, Wallop MSS, 15M84, Box 30.

[163] Rutland to Frances Anne Londonderry, 12 Feb. 1854, Londonderry MSS, D/Lo Acc 451 (D) File 18.

[164] Hewett, Strawberry Fair, 170.

[165] John Parfitt to Frances Waldegrave, 12 June 1856, Strachey MSS, DD/SH C1189 G214.

And this in a letter announcing that Lady Waldegrave's share of the profits for that quarter would be £2,000.

Although her personal involvement in the mining concerns of her estates was limited, Frances Waldegrave was very much associated with the product. The bishop of Carlisle 'was struck by your name which your agents have made very public in all this neighbourhood [Salisbury, Wiltshire] by means of large placards advertizing the Radstock Coal', and took the opportunity to ask for a gift of coal for his schools.[166] Harriet Sutherland's papers also reveal very little interest in the management of the great industrial concerns of her family, contrasting with the extent of her involvement with the agricultural estates; a letter from George Loch outlining the costs of improving the harbours at Brora and Little Ferry in 1856 provides an exception.[167]

There were exceptions to this rule of aristocratic female indifference to trade and industry. Sarah, countess of Jersey, inherited the London banking house of Child & Co. from her maternal grandfather, and from 1806 until her death, 'Lady Jersey was both the owner and the very active senior partner of the bank.'[168] Frances Anne, marchioness of Londonderry, and Lady Charlotte Guest provide the most striking, and best-documented, examples of aristocratic women in business. The situations of these two women were similar in so far as they both took control of huge heavy industrial interests as widows in the 1850s, taking day-to-day responsibility for the management of their industries, and gaining public recognition, if not approbation, for their activities. There the similarities cease; Lady Londonderry had been a great heiress in her own right, and the mining properties she managed had been hers originally, and returned to her for her lifetime after the death of her husband in 1854. She had spent some time after Waterloo as wife of the ambassador in Vienna (where she had included the Russian tsar among her conquests), and had for many years been one of the leaders of fashionable Tory society: Disraeli recalled her after her death as 'a grande dame who was kind to me when a youth, though she was a tyrant in her way'.[169] Lady Charlotte, on the other hand, was the daughter of the impoverished ninth earl of Lindsay, whose widow's second marriage to a clergyman was regarded as a *mésalliance*. Marriage to the Dowlais ironmaster, Josiah John Guest,

[166] Samuel Waldegrave, bishop of Carlisle, to Frances Waldegrave, 11 Sept. 1856, Strachey MSS, DD/SH C1189 G292.
[167] George Loch to Harriet Sutherland, 22 Oct. 1856, Sutherland MSS (Staffs.), D593 P/22/1/25.
[168] 'Child & Co.: Three Hundred Years at No. 1 Fleet Street', *Three Banks Review*, 98 (June 1973), 46–7. I owe this reference to Robert Brown.
[169] Disraeli to Selina Bradford, 20 Apr. 1874, in the Marquess of Zetland (ed.), *The Letters of Disraeli to Lady Bradford and Lady Chesterfield* (2 vols., Ernest Benn, 1929), i. 74.

provided her with an escape from an unhappy family life, while giving the socially-aspiring industrialist and member of parliament an *entrée* into fashionable and political society. During his protracted illness in the 1840s, an increasing amount of the business of Dowlais fell on Lady Charlotte's shoulders, and after his death in 1853, she was appointed trustee of the ironworks for as long as she remained a widow. The freehold estates also came under her sole jurisdiction during her lifetime. Thus Lady Londonderry approached her industrial management from a totally secure social position, with an immovable place in the aristocracy, while Lady Charlotte, apparently downwardly mobile, struggled against becoming *déclassée*: her success may be measured by the barony bestowed on her son, the first Lord Wimborne, and the marriage of that same son to Lady Cornelia Spencer-Churchill, daughter of the duke of Marlborough, and Frances Anne Londonderry's granddaughter.[170]

Lady Londonderry had early taken an interest in the collieries which were the source of much of her inheritance;[171] during her marriage, the additions and improvements to the Vane-Tempest properties were generally carried out in the name of the marquess, such as the purchase of the Seaham estate in 1821 and the building of Seaham Harbour to facilitate the export of coal. None the less, these actions were seen as being on Frances Anne's behalf. Thus, in 1821, Castlereagh wrote to his brother, the future Londonderry (then known as Lord Stewart), on the Seaham purchase, that 'It certainly will be a service rendered to *Lady Stewart's interest* to have so largely added to her landed estate, which I am sure you will have a particular pride in having accomplished after all her devotion to you.'[172]

So in industry, as in other areas of economic life, it is useful to resort to the notion of incorporation to discuss the relationship of the married woman to the family property, to see the enterprise in terms of the benefits to both members of the partnership, and to see the roles within the enterprise as distinct, with different emphases. In the Londonderry case, there was a surprising reversal of the usual hierarchies: Frances Anne was the transmitter of the property, her husband her active agent. This, if not a total reversal of the expected gender roles, was a reversal of the social hierarchy, with the marquess appearing in a symbolically inferior position to his wife. His position was revealed in the edict he issued to the striking Durham and Northumberland pitmen in 1844, after the expiry of an ultimatum:

---

[170] See Londonderry, *Frances Anne*, esp. ch. 9, and Guest and John, *Lady Charlotte, passim.*
[171] Londonderry, *Frances Anne*, 26.
[172] Ibid. 71, emphasis added.

I found you dogged, obstinate and determined:- indifferent to my really paternal advice and kind feelings to the old families of the VANE and TEMPEST Pitmen who had worked for successive ages in the Mines. I was bound to act up to my word,—bound by duty to my property, my family and station. I superintended then many ejections, it had no avail.[173]

Besides being an example of Londonderry's managerial style, this document charts the ambiguities in the marquess's position: he could not call on long years of service to his own family, but only to that of his wife. His paternalism, arguably, had less symbolic effect in this instance than the maternalism of his wife, which had the longer pedigree. Although Londonderry stated his duty to be to 'my property', he clearly found it necessary to refer obliquely to the authority of his wife in the qualifying 'my family'. Similarly, when he threatened the local tradesmen who were giving credit to the striking miners, it was with the loss of his own *and* his wife's custom.

While Londonderry was the more active figure in the industrial concerns, his wife exerted herself through the political connections she had cultivated as a hostess on behalf of the coal interest. It was she who had a correspondence with Disraeli (of whose protectionist views Londonderry was a zealous supporter) in 1850 over the Mines Bill; Londonderry had opposed the Act of 1842 restricting the labour of women and children underground, and the new bill, to improve inspection, was supported by the miners and opposed by the mine-owners. Disraeli's assistance was sought by the Londonderrys, and he wrote to Frances Anne that

I have prevented the 2nd Reading of the Mines bill on two occasions, but fear I shall not succeed in obtaining further delay to night. Delay is our only chance, as there is no hope of opposition to it, the philanthropists on our own side & the political economists on the other, being, strange to say, united in favor of it.[174]

There can be little reason for thinking that Lady Londonderry did not share her husband's authoritarian views on industrial management; she certainly continued his rhetoric. After his death, she wrote to their tenants at Garron Tower in Ireland that he had been devoted to the 'improvement of the districts he became connected with'. The works were a memorial to his 'desire to do his duty towards those amongst whom he lived', which were 'foremost in the impulses of his generous nature'.[175] The Londonderrys'

---

[173] Public statement by Lord Londonderry, 3 July 1844, quoted in Londonderry, *Frances Anne*, 233–4.

[174] Benjamin Disraeli to Frances Anne Londonderry, 2 Aug. 1850, Londonderry MSS, D/Lo/C 530 (89).

[175] Londonderry, *Frances Anne*, 263.

approach to industrial relations contrasts strongly with that of Lady Charlotte Guest, although both were firmly in the paternalist tradition of treating the working classes like recalcitrant children. Unlike the Londonderrys, Lady Charlotte did not like 'to treat the people de haut en bas. They are generally very reasonable—and a few firm, kind words often puts matters on the proper footing and in the right light with them.'[176] The Guest approach to the marital business partnership was in some respects more complex, for although the property hierarchy was maintained, Lady Charlotte took social precedence of her husband. Further, during 1844, Guest was stricken with a debilitating disease which limited his capacity for involvement in the daily business of the ironworks, business which increasingly was overseen by Lady Charlotte. Placed in a socially equivocal position, Lady Charlotte was one of the few aristocratic women who explicitly articulated thoughts about gender and class, and the indeterminacies of her position as an aristocratic woman involved in industry. It is worth quoting her at length:

How deeply I have felt this inferiority of sex and how humiliated I am when it is recalled to my mind in allusion to myself . . . since I married I have taken up such pursuits as in this country of business and ironmaking would render me conversant with what occupied the male part of the population. Sometimes I think I have succeeded pretty well—but every now and then I am painfully reminded that toil as I may, I can never succeed beyond a certain point and by a very large portion of the community my acquirements and judgements must always be looked upon as those of a mere woman.[177]

It is interesting that, in this moment of reflection at least, Lady Charlotte was more concerned at being thought incompetent 'beyond a certain point' in business because she was a 'mere woman' than she was in the propriety of being engaged in such business at all.

In the industrial world, then, as nowhere else, the aristocratic woman was most subject to the prescriptions of woman's sphere, because industry was essentially a middle-class preserve, and the aristocratic woman had no traditional role to play in it. Lady Londonderry in many respects treated her industries as a simple extension of her landed estate; the great feast for between three and four thousand pitmen on Chilton Moor in March 1856 can be seen as a large-scale version of the tenants' ball or the labourers' dinner provided for the agricultural dependants.[178] Lady Charlotte was obliged to work within the framework of middle-class expectations, although she remarked that walking through the ironworks, 'I always feel here in my proper sphere'.[179]

[176] Guest and John, Lady Charlotte, 173.   [177] Ibid. 31.
[178] Londonderry, Frances Anne, 276–80.
[179] Guest and John, Lady Charlotte, 123.

As widows, both women took a very active role in the management of the industries under their care. Both were appointed to sole authority over vast concerns, in spite of the prevailing practices of property transmission. In neither case was the control granted to be terminated by the coming of age or marriage of a son, but rather was granted, in Lady Londonderry's case, for her lifetime, and in Lady Charlotte's, for so long as she remained a widow. Lady Charlotte had undergone a long apprenticeship in the works, acting as her husband's secretary from 1836. The tasks of letter writing, copying, accounting and arranging went on for many years, interrupted only by her ten confinements in thirteen years.[180] The extent of her husband's dependence on her activities was indicated by the 'immense pile of letters' which Guest brought for his wife to deal with, which had accumulated during the final stages of one pregnancy. Similarly, when Lady Charlotte gave up doing their private accounts, Guest found the activity so time-consuming and uncongenial that she was obliged to take it on again.[181] Such was the extent of Lady Charlotte's involvement that she could write in 1838 that 'Merthyr [Guest] has weaned me from all my own pursuits and taught me to be fond of his business and now . . . I have got into such habits that business is almost the only thing that interests me.'[182] The following year she reinforced her sense of the gendered nature of the change in her priorities, observing that she was 'so schooled . . . into habits of business' that she would rather 'calculate the advantage of half per cent commission on a cargo of iron than . . . go to the finest Ball in the world'.[183] In 1839, the Dowlais premises in the City of London included an office for Lady Charlotte. This training held her in good stead during the 1840s, when Guest's illness caused his wife to take on more and more of the daily business of the ironworks, and after his death in 1852, when she became the active head of the works.

The labour difficulties experienced in the summer of 1853 in South Wales are worth some examination, for the light they shed on the peculiar problems experienced by a woman in industry.[184] Faced with inflationary wage demands from the miners and a strike at the Penydarren pit, the owners of four South Wales collieries met at Lady Charlotte's London house to plan concerted action. One of the owners suggested stopping work at all their sites until the Penydarren men returned to work at no increase of wages, a proposal which outraged Lady Charlotte, who thought it 'monstrous to tell

---

[180] Earl of Bessborough (ed.), *Lady Charlotte Guest: Extracts from her Journal 1833–1852* (John Murray, 1950), 43, 110–11.

[181] Guest and John, *Lady Charlotte*, 130–1.   [182] Ibid. 131.

[183] Bessborough (ed.), *Lady Charlotte Guest*, 89.

[184] The discussion which follows is based on Guest and John, *Lady Charlotte*, 173–8.

our steady good men that unless . . . they *compelled* their refractory neighbours to go to work we would revenge it upon them and throw them out of bread'. However, opposed by all the iron- and coal-masters, including her own foreman, John Evans, and feeling that 'my objections might arise from a woman's weakness', Lady Charlotte accepted the principle, although without signing the agreement. Overnight, she changed her mind, for 'though I might plead the extenuating circumstances of being a woman and in argument *alone* against the opinion of *five* experienced men of business who hurried matters unduly to an assumed conclusion, yet I cannot but own that I had the *power* to say no'. The strike was ended by agreement to higher wages, and some of the other pits followed suit. In July the Dowlais men also demanded increased wages, but in a show of determination aimed in part at her workers, but also at the other owners, Lady Charlotte resisted, saying 'all the more I have declined all aggressive meanness towards them, the more I shall feel not only justified, but bound, to resist any movement of this kind [i.e. a strike] on their part. *I will be their master* [my italics].' This determination was met with resistance, and 1,500 colliers went out on strike, and received their month's notice; Lady Charlotte herself supervised the stopping of thirteen blast furnaces. By September, the men returned to work, on terms dictated by their employer: that is, with no new rise in pay. Thus we see Lady Charlotte, afraid of having been unduly influenced by feminine considerations in her dealings with the industrialists, resolved on playing an unequivocally masculine role with regard to her workers—'I will be their master'—which role she pushed to its limits, breaking the strike of the exclusively and aggressively masculine mining community.

For Lady Londonderry, taking over the Durham collieries in 1854, the whole activity was novel. She wrote to Disraeli that she fancied 'I am turned into a clerk', and pointed to the vast range of business with which she had now, and rapidly, to become acquainted: 'I silently suck everybody's brain and go home and digest it all. I think I could manage any one subject but I have so many to go for Estates to Docks, from draining to Railways, quarries to timber and so on till I get hopelessly bewildered.'[185] She could, of course, have entrusted the whole business to her agents, or to one of her sons, but chose not to. The measure of her success in coming to terms with her new role may be found in the description left by Disraeli of the marchioness in 1861:

She prefers living in a hall on the shores of the German Ocean [North Sea], surrounded by her collieries and her blast furnaces and her railroads and the unceasing

---

[185] Frances Anne Londonderry to Benjamin Disraeli, 24 July [1854], Londonderry MSS, D/Lo/C 530 (112).

telegraphs, with a port hewn out of the solid rock, screw steamers and four thousand pitmen under her control. . . . she has a regular office, a fine stone building with her name and arms in front, and her flag flying above; and here she transacts, with innumerable agents, immense business—and I remember her five-and-twenty years ago a mere fine lady; nay, the finest in London! But one must find excitement if one has brains.[186]

Frances Anne was by no means a figure-head; her biography is full of incidents demonstrating her personal grasp of the affairs of her business, her interest in all that concerned her properties. The idea of setting up blast furnaces at Seaham was her own, and she initiated the connection of the Seaham and Sunderland Railway with the London and North-Western Railway.[187]

The occasion on which Frances Anne's activities were drawn to general attention, the feast for the pitmen on Chilton Moor in 1856, has already been noted. Aside from the paternalist implications of the occasion, it was significant for the speech which Lady Londonderry made. At a time when women, even aristocratic ones, seldom made speeches, the event aroused considerable public interest. The duke of Rutland commented that 'A new Era seems coming on & Women's Empire is I think wholly to come back in all its glory',[188] Disraeli found 'your address very telling, and, both in spirit and expression, without a fault'.[189] Lady Charlotte Guest, who had by this time remarried and given up the Dowlais business to her son, read reports of the occasion, and was reminded of 'my old days of power'. She found the speech 'a most excellent and sensible one—No man could have done better . . . It is a move in the right direction and as coming from a woman is deserving of greater consideration. If our aristocracy will avail themselves of such occasions to mingle with and advise the people, they will do much good for both classes.'[190] The speech, which had expressed Lady Londonderry's regret at not being allowed to go down the mines herself, was essentially a homily against striking (she pointed to strikers from other pits turned from their homes, and the pitmen must have been reminded of the evictions from the Londonderry estates in 1844), advocating increased caution in the pits, and an exhortation to virtue, concluding with the wish that 'we may each . . . do

---

[186] Quoted in Londonderry, *Frances Anne*, 268.

[187] Ibid. 272; Ralph Ward Jackson to Frances Anne Londonderry, 12 Dec. 1861, Londonderry MSS, D/Lo/C 182 (19).

[188] Rutland to Frances Anne Londonderry, 6 Mar. 1856, Londonderry MSS, D/Lo Acc 451 (D) File 18.

[189] Disraeli to Frances Anne Londonderry, 4 Mar. [1856], Londonderry MSS, D/Lo/C 530 (162).

[190] Guest and John, *Lady Charlotte*, 71–2.

our duty in that state of life to which it has pleased God to call us'.[191] Although Lady Londonderry's state in life was in many ways a peculiar one, the calm acceptance of her active commercial and industrial life—it was even reported in *The Times* without criticism or comment[192]—shows that, although it was unusual, industry and business were not so far removed from aristocratic women's usual activities as to prohibit their active involvement.

Households and estates, and their attendant business, occupied most aristocratic women in great measure. Providing the physical and territorial basis of aristocratic authority, maintaining ties of dependency and patronage, and creating the economic security which underpinned the edifice of aristocratic culture, the great houses and estates were much more than homes, and the women who ran them much more than the glorified housekeepers of the 'sacred temples'. Their contributions to the management of estates were rarely strategic, but in the less easily quantifiable realm of daily observation and supervision. A similar pattern may be discerned in the involvement of aristocratic women in the institutional and spiritual concerns of those who surrounded them, in the schools and churches of their parishes.

---

[191] Londonderry, *Frances Anne*, 277–9.
[192] *The Times*, 3 Mar. 1856, p. 7 col. f.

2

'The Business and Charities of the Parish': Churches, Schools, and Local Authority

Authority in rural areas rested on control of much more than the home and estates of the aristocratic family. The instruments of rural order—the local magistracy, justices of the peace, local militias, and church vestries, for example—were exclusively male in the period until 1880; in religion and education, however, women could play a significant part. Churches and schools, which sought to reinforce the social hierarchies and the stability of society, were also under aristocratic patronage, influence, or direct authority. Moreover, religion and the education of the young were considered to be especially feminine occupations, deriving from their maternal and moral responsibilities.[1] In this respect, the aristocratic woman shared her role with the domestic middle-class woman. But while the middle-class woman sought to extend her domestic role into the public sphere of schools and church organization during the course of the later nineteenth century, in part as an escape from the confines of the home, the aristocratic woman, who generally handed over the education of her own children to a succession of nurses, tutors, governesses, clergymen, and schools, was expected, as a natural part of her role, to act in a maternal capacity towards the dependants on her husband's or her own estate.

In contrast to the commercial activities of Lady Londonderry and Lady Charlotte Guest, interest and involvement in the intellectual and spiritual needs of the local community were sanctioned for all women, as they could be constructed as an extension of a feminine sphere. This sort of sleight of hand has not gone unremarked, and has indeed proved one of the earliest criticisms of the notion of the separate spheres.[2] The engagement of many aristocratic women with schools and churches, however, derived less from any idea that they were fulfilling their womanly obligations than from their

---

[1] Davidoff and Hall, *Family Fortunes*, ch. 2; Brian Heeney, *The Women's Movement in the Church of England 1850–1930* (Oxford: Clarendon Press, 1988), 9–10 and 84–6.

[2] Frank K. Prochaska, *Women and Philanthropy in Nineteenth-Century England* (Oxford: Clarendon Press, 1980), 7–13; Vickery, 'Golden Age', 388–91.

firmly-rooted commitment to paternalism, which in turn derived from their social position.[3]

While activities in these areas can in some senses be regarded as an extension of charitable duties, they call for separate treatment, as the institutional structure of church and schools differentiates them from personal and individual charity, while the informal nature of aristocratic women's involvement with the rural institutions separates them from the highly organized philanthropies, causes, and structures which tended to flourish under middle-class inspiration in urban contexts. The patterns of aristocratic residence on their estates gave their involvement with local institutions a spasmodic character, quite contrary to the demands of organized, regular philanthropy: discussion of their activities in rural schools and churches shares this disjointed and fragmentary nature, for they formed no committees and kept no regular records of the institutions of which they were patrons. While aristocratic men often interested themselves in urban schools and missions to the poor, both in London and in the provinces, aristocratic women seem to have confined their interests to the villages on their estates, where their involvement constituted one of the faces of a 'benevolent' county society.

Religion and education were closely intertwined during the nineteenth century, popular education often being seen more in terms of religious than of secular, vocational instruction, and as a means of confirming denominational support. More contentiously, some historians have argued that education was intended to reinforce the social hierarchy, to create a docile populace, and to prevent the acquisition of dangerous knowledge.[4] Auberon Herbert summed up aristocratic ambitions for the schooling of rural labourers in a letter to his sister, Eveline, countess of Portsmouth, calling for 'a really thoroughly satisfactory system of education', which would 'especially br[ing] out the idea of duties and obligations—I so fear that at present we are as iron badly welded—which flies whenever the strain comes.'[5] Herbert, a radical Tory in his politics, at once set out his understanding of the purposes of mass education: namely, the maintenance of the social order, and also admitted that the education system as then constituted was failing in this

---

[3] The term 'paternalism' has been preferred here to 'maternalism', to avoid quaintness; but it is used here in a gender-inclusive sense.

[4] The extent of their success has been questioned in the later literature of social control. Laqueur, for example, has argued that the Sunday school movement may have been started with the intention of providing an instrument of bourgeois control, but that it was rapidly co-opted by the working classes to meet their own educational, cultural, and social needs: Thomas Walter Laqueur, *Religion and Respectability: Sunday Schools and Working-Class Culture 1780–1850* (New Haven: Yale University Press, 1976).

[5] Auberon Herbert to Eveline Portsmouth, n.d., Wallop MSS, 15M84, Box 30.

aim. Although the movement for mass education resulted principally from concerns about the disintegration of society wrought by the effects of the industrial revolution and the need to instil religion into the urban workforce, it spread through rural areas also, provision of schools remaining in private or charitable hands, even where government subsidy was available.[6] Aristocrats, both male and female, as landowners and patrons of rural communities, were thus drawn into the process of providing schools and schooling for the children of their poorer· tenants and labourers. Religious motivation, however, must not be trivialized, even where there is clear evidence or a strong presumption of the desire to maintain social order and hierarchies.

PERSONAL RELIGION

Aristocratic women were by no means exempt from the Victorian preoccupation with religion. Indeed, it was a central area for the making of independent decisions by aristocratic women, often in the teeth of family opposition: religious compatibility was usually a criterion for an acceptable marriage, but changing convictions after marriage could be a source of great tension. The vast majority of aristocratic women in this period belonged to the Churches of England, Scotland, and Ireland, but women of the established faith participated fully in the differences of religious opinion of the period. The whole gamut of religious opinion and school was to be found among aristocratic women, from the high church Harriet Sutherland and Charlotte Canning, through the broad church of Georgiana Somerset and Lady Augusta Stanley, to the Protestant evangelicalism of Eveline Portsmouth and Anne Sutherland, and the active anti-Catholicism of Lady Charlotte Guest. There was a significant minority of Roman Catholics, such as the Norfolk, Clifford, and Camoys families. The active commitment of Roman Catholic aristocratic families to their faith may be charted through the numbers of their members who joined religious orders: of the families mentioned above, two daughters of the fourteenth duke of Norfolk became nuns, as did two daughters and two granddaughters of the sixth baron Clifford, and four daughters of the third baron Camoys; the same generations of these families also produced five Roman Catholic priests.[7] In Scotland the established church was Presbyterian, and as such provided the usual forms

---

[6] Little attention has, as yet, been focused specifically on the provision of rural education, and none on rural proprietary schools. See Pamela Horn, *Education in Rural England 1800–1914* (Dublin: Gill & Macmillan, 1978), esp. 119–21, and J. S. Hurt, *Elementary Schooling and the Working Classes 1860–1918* (Routledge & Kegan Paul, 1979).

[7] Joseph Foster, *The Peerage, Baronetage and Knightage of the British Empire for 1881* (2 vols., Nichols & Sons, 1881), i.

of devotion for aristocratic women, including Anne Athole. The degree of religious enthusiasm of the women varied considerably: for some, such as Cecil Lothian, it was the guiding force and chief motivation of their lives; while for others, such as Mary Derby and Emily Palmerston, it was at best a social obligation rather than a spiritual necessity. Moreover, religion could play a different part in their lives at different times: thus Harriet Granville lived a worldly life in London and Paris until the death of her husband in 1846, after which she withdrew from Society to find solace in evangelical religion.[8]

It is difficult to reduce this great variety of religious involvement to an overall pattern, but in order to discuss it, it is necessary to make some effort to understand their religious positions and to place them in the context of the religious practices of the nation as a whole. The overlapping lives of Ladies Palmerston, Canning, Granville, and Shaftesbury, who all responded very differently to religious matters, suggests a greater confusion than actually existed if we consider them by generation. On the whole, the generation which married in the late eighteenth and early nineteenth centuries took little interest in religion, observing its forms where necessary and approving of it for others but not necessarily for themselves. As young women, they reflected the Enlightenment dislike of 'enthusiasm', and distanced themselves from any extreme display of religious sentiment. Visiting Paris in 1846, Lady Palmerston was disgruntled to find that religious devotion was the current fashion, and that 'nobody will dine at all tomorrow and it is even a stretch for Mde. de Lieven to give us dinner Saturday and half her company will eat nothing but fish'.[9] Emily Palmerston could be rallied to the Protestant cause, however; in 1851 she joined in the general outcry against 'papal aggression', writing to her husband on the 'dangers of Popery', maintaining that it was 'impossible for the well-being of any Protestant Country to allow the System which the Pope is trying to introduce here'.[10]

Lady Londonderry's papers reveal little evidence of personal belief, although a great deal about institutional involvement. Her speech to her miners at the Chilton Moor feast contains a typical sermon to the working classes, bidding them to seek God's blessing, and to 'fail not to do all in your humble power to deserve it', by the rational use of their leisure time and by being 'orderly, industrious, religious'. She concluded with what Jenifer Hart has identified as one of the most frequently used exhortations in Victorian

[8] Askwith, Piety and Wit, ch. 12.
[9] Emily Palmerston to Frederick, Lord Beauvale, 9 Apr. 1846, Broadlands MSS, BR30.
[10] Emily Palmerston to Lord Palmerston, [31 Jan. 1851], Lever, Letters of Lady Palmerston, 313.

sermons, that 'we may each individually and collectively continue to endeavour to do our duty in that state of life to which it has pleased God to call us'.[11] At the same time, an evangelical minority fostered a different outlook, more in common with the generation which was to follow. This group is represented by Harriet Granville, who had grown up in a nursery filled with the legitimate children of her parents (the duke and duchess of Devonshire) and her aunt (Lady Bessborough), and the miscellaneous collection of children who resulted from their various affairs: despite the unconventional nature of their family, Lady Granville was educated by the daughter of the evangelical novelist Sarah Trimmer, and was associated closely with her pious grandmother, Georgiana Spencer.[12]

The next generation reveals the deepening interest in religion of the early Victorians, in particular the influence of the Oxford Movement on some women of this class. Alongside Emily Shaftesbury, who abandoned her mother's religious apathy for the evangelical fervour of her husband, the reforming earl, and Georgiana Somerset, who greeted news of a new clergyman with the query, '[Is he] High church, Low church or a Happy medium?'[13] stood the high church Harriet Sutherland, whose interests were reinforced by her friendship with W. E. Gladstone. Their long correspondence frequently emphasizes religion, and reveals the influence of high church thought: reflecting on her recent illness, she expressed the peculiarly Catholic sentiment that 'my thoughts have been with the Saviour's wounds'.[14] That the duchess remained within the Anglican communion when so many converted to Rome is perhaps attributable to Gladstone's influence; in turn, she cautioned him against a resumption of intimacy with Manning in the 1860s.[15]

Lady Canning was another of the high Anglicans for whom religion played a central role. On her death in 1861, she was likened to the wise virgins, 'one of those whose lamp was always burning & she was ready'.[16] Charlotte Canning was fully aware of the suspicion with which the high church was regarded, and, visiting the newly established Anglican sisterhood at Clewer in 1849, she was careful to note 'a quiet holy tone', with 'nothing

[11] Londonderry, *Frances Anne*, 279; Jenifer Hart, 'Religion and Social Control in Nineteenth-Century Britain', in A. P. Donajgrodzki (ed.), *Social Control in Nineteenth-Century Britain* (Croom Helm, 1977), 108–37.

[12] Askwith, *Piety and Wit*, 17–22.

[13] Georgiana Somerset to unknown correspondent [fragment], [n.d.], *c.*1860, Bulstrode MSS, D/RA/5/22A.

[14] Harriet Sutherland to Gladstone, 3 Sept. 1863, BL Add. MS 44,327, fos. 242–3.

[15] Harriet Sutherland to Gladstone, 27 June [n.y.1864?], BL Add. MS 44,328, fos. 95–100.

[16] Catherine Gladstone to Anne Athole, 11 Dec. 1861, Atholl MSS, Box 61.

calculated to alarm the most zealous Protestant'.[17] At a time when religion and politics were closely connected, adherence to any unusual form of belief, even within the established church, could cause political difficulties; Lord Granville informed Lord Canning, the first viceroy of India, who was making a case for missionary subscriptions in the House of Lords, that 'there still seems to be a run against you by the Low Church, I presume on account of Lady Canning's Church principles'.[18] The expectation that whole families would subscribe to the same religious practices is implicit in this comment; the cases of two converts to Roman Catholicism demonstrate the difficulties which the fallacy could cause.

Mirroring the experience of men, a number of aristocratic women followed the example of John Henry Newman and Henry Manning and converted to Roman Catholicism, in spite of widespread fear and hostility towards the Church of Rome. Because of their potential influence, they were energetically courted by the Roman Catholic clergy. Cecil Lothian and Charlotte Buccleuch were among the most socially prominent of the converts.[19] Neither found the conversion easy, despite deeply held convictions: Cecil Lothian, who was widowed, endangered her guardianship of her sons by her conversion. The other guardians appointed under her husband's will planned to take the boys away from her, to avoid the danger of her promoting their conversion to Rome; the boys were a matter of concern in a way that the girls were not, principally because it was possible that they or their children might inherit the title and the seat in the House of Lords. In a midnight adventure, she escaped with the younger children from Newbattle Abbey to Edinburgh, where the children were received into the Roman Catholic Church, making their removal by the other guardians redundant. (The eldest son, the marquess, was away at college, and remained within the Anglican church.[20]) Charlotte Buccleuch, who was mistress of the robes to Queen Victoria between 1841 and 1846, faced strenuous opposition from her husband, who succeeded in delaying her reception into the Roman Catholic Church for over ten years, adding to the trauma of the change. The duchess recognized the pain she was causing, 'for with the Duke's opinions

---

[17] Charlotte Canning to Catherine Gladstone, 20 Oct. [1849], BL Add. MS 46,226, fos. 282–3, 287.

[18] Lord Granville to Lord Canning, 9 Jan. 1858 quoted in Lord Edmond Fitzmaurice, *The Life of Lord Granville, 1815–1891* (2 vols., Longmans, Green & Co., 1905), i. 287.

[19] Cecil Lothian specifically linked her progress to that of Manning, writing to her sympathetic brother that 'I have for very long *all but* settled that Archdeacon Manning's course should decide mine': quoted in Kerr, *Cecil Lothian*, 90. See also Cecil Lothian to Manning, 10 May 1851, Bod., MS. Eng. lett. c. 664, fos. 217–20.

[20] Kerr, *Cecil Lothian*, ch. 8.

& feelings my views must be very distressing to him—for I do not suppose he would mind my becoming a presbyterian', but felt that 'for the sake of my soul' she had to convert.[21] The duke, who was active in politics, was afraid of the effect such a conversion would have on his career—particularly as he was involved in the sensitive negotiations over the Disruption of the Church of Scotland in the 1840s, and because of the effect it would have on his relations with the queen.[22] As a consequence, the duchess did not join the Roman Catholic Church until 1860. Such conversions, which also included Elizabeth Herbert of Lea (1862), Adelaide Gainsborough (1851), Mary Holland (1850), and Elizabeth Londonderry (1855) among peeresses, had an importance beyond the conscience of the individual woman, as the Lothian case demonstrates, because of the implications for the upbringing of children and the installation of Roman Catholic chaplains in the great houses. More importantly, the charitable activity and the pious influence which an aristocratic woman was supposed to exert were no longer exercised in the name of the established church, but in that of the Roman Catholic Church.

The number of aristocratic conversions in the 1850s, which coincided with one of the periodic anti-popery crusades, caused public comment and periodic rumours about further conversions: in November 1856 reports appeared in the newspapers that the duchess of Athole was among the converts, and she received a large number of anxious letters from friends and connections, which she bundled together, labelling them 'Letters &c on my reputed Perversion to the Roman Catholic Faith, 1856&7'.[23] She also wrote to her husband saying, 'I *do* believe if *all* the world became Roman Catholics, I should be found a firm Protestant still!', and suggesting that a letter of contradiction be sent to the papers.[24]

Few, if any, women of this generation could be indifferent to religious questions, whether they followed Catholic or Protestant doctrine. This trend continued into the next generation, as the highly coloured religious correspondence between Lady Beauvale and Georgina Cowper-Temple

---

[21] Charlotte Buccleuch to Manning, 6 and 7 June 1850, Bod., MS. Eng. lett. c. 664, fos. 61–4, 65–7.

[22] Kerr, *Cecil Lothian*, 151–3; G. I. T. Machin, *Politics and the Churches in Great Britain, 1832 to 1868* (Oxford: Clarendon Press, 1977), 141. For the Disruption, see Andrew L. Drummond and James Bulloch, *The Churches in Victorian Scotland 1843–1874* (Edinburgh: St Andrew's Press, 1975), ch. 1.

[23] Atholl MSS, Box 58.

[24] Anne Athole to Athole, n.d. [Nov. 1856], and 21 Nov. 1856, Atholl MSS, Box 58. See also Charlotte Canning to Mary Bulteel, 8 Mar. 1857, in Magdalen Ponsonby (ed.), *Mary Ponsonby: A Memoir, Some Letters and a Journal* (John Murray, 1927), 27–33, for another wrongly suspected conversion.

attests.[25] The first fervour of the Oxford Movement had passed, and those professing high church principles later in the century tended to be children of high church parents, rather than converts—for example, Elizabeth Argyll and Lady Frederick Cavendish were both daughters of high church families.[26] The evangelical revival of the 1870s and 1880s is represented by Anne Sutherland and Eveline Portsmouth. The former attended the Moody and Sankey revivalist meetings in the 1870s, and pressed Protestant causes and literature on the prince of Wales and the queen, who declared 'the strongest interest in everything wh. can tend to the Unity of the Protestant Churches', while declining an invitation to send a message to an evangelical conference, on political grounds.[27] Eveline Portsmouth grew up in an evangelical household, and was distressed on a visit to some relatives in Scotland to find herself in the middle of religious controversy; she recommended that her mother, Lady Carnarvon, 'do, say or write nothing which can stir up the tiniest spark on Religious subjects', and to '*dwell* on all the great Spiritual Truths of the Bible without dwelling on the *Untruths'*.[28] Marriage to Lord Portsmouth did not change Eveline's religious persuasions, and she shared his disapproval of the appointment of the high churchman Henry Phillpotts to the see of Exeter. When Portsmouth was required to give a toast to the clergy of Devon at a public meeting, he told his wife that he had avoided the difficulty by resolving 'to *propose* the ArchBishop of Canterbury & the *Protestant* Clergy of this Realm more particularly the working Clergy of the County of Devon. That will not include Hy. of *Exon.'*[29]

Although, as has been seen, women's religious convictions sometimes diverged widely from those of their husbands, there was a presumption that, as in politics, they would conform to the practices of the family into which they married. Marriage from an English family into an Irish one could involve a dramatic change of perspective, as Lady Palmerston's daughter, Lady Frances Cowper, found when she married Lord Jocelyn, the heir to the Calvinistic earl of Roden.[30] The established church in Scotland provided

---

[25] Adine Beauvale to Georgina Cowper-Temple, 1853–4, Broadlands MSS, BR55/66, *passim*.

[26] See e.g. Anthony, 7th earl of Shaftesbury, to Elizabeth Argyll, 23 Jan. 1864, Broadlands MSS, SHA/PC/6. See also John Bailey (ed.), *The Diary of Lady Frederick Cavendish* (2 vols., John Murray, 1927).

[27] Victoria to Anne Sutherland, 3 and 13 June 1870, Sutherland MSS (Staffs.), D593 P/28/1, and Prince of Wales to Anne Sutherland, 28 Dec. [n.y.], D593 P/28/2, Bundle 2. See also Victoria to Frances Gainsborough, 27 Apr. 1875, also on Moody and Sankey, in *LQV*, 2nd ser. ii. 385–6, and *The World*, 5 May 1875, 413.

[28] Eveline Portsmouth to Lady Carnarvon, n.d. [Nov. 1853], Wallop MSS, 15M84, Box 30.

[29] Portsmouth to Eveline Portsmouth, n.d. [1856?], Wallop MSS, 15M84, Box 30.

[30] Countess of Airlie (Mabell Ogilvie), *Thatched with Gold: The Memoirs of Mabell, Countess of Airlie* (Hutchinson, 1962), 16; Airlie, *Lady Palmerston and her Times*, ii. 48–9.

another different religious outlook for a significant number of aristocratic women. The Scottish Leila, Lady Erroll shared the Calvinism of the Rodens; her attempt to comfort the queen in one of her many bereavements with the thought that ' "We will all meet in Abraham's bosom" ' was met with a sharp rebuff from Victoria, who declined to meet Abraham, and noted in her diary that Lady Erroll was 'not at all consolatory in moments of trouble'.[31] Anne Athole was a member of the Church of Scotland, remaining within the established church after the Disruption of 1843 (which led to the formation of the breakaway Free Church of Scotland), unlike Lady John Russell, who believed that theology was an obstacle to true religion, and joined the Free Church.[32] Prior to the queen's first visit to Blair Castle in 1844, Prince Albert was obliged to confirm 'whether the Blair minister was "all right"—or one of the *Free Church*'.[33] During the visit, Anne and her husband (then Lord and Lady Glenlyon) were commanded to sit in the same pew as the queen, so 'Lady Glenlyon should be near her [i.e. Victoria] in order that she may be able to give any hint which may be required as to the forms of the service which Her Majesty is not used to'.[34] This was in fact the first time that Victoria had attended a service outside the Church of England, and it caused unfavourable comment. The queen, despite her position as head of the Church of England, came to evince a strong preference for Presbyterianism, encouraged by Albert's Lutheran background and supported by her own well-documented dislike of bishops. In Scotland she regularly attended Presbyterian services rather than those conducted by the Episcopalian Church, which had closer connections with the Church of England.[35]

The move away from institutional religion, and the predominance of religious doubt in the late nineteenth century, may be seen in Kate Amberley (daughter-in-law to Lady John Russell and mother of the philosopher Bertrand Russell), who described herself as a theistic humanitarian; while the increasing heterodoxy of belief in aristocratic circles is reflected in the marriages of Lord Rosebery and Cyril Flower (later Lord Battersea) to

---

[31] Stanley Weintraub, *Victoria: Biography of a Queen* (Unwin Hyman, 1987), 633; Longford, *Victoria R. I.*, 402, 452.

[32] John Prest, *Lord John Russell* (Macmillan, 1972), 182.

[33] Lord James Murray to Glenlyon, 8 Aug. 1844, Atholl MSS, Bundle 9.

[34] George Anson to Glenlyon, 14 Sept. 1844, Atholl MSS, Bundle 9.

[35] Walter L. Arnstein, 'Queen Victoria and Religion' in Gail Malmgreen (ed.), *Religion in the Lives of English Women, 1760–1930* (Croom Helm, 1986), 88–128. See also Longford, *Victoria R. I.*, 361. The queen did, of course, have an official relationship with the Established (Presbyterian) Church of Scotland (although she was not its head in the English sense), and appointed a Lord High Commissioner to its annual assembly.

daughters of the Jewish Rothschild dynasty, although the latter marriages were not effected without causing some dismay among the anti-Semitic upper classes: Helen Gladstone thought that 'marrying a Jewess isn't very nice', although the fact that she was 'perfectly gigantically rich' was some mitigation.[36]

With this great variety of personal belief, denominational affiliation, and degrees of fervour, a similar variety of activity within the institutions of the churches is to be expected. Four categories of interest may be discerned: ecclesiastical politics, patronage, control over the form and content of services, and education. Excluded from this discussion are those women who were married to clergymen, such as Lady Caroline Somers-Cocks, who married the Revd and hon. Charles Courtenay, and Lady John Thynne, whose husband was rector of Backwell in Somerset and subdean of Westminster, since their experience as wives of active clergymen diverged considerably from that of their lay sisters. For instance, Lady Augusta Stanley, wife of the dean of Westminster and celebrated broad churchman A. P. Stanley, was hostess for many church functions, and provided a link for her husband with the queen, whom she had previously served as woman of the bedchamber.[37]

THE CHURCHES

The church provided an approved field of action outside the home for women of all classes, and provided the training ground for many middle-class women who later in the century sought public acceptance of their work outside the home.[38] The aristocratic woman's experience of church affairs differed from that of the middle-class woman in several respects: firstly, very few, if any, aristocratic women belonged to Protestant nonconformist churches, to which many middle-class women belonged. Secondly, their regular connections with particular churches were likely to be either in rural parishes where they were the principal patrons, or with one of the fashionable London churches which they attended during the season, rather than as anonymous members of a large urban congregation. Thirdly, their social and economic status tended to put them in positions of authority over the clergy, which was seldom, if ever, the case for less socially elevated women, whose church activities were generally closely supervised by the

[36] Quoted in Jalland, *Women, Marriage and Politics*, 89.

[37] See her correspondence with Victoria, Lady Augusta Stanley Papers, Westminster Abbey Archives (hereafter Augusta Stanley MSS), *passim*, esp. Lady Augusta to Victoria, 29 Apr. 1864 and 24 Mar. 1873. Also see A. V. Baillie and Hector Bolitho (eds.), *Later Letters of Lady Augusta Stanley 1864–1876* (Jonathan Cape, 1929), esp. ch. 6.

[38] Prochaska, *Women and Philanthropy*, 1–17, and *passim*; Davidoff and Hall, *Family Fortunes*, 140–8; Heeney, *Women's Movement in the Church of England*, chs. 2 and 3.

clergy. And finally, their social position and political connections put aristo-cratic women in a position to discuss religious questions with men of influ-ence in church and state.

In England, the interests of aristocratic women in ecclesiastical politics during this period generally took the form of intense partisanship over the issues raised by the Oxford Movement in the 1840s, issues which were raised to fever pitch by the secession of many of the leaders of that movement to Roman Catholicism and, in the early 1850s, by the issue of ecclesiastical titles in the Roman Catholic Church in Britain. In Scotland, the issues were some-what different, the emphasis being on the schisms within the Presbyterian Church of Scotland. Lady John Russell, following the Whig principle of con-current endowment, supported the Maynooth Grant (for Roman Catholic education) in 1845, writing to her father, Lord Minto, that she was 'glad Mr Rutherford voted right in spite of his free Kirk & constituents', although she was glad for the general Scottish opposition to the bill, believing it to show 'good protestant feeling'.[39] Similarly, following Gladstone's second Home Rule Bill in 1893, she wrote to her son that an acquaintance 'did not under-stand how Gladstone cd ever again read the Sunday Lessons after bringg. in such a bill!!! Such is Church Christianity!'[40] It had been her husband who had raised the great 'No Popery' cry in 1850, which lead to the Ecclesiastical Titles Act of 1851, a measure intended to prevent the establishment of a Roman Catholic diocesan structure in England with episcopal sees given British territorial designations. Anti-Catholicism, whether of the Roman or the home-grown variety, was at the forefront of the political agenda in the late 1840s and 1850s, Disraeli writing to Lady Londonderry in 1850 of the queen's pleasure at the outcome of the Gorham case, which gave support to the opponents of the Oxford Movement in the Church of England.[41] Exactly a year later, as the Ecclesiastical Titles Bill came before parliament, he reported that 'The struggle after Easter will, I anticipate, be rather of a reli-gious, than a fiscal or agricultural character. . . . There is no lull in the Anti-Catholic feeling in this country, on the contrary, the middle classes are more alarmed than ever.'[42]

It was not only the middle classes who worked themselves into a frenzy over the wave of conversions and the 'papal aggression': Lady London-derry's correspondence contains letters from Lady Westminster, the duke

[39] Lady John Russell to Minto, 21 Apr. 1845, Minto MSS, MS11774, fos. 72–6.
[40] Lady John Russell to Rollo Russell, May 4 [1893], Bod., MS. Eng. lett. e. 113, fo. 166.
[41] Disraeli to Frances Anne Londonderry, 20 Apr. 1850, Londonderry MSS, D/Lo/C 520 (87).
[42] Disraeli to Frances Anne Londonderry, 20 Apr. 1851, Londonderry MSS, D/Lo/C 530 (100).

of Rutland, and Lady William Powlett, all betraying the hysterical note of anti-Catholicism, Lady Westminster speaking of converts going 'out of the way to do mischief & make themselves ridiculous', and the duke describing the pope's effort to restore diocesan titles to his bishops as the 'Papal Impertinence'.[43] Further, Lady Londonderry herself became embroiled in controversy when she declined to make a grant of land for a Roman Catholic burial ground, being accused of religious intolerance.[44] Lady Charlotte Guest, who in the 1840s had waged a campaign against the Puseyite tendencies of the priest at Canford in Dorset, Walter Ponsonby (later seventh earl of Bessborough), going so far as to consult the archbishop of Canterbury, was reassured by his preaching 'strongly on our Church being *Protestant* as well as Reformed', on the occasion of the 'late popish movement'. She was to be greatly embarrassed and personally distressed when her husband's nephew (who was married to a Catholic) invited the Roman Catholic bishop of Merthyr to Dowlais House at the height of the controversy, and spent several days confined to her room in an effort to avoid meeting him.[45] In the 1860s, Harriet Sutherland expressed a continued 'repugnance' towards the Catholic convert Lady Lothian, whom she considered to be 'among the *non* straight forward among roman catholics', particularly because Lady Lothian's daughter was in a French convent, reputedly 'for the repression of her spirit'.[46] Convents exerted a strange fascination for Victorian aristocratic women, who, while professing to be repelled by the idea, not infrequently visited convents on the Continent, as, for example, did Lady Morier in 1864, when she went early in the morning to 'see two nuns take the veil at the Convent of the Ursulines' in Berlin, breakfasting in the convent after the ceremony.[47]

The churches in Scotland provided a different set of political problems for their supporters, the result of their different theologies and perpetual

---

[43] Elizabeth Westminster to Frances Anne Londonderry, 7 Sept. 1850, and Rutland to Frances Anne Londonderry, 7 Nov. 1850, Londonderry MSS, D/Lo Acc 451 (D) File 34; Lady William Powlett to Frances Anne Londonderry, 6 Mar. 1851, D/Lo Acc 451 (D) File 35.

[44] Londonderry MSS, D/Lo/C 216 (3–7), Jan.–Mar. 1862. A detailed analysis of this incident is provided in R. J. Cooter, 'Lady Londonderry and the Irish Catholics of Seaham Harbour: "No Popery" out of Context', *Recusant History*, 13/4 (1976), 288–98. Obviously such intolerance was not confined to women: for an interesting example of the potential consequences of denial of land to non-established churches, see L. A. Ritchie, 'The Floating Church of Loch Sunart', *Records of the Scottish Church History Society*, 22 (1985), 159–73.

[45] Bessborough (ed.), *Lady Charlotte Guest*, 178–9, 252, 254–9.

[46] Harriet Sutherland to Gladstone, 9 Nov. [n.y.], BL Add. MS 44,329, fos. 31–4.

[47] 'Extracts from the Diary of Lady Morier', 31 Mar. 1864, Morier Papers, Balliol College, Oxford (hereafter Morier MSS). For attitudes to convents, see Walter L. Arnstein, *Protestant versus Catholic in Mid-Victorian England: Mr Newdegate and the Nuns* (Columbia, Mo.: University of Missouri Press, 1982), and Susan P. Casteras, 'Virgin Vows: The Early Victorian Artists' Portrayal of Nuns and Novices', in Malmgreen (ed.), *Religion in the Lives of English Women*, 129–60.

schism. Anne Argyll bemoaned the lack of success of the Episcopalian Church in Scotland and the rejection of the doctrine of apostolic succession (and thus of the authority of the bishops) by rich and poor alike, in a long letter to Bishop Wilberforce: 'Not one do I speak to, who seems to know any thing beyond this, that they have a Bible and that *their* Minister takes his Religion from the Bible—And that the Church is Popery *modified*—without knowing what that is, or having the most remote idea of the virtue of either Sacraments. . . .'[48] Religion in Scotland was a central family concern with the Argylls: the next duchess, Elizabeth, wrote to the prime minister, Lord John Russell, in 1848, suggesting that the lord chancellor 'be sent to Scotland to see the workings of Schism, for he seems to be provoking Free Churchism in Wales, with a Vengeance, by his extraordinary wish of giving them Clergymen who cannot speak the language'.[49]

The right of church patronage was an important one to the aristocracy throughout Britain, as it provided them as a class with the means of rewarding their friends and dependants with considerable livings.[50] In 1865, for example, the Sutherlands had the patronage of fourteen livings, worth in total £3,169 annually; Frances Anne Londonderry's four livings were worth £1,481; the Bradfords controlled £5,214 annually in twelve livings; and even the impoverished Portsmouths had eight livings worth £2,255 in their gift.[51] Patronage was a source of income through the sale of advowsons, and also gave a significant degree of control over the local communities; as such, the aristocracy did not give up the right to present incumbents to parishes without a struggle which lasted well into the twentieth century.

The issue of patronage featured largely among the causes of the Disruption of the Church of Scotland, with congregations which demanded the right to veto the appointment of particular clergymen to their parishes seceding from the established church to form the Free Church of Scotland. According to a study made by Lord Dalhousie in 1840, in the preceding six years, four Scottish livings had been presented with ministers by aristocratic women, uncontested by the parishioners. This was a small percentage of the 179 vacancies that were filled, but a significant proportion of the

---

[48] Anne Argyll to Bishop Samuel Wilberforce, 15 Aug. 1855, MS. Wilberforce Papers, Bodleian Library, Oxford (hereafter MS. Wilberforce), c. 11, fos. 172–5.

[49] Elizabeth Argyll to Lord John Russell, 2 Dec. [1848], Russell MSS, PRO 30/22/6E, fos. 269–70.

[50] Alan Haig, *The Victorian Clergy* (Croom Helm, 1984), ch. 6, has shown that livings presented by personal patronage tended to have higher stipends than those given by other patrons, and that the recipients were likely to be young men related to the patron, throughout the nineteenth century.

[51] *Crockford's Clerical Directory* (1865).

presentations made by aristocrats (twenty-nine).[52] The authority of Church courts also featured in the Disruption, and legal disputes over rights of presentation and veto made the task of the patron more complex: in 1857, Anne Athole reminded her husband to recommend that the duke of Leeds 'put his *Manse Case* in the hands of a respectable agent (a Scotch Lawyer *only* will do). . . . Do advise the Duke to get good advice at once, otherwise he will get into endless difficulties.'[53]

Compared to the difficulties of Scottish presentations, patronage in the Church of England was straightforward. Livings were in the gift of the Crown or of private individuals, and were disposed of largely according to the will of the patron, regardless of the inclinations of the congregation. Bishoprics, of course, were Crown appointments. Gladstone's high church beliefs were reflected in a number of his appointments; it was one of these appointees who consecrated Disraeli's rebuilt church at Hughenden in 1875. Disraeli was not a little discomfited by the presence of a high church bishop, belonging to the anti-ritualist school himself, and sent an invitation to Anne Sutherland to join him at the ceremony, as 'I want a good Protestant to support me in a difficult position'.[54] Worse was to follow: in 1879 Disraeli informed the duchess that 'my own spiritual pastor & master has become an absolute Ritualist . . . the Manchester Protestant Association, once my warm supporters, have withdrawn their confidence from the Government in consequence of the Vicar of Hughenden wearing a violet-coloured surplice in Lent!'[55]

Crown patronage, by definition, could not be exercised directly by women except in the case of the queen herself, but indirect influence was another matter: Mary Gladstone, for example, took particular responsibility for matters of church patronage when acting as unofficial private secretary to her father during his terms of office as prime minister.[56] Aristocratic women made extensive use of their contacts in political circles to seek such patronage for their friends or relatives. Thus in February 1845 Charlotte Buccleuch took advantage of her position as mistress of the robes and wife of

[52] 'List of Presentations by Patrons to Parishes within the Church of Scotland; and of cases in which the Veto has been exercised. Between May 1834 and April 1840': Dalhousie MSS, GD45/13/380.

[53] Anne Athole to Athole, 20 July 1857, Atholl MSS, Box 58.

[54] Disraeli to Anne Sutherland, 1 Sept. 1875, Sutherland MSS (Staffs.), D593 P/28/8/15. See also Zetland (ed.), *Letters . . . to Lady Bradford and Lady Chesterfield*, i. 288.

[55] Disraeli to Anne Sutherland, 20 Sept. 1879, Sutherland MSS (Staffs.), D593 P/28/8/15.

[56] See Lucy Masterman (ed.), *Mary Gladstone (Mrs Drew): Her Diaries and Letters* (Methuen, 1930), 184, and H. C. G. Matthew, *Gladstone, 1875–1898* (Oxford: Oxford University Press, 1995), 270.

a cabinet minister to request that Peel appoint her brother, Lord Charles Thynne, to the next vacant canonry in Canterbury. Peel responded that he made it an absolute rule to give no assurances 'with regard to Church Preferment not actually vacant', explaining further that such patronage caused him the 'greatest Embarrassment'.[57] In October, however, the duchess was writing to Peel to thank him for presenting her brother with precisely that stall at Canterbury which she had requested, reiterating her thanks in December.[58] Lady Palmerston wrote to Lord John Russell in 1847 to 'remind you of an Old friend, Robert Eden—a most excellent Clergyman . . . and with Nine Children on his Shoulders', hoping that the canonry at St Paul's was still vacant.[59] Some years later, Elizabeth Argyll suggested, tongue in cheek, that Gladstone appoint the ageing Christian Socialist, F. D. Maurice, to a canonry, pointing out that doctrinal objections could be overcome as 'he wd *teach* less as a Canon than as a Preacher'; in this instance, the suggestion was not taken up.[60] Disraeli used his church patronage for the benefit of his female admirers, writing to Lady Chesterfield in 1874: 'There is a vacant canonry at York. You shall give it to Orlando [her brother, the Revd and hon. Orlando Forester].'[61]

Personal patronage provided many aristocratic women with their principal role in the religious affairs of their parishes. Such patronage could take the form of small-scale donations—for example, in 1888, the duchess of Athole was asked to 'join in the presentation of a Gown to the Minister of Dunkeld'[62]—or very large ones: Lady Lothian built an elaborate Puseyite church in Jedburgh in 1843, and then, following her conversion, set up a Roman Catholic mission chapel and church in the same town, as well as

[57] Charlotte Buccleuch to Sir Robert Peel, 6 Feb. 1845, and Peel to Charlotte Buccleuch, 7 Feb. 1845, BL Add. MS 40,559, fos. 104–5 and 106–7.

[58] Charlotte Buccleuch to Peel, 22 Oct. and 15 Dec. 1845, BL Add. MS 40,576, fos. 138–9 and 40,581, fos. 9–10.

[59] Emily Palmerston to Lord John Russell, Thursday 25 [May 1847], Russell MSS, PRO 30/22/6C. On this occasion the request was not granted, but Eden was subsequently appointed chaplain to the bishop of Norwich, a canon of Norwich Cathedral, and, in 1854, vicar of Wymondham, with a gross annual income of £761, by the patronage of the bishop of Norwich. See also Emily Palmerston to Lord John Russell, 21 Jan. [1848], Russell MSS, PRO 30/22/7A, fos. 163–5.

[60] Elizabeth Argyll to Gladstone, 21 June [1869], BL Add. MS 44,421, fos. 59–60. See also Sir Robert Peel to Frances Anne Londonderry, 25 June 1846, Londonderry MSS, D/Lo Acc 451 (D) Correspondence File 28.

[61] Disraeli to Anne Chesterfield, 8 July 1874, in Zetland (ed.), *Letters . . . to Lady Bradford and Lady Chesterfield*, i. 115.

[62] Mrs McGillurie to Anne Atkole, 27 Aug. 1888, and Anne Atkole to Mrs McGillurie, 28 Aug. 1888, Atholl MSS, Bundle 1652.

purchasing a site and building a Roman Catholic church in Dalkeith.[63] Laura Phillipps de Lisle, a granddaughter of the fourth Lord Clifford, was active with her husband Ambrose in the still more grandiose attempt to convert the Midlands to Roman Catholicism.[64] On a lesser scale, Anne Argyll commented that 'the [Episcopal] Church also in this place mainly looks to the means God has placed in my power'.[65] Aristocratic women were frequently involved in appointments to church livings, even where there were active males in the family, demonstrating their often dominant voice in matters of practical religion. The duke of Argyll consulted his wife's sister-in-law, Anne Sutherland, over the suitability of a Mr McLennan for a vacant living, congratulating her on her prompt and 'business-like' response, and deciding in consequence to offer the living to McLennan.[66] Anne Sutherland, as the heiress to her father's great Cromartie estates, had herself considerable church patronage to command; in 1851, she commissioned Donald Mac-Donald to find her a suitable candidate for a parish, settling on one, William McPherson, who was described as meeting her wishes, being 'modest & unassuming in his manner—& evidently possesses more than ordinary talents and [acquirements?]'.[67]

Frances Anne Londonderry once again provides instructive material for a case-study of the involvement of an aristocratic woman in the ecclesiastical affairs of her community. A detailed examination of her dealings with clergymen of all ranks and her use of patronage in the church shows how social status could overcome the limits placed on public action by women. It also sheds some light on the relationship between an aristocratic woman and the clerical authorities in her parish, and on the ways in which aristocrats expected the church to reinforce social hierarchies.

During the lifetime of the marquess, the Londonderrys acquired a reputation for religious intolerance (strongly contested by later members of the family), and Frances Anne was certainly a prominent supporter of the Church of England, with influence in the highest church circles, and was

[63] Kerr, Cecil Lothian, 45–6, 100; Peter Gallwey, 'Cecil, Marchioness of Lothian', in Salvage from the Wreck: A Few Memories of Friends Departed, Preserved in Funeral Discourses (Burnes & Oates, 1889), 142. See also Priscilla Westmorland to Pauline Neale, 28 Sept. 1862 in Weigall (ed.), Correspondence of Priscilla Westmorland, 435–6.

[64] Bernard Elliott, 'Laura Phillipps de Lisle: A Nineteenth-Century Catholic Lady', Recusant History, 20 (May 1991), 371–9.

[65] Anne Argyll to Samuel, Bishop Wilberforce, 15 Aug. 1855, MS. Wilberforce c. 11, fos. 172–5.

[66] Argyll to Anne Sutherland, 25 Mar. and 4 Apr. 1857, Sutherland MSS (Staffs.) D593 P/28/14.

[67] Donald MacDonald to Anne Sutherland, 12 May 1851, and William McPherson to Anne Sutherland, 2 Aug. 1851, Sutherland MSS (Staffs.), D593 P/28/11.

somewhat embarrassed by the conversion to Roman Catholicism of her stepson's wife in 1855. Bishop Edward Maltby of Durham wrote to her that he was glad to have appointed a clergyman 'who was acceptable both to your Ladyship & Lord Londonderry, and with whom you could co-operate in the business and charities of the Parish'.[68] Between 1855 and 1860, Frances Anne became involved in a three-way conflict between herself, the bishop of Durham, and the Revd Robert Houghton Baxter of Seaham, which illustrates the potential consequences of conflicting social and political hierarchies.[69] The bishop had spiritual authority over the diocese, but no direct control over appointments. A clergyman could claim authority and precedence over persons of all classes by virtue of his calling, regardless of his own social class, and exercised spiritual authority within his parish. A patron, on the other hand, could expect a degree of deference from someone who owed his position to her good offices, and was in a position to confer benefits on the parish, and hence felt a right to dictate the terms in which the gift was to be received.

Frances Anne determined upon building a church in New Seaham, the town which had come into existence largely as a result of Londonderry industrial enterprises. Aside from the question of a large population which had no established church clergyman, the clergyman in Old Seaham, Robert Baxter, did not meet with Lady Londonderry's approval: she complained to the bishop of his church being empty, and of Baxter being personally troublesome. At the time of her decision, the bishop was recovering from a cataract operation, and did not personally accede to the plan, although, as Frances Anne later showed, his wife wrote expressing the bishop's pleasure at the endeavour. In August 1855, Baxter complained to the bishop that he had not been informed of the proposed building in his parish until he received an invitation to the ceremony of laying the foundation-stone, and the bishop wrote to Frances Anne, rebuking her for beginning such a project without authority. Frances Anne responded in kind, pointing out the need for the church, her own generosity in giving the land, the building costs, and meeting the salary of the incumbent, reminding the bishop of Baxter's deficiencies, and concluding with the threat that 'it would be very annoying to make a public announcement that I have been forbidden to build the Church and I cannot stop all the arrangements contracts &c without doing so'. The bishop denied any intention to offend, denied that he was supporting the

---

[68] Edward Maltby to Frances Anne Londonderry, 11 Jan. [n.y.], Londonderry MSS, D/Lo Acc 451 (D) Correspondence File 27.

[69] This discussion is based on Londonderry MSS, D/Lo/C 552 (1–19), D/Lo/C 176 (1–9), and D/Lo/C 201 (1–7).

insupportable Baxter, and denied that he wanted to inhibit her 'munificent design', claiming merely to be trying to smooth over the difficulties she was experiencing with Baxter. Further, he engaged his archdeacon, Charles Thorpe, to communicate with Baxter, informing him of the wish to avoid delay or the withdrawal of Lady Londonderry's project, which would 'bring upon us the suspicion that needless impediments on the part of the Church vicars have deprived the Parish of the great boon & privilege offered to us by her Ladyship's liberality'. Baxter replied in unrepentant terms, expressing his willingness 'to pay ready obedience to my superiors *in the Church*' [my italics]: by implication, Baxter refused to pay such obedience to his social superiors and patrons in matters relating to church business in his parish. There was then something of a stand-off for a few weeks, until Frances Anne wrote to the bishop that building had gone ahead, despite her sense of ill use, and that when it was finished, she would apply for a licence and consecration. If this request was refused, she would 'have the satisfaction of knowing I am not to blame if the population of New Seaham are deprived of the advantage of religious worship in a Church of England of which I am prepared to pay the Minister's stipend'. After this heavy-handed reminder of her generosity, the bishop declined any further personal correspondence, suggesting that they leave the matter to their agents, indicating that on the strength of all the communications he had received, and in the light of his professed ignorance of Lady Londonderry's intention, she had been 'acting very irregularly'. At this point, Frances Anne produced the letter she had received from Mrs Maltby, which clearly stated that the bishop had been told of the planned church, and assured her of 'his best wishes and earnest prayers on the occasion'. The correspondence then falls silent until April 1857, when the Revd William A. Scott accepted the living of New Seaham, worth £788 per annum with a house, from Frances Anne. His letter of acceptance was a succinct expression of the priorities of a clergyman likely to receive the approval of an autocratic aristocratic patron. 'I earnestly trust', he wrote, 'that I may be enabled by God's blessing to labour for His Glory, to your Ladyship's satisfaction and for the spiritual welfare of the people.'

There was, by this time, a new bishop of Durham, Longley, who sought to restore good relations with Lady Londonderry. He informed her that 'the difficulties in the way of the consecration of Seaham Church do not seem insurmountable', and sent her a copy of the legal advice he had received. Even with a new bishop and a personally appointed minister, the difficulties over the New Seaham church were not at an end, however. In February the marchioness was complaining to the bishop that Scott was holding prayer-meetings in his house rather than in the church, and in July 1860 Scott received a reprimand from his patron, for informing the bishop of the appointment of a curate before writing to Frances Anne. Then in September of the same year, there were difficulties over the arrangements for the consecration of the church: the ceremony was finally fixed by Scott to take place at a time when Lady Londonderry would be absent, which caused her great annoyance, although Scott believed he was acting in accordance with her wishes, having himself 'very many powerful motives for avoiding all that would give you pain'. The correspondence at this time gives a very clear picture of the different conceptions of the rights and obligations and the tensions of hierarchies between church and patron. In the course of the dispute, Scott had written that Lady Londonderry was 'sometimes not quite as considerate as might be expected of the feelings of us poor clergymen and of what is due to our office'. Frances Anne replied with all the considerable hauteur of which she was capable that 'upon reflection you will admit that yr letter of the 5th is not a proper one to Write to me'.[70]

Frances Anne Londonderry had a less problematic relationship with the parish of St Nicholas, Durham, which was also in her gift. She bestowed the perpetual curacy (of £84 a year) on the Revd George Townshend Fox, under whose supervision the church was largely rebuilt, and a school and a Female Training School established. There were no differences of dogma between cleric and patron in this instance, Fox sharing Frances Anne's horror of 'the frivolities indulged in by the Tractarians', and the only difficulty to cloud the horizon was the adultery of his curate, 'a hypocrite a scoundrel & a most depraved character', whom Fox forced from the town 'in company with the vile woman for whom he had forsaken his poor unhappy wife'.[71]

This kind of reporting by a minister or priest to a patron was not uncommon, providing a mechanism of control over the form and content of religious practice in a parish. Of course, where a living was in the gift of a patron, whether male or female, aristocrat or commoner, the patron was likely to present the parish to a clergyman who shared his or her own religious preferences: thus, for example, the controversial appointment by the dowager Lady Bath of a Tractarian to the parish of Frome in 1852, despite the opposition of many parishioners and the general unpopularity of the high church,

---

[70] Another of the *grandes dames*, Lady Jersey, broke off relations with her local minister, whom she regarded as having treated her with 'undue familiarity'. Countess of Jersey (Margaret E. Child-Villiers), *Records of the Family of Villiers, Earls of Jersey* (Morton, Burt & Sons, 1924), 49. Similarly, Lady Stanley of Alderley and her husband maintained a long-running feud with their local cleric, which began with a dispute over tithes: Mitford (ed.), *Ladies of Alderley*, 9, 104, 148–50.

[71] George Fox to Frances Anne Londonderry, 1856–60, Londonderry MSS, D/Lo/C 194 (1–9).

was in sympathy with the patron's beliefs.[72] Once the appointment was made, however, the patron had no power to remove the incumbent. Where the relationship between clergyman and patron was good, the clergyman could provide a useful link between the parish and the great house, informing the patron of cases where charitable aid would be of value, and keeping him or her in touch with the sentiments of the parish, which might otherwise pass them by, for reasons of social hierarchy and frequent absence.

The minister at Minto, David Aitken, kept Lady Minto informed of all that was going on in the parish, reporting on local incidents, the state of the harvest, charity cases, wage levels, and local politics.[73] The relationship had a price for the aristocratic woman: Lady Constance Stanley (later countess of Derby) noted that 'We did some duty last night', in having the clergyman and his family to dinner, adding, 'Need I say we were much bored!' The boredom was not entirely without its uses, however, as Lady Constance took the opportunity to outline her preferences for the form of service, clearly with the expectation that they would be taken into serious consideration, if not instantly complied with: 'I had an opportunity of saying I liked short sermons & quick service & I advised the leaving out of the Litany.'[74] Charles Kingsley, rector of Eversley, kept Lady Mildmay abreast of local events, gossiping under the licence of his dog-collar, relating the breakdown of the marriage of Sir John and Lady Cope, and the case for and against a schoolmistress, Esther Warner, who was accused of drunkenness.[75] The case for the churches as instruments of social control is, at best, unproved; but the relationship between clergy and aristocratic women does provide considerable evidence for the church as an instrument of social observation and reportage.

In this central institution of community life, then, aristocratic women can be seen to have played a role which was not limited by their gender to one of passive support and obedience to male authority. They enjoyed considerable autonomy in the matter of their own religious preferences, and were often in a position to impose those preferences on the local hierarchy of the church. They used their social position and political connections to advance the interests of their families and clients, and sought, through the various churches to which they belonged, to reinforce the social order. Similar issues

[72] W. N. Yates, ' "Bells and Smells": London, Brighton and South Coast Religion Reconsidered', *Southern History*, 5 (1983), 122–53.

[73] David Aitken to Mary Minto, 1846, Minto MSS, MS11908, fos. 10–37, *passim*.

[74] Lady Constance Stanley to Katharine Clarendon, 2 Sept. 1871, Hobbs (Derby/Gathorne Hardy) Papers, Corpus Christi College Library, Cambridge (hereafter Hobbs MSS), 30/40.

[75] Charles Kingsley to Lady Mildmay, 22 May 1882 and Apr. 1866, Mildmay (Dogmersfield) Papers, Hampshire Record Office (hereafter Mildmay MSS), 15M50/1204/2.

are raised in a consideration of aristocratic women's involvement in the provision of schools for the rural poor.

EDUCATION

Until the 1870 Elementary Education Act, which allowed (but did not compel) school-boards to levy a special rate for the provision of a school, education for the masses was organized on a voluntary basis, with churches, both established and nonconformist, taking the lead. By mid-century, some landowners were also engaged in educational provision for their labourers and tenants, also on this voluntary basis, and schools were found to be a particularly suitable interest for the wives and daughters of the aristocracy. The extent of such provision by the landowning classes should not be overstated; indeed, their failure to contribute to the education of children on their estates was commented on and criticized by the 1861 Newcastle Commission on popular education: 'The general cause of apathy is the non-residence of the landowners. . . . In the thinly peopled rural districts the higher classes consist of the landlords and the clergy, the farmers forming the middle class. The farmers are often hostile to education; the landlords, unless resident, are indifferent.'[76]

Thomas Laqueur, in his study of the rise of the Sunday school in the late eighteenth and early nineteenth centuries pointed out that the stereotype of the organization of these institutions were of the kindly vicar assisted by a middle- or upper-class 'lady bountiful'. In fact, as Laqueur demonstrates, upper-class teachers were vastly outnumbered by working-class, Sunday school-educated teachers, particularly in urban areas, with a resurgence of middle-class activity during the mid-Victorian period.[77] Although the number of aristocratic women involved in teaching in Sunday schools was not particularly significant for the Sunday school movement, for the women themselves, particularly for the daughters of the house, it had great importance. Teaching in Sunday schools was considered appropriate for young, unmarried women, training them in public service, and reinforcing the ties between the classes. For example, the daughters of Henrietta Stanley of Alderley taught Sunday school classes at Alderley in the 1850s, and the young Ishbel Marjoribanks, later countess of Aberdeen, taught at a London Sunday school in the 1870s, teaching a morning and an afternoon class every Sunday that she was in London until her marriage. Further, in 1874 at the age of 17 she founded the first Sunday school on her father's Scottish estate, Guisachan. She described the classes she lead:

[76] *Parliamentary Papers*, 1861 [2794–I] xxl, part 1, 279, 'Report of Her Majesty's Commissioners appointed to Inquire into the State of Popular Education in England'.

[77] Laqueur, *Religion and Respectability*, esp. 93.

I could find no helpers as teachers, and so divided the children according to age, and after roll call, marks for attendance, and opening prayer, placed a monitor over each class, to hear and award marks for correct repetition of Bible portion, hymn, and catechism, then a hymn sung all together and a general talk given by myself, another hymn, and then to Church.[78]

The ladies of the family of Stanley of Alderley were committed to the education of their local children; in addition to Sunday schools, they supported day schools in Northwich and Baintree, and Maria Josepha Stanley agreed to contribute to a local 'Ragged School', despite disapproving of the name which she considered 'a sort of opprobrium'.[79] Her successor, Henrietta Stanley, took her interest in education into a different sphere, becoming one of the founder-patrons of Girton College, Cambridge. Eveline, Lady Portsmouth was one of the women who continued to teach in schools after her marriage, combining teaching with the general supervision in which more married women engaged. Her diary for 1871 finds her doing the school registers for an impending visit by the inspectors, superintending a school fete, and taking 'a large class for English reading in the School'.[80]

Frequent absence could restrict regular commitment to the superintendence of schools. In 1843, Charlotte Canning reported that she was returning to her parental home 'for a day or two, to look after the place, the poor people, and the school'.[81] In the absence of extensive documentation, the extent of aristocratic women's interest in schooling for 'their' poor can perhaps best be gauged by the regular inclusion of a visit to the schoolhouse on the itinerary of many of their visitors: on a visit to an aunt in Dundee, the future Lady Portsmouth was taken to visit the school, where she particularly admired the pupils' singing.[82] Lady Harriet Elliot, visiting her sister, Lady John Russell, in London in 1844, recorded accompanying Lord and Lady John to a number of schools 'which are very well worth it', commenting on the excellence of the boys' drawing, swimming, and singing, adding that 'the girls['] school less interesting'.[83] Lady Lyttelton reported to her daughter on

---

[78] Earl and countess of Aberdeen (John and Ishbel Gordon), 'We Twa': Reminiscences of Lord and Lady Aberdeen (2 vols., W. Collins, 1925), i. 146–51. From a different religious tradition, Constance Rothschild and her sister Annie began the first school in Aston Clinton in Buckinghamshire in the face of the opposition of the rector, and taught at the Jews' Free School: Battersea, Reminiscences, 25–7, 409–10.

[79] Maria Josepha Stanley to Henrietta Eddisbury, 20 Nov. 1849, quoted in Mitford (ed.), Ladies of Alderley, 264.

[80] Eveline Portsmouth's diary, 21 Jan., 18, 28 Feb. 1871, Wallop MSS, 15M84, Box 38.

[81] Charlotte Canning to Lady Stuart de Rothesay, 13 Sept. 1843, quoted in Hare, Two Noble Lives, i. 269.

[82] Lady Eveline Herbert to Lady Carnarvon, 16 Nov. 1853, Wallop MSS, 15M84, Box 30.

[83] Lady Harriet Elliot's journal, 10 May 1844, Minto MSS, MS12014.

her visit to the queen's school in Windsor,[84] while the princess royal commented to Lady Canning, then in India, that 'Your visits to the native schools must be a great source of interest to you, and the difference between them and those in England must be most striking.'[85]

Such visiting provided a link between the classes, offering an opportunity for the aristocracy to show concern and interest in their tenants' welfare, and providing the schools with the opportunity to show gratitude and deference to their patrons.[86] Anne Summers has noted in the broader context of upper-class women's philanthropy that 'the Lady Bountiful is a legitimate object of popular resentment and literary satire'; but it could be argued that the very infrequency of aristocratic visits to 'their' schools lent mystique and authority to the aristocratic visitor, which the familiar supervision of the middle classes could not obtain.[87]

A concomitant to church building was school building, many patrons taking the opportunity to provide religious and secular education at the same time. Most of these schools would fall to the day-to-day administration of the local clergyman, unsurprising at a time when the principal providers of education were the Church of England National Society and the nonconformist British and Foreign Society. After 1870 and the rise of the board schools, the domination of the church declined, but the two systems ran alongside each other (as in some respects they continue to do). On the same day that Lady Westmorland's chapel in Sharlston, near Wakefield, was inaugurated, she also opened a school, 'really pretty and picturesque, although plain, as I wished'.[88] Anne Argyll, while despairing for the Episcopal Church in Scotland, had provided 'a School in connection with the little Church, in which above 80 Children are in training in Ch. principles', although she noted that most of the pupils were from Roman Catholic families.[89] Lady Charlotte Guest was involved in reorganizing the schools set up by her husband at Dowlais and Merthyr Tydfil, and took particular interest in adult education, forming a night school for young women in 1848, from which

---

[84] Sarah Lyttelton to Caroline Lyttelton, 14 Oct. 1848, Wyndham (ed.), *Correspondence of Lady Lyttelton*, 387.

[85] Victoria, princess royal, to Charlotte Canning, 23 Sept. 1856, Canning Papers, Oriental and India Office Collections, British Library, (hereafter Canning MSS), Photo Eur 31 / 1.

[86] See Lady Waldegrave's letter of thanks for a quilt worked by the girls of Nuneham school, Frances Waldegrave to Mrs Hutchinson, 26 Feb. 1862, Strachey MSS, DD/SH C1189 G217.

[87] Anne Summers, 'A Home from Home—Women's Philanthropic Work in the Nineteenth Century', in Sandra Burman (ed.), *Fit Work for Women* (Croom Helm, 1979), 33.

[88] Priscilla Westmorland to Pauline Neale, 28 Sept. 1862, in Weigall (ed.), *Correspondence of Priscilla Westmorland*, 435–6.

[89] Anne Argyll to Samuel Wilberforce, 15 Aug. 1855, MS. Wilberforce c. 11, fos. 172–5.

year she also taught in the schools in emergencies.[90] The extent of Frances Anne Londonderry's involvement in the churches of her neighbourhood almost necessitated a like degree of involvement in the educational mission of the church, although she does not appear to have devoted a similar attention to detail in her schools as in other areas of her activity. In 1853, she had a sum of money to dispense, and sought advice on the most suitable way of spending it. Her correspondent responded that

> though, I fear, we do not exactly agree on the subject of the National Schools, you have, if I mistake not, expressed to me your approval of the five [illeg.] principles of the Church Edn Socy—namely that every child, capable of reading, shall read the Scripture Daily, & the Church Children be taught *its* (the Church's) catechism &c.[91]

In 1855, the Revd A. Bethune sent Lady Londonderry the outline of two schemes for schools in Seaham Harbour and their relative costs, one which would provide exclusively for the children of people employed in the Londonderry collieries, the other providing for all the children in the locality. The latter scheme, surprisingly, would prove the least expensive to Frances Anne, as a larger government grant would be available if the school were not restricted to her employees.[92] The schools were set up, and little correspondence on the subject remains beyond a few letters from the minister of New Seaham, W. A. Scott, to Lady Londonderry seeking her approval—and presumably her financial support—for the appointment of new teachers.[93] In addition, she was involved in setting up schools in the vicinity of her Garron Tower retreat in Ireland and with the Female Training School in the city of Durham.[94]

Anne Athole, on the other hand, was not content with merely financing the building of a school, but played an active part in its supervision, finding suitable schoolteachers and mediating in disputes. In 1854 (the same year that she was appointed lady-in-waiting) the duchess determined on founding a school for girls in Dunkeld, building both school and a house for the schoolmistress at a final cost of £1139. 1s. 5d.[95] Her diary for the year notes

---

[90]   Guest and John, *Lady Charlotte*, 61–9; Bessborough (ed.), *Lady Charlotte Guest*, 222–4.

[91]   J. Blackwood Price to Frances Anne Londonderry, 24 Feb. 1853, Londonderry MSS, D/Lo Acc 451(D) File 42.

[92]   Revd A. Bethune to Frances Anne Londonderry, 13 Jan. 1855, Londonderry MSS, D/Lo/C 525.

[93]   W. A. Scott to Frances Anne Londonderry, 15 Sept. 1860 and 25 Sept. 1860, Londonderry MSS, D/Lo/C 201 (4) and (8).

[94]   Frances Anne Londonderry to Benjamin Disraeli, 18 Sept. [1850], Londonderry MSS, D/Lo/C 530 (92); and Revd George Fox to Frances Anne Londonderry, 21 Feb. 1857 and 10 June 1858, D/Lo/C 194 (1) and (6).

[95]   'Building Expenses for the Duchess's School, Dunkeld', R. C. Carrington (Factor), [1854], Atholl MSS, Bundle 1288.

the visits of Mr Dickson the architect and her interest in all the details of the new buildings down to the desks and furnishings.[96] She also engaged the schoolmistress, commenting to her husband that she 'liked her much & hope you will'.[97] The buildings were not ready for the opening of the academic year in September, and Anne noted that 'my school opened in Dunkeld in Sunday School room. 36 girls'.[98] By December, the buildings were ready, and the duchess attended a general meeting in the schoolhouse to arrange the opening ceremony, which took place on 21 December. She recorded the day's events in her diary: 'Constant arrangements all day—in & out—Miss Grant arrives about 1.30.—Lunch at 3—all repair to open my school at 6pm—76 girls at tea—magic lantern, xmas tree &c till 8.30. Tea & mutton chops on return home.'[99]

The duchess's interest did not wane after the opening, and, particularly after her husband's death, when she made her principal home in Dunkeld, she closely supervised the activities of the school, which was known as 'The Duchess's School'. She received regular reports from the minister on the progress of the school, one in 1856 expressing the minister's relief that the reports of her conversion to Rome were being contradicted, as 'the girls were in the state of highest excitement for a day or two'.[100] This incident highlights the extent of the connection felt between patron and school, and the patron's potential for influence. In 1888, a later minister's wife, Mrs Rutherford, found cause for complaint in the treatment of her daughters by the schoolmistress, Miss Illingworth. She wrote to Emily Murray Mac-Gregor, Anne Athole's cousin and companion, setting out the local perception of the duchess's role in her school.

Were she [Miss Illingworth] under a School Board she wd not *dare* act in the way she does, for a complaint wd be immediately made at Headquarters—but seeing the Duchess is practically *our* School Board so to speak tho' I use the word in all respect, I feel sure she will excuse me bringing this case before her.[101]

In an interview with Miss Murray MacGregor in September, during a second round of complaints, Mrs Rutherford again outlined some of the stresses on the community that the direct connection of the duchess with her school entailed, suggesting that

[96] Anne Athole's diary, 28 Feb. and 14 Aug. 1854, Atholl MSS, Bundle 639.
[97] Anne Athole to Athole, Tuesday [n.d., 1854], Atholl MSS, Box 43.
[98] Anne Athole's diary, 1 Sept. 1854, Atholl MSS, Bundle 639.
[99] Anne Athole's diary, 21 Dec. 1854, Atholl MSS, Bundle 639.
[100] Revd J. C. Wilson to Anne Athole, 2 Dec. 1856, Atholl MSS, Box 58.
[101] Mrs Rutherford to Emily Murray MacGregor, 10 May 1888, Atholl MSS, Bundle 1290.

The Parents were afraid to speak it was a question of bread & butter to them the future both of their *boys* & girls might depend upon it—although of course Her Grace would not make any difference . . . Even the School Inspectors are influenced by its being Her Grace's school Walker wd pass over things which would not be stood in a board school.[102]

The nature of Mrs Rutherford's complaints were trivial, and it seems that she was generally being unreasonable—complaining that the rules for attendance were applied to her daughters as to all other children, when she wanted to keep them at home, and complaining that the windows in the school were kept open, forcing her children either to sit in draughts or to be placed away from the draught in the 'dull scholars' seats'.[103] None the less, the correspondence demonstrates belief in the power of the duchess to intervene in the school—she was 'practically *our* School Board'—and the dominion which she was in a position to exercise in the lives of the local community and on a wider stage, particularly on the employment prospects of the children, by virtue of her rank. Moreover, it demonstrates a firm conviction that the rank of the patron exempted her and her school from the state supervision bestowed on grant-maintained schools, giving them a freedom of action unavailable in schools without such highly placed patrons.[104] The duchess, and her faithful aide, Miss Murray MacGregor, stood firmly behind the schoolmistress, turning aside the complaints with the assurance that 'We should never think of investigating from the parents what they thought unless any actual moral offence was in question'.[105] The second round of complaints was met with the assurance that 'the school having been open for so many years, we have full experience of what is necessary for the general comfort'.[106] Mrs Rutherford continued to express her discontent, finally drawing a response from the duchess herself that 'I must however beg to decline discussing the conduct of my school-mistress & cannot enter into any further correspondence on the subject'.[107]

A similar degree of absorption in the business of educating the tenantry

[102] 'Rough Notes of a Conversation with Mrs Rutherford', A. M. M. [Emily Murray MacGregor], 29 Sept. 1888, Atholl MSS, Bundle 1290.

[103] Atholl MSS, Bundle 1290, *passim*.

[104] The impact of inviting state supervision by accepting government grants is discussed in Michael J. Gray-Fow, 'Squire, Parson and Village School: Wragby 1830–1886', in Patrick Scott and Pauline Fletcher (eds.), *Culture and Education in Victorian England* (Lewisburg, Pa.: Bucknell University Press, 1990), 162–73.

[105] 'Rough Notes', 29 Sept. 1888, Atholl MSS, Bundle 1290. A similar case involved a school run by Mrs Withers in Romsey, where a complaint was treated in a similar way by the Palmerstons: Henry Palmerston to Emily Palmerston, 11 July 1865, Broadlands MSS, BR23 AA/1.

[106] Emily Murray MacGregor to Mrs Rutherford, 2 Oct. 1888, Atholl MSS, Bundle 1290.

[107] Anne Athole to Mrs Rutherford, 15 Oct. 1888, Atholl MSS, Bundle 1290.

was exhibited by Frances, Lady Milton, on the family's Coollattin estates in Ireland. To Lady Milton fell the task of keeping her father-in-law, Lord Fitzwilliam, informed of the condition of the people on the estate, and of the activities which she and her husband were instituting or supporting for the benefit of the tenants: for example, a Sunday school library and a bible depot for the cheap purchase of bibles.[108] The sectarian nature of Irish politics and society added complications to the work of creating competent educational establishments, Lady Milton assuming that the library would have to be exclusively Protestant, for example. More important were the difficulties over plans for a new mixed (Protestant and Catholic) school in 1852, to which the Protestant minister objected. A new plan was devised, whereby 'the children are . . . to separate into Prot. & R.C. classes at opposite ends of the room so as not to interfere with each other's reading—& tho' no catechisms are to be taught inside the walls of the school you [Lord Fitzwilliam] are to send a teacher with the children to see that they learn them elsewhere.'[109] The difficulties had been considerable and the debate protracted, and Lady Milton concluded that 'you must be sick of the school subject'.[110]

Much of Lady Milton's educational interest focused on the search for suitable teachers for the Shellelagh school, again a particular difficulty because many English teachers were unwilling to go to Ireland. The teacher in 1850, Mrs Burke, informed Lady Milton that 'she and her daughter had determined to go to America, where they have relations', and sought Lord Fitzwilliam's assistance with the passage. Lady Milton urged that Mrs Burke not be allowed to stay on until the following May, as her class-room was 'in such confusion', partly owing to the greatly increased number of students attending once the harvest was over.[111] Then began the process of selecting a replacement. A 'Native, the daughter of a tenant of yrs', a Miss Grange, offered her services, but although 'clean & respectable', Lady Milton did not think her up to the management of a large school, because Miss Grange had herself never been to school before attending the 'church education training school'.[112] Frances Milton received a recommendation for a Miss Baird, a Scottish woman with excellent credentials, who appeared 'willing to go to Ireland', something of a rarity. This letter also makes clear that earl

---

[108] Frances Milton to Fitzwilliam, 8 Sept. [n.y., 1840s], Wentworth Woodhouse Muniments, WWM MF67 G75/5.

[109] Frances Milton to Fitzwilliam, 6 Feb. [1852], Wentworth Woodhouse Muniments, WWM MF67 G75/13a.   [110] See also Foster, *Paddy and Mr Punch*, 50–1.

[111] Frances Milton to Fitzwilliam, 1 Oct. 1850, Wentworth Woodhouse Muniments, WWM MF67 G75/10.

[112] Frances Milton to Fitzwilliam, 13 Jan. [1851?], Wentworth Woodhouse Muniments, WWM MF67 G75/12a.

Fitzwilliam did not decide these matters alone, but was in the habit of consulting his unmarried daughter. Lady Milton wrote: 'you & Charlotte [my italics] had better decide soon, please, as it is not fair to keep the woman waiting.'[113] The mistress who was eventually appointed, a Miss Macdougal, did not meet with Frances Milton's approval, despite being 'well-informed and quite competent to instruct', having 'a disagreeable remark for every child in the school' and a 'snarling' manner. In the event of a 'good mistress or even a good & clever master' being discovered, Lady Milton recommended appointing them to the Shellelagh school.[114]

Lady Mildmay took great interest in local affairs, being kept informed by her diligent rector, Charles Kingsley, who in 1866 reported on the affair of Esther Warner, the schoolmistress, which reveals the moral surveillance carried out over schoolmistresses in much the same way that domestic servants' morals were supervised. She was accused of staying out late at night and of being drunk, and was threatened with dismissal. After the first shock, however, Kingsley wrote that the matter was not so dreadful. Although Miss Warner admitted to being out late, it was at a party, where she was chaperoned by her young man, and she strongly denied having been tipsy, which explanation Kingsley accepted. Nevertheless, Miss Warner's position was considered untenable after the lapse: ['O]f course, she must go . . . But I think Sir Henry would agree with me, that a happy wedding, & as graceful & merciful a dismissal as possible, will be the best solution of the difficulty.'[115]

The provision of the annual school treat was a widespread practice in the nineteenth century: the duke of Athole marked his wife's birthday each year with some kind of festival for her school, in 1855 dispensing '11 shillings worth of Sugar Plums'.[116] Lady Augusta Stanley described a treat given to local schoolchildren by her sister to celebrate the birth of a child:

I wish you had been here today to see all the children . . . dining on beef, mutton, potatoes & apple tart in the Servants Hall. . . . They eat more than you can fancy, one little Boy I saw set to work to eat his *third* helping as 'si de rien etait'—using a spoon but in the first place putting the meat into said spoon with his fingers!! They had a glass of wine each to drink the health of the parents, & then a little glass for the Baby's health.[117]

[113] Frances Milton to Fitzwilliam, 15 Oct. [1850], Wentworth Woodhouse Muniments, WWM MF67 G75/11a.

[114] Frances Milton to Fitzwilliam, 31 Oct. [1853], Wentworth Woodhouse Muniments, WWM MF67 G75/20.

[115] Charles Kingsley to Lady Mildmay, 3 Apr. 1866, Mildmay MSS, 15M50/1204/2.

[116] Athole to Anne Athole, 24 June 1855, Atholl MSS, Box 58. See also Athole to Anne Athole, 17 June 1856, Box 58.

[117] Lady Augusta Bruce to Lady Frances Bruce, 27 Oct. [1843?], Augusta Stanley MSS, vol. 1,

By such means was the prosperity of the ruling family tied to pleasant recollections on the part of the labourers, and the patterns of deference replicated. (Of course, this is not to make any assessment of the degree to which such deference was actually internalized; but aristocratic society could function perfectly well on the basis of a show of deference.)

Schools were unofficially segregated along class lines,[118] and while the working-class pupils would be treated to a feast or, later in the century, to a day trip, middle-class pupils would be treated to a visit by a 'great man', who would be called upon to address the scholars, remind them of their obligations, and by his presence, reinforce the status of the aristocratic patrons of the school. Lord Houghton, a middle-ranking politician and man of letters, was typical of the kind of person in demand, receiving an invitation from Eveline Portsmouth to speak 'on the occasion of an annual Examination of a Middle Class School for boys' in North Tawton. Also to be present was the dean of Westminster, A. P. Stanley.[119] The same gentleman was invited by Lady Frederick Cavendish to 'be the Great Man' at a joint function of the convalescent home at Woodford in Essex and 'a good upper-middle class private school'.[120] An aristocratic patron could also take advantage of her contacts to publicize the activities of her school, as did Eveline Portsmouth, who sent a report to John Thaddeus Delane of *The Times*, who 'took much pleasure' in publishing it.[121]

Aristocratic women's involvement in the schools for their tenants' children thus ranged from financing schools, selecting teachers, and daily management, to holding classes, to the provision of, and occasional presence at, an annual treat. We have seen how the duchess of Athole's engagement with her school was regarded in the local community, and there is no reason to suppose that this was exceptional: Sarah Sophia, countess of Jersey, issued a dictate that the children of Middleton Stoney should begin attending school at the age of 2, and some years after her death a future countess discovered the instruction still being obeyed.[122] Lady Minto received reports on the state of the local school from the minister, who enquired 'if there are any

---

fo. 21. See also Katherine Clarendon to William Vernon Harcourt, 28 Sept. 1871, Harcourt Papers, Bodleian Library, Oxford, (hereafter MS. Harcourt), dep. 633, fos. 218–21; Louisa, countess of Wemyss, to Frances Waldegrave, [n.d.], Strachey MSS, DD/SH C1189 G251; and Susan Wharncliffe's diary, 29 Jan. 1861 and 6 Jan. 1865, Wharncliffe Muniments, WhM 485.

[118] See David Allsobrook, *Schools for the Shires: The Reform of Middle-Class Education in Mid-Victorian Britain* (Manchester: Manchester University Press, 1986).

[119] Eveline Portsmouth to Lord Houghton, 8 Oct. 1874, Houghton MSS, 33/93.

[120] Lady Frederick Cavendish to Houghton, 15 July 1869, Houghton MSS, 29/117.

[121] John T. Delane to Eveline Portsmouth, 4 Jan. [n.y.], Wallop MSS, 15M84, Box 30.

[122] Jersey, *Records of the Family of Villiers*, 49.

particular directions you would like observed'.[123] Patronage of local institutions such as churches and schools reinforced the authority of the aristocracy in the country—as critical commentary on its absence highlights. Aristocratic women often played a crucial part in maintaining the relationship, whether it is viewed as essentially benevolent or fundamentally exploitative. Such involvement could be construed as appropriate feminine behaviour; but at the same time their social position enabled these women to have a wide impact on their local communities. The exploration of the functions of patronage as exercised by early Victorian aristocratic women will be pursued in the next chapter, which examines their uses of charity.

[123] David Aitken to Mary Minto, 16 Sept. 1846, Minto MSS, MS11908, fos. 29–32.

3

'Many to Take Care of': Charity, Philanthropy, and Paternalism

Aristocratic charity, like patronage itself, does not have a good image. The 'Lady Bountiful', supercilious and condescending, slumming with the poor in a quest for novelty or dispensing benevolence like unpleasant medicine, with no understanding, little compassion, and small consistency, is a familiar figure in nineteenth-century fiction. Consider Lady Catherine De Bourgh, who 'whenever any of the cottagers were disposed to be quarrelsome, discontented, or too poor, . . . sallied forth into the village to settle their differences, silence their complaints, and scold them into harmony and plenty'.[1] The Jesuit priest Father Gallwey warned his congregation that 'a suspicion not infrequently attaches to the good works of those in high stations', contrasting by implication the hardships which charitable activity imposed on his subject, Cecil, Lady Lothian, with the 'mere honorary charity, which does no real work, and merits only small reward' of many aristocratic ladies.[2]

Anne Summers, in the context of the lady volunteers for service in the Crimean War, enjoins her readers to 'stifle the instinctive groans and laughter, and to take the ladies as seriously as they took themselves'.[3] It is sound advice. For while the charity of aristocratic women did not conform to the emerging standards of the New Poor Law and of organized philanthropy, it is an index of aristocratic attitudes, and serves as a reminder that the era was marked by continuity as well as change.

The satirical version of the Lady Bountiful undoubtedly had her counterparts in real life; the well-meaning gush of Lady Battersea was ripe for caricature. On her marriage in 1877, she was 'disappointed that we did not settle down in Battersea amongst the working classes', where she proposed 'making a "House Beautiful" . . . allowing of closer intercourse with and better knowledge of the men and women whose paths were so different from mine', which she thought would have been 'a splendid

---

[1] Jane Austen, *Pride and Prejudice* (1813), ch. 30.
[2] Gallwey, 'Cecil, Marchioness of Lothian', 125–63.
[3] Anne Summers, 'Pride and Prejudice: Ladies and Nurses in the Crimean War', *History Workshop*, 16 (Autumn 1983), 54.

experience.'[4] Similarly, the accusations of hypocrisy aimed at Harriet, duchess of Sutherland's anti-slavery activism (see below) were not without foundation, and acceptance of the 'Lady Bountiful' label as one of uncritical approbation[5] should not be reinstated unreflectively. Many aristocratic women, did, however, sincerely interest themselves in works of charity and public benevolence.[6] The purpose of this chapter is to examine these women and their works, assessing the rationale behind the extensive involvement of aristocratic women in charities, an involvement which continues to the present day.[7]

The chapter is in three parts. The first considers personal charity—direct involvement with the individual in need—and examines the ways in which aristocratic women constructed their responsibilities and obligations towards the poor, relating it to an understanding of the functioning of a paternalist society. The second looks at the interaction between aristocratic women and organized philanthropy, arguing that in the context of middle-class philanthropic activity, aristocratic women continued to treat the poor as beneficiaries of patronage and to take advantage of their social position for the benefit of their dependants. The third section turns to the national stage, to their engagement with public causes and crises, suggesting through a pair of case-studies that, once more, the combination of class and gender gave aristocratic women a unique voice.

PERSONAL CHARITY

Charitable activity by aristocratic women on their estates was part of a wider system of social relations. The delivery of soup and blankets to the poor was part of the structure of paternalism which embraced balls given for county society, tenants' dinners, Sunday school treats, and the patronage of church

---

[4] Battersea, *Reminiscences*, 172.

[5] Encountered most recently in Horn, *Ladies of the Manor*, ch. 5: 'The Role of "Lady Bountiful" '.

[6] Jessica Gerard, 'Lady Bountiful: Women of the Landed Classes and Rural Philanthropy', *Victorian Studies*, 30 (Winter 1987), 183–210. Gerard's conclusions, here based largely on published sources, are broadly borne out by archival research, although with significant differences of emphasis. Many of her subjects come from the permanently resident, parochial gentry class, rather than from the peripatetic national aristocracy. Moreover, she places greater influence on the 'cult of True Womanhood' as the inspiration for country-house charity than I think is appropriate in the case of the aristocratic woman.

[7] Frank Prochaska's *Royal Bounty: The Making of a Welfare Monarchy* (New Haven: Yale University Press, 1995) undertakes a similar task with respect to the royal family. There are some parallels between his thesis that the royal family turned to large-scale philanthropic work to justify its position in a period of declining actual power, and the uses to which aristocratic families put charitable work.

and school discussed in the previous chapters.[8] Seeking to reinforce a social order characterized by interdependence, it is unsurprising that aristocratic women continued to dispense personal charity long after the implementation of the New Poor Law sought to regulate the poor into prosperity by removing outdoor relief.[9]

The hallmark of personal charity was that it entailed direct contact between the donor and the beneficiary; the direct charity of aristocratic women in this period was thus almost exclusively confined to their country estates. The very term 'charity' implies this kind of personal knowledge and contact, in contrast to the general, impersonal, and dangerous benevolence which 'philanthropy' implied to the early Victorian paternalists.[10] Harriet Ashburton was praised for avoiding the 'common currents of charity' and for devoting her resources 'to the comfort of those with whom she had some local relation, and over whose interests she exercised a close personal superintendence'.[11] Emphasis on personal knowledge precluded aristocratic women from direct charity in the towns and cities, where there was little tradition of engagement with communities and individuals. This personal contact in the countryside was maintained through the rituals of visiting. M. Jeanne Peterson has commented that 'Visiting the poor was one of the commonest forms of charity throughout the Victorian period. . . . Even when we know only the barest facts about a woman's charitable work, we know that she visited the poor.'[12] Like the upper-middle-class Paget family of Peterson's study, most aristocratic women either visited their poor tenants themselves, or sent their daughters or other agents, often clergymen, to do so. Eveline Portsmouth's visitors' book for the 1870s, interestingly, alongside the names of her eminent house guests, also contains records of school treats and occasional accounts of her visits to tenants and the poor: at Enniscorthy in 1871, part of the record reads: 'Called on the *Roberts*, visited the *Almshouses* left 2/ a piece for the old Women—Called upon the *Corvans*,

---

[8] See also Beckett, *Aristocracy in England*, ch. 10, and Thompson, *English Landed Society*, ch. 7.

[9] A possible exception to this net of social relations is suggested by Jane Austen's *Emma*: 'The yeomanry are precisely the order of people with whom I feel I can have nothing to do. A degree or two lower, and a creditable appearance might interest me; I might hope to be useful to their families in some way or other. But a farmer can need none of my help, and is therefore in one sense as much above my notice as in every other he is below it': *Emma*, ch. 4. Emma, unlike Mr Knightley, of course, has no professional relationship with Martin to justify their contact.

[10] See Roberts, *Paternalism in Early Victorian England*, 34–5 and 42–3.

[11] 'Obituary Notice of Ly. Ashburton' [Richard Monckton Milnes, 1857], Houghton MSS, 1/224. See also 'Lady Brownlow', in Lady Battersea (Constance Flower), *Waifs and Strays* (A. L. Humphreys, 1921), 151–2.

[12] Peterson, *Family, Love and Work*, 133.

the *Heeneys & Hardens* (curates) *Corcorans, Flynns, Mahoneys*, Mrs [illeg.]—
left with her 4/ for beggars—Gave [illeg.] 3/6 & Brogan 4/. Leave £2 with
Father Furlong.'[13] This was no inconsiderable visiting list, even if we must
assume, from the presence of the curates on the list, that not all were families of the poor. From an early age women were taught that the care of the
poor was their responsibility. Georgiana Liddell's mother advised her to 'be
kind and benevolent to all persons under you, and so regulate your expences
[sic] as to be able to set aside a certain portion of your income for charitable
purposes'.[14] Lady Battersea likewise remembered that she had been brought
up to regard charitable work as a privilege, 'not as a hardship, nor as anything meritorious in itself'.[15] Nor, most importantly in the light of developments among the middle classes, was charity a career, a vocation, or a
full-time occupation; rather, it was a part of the whole series of aristocratic
duties through which the fabric of society was maintained.

It is impossible to assess how successful this systematic visiting was in fos-
tering deference, even in the restricted context of the estates. Evidence of
the reponses of the poor simply does not exist.[16] It is fair to assume, however,
that while some kinds of charity met with gratitude—such as, for example,
the medical care offered by Lady Marjoribanks in the Scottish Highlands,
twenty miles from the nearest doctor[17]—others could arouse resentment in
the recipients. An example of charity which must have been received as a
blow to pride and dignity is given in the memoirs of Consuelo, duchess of
Marlborough, who, late in the century, was appalled to discover the long-
standing practice at Blenheim Palace of packing the remnants of luncheon
into tins for distribution among the local poor, 'meat and vegetables and
sweets in a horrible jumble in the same tin'.[18]

If visiting was intended to promote emotional and psychological ties
between great house and cottage, it also served a more pragmatic purpose.
Regular monitoring enabled the aristocratic woman to discover where
practical assistance was needed, and to determine its most suitable form. As
Summers has said, 'Visitors constituted not an intangible spiritual force, but
an important patronage group'.[19] The patronage which aristocratic women
offered to their dependants took a number of forms, including running

---

[13] 'Visitors' Book 1870s', Wallop MSS, 15M84, Box 30.
[14] Bloomfield, *Reminiscences*, i. 23.   [15] Battersea, *Reminiscences*, 409.
[16] Gerard, 'Lady Bountiful', 206.   [17] Aberdeen, 'We Twa', i. 131–2.
[18] Balsan, *The Glitter and the Gold*, 68. See also Flora Thompson, *Lark Rise* (Oxford:
Oxford University Press, 1939), 7, for the preference for independence felt by many rural
labourers.
[19] Summers, 'A Home from Home', 45. See also James Obelkevich, *Religion and Society:
South Lindsay 1825–1875* (Oxford: Clarendon Press, 1976), 33–9.

clothing clubs, assisting with emigration, and supporting needy crafts- and tradespeople.[20] The most common, however, was the gift in kind to meet immediate, short-term needs. Mary, Lady Minto kept a daily record of the charitable donations which she made to the poor of Minto between 1848 and 1851; it is probably a typical example of the kind and extent of personal charity by aristocratic women.[21] The Mintos were in financial difficulties at this time, and were obliged to go abroad in 1852 to retrench; the support offered to the local community by way of charity did not appear to be considered as an area in which savings could be made.[22] The most common offerings were dresses, shawls, bonnets, and blankets, along with coals and meal. Money was sometimes given, usually with a specific purpose in mind. Interestingly, the recipients of Lady Minto's charity were usually women: between September and December 1848, nineteen women received goods, and only two men. The fact that Lady Minto recorded the names of the recipients of her bounty reinforces the idea that this was personal charity, bestowed on known individuals who were construed as dependants of the Minto family, and not a general dispensation for the good of an unspecified 'poor'. Many names recur frequently on the list, probably those of long-term dependants, widows and the elderly who had no hope of improving their condition. Betsey Melville is recorded as receiving an old bonnet, a new shawl, and ten shillings in September 1848, one pound in November 1849, a warm gown, a blue flannel petticoat, two cotton shifts, coals, meal, and '£1 to buy clothes for the children' in December 1850, and a gown in the following winter. Over the same period, Nelly Fairbairn received a new gown each year and two pairs of stockings. The dating of the majority of these gifts indicates not only the times of greatest hardship for the poor, but also the seasonal presence of the aristocratic woman on her estates.

Frequent absence did not mean an absence of supervision, however. While Mary Minto was away from Scotland, she received regular reports from the minister, David Aitken, outlining the condition of the people and their needs, the detail of which confirms her own familiarity with the people on the estates.[23] Rather later in the century, W. A. Durnford reported regularly to Lady Fitzwilliam on the hardships being suffered by striking

[20] See e.g. Lady Constance Stanley to Katherine Clarendon, n.d. and 12 Nov. 1879, Hobbs MSS, 30/48, 35/5/7; Frances Milton to Fitzwilliam, 7 Oct. 1845 and 1 Oct. 1850, Wentworth Woodhouse Muniments, WWM MF67 G75/10; Harriet Sutherland to Mary Minto, n.d. [1838?], Minto MSS, MS11908, fo. 302; and Charlotte Buccleuch to Sir Robert Peel, 18 Oct. 1842, BL Add. MS 40,517, fo. 106.

[21] 'Poor People', 1848–51 [Mary Minto], Minto MSS, MS12010A.

[22] Mary Minto's journal, 7 May 1852, Minto MSS, MS12011, fos. 6–7.

[23] David Aitken to Mary Minto, 1846, Minto MSS, MS11908, fos. 10–37.

miners at the Elsecar collieries, and administered her donations for relief works.[24] Frances Fitzwilliam was aware of the problems caused by the absence of supervision, and, in setting up a clothing club and working fund at Coollattin in 1845, was anxious not to 'begin any thing that cannot be satisfactorily carried on in our absence'.[25]

With charity of this kind, aristocratic women continued to relate to their tenants in a paternalist fashion, regardless of the attempts of the New Poor Law to treat poverty in a more utilitarian fashion. Of course, the context of their charity was conditioned by the responses of their husbands and fathers to their responsibilities as landlords: where a landowner pulled down the cottages of the poor or made no repairs in order to keep the poor-rates low, thereby driving the impoverished out of the parish, his wife and daughters had less scope for their bounty.[26] Women had little or no voice in the formulation of state policy on poverty, and were distanced through their own often chronic lack of education from participating in the intellectual debates which led to the revolution in thinking about poverty and the economy more generally.[27] It is therefore scarcely surprising that they continued to hold on to a method of poor relief which was increasingly condemned as unsystematic, wasteful, and a factor in pauperizing the labouring classes.

Of course, aristocratic women did come into contact with the new ideas about poverty, and, as will be seen, increasingly engaged in new kinds of philanthropic activity. The intermediaries—clergymen and land agents— who reported to aristocratic women about the poor on their estates often adhered to the view that poverty was a moral failing, and hence should not receive the benefit of aristocratic relief. The Sutherlands' factor, Loch, commenting on the state of some of their cottages and their inhabitants, applied the criteria of moral worth in recommending assistance. Widow Mackenzie was a 'nice respectable old person', and her son an industrious labourer, but their acute poverty was exacerbated by their caring for a chronically ill distant relative. 'These people', Loch wrote, 'have always struggled to be independent, and have never applied for parochial relief—

[24] W. A. Durnford to Frances Fitzwilliam, 13 and 15 Sept. 1893, Wentworth Woodhouse Muniments, WWM T29.

[25] Frances Milton (later Fitzwilliam) to Fitzwilliam, 7 Oct. 1845, Wentworth Woodhouse Muniments, WWM MF67 G75.

[26] Roberts, *Paternalism in Early Victorian England*, 118–19.

[27] On the changing understanding of poverty and its treatment, see Boyd Hilton, *The Age of Atonement: The Influence of Evangelicalism on Social and Economic Thought 1785–1865* (Oxford: Clarendon Press, 1988); Gertrude Himmelfarb, *The Idea of Poverty: England in the Early Industrial Age* (Faber & Faber, 1984; 1st pub. 1983); David Eastwood, *Governing Rural England: Tradition and Transformation in Local Government 1780–1840* (Oxford: Oxford University Press, 1994), pt. 2.

they would well deserve some little aid at His Grace's hands.'[28] David Aitken's report to Lady Minto on the recipients of her charity indicates a mid-point between paternalist and Poor Law: 'We are not overlooking Jeanie Galloway, tho' I am not quite pleased with her nor Nannie Bert: tho' still less am I pleased with her daughter and family, who are ungrateful for all they have got, & constantly clamouring for more.'[29] Moral condemnation of the poor was here accompanied by continued relief rather than banishment to the workhouse for the 'undeserving'. A more vigorous statement of the pauperizing effects of personal charity was given to Frances Anne Londonderry by her land agent in Ireland at the height of the Famine. The Londonderrys proposed visiting Ireland, and Andrews, the agent, was urging them to put off their visit. The reasons he gave for pressing the delay demonstrate clearly that the Irish tenants were clinging to the idea of the interdependence of landlord and tenant in the hope of personal relief. It was their 'well-known propensity' in all emergencies,

to throw the burden entirely on their Landlords, and to contend that they are free from blame, that they have done all they could, that they can do no more. . . . they would expect and seek much more than your Ladyship may be inclined to grant . . . and that while the refusal must be painful to your Ladyship, the disappointment could not but militate against that contentment and affection which your Ladyship must desire to promote.[30]

Andrews proceeded to warn the marchioness specifically against the kind of personal charity which was most frequently dispensed on English estates, the distribution of food and clothing. Charity should 'ameliorate the condition, and elevate the character of the Recipients', while 'the gratuitous distribution of articles of consumption, . . . though it may be admitted as an opiate or Palliative in cases of acute Pain and suffering, should be carefully avoided in general practice' except in the case of the old or the ill; it should in no circumstances be given to 'those whose duty and interest require that they should learn to provide for themselves'. The Londonderrys visited Ireland in the following year, and while it is not clear whether they followed Andrews' advice, they did engage in a massive programme of works on Lady Londonderry's Antrim estates, providing employment for many of the impoverished tenants.

If aristocratic women treated their gifts to the poor as one side of an arrangement whereby the poor received the necessities of life in exchange for at least a semblance of deferential behaviour, then their use of

[28] Memorandum [George Loch], 28 Sept. 1856, Sutherland MSS (Staffs.), D593 P/22/1/25.

[29] David Aitken to Mary Minto, 26 Nov. 1846, Minto MSS, MS11908, fos. 33–7.

[30] John Andrews to Frances Anne Londonderry, 15 Nov. 1846, Londonderry MSS, D/Lo Acc 451(D), Correspondence File 28.

employment was an explicit form of patronage. Moreover, it appears that a significant number of their clients shared their view of their mutual relationship. As demonstrated in Chapter 1, a patron–client relationship could last beyond the termination of employment; it also applied to tenants and dependants, and could cross generational boundaries. Aristocratic women were particularly, perhaps uniquely, well placed to find employment for their dependants. The networks which enabled them to place former servants in new positions could also be used for the benefit of both the independent and the destitute poor. The absence of rigid boundaries in the bestowal of patronage once again indicates that the personal charity of the aristocratic woman was part of a general web of social relations and not an isolated response to the particular problem of charity.

At its most basic, employment was offered as a means of supplying a needy family with a wage, thereby removing the necessity to support them directly. The large scale of the aristocratic household often meant that work could be offered directly, not least because, as Thompson has pointed out, many of those employed were far from functionally necessary; positions could be invented for appropriate applicants, without waiting for vacancies.[31] Loch received a petition for assistance from one of the Sutherland tenants, and decided that 'the best thing to be done for this woman is to give employment to her eldest son', and noted that the duchess had agreed to his working in the gardens at Dunrobin.[32] If the patron was unwilling or unable to employ the dependant directly, she could make use of her contacts to find an appropriate position elsewhere. Thus Anne Athole sought a position for a schoolmistress, Agnes Fisher, while she was in waiting at Balmoral, as 'it will be a great thing if she can be made independent'.[33] Indeed, the duchess of Athole's court connections gave her extensive patronage in matters of employment, for she was regularly consulted by the queen and her family when they required new servants. Sometimes the Scottish connection is obvious, as, for example, in the hiring of bagpipers for the crown princess of Prussia and the prince of Wales; but the duchess was also regularly consulted about potential lady's maids, a result of Victoria's well-known approval of Scottish servants.[34] Lady Londonderry also exercised considerable patronage over employment: she

[31] Thompson, *English Landed Society*, 187–90.

[32] 'Memorandum', [George Loch], 28 Sept. 1856, Sutherland MSS (Staffs.), D593 P/22/1/25.

[33] Anne Athole to Athole, 23 May 1862, Atholl MSS, Box 58.

[34] See e.g. Princess Helena to Anne Athole, 16 Nov. 1865, and Victoria to Anne Athole, 9 Apr. 1866, Atholl MSS, Box 58. The first of these letters makes clear that even John Brown respected the advice of the duchess with regard to finding appropriate servants for the royal family.

was assured that her nomination for the postmastership at Carnlough, Co. Antrim, would be respected, and she was offered the nomination to a cadetship as 'you are under the necessity of employing so many persons in confidential situations, that you cannot fail to have frequent requests addressed to you for assistance in providing for their families'.[35]

Applications made to aristocratic women for assistance frequently took the form of requests for money, work, or purchase of goods manufactured by the applicants. It is difficult to gauge the extent of either the applications or their success rate, because the information that has survived is patchy. In the collections of papers examined, only two yielded substantial collections of begging letters, and in neither case were the outcomes recorded.[36] However, it is clear that, while many solicitations for support were made solely on grounds of the prominence and supposed wealth of the lady, a significant number drew on personal ties, however slight, to support their applications. Among the Waldegrave Papers, for example, is an application on behalf of John and Eleanor Lash, tenant farmers on Frances Waldegrave's Navestock estate, who were in their eighties and needed five pounds a year to keep them from the workhouse; Margaret Mitchell asked for money, while mentioning her acquaintance with Lady Waldegrave's father, John Braham, while A. Nicholson, who needed money for medical treatment, claimed to have been her father's coachman. Other applications included those of her former servant, John Collins's fiancée, who wanted the lease of the Harcourt Arms in Nuneham, and of Sophie Taylor, who wanted the countess to buy her house in East Harptree.[37]

Anne Sutherland's collection included requests from Isabella Mackenzie, widow of a former tenant, for replacement fishing nets for her son; from 82-year-old Joseph Fowler, who had been coachman to the duke and who needed money for his wife's funeral; and from the daughter of a former tenant of her father's, who was seeking employment. Jane Jordan wrote to the duchess from the St Pancras workhouse, including a sample of her needlework, seeking her help in obtaining employment, having lost everything in a fire and subsequent illness. The application is reinforced by the presentation of Jordan's credentials and connections with the Sutherlands:

[35] Sir William Somerville to Frances Anne Londonderry, 25 Sept. 1845, Londonderry MSS, D/Lo Acc 451 (D) File 32, and [J?] Hogg to Frances Anne Londonderry, 6 June 1856, D/Lo/C 548 (15).

[36] The two substantial collections were those of Frances Waldegrave and Anne Sutherland. An instructive comparison can be made with begging letters in New York, which points to the near-universality of the search for personal patronage. See Dawn M. Greeley, 'Beyond Benevolence: Gender, Class and the Development of Scientific Charity in New York City, 1882–1935' (unpublished Ph.D. thesis, State University of New York at Stony Brook, 1994), ch. 4.

[37] Begging Letters and Charity Appeals, Strachey MSS, DD/SH C1189 G316.

not known personally to Anne Sutherland, she had known her mother-in-law, the duchess Harriet, when she (Jordan) had been nurse to some of the ladies of the court. These ladies, Lady Bertha Clifton and the duchess of Norfolk (who was also the sister of the second duke of Sutherland) were both dead by the time of the application (1888), and Jordan was looking beyond those whom she must have considered her natural patrons. The most tenuous connection invoked in these letters is in that of Kenneth M. Black, an actor, who wanted money for rest and recuperation after an illness. He pleaded '[t]he recollection of a few kind words you addressed to me when I was a boy on the occasion of your paying a visit to the Schoolhouse at Golspie' as the connection on which he based his appeal.[38] While it is not possible to say whether the assertion of this kind of personal connection was effective in securing assistance, it is evident that the applicants believed it could, or should be. Even if aristocratic women wanted to distance themselves from the personal ties of a paternalist society, and even if those ties were weakening, their dependants continued to act as if the patronage of aristocratic women was important.[39] Any organized philanthropic work which they undertook was therefore in addition to the basic expectation of personal charity.

ORGANIZED PHILANTHROPY

The role of philanthropy in defining and expanding the later Victorians' idea of 'woman's mission' has been the subject of a number of studies, notably by F. K. Prochaska.[40] They argue that philanthropic work was construed as an extension of women's maternal functions, extending concern for children, health, and moral welfare beyond the confines of their own homes into those of the poor; further, they contend that the very extension of this 'feminine' role beyond the confines of the middle-class home altered the nature and understanding of womanly roles, giving women a voice in the previously masculine political arena. Catherine Hall has argued more fundamentally that the excursion into philanthropy was an essential part of

---

[38] Begging letters to Anne Sutherland, Sutherland MSS (Staffs.), D593 P/28/13. See also Elizabeth Lose to Frances Milton, 12 Nov. 1849, Wentworth Woodhouse Muniments, WWM T9/4.

[39] The same phenomenon in the context of the assumed political patronage and power of aristocratic women will be discussed in Chs 4 and 5.

[40] Prochaska, Women and Philanthropy, esp. 1–17; F. K. Prochaska, 'Women in English Philanthropy, 1790–1830', International Review of Social History, 19 (1974), 426–45; Summers, 'A Home from Home'; Judith R. Walkowitz, Prostitution and Victorian Society: Women, Class and the State (Cambridge: Cambridge University Press, 1980); Cott, Bonds of Womanhood; Martha Vicinus, Independent Women: Work and Community for Single Women, 1850–1920 (Virago, 1985); Barbara Corrado Pope, 'Angels in the Devil's Workshop: Leisured and Charitable Women in Nineteenth-Century England and France', in Renate Bridenthal and Claudia Koonz (eds.), Becoming Visible: Women in European History (Boston: Houghton Mifflin, 1977).

the effort of the middle classes to define themselves as distinct from the aristocracy, 'rejecting aristocratic values and the old forms of patronage and influence', and setting themselves up, particularly in the towns and cities, as a new, challenging source of authority.[41] The point that has not been clearly made is that, in adopting philanthropy as their own province, middle-class women both emulated and altered the nature of the charity of the aristocratic woman. Middle-class philanthropy, based in towns rather than rural communities, tended to be directed not at known individuals but at categories (single mothers, chimney-sweeps, sufferers from tuberculosis, and so on), and the assistance was generally not offered directly, from patron to client, but was mediated through one of thousands of organizations dedicated to specific causes. The movement for visiting the urban poor which escalated towards the end of the nineteenth century was, in effect, an attempt to re-create the communities of dependence which were perceived as already existing in the countryside. But in these new communities of dependence, the patron was to be, not the aristocrat or the landowner, but the rational, bourgeois philanthropist. Moreover, the whole issue of philanthropic work was tied up with questions of status. Aristocratic women were unequivocally ladies, and had no need to prove their status by any action of their own.[42] Middle-class women, who sought to be recognized as ladies, imbued that status with moral qualities, and attached to it appropriate behaviours. Aristocratic women proferred charity to their dependants; therefore middle-class women adopted charity as one of the qualities of both femininity and social status.

There was no complete severance between aristocratic and middle-class ladies in the pursuit of 'good works'. While the middle classes adopted the aristocratic model of visiting and personal contacts, aristocratic women increasingly involved themselves in organizations for impersonal philanthropic works. The parts that they took in these organizations reflected their different social status and expectations; here too patronage was central to the aristocratic woman's contribution.

Before the 1880s, few aristocratic women took an active part in the work of organized middle-class charities.[43] In common with middle-class women,

---

[41] Hall, *White, Male and Middle Class*, 143.

[42] Revel Guest and Angela V. John make this point with relation to Lady Charlotte Guest; see *Lady Charlotte*, 246.

[43] The main exceptions were Lady Byron and Angela Burdett-Coutts. Both made philanthropy their career; because of their almost professional attitude to charity, they are excluded from this study. Burdett-Coutts was created a baroness in her own right in consequence of her philanthropic activity. See Ethel Colburn Mayne, *The Life and Letters of Anne Isabella, Lady Noel Byron* (Constable, 1929); Joan Pierson, *The Real Lady Byron* (Hale, 1992); Healey, *Lady Unknown*.

they did not attend or chair public meetings, but, unlike them, they did not sit on ladies' committees. They did not, on the whole, supervise hospitals, reformatory schools, or penitents' institutions, although a few, like Catherine Gladstone, did. Lady Londonderry and Lady Westminster expressed an interest in visiting the poor in London personally, and made enquiries as to how they could be of most use. The reply they received is instructive:

W[estminster?]'s opinion strongly is that if we Ladies *support* the Associations already established in London, by *giving* to them, we shall do more good than by personally visiting, which we could never do with [illeg.] enough to be of real use—it requires those who are completely conversant with them—& seeing them daily, which we never could do, to be of efficient use.[44]

While the aristocratic woman was the natural patron of the rural poor, a combination of factors meant that she did not perform the same role *vis-à-vis* the urban poor. Most important of these was the determination of middle-class philanthropists to regulate the poor through an organized philanthropy. As Elizabeth Westminster pointed out, daily visiting of the urban poor was impossible for the peripatetic aristocratic woman, who, moreover, had other significant claims on her time. This insistence on constant supervision as the prerequisite for assistance can be understood not only as part of the attempt to place charity on a 'scientific' basis, but also as an integral aspect of the middle-class effort to differentiate themselves from the aristocracy, and to create for themselves specific arenas of moral authority and power. However, aristocratic women did support the work of the active philanthropists in three significant ways: they provided money, they turned social events to philanthropic purposes, and they sanctioned the use of their names in connection with good causes.

Financial support was essential to the work of most charities, and fund raising became a major preoccupation of most organizations. Belonging to the wealthiest families, aristocratic women were constantly solicited for donations and subscriptions to philanthropic causes, particularly those concerned with the relief of women and children, and medical charities. For example, surviving cheques for donations made by Harriet Sutherland between 1848 and 1850 record, alongside regular donations to clothing clubs on the Staffordshire estates, one guinea to the British Ladies' Society for the Reformation of Female Prisoners, three guineas to the Brompton Hospital for Consumption and Diseases of the Chest, and two guineas to the School

---

[44] Elizabeth Westminster to Frances Anne Londonderry, n.d., Londonderry MSS, D/Lo Acc 451 (D) File 13.

of Discipline, Chelsea.[45] Frances Milton's papers include solicitations on behalf of the London Benevolent Repository (which assisted distressed gentlewomen by selling the fancy goods which they manufactured), the Grosvenor and Berkeley Squares' Medical Relief Society, and the Watercress and Flower Girl Mission.[46]

Financial support, while invaluable, was also symptomatic of the distance between the donor and the recipient of the charity, demarcating the difference between personal and organized charity.[47] The assumption that such donations were always an easy way to salve the consciences of the rich at little personal cost is undermined, however, by a brief examination of the difficulties encountered by aristocratic women in finding the money to meet the demands on their benevolence. The advice to Georgiana Liddell regularly to lay aside a portion of her income for charity has already been cited; but she was a maid of honour, and the income to which her mother referred was the annual salary of £400 which went with that post. Few unmarried aristocratic girls could count on so large an independent income, while married women were generally given a quarterly allowance by their husbands.[48] Surrounded by all the trappings of great wealth, it was often difficult actually to produce cash. Charlotte Canning wrote to the inveterate charity fund-raiser Catherine Gladstone that 'I am sorry to say I meant not to give you my donation till after New Year's Day, when I will have a fresh quarter [i.e. quarterly allowance] & I do think it will suit me best still to do. . . . I am not fond of annual subscriptions for I am apt to get involved in too many.'[49] Likewise, Harriet Sutherland explained to an anti-slavery campaigner that there were limits to the financial resources of even the most apparently wealthy women: 'You know that no Woman has much to give,' she wrote; 'those that would seem to have more, the Wives of large proprietors have always many claims, for with means never very large, the Poor are considered particularly their own, & I have many to take care of in England, & more in Scotland.'[50] This clear exposition of the demands on the purse of the aristocratic woman also makes clear her priorities: the personal responsibility for

[45] Cheques, Sutherland MSS (Staffs.), D593 R/2/41.

[46] Charity circulars and receipts among the papers of Frances Fitzwilliam, Wentworth Woodhouse Muniments, WWM T9/1, T9/2, T9/25.

[47] Thomas Carlyle's diatribe against the substitution of cash for personal relationships could be applied as easily in the field of charity as in the work-place. 'A man has other obligations laid on him, in God's Universe, than the payment of cash': Past and Present, 195.

[48] See Holcombe, Wives and Property, for an account of the legal and economic position of aristocratic and other married women.

[49] Charlotte Canning to Catherine Gladstone, 1 Dec. [1851], BL Add. MS 46,226, fos. 288–9.

[50] Harriet Sutherland to Sir Thomas Fowell Buxton, 21 Dec. 1840, Buxton Papers, Rhodes House Library, Oxford (hereafter Buxton MSS), MSS Brit. Emp. s444, vol. xx, fos. 91a–h.

the poor on her estates came before the needs of the undifferentiated mass, even in the interests of a cause to which she might personally be much attached.

The shift from donating money to raising funds for philanthropic causes was made by many aristocratic women, and if offering financial support to good causes placed few demands on their time and energies, the same could not be said of fund raising. Some women—Catherine Gladstone is perhaps the most prominent example—became notorious for constantly soliciting friends and guests for support for their good causes. Mrs Gladstone was well aware of her own reputation, and welcomed the support of Frances Waldegrave for a hospital for incurables: 'When *you* take up a thing warmly you succeed I am sure of this & this is the first thing of the kind you have undertaken—whilst people are tired of *me*; & my wish is to appear as little as possible.'[51]

Aristocratic women could be expected to make use of their extensive family and social ties to gain new, influential, wealthy supporters for particular causes, and their correspondence testifies to their willingness to do so.[52] Enjoying large houses with suites of reception rooms and extensive gardens, both in London and in the country, aristocratic women were in a position to play host to large-scale fund-raising activities impossible in the less spacious residences of most middle-class activists. Stafford House, for example, was used for an important anti-slavery meeting in 1852; in 1886 the Saturday half-holiday movement thanked Anne Sutherland for lending the same house for their meeting.[53] More important were the gardens, which were frequently used as venues for bazaars and fêtes, as well as for the entertainment of large numbers of beneficiaries of associations and the local 'treating' which was part of the personal charity of the aristocratic woman. For example, the bazaar in aid of Holy Trinity Church, Twickenham, was held in the gardens of Frances Waldegrave's Strawberry Hill, while that in aid of the Children's Sea Convalescent Home in North Wales was held at Grosvenor House.[54]

The charity ball, such as that in 1848 organized in aid of the Spitalfields weavers and patronized by Lady Londonderry, and the bazaar were the

[51] Catherine Gladstone to Frances Waldegrave, 13 Dec. 1872, Strachey MSS, DD/SH C1189 G253.

[52] Anne Athole to Lady Anna Maria Dawson, n.d., Bod., MS. Eng. lett. d. 378, fos. 27–8; Charlotte Canning to Catherine Gladstone, n.d. [1854?], BL Add. MS 46,226, fos. 290–1; Victoria to Charlotte Canning, 28 July 1847, Canning MSS, Photo Eur 321/1; Mary Ponsonby to Frances Waldegrave, n.d., Strachey MSS, DD/SH C1189 G279.

[53] Early Closing Association to Anne Sutherland, 26 July 1886, Sutherland MSS (Staffs.), D593 P/28/14, 1st bundle.

[54] Advertisement, Strachey MSS, DD/SH C1189 G318, and Catherine Gladstone to Frances Waldegrave, n.d., DD/SH C1189 G253.

most popular exercises in practical philanthropy for aristocratic women.[55] They were not alone in favouring these sociable methods of fund raising. Frank Prochaska has demonstrated the burgeoning enthusiasm for the bazaar or fancy sale from the inception of the idea in 1804 until the end of the century, in London and the provinces alike.[56] Of the hundred such events which he found advertised each year in London, very few would have enjoyed the patronage of aristocratic women, and it would not do to over-state their importance in the wider picture of philanthropic fund raising. From the perspective of aristocratic women, however, the bazaar was an important instrument of charity, which had a dual identity as fund-raiser and social event. That the bazaar was an important public activity for aristocratic women is confirmed by the comment of Richard Acton on the death of Lady Lascelles in Berlin in 1897. He wrote: 'It will be remembered to her glory that she died as it were in the field of battle, as it was the fatigue of the Embassy bazaar last Wednesday week which caused her illness.'[57]

The aristocratic bazaar was undoubtedly a social occasion for many, if not most, of the participants, who would buy or sell any number of 'fancy goods' rather as a form of entertainment than as an act of solemn charitable duty. Aside from the few occasions when aristocratic women undertook the com-plete organization of a bazaar (as, for example, when Frances Anne Lon-donderry organized a bazaar in aid of the starving Irish in 1847, ironically at the same time as her husband was opposing the repeal of the Corn Laws which was intended to have much the same effect[58]), buying and selling were the main contributions of aristocratic women to such events, although some also contributed goods they had made—for example, the kites made by Katherine Clarendon and Lady Waterpark's penwipers.[59] Rather than manufacture goods themselves, most contributors purchased their offerings from one of the many organizations which supported distressed gentle-women by selling their manufactures, the 'embroidered or braided table covers, or borders for ditto; knit articles of all kinds; spencers for children,

[55] The silk weavers of London to Frances Anne Londonderry, 18 July 1848, Londonderry MSS, D/Lo Acc 451 (D) Correspondence file 30. I have not, however, found a great many papers concerning charity balls, while bazaars are well documented.

[56] Prochaska, *Women and Philanthropy*, ch.2.

[57] Richard Acton to John, first Lord Acton, 3 Apr. 1897, Acton Papers, Cambridge University Library, Add. MS 8121 (10)/53. I am grateful to John Wells for this reference.

[58] See Charlotte Canning to Frances Anne Londonderry, n.d. [June 1847]; bishop of Armagh to Frances Anne Londonderry, 28 June 1847; Victoria to Frances Anne Londonderry, 7 Mar. 1847, Londonderry MSS, D/Lo Acc 451 (D) File 29.

[59] Lady Constance Stanley to Sir William Vernon Harcourt, 16 Oct. 1866 and n.d., MS. Harcourt, dep. 633, fos.148–51; Elizabeth Waterpark to Houghton, 7 Oct. 1884, Houghton MSS, 35/33.

shawls, carriage boots, etc; . . . arranged specimens of minerals, shells, dried plants, etc.' which were among the most popular items sold at bazaars.[60] It seems unlikely that many of these goods were destined to adorn either the persons or the houses of their purchasers; instead, they would be contributed to the next bazaar for resale, or, in the case of items of clothing, given directly to a needy person. Thus, instead of purchasing a shawl from a commercial enterprise to give in personal charity, the same result could be achieved to the benefit of a number of causes. The shawl could be purchased from the Benevolent Repository (most of the purchase price going to the distressed gentlewoman who had manufactured it), and then be donated to a bazaar in aid of another cause or institution. The shawl would be purchased (the profit after overheads benefiting that cause), and then given to a needy tenant. Thus three charitable purposes could be effected in what was essentially one transaction. Considerable sums of money could change hands at a bazaar; the account of the bazaar in aid of the Convalescent Hospital, Blackrock, Brighton, in 1872 made a total profit of £1080. 7s. 2d.[61] The account also specifies the amounts paid by aristocratic women during the three days of the sale. Princess Mary of Cambridge was the most prolific purchaser, spending £119. 13s. 6d. on the first day, £107. 5s. 0d. on the second, and a token £8. 8s. 0d. on the third day. The duchess of Argyll, who also attended every day, spent £26. 6s. 6d.; Lady Sydney spent £41. 11s. 0d. over the three days, while Lady Aberdeen spent £5. 0s. 0d. and the duchess of Wellington £14. 0s. 0d. when they attended on 3 July, the first day of the bazaar. Few women outside the aristocracy would have such sums available to spend in this way, and hence the latter's presence and patronage of bazaars was much sought after.

Lady Harriet Elliot's journal of her first London season, that of 1844, contains a description of a three-day bazaar in Chelsea, held to raise funds for a hospital, which conveys the social aspects of these events.[62] The event was held outside, 'all the stalls in tents on the grass, a great many people & most excellent fun'. Her sister, Lady John Russell, had a stall at the bazaar, and the sisters acted as saleswomen, eventually growing 'very bold in offering and puffing things', making £39 on the one stall by the end of the first day. The second day was less well attended, but by dint of holding raffles for the goods, which drew crowds to their stall as it was 'the most amusing of all', they

---

[60] London Benevolent Repository, Wentworth Woodhouse Muniments, WWM MF T9/1. Purchase was preferable to manufacture, as it created work, and hence an income for persons who needed it, rather than diversion for the rich.

[61] Bazaar Account in aid of the Convalescent Hospital, Blackrock, Brighton, 1872, Sutherland MSS (Staffs.), D593 P/24/9/4.

[62] Lady Harriet Elliot's journal, 11–13 June 1844, Minto MSS, MS12014.

raised a further £22. The final day was poorly attended, and it was only with 'very hard work' that £12 was made, with only the duchess of Norfolk's stall doing better. Thus the bazaar in this instance served as a source of entertainment for the young woman recently arrived in London, provided her with a kind of introduction to the social scene, and, perhaps incidentally, raised over £70 towards building a new hospital. The acclimatizing effects of the bazaar for the newly 'out' young woman should not be underestimated: they provided a safe, controlled atmosphere for her to appear, and, more importantly, to act, in public, in a capacity different from that usually expected of the young débutante. Thus, although Lady Harriet appeared thoroughly to enjoy 'offering and puffing' items to strangers from behind the bazaar table, when, a week later, she was taken to a breakfast at the duchess of Bedford's, she recorded that she was 'in a great fright & very glad to get into the carriage on our way home'.[63] A similar experience is recorded in Harriet Gurney's journal for 1842, when she attended a bazaar organized by her aunt, the Quaker, Mrs Fry, at the Mansion House. Harriet Gurney too acted the saleswoman, alongside her Aunt Isabella and Lady Winchilsea. The duchess of Sutherland, then mistress of the robes, attended this bazaar, which 'excited much commotion', although Miss Gurney considered her own aunt to be more 'worth looking at than the Duchess who came for a show'.[64]

Harriet Gurney was in a minority in condemning Harriet Sutherland's appearance at the bazaar, for it was precisely this 'show' which was attractive to the fund-raisers, and made them eager to secure aristocratic patronage for their events and organizations. Prochaska has noted that, while a member of the royal family was the biggest draw, 'failing the Queen any distinguished lady, preferably with a title, ensured an increase in sales'.[65] Before the advent of a truly national entertainment business, titled women formed one of the largest groups of recognizable 'names' who could be called upon to add glamour to an event. The patronage of a prominent member of the aristocracy or royal family would, it was believed, ensure the attendance of members of the élite and of those who desired to be seen in their company.[66] Such was the

---

[63] Ibid., 19 June 1844. It is possible that, after the public pleasure-grounds became off limits to the aristocracy, bazaars were the closest that aristocratic women came to the social freedom and intercourse of those places—although in a more respectable, attenuated form.

[64] 'Journal of Harriet Gurney in London', Tuesday [18 Apr. 1842], Broadlands MSS, BR55/39.

[65] Prochaska, *Women and Philanthropy*, 65.

[66] The roles of patrons of organizations in fund raising are too broad to be discussed here. Anecdotal twentieth-century evidence and Prochaska's *Royal Bounty* suggest that having a prominent 'name' at the head of the list of patrons generated additional revenue, which was boosted by their personal attendance at events, in addition to affecting the commitment of other workers to the cause.

power of this belief that, by the end of the century, few philanthropic organizations with any pretensions to national or metropolitan significance were without an aristocratic patron. It is worth noting that aristocratic men and women took different roles in their sponsorship of charities; while both sexes acted as patrons to such organizations, in the period until 1880 at least, few aristocratic women also acted as presidents of charities. The president of a charity committee might play an active part in the formulation of policy, and while a few aristocratic women in this period were active members of ladies' committees, their numbers were greatly surpassed by the number of aristocratic men holding similar positions. *Low's Charities of London* for 1850, for example, lists thirty-three hospitals with male aristocratic presidents and chairmen, and only three presided over by women. One of these latter, the St George's Hospital, had the queen as both president and patron, indicating that neither position was executive.[67] Of the other two, Lady Mandeville was president of the Invalid Asylum for Respectable Females in London and its Vicinity, an organization which also had women as treasurer, honorary secretaries, and collector, while Lady Inglis presided over the Institution of Nursing Sisters, which likewise had a female executive.[68] It is clear that after about 1880, this pattern altered significantly, and that large numbers of aristocratic women took a more active role in the organizations which they supported. The collection of papers edited by Lady Burdett-Coutts, *Woman's Mission: Papers on the Philanthropic Work of Women* in 1893 contains accounts of philanthropic work by women such as Mary, countess of Meath, the Hon. Maude Stanley, Lady Marian Alford, and the Hon. Mrs Stuart Wortley, and in an appendix lists a vast number of organizations and their female founders, presidents, or patrons.

The increasing connection between aristocratic women and philanthropic organizations supports the view that, by the end of the century, the aristocracy had moved away from the practice of personal charity based on reciprocal rights and duties, and hence points to a diminution of the bonds of community which had been a feature of aristocratic society. In the period under consideration here, these social relations, although under challenge, continued to dominate the perceptions of the aristocratic woman, who persisted in making personal charity her main priority. Just as they preferred to offer charity to named and known individuals, so they treated their patronage of organizations; rather than allowing their names to be used in connection with philanthropies in which they were not personally involved,

---

[67] Without an examination of the constitutions of all the charities, it is impossible to say how many of the male presidents took an active, rather than a symbolic, leadership role.

[68] *Low's Charities of London* (1850), ch. 1.

they were selective about the charities to which they gave support. In 1837, the duke of Wellington explained to Frances Salisbury why he would not allow his name to be used unless he had personal knowledge of the cause: 'I do not think it right. I had much rather give the money myself, I have a right to do what I like with my own money, but I have no right to give my name as an inducement to others to contribute.'[69] The duchess of Athole agreed to add her name to the list of patrons for 'Mr Brown's Home', when invited to do so by Lady Anna Maria Dawson (with whom she also shared other charitable interests); but she noted that 'Altho' in general it is not in my power to aid many institutions *substantially* , I refrain from giving my *name* only—In this case I will do what I can.'[70] Patronage of organizations could thus be reconciled with an understanding of charity as personal benefaction. Understanding the market value of their names, aristocratic women were reluctant to allow them to become common currency, and, as the case of Mrs Gladstone, quoted above, indicates, recognized that, in the context of charity as elsewhere, familiarity could breed indifference, if not contempt. They were, nevertheless, in an almost unique situation in that their names had both novelty value and social appeal, and philanthropists sought to exploit these characteristics for the benefit of their organizations. A few aristocratic women were prepared to take advantage of their own position and connections to engage in charitable or philanthropic causes that went beyond the local to the national sphere. Such causes included the relief effort for those who fled the Continent in the wake of the revolutions of 1848, the efforts directed towards the comfort of the army in the Crimean War (which embraced more than just the nursing of Florence Nightingale, who was herself supported by a number of aristocratic women, including Charlotte Canning), and the assistance offered in the wake of the Franco-Prussian War of 1870. Two such causes, the Irish Famine and the campaigns for the abolition of slavery, will be treated as case-studies here.

NATIONAL CAUSES AND CRISES

One of the biggest humanitarian crises of the first forty years of Victoria's reign, the Irish Famine of the 1840s, drew an active response from aristocratic women. Although the New Poor Law of 1834 established in England a national network of workhouses, it coupled this relief with the concept of 'less eligibility'. There were no mechanisms for, and no tradition of, an

---

[69] Frances Salisbury's diary, 14 Aug. 1837, quoted in Carola Oman, *The Gascoyne Heiress: The Life and Diaries of Frances Mary Gascoyne-Cecil, 1802–1839* (Hodder & Stoughton, 1968), 254.

[70] Anne Athole to Lady Anna Maria Dawson, n.d., Bod., MS. Eng. lett. d. 378, fos. 27–8. See also Anne Athole to Lady Anna Maria Dawson, 13 Dec. 1858, fos. 11–13.

organized state response—beyond programmes of public works—to crises such as the Irish Famine, and indeed, a general reluctance to accept that there was anything that could or should be done prevailed. Personal charity took on a wider significance in the context of famine and starvation, and while it could do little to stem the devastation caused by landlord neglect and government hostility to intervention, in many places it was the only relief available.

Ireland in the 1840s stood as a witness to the disasters consequent upon the failure of the estate system: absence of supervision and example led to demoralization and economic disaster. Of course, much of the blame was laid on the Irish themselves: English racial stereotyping, shared by many aristocratic women, produced an image of the Irish as feckless, greedy, and irresponsible.[71] In 1846, at the height of the Famine, Lady Palmerston observed that 'The accounts from Ireland are very various. We believe the distress is exaggerated—There never was such a people instead of helping themselves They try what they can get from us—when a Sub[scriptio]n for the Starving people was talked of, Irishmen in employment in Liverpool & elsewhere threw up their work to go home and see what they could get.'[72] The chief measures of relief offered were those traditionally used in hard times, and were largely left to the initiative of landlords: programmes of public works, such as the coast road built through the Antrim estates of Lady Londonderry, and piecemeal relief offered in soup kitchens on the estates of the landed. Lady Roden and the women of her family opened a soup kitchen in Bryansford, the village next to their estate of Tullymore Park, where they personally supervised the feeding of the hungry.[73] In Curraghmore, Louisa Waterford devoted considerable energies to the relief of the starving, initiating a clothing factory on the estate of provide employment, and improving the houses of the tenants.[74] In addition to these efforts at disaster relief, Louisa Waterford served as an unofficial publicity agent for the relief cause, writing regularly to her sister, Charlotte Canning, then a lady-in-waiting to the queen, outlining conditions in Ireland. The letters were intended to be read to the queen, who was thus kept informed of the state of affairs from a more direct source than her political ministers. More practically, she sent donations for Lady Waterford's work with the starving.[75]

---

[71] Foster, *Paddy and Mr Punch*, 171–94.

[72] Emily Palmerston to Frederick Lamb, n.d. [1846] Broadlands MSS, BR30.

[73] Airlie, *Thatched with Gold*, 16. It is worth recording that famine and pestilence also struck Scotland in these years. It drew a similar response from the more regularly resident aristocracy. See e.g. David Aitkin to Mary Minto, 26 Nov. 1846, Minto MSS, MS11908, fos. 55–8.

[74] Hare, *Two Noble Lives*, i. 238–40.

[75] Victoria to Charlotte Canning, 28 July 1847, Canning MSS, Photo Eur 321 / 1.

The implementation of 'English' charitable practices in Ireland could do little to stem the Famine, given the limitations of scale and the reluctance of most landowners to spend any time in Ireland: the Waterfords and Rodens were exceptions rather than the rule. Others committed themselves to relief at a distance: the bazaar of 1847 organized by Frances Anne Londonderry has already been mentioned, as has the critique of Irish poverty offered by her Irish land agent. Congratulating her on her visit to Ireland, which took place in 1847, despite the agent's advice the previous year, the duke of Rutland commented that 'Such an Excursion as you have made, if followed up by all the Owners of Irish Property, would soon solve the Riddle of Irish *ungovernableness*'.[76] Laura Palmer, later Lady Selborne, received a plea for help from 'some really nice friends of ours in Ireland' which dispelled her doubts about the accuracy of newspaper reports of the Famine, and decided that 'we really ought to see what we could do for our fellow starving creatures, so I determined I would make the attempt amongst ourselves & with our friends'.[77] Lady Dover wrote to her sister, Harriet Sutherland, about the scale of public works to be carried out in the barony of Gowran, in County Kilkenny; after a barrage of figures, she concluded: 'It does not convey much idea to me; and I never understand anything but on the spot.'[78] Inability to understand, 'except on the spot', severely curtailed all responses to the Famine, and that of aristocratic women was thus essentially restricted to implementation of the kinds of poor relief which they were accustomed to offering on their estates, albeit without the expectation of personal acquaintance with the recipients. It was restricted, and it is doubtful that it made any significant impact on the outcome of the Famine; but, such as it was, it did not rely on theories of political economy or on moral judgements about the starving. This relief was paternalist in the fullest sense of the word, the Irish being treated as children, wilful and foolish perhaps, but above all else, in need of nurturing and protection.

Similar attitudes are to be found towards the Africans who had been carried off into slavery in the New World, on the part of large numbers of anti-slavery campaigners.[79] Catherine Hall has argued that the struggle against slavery was also an essential part of the struggle for a distinct identity

[76] Rutland to Frances Anne Londonderry, 8 Dec. 1847, Londonderry MSS, D/Lo (Add) Correspondence File 29. See also Baillie and Bolitho (eds.), *Later Letters of Lady Augusta Stanley*, 65.

[77] Laura Palmer to Frances Waldegrave, 2 Feb. 1846, Strachey MSS, DD/SH C1189 G283.

[78] Georgiana Dover to Harriet Sutherland, 20 Oct. [1846?], Sutherland MSS (NLS), Dep. 313/905.

[79] Catherine Hall argues that Africans were seen as 'children who needed the care and protection of their older brothers and sisters, fathers and mothers in the abolition movement. The ending of slavery meant the beginning of adulthood': *White, Male and Middle Class*, 32.

for the middle classes during the early years of the nineteenth century.[80] In the light of this very plausible view, the support of the quintessentially aristocratic Harriet, duchess of Sutherland, for the movement appears more than a little anomalous. Accounts of the anti-slavery movement seldom give her more than a passing mention, and, in light of the scale of the campaign, this is scarcely disproportionate. But her support for anti-slavery had significance in a number of respects: her prominence gave the movement publicity, and her contacts with politicians, particularly Gladstone, helped keep the issue on the political agenda. The intensity of the opposition to her public advocacy of abolition, moreover, is an important indicator of attitudes to aristocratic philanthropy.

Connected by birth and marriage to the Whig political aristocracy, and by her position as mistress of the robes to the court and the person of the queen, Harriet Sutherland's prominence in society was undisputed, and the immense wealth of her family was no small consideration for the movement, as W. C. Dowding recognized in soliciting her support for the cause of the freed slaves of Bermuda, informing her that 'it has been felt from the first . . . that your Grace's name and influence would be very valuable to our cause'.[81] Thus, as a patron the duchess contributed to the abolition movement; but she also took more active steps. She lent Stafford House for anti-slavery meetings, notably those attended by Harriet Beecher Stowe; arranged meetings between prominent abolitionists and British politicians; and, in 1852, issued an address on slavery, which was signed by 571,352 British women and presented to an American anti-slavery meeting in the following year.[82] She kept in contact with the British anti-slavery movement, corresponding with Sir Thomas Fowell Buxton, through whom she became involved with the Ladies' Negro Education Society and the organizations which supported mission work in Africa.[83] The duchess's reputation as a 'friend of the negro' led to her being wooed as a patron by other organizations, tangentially concerned with the slavery question, as for example in the request that she subscribe to a 'Negro College at Bermuda'.[84] But

---

[80] Ibid. 25–34. See also Clare Midgley, *Women against Slavery: The British Campaigns, 1780–1870* (Routledge, 1992), and Jane Rendall, *The Origins of Modern Feminism: Women in Britain, France and the United States, 1780–1860* (Macmillan, 1985), 243–54.

[81] W. C. Dowding to Harriet Sutherland, [n.d.], Sutherland MSS (Staffs.), D593 P/20.

[82] *Weekly Commonwealth*, 14 May 1853, enclosed in John Graham Palfrey to Harriet Sutherland, 19 Apr. 1853, Sutherland MSS (Staffs.), D593 P/22/1/32.

[83] Sir Thomas Fowell Buxton to Harriet Sutherland, 26 Dec. 1840, and Harriet Sutherland to Sir Thomas Fowell Buxton, 1 Jan. 1841, Buxton MSS, MSS Brit. Emp. s444, vol. xx, fos. 92–4.

[84] W. C. Dowding to Harriet Sutherland, quoted above, n. 81. See also Harriet Martineau to J. A. Collins, 9 Nov. [1840], in Clare Taylor, *British and American Abolitionists. An Episode in Transatlantic Understanding* (Edinburgh: Edinburgh University Press, 1974), 123.

probably her greatest contribution to the cause of abolition was her friendship with Gladstone, for whom she acted as patron and confidante, sponsoring his movement from Tory to Whig circles.[85]

From the beginning of her long and intense friendship with Gladstone, the issue of slavery featured prominently in their correspondence, despite the fact that here was a subject on which the correspondents were not natural allies. Unlike questions of religion and support for the liberation and unification of Italy, the duchess and the politician approached slavery from opposite viewpoints. The duchess belonged to the party which had outlawed slavery in the British Empire in 1833, and had family connections with the opponents of slavery. Gladstone, by contrast, had made his parliamentary début defending the right to adequate compensation of the West Indian slave-owners, of whom his father was one. Moreover, during the American Civil War, Gladstone's sympathies were predominantly with the Confederacy, on constitutional grounds, whilst the duchess resolutely supported the Union as the means to abolish slavery. In attempts to woo him over, the duchess invited Gladstone to meet luminaries of the anti-slavery campaign at breakfasts, lunches, and evening parties, both at Stafford House and at Dunrobin. For example, Gladstone met Charles Sumner, the Massachussetts senator and abolitionist, at Stafford House in July 1855; Gladstone disagreed with the duchess over Sumner's methods, occasioning her impassioned defence that 'Some men are made to batter the wall—to blow the Trumpet—to blast the wicked—to say to each of a multitude—Thou art the man—I think it magnificent'.[86] He was likewise invited to meet Harriet Beecher Stowe, the author of Uncle Tom's Cabin, at a reception at Stafford House in May 1853.[87] He was invited to meet her more informally at Dunrobin in September 1853; the meeting did not take place on this occasion, as Mrs Stowe was urgently recalled to America, perhaps fortunately, as Gladstone suffered from an acute attack of erysipelas during the visit and was confined to his room.[88] Although Mrs Stowe and Gladstone do not appear to have met again, Harriet Sutherland and her daughter, Elizabeth Argyll, continued to entertain Mrs Stowe on her visits to England

---

[85] H. C. G. Matthew, Gladstone, 1809–1874 (Oxford: Oxford University Press, 1988), 150.

[86] Harriet Sutherland to W. E. Gladstone, [1 July 1855] and [20 June 1856], BL Add. MS 44,324, fos. 109–10 and 223–4.

[87] M. R. D. Foot and H. C. G. Matthew (eds.), The Gladstone Diaries (14 vols., Oxford: Oxford University Press, 1968–94), 7 May 1853. The previous year, he had written of Uncle Tom that it was 'a good book which scarcely denies exaggeration, which under the circumstances would be a serious error': 15 Oct. 1852.

[88] Sutherland to Anne Stafford, 8 Sept. 1853, Sutherland MSS (Staffs.), D593 P/28/9; Matthew, Gladstone, 1809–1874, 95.

and to introduce her to senior politicians—in 1856 she visited Inveraray and Dunrobin, at the latter of which she was to meet Lord Lansdowne and Henry Labouchère.[89]

The slavery question was thus one over which the duchess did not sit at Gladstone's feet; rather, she disagreed forcefully with him over issues and personalities, and constantly brought the question to his attention. How far she succeeded in influencing his views, it is impossible to say, particularly because Gladstone's side of their frequent correspondence is missing. It would not be reckless to assert that Harriet Sutherland played a leading role in keeping the issue alive in Gladstone's mind, a role of some importance during the Civil War. The duchess consistently interpreted the Civil War as a struggle primarily about the slavery issue, and not, as Gladstone believed, a political struggle over the Confederacy's right to secede from the Union. In this difference of opinion, Harriet Sutherland's and Gladstone's views prefigured the historians' debates which continue to the present about the meaning of the Civil War. On its outbreak in 1861, the duchess wrote:

If the canker of the irritation of Slavery has produced this war—one must feel it to be a natural result—not too horrible for that which has caused it—& if the bloody road is to lead to emancipation in some way not yet apprehended still the curse of war will sweep [away] a curse greater still.[90]

A few days later, the duchess was horrified to hear Gladstone 'quoted for saying you think the Southern states most in the right—I did not hear you say so: I do not believe it'.[91] Gladstone's position, that the South had a right to secede and that slavery was only incidental, drew a series of rebuttals from the duchess over the next year: when the Union states declared gradual abolition, she remarked that 'England must believe now that Slavery has something to do with it'.[92] She reiterated her disagreement with Gladstone's view: 'That the War is mainly political I cannot feel. Surely it was the horror of an Anti-Slavery Parlt. that raised the South.'[93] She also provided a channel of communication with pro-Unionists, passing on letters from Harriet Beecher Stowe and involving herself with the relief effort directed towards the Lancashire cotton mill workers, who were adversely affected by the blockade of the South, but who none the less supported the Union cause of free labour.[94]

[89] Sutherland to Anne Stafford, 7 Sept. 1856, Sutherland MSS (Staffs.), D593 P/28/9.
[90] Harriet Sutherland to Gladstone, 25 May 1861, BL Add. MS 44,325, fos. 137–9.
[91] Harriet Sutherland to Gladstone, 28 May [1861], BL Add. MS 44,325, fo. 144.
[92] Harriet Sutherland to Gladstone, [Feb. 1862], BL Add. MS 44,326, fos. 64–5.
[93] Harriet Sutherland to Gladstone, 30 June 1862, BL Add. MS 44,326, fos. 178–9.
[94] Harriet Sutherland to Gladstone, 2 Oct. [1862] and n.d., BL Add. MS 44,326, fos. 204–7 and 210–11.

The duchess of Sutherland's advocacy of the cause of abolition was widely condemned, from a variety of perspectives; the nature of those criticisms offers insight into differing perceptions of the role of aristocratic women in philanthropy at mid-century. They also presage the criticisms which were to be directed against middle-class women who sought a public role through the championing of the poor and oppressed. Here, once more, the fundamental difference is that while the middle-class woman had to struggle to assert her right to a public platform, Harriet Sutherland enjoyed such a platform already, by virtue of her social position. Whatever the justifications for the criticisms which were levelled against her, her use of her public persona in the interests of abolition may be read also as a courageous example.

While she was supported actively by members of her family, notably Elizabeth Argyll, who shared a commitment to the cause of abolition, Harriet Sutherland's anti-slavery activities provoked widespread criticism. Public criticism of women was unusual and unacceptable, because of the protected status which their general absence from public discourse conferred on them. The adoption of middle-class lobbying tactics by an aristocratic woman on an issue which could not be explained in terms of personal, paternal conduct, and which, unlike the political activity which will be discussed further below, took place outside the protective boundaries of her class, made personal criticism and public debate of her activities possible.

The occasion for the bulk of this criticism was the meeting at Stafford House on 26 November 1852, at which the duchess read a draft address from the women of England to those of America on the subject of slavery, which was eventually to be signed by half a million British women. The address, outlining humanitarian and Christian arguments against the perpetuation of slavery, self-consciously invoked the femininity of its signatories, appealing to its recipients 'as sisters, as wives, and as mothers':

We shall not be suspected of any political motives; all will readily admit that the state of things to which we allude is one peculiarly distressing to our sex; and thus our friendly and earnest interposition will be ascribed altogether to domestic, and in no respect to national, feelings.[95]

This kind of argument for female engagement in the anti-slavery movement paralleled arguments made by American abolitionists, who found in their gender not only a justification, but a moral imperative, to resist slavery.[96] The arguments were rejected by those who believed that even in a benevolent cause, public exposure and apparent similarity to the business world

[95] *The Times*, 29 Nov. 1852, p. 8 col. c.
[96] Rendall, *Origins of Modern Feminism*, 248–50; Clinton, *Other Civil War*, 67–71.

which philanthropic organization could entail would demean womanhood and destroy its moral superiority. The immediate responses to *The Times* report, reflected in its letter columns, included the fervent wish of 'Common Sense' that the ladies had been persuaded 'for the first, and I trust for the last, time in their lives . . . to address a public audience, to move, to resolve, to form committees and subcommittees, and to engage offices and a secretary'.[97] Another letter-writer attacked the methods of the meeting, suggesting that if the women were to renounce 'luxurious habits of dress and furniture', they would do more for the abolition of slavery by reducing the demand for the cotton goods produced by slave labour. A female critic considered the meeting and the interference in legislative matters by its supporters which she inferred from it to be an 'entire . . . misconception of their own peculiar character and provinces', and recommended that women confine themselves to the reform of sentiment in their own circles, particularly in ending prejudice of colour and race.[98]

But by far the majority of the criticisms were aimed at the duchess and her co-signatories (who included the duchesses of Bedford and Argyll and the dowager duchess of Beaufort, Ladies Palmerston, Shaftesbury, Dover, Cowley, Ruthven, and Belhaven, and Lady Constance Grosvenor), not on account of their gender, but because of their social status. 'R. G. D.' suggested that English aristocrats had no grounds for criticizing slavery while they ignored the condition of the British urban poor; Janet Kay Shuttleworth pointed to the 'neglect, ill-usage, and starvation payment' of governesses employed in upper-class English families as a reason for American women to ignore the protests of the meeting, adding: 'Let us reform our schoolrooms, and we may expect them to reform the cabins of their slaves.'[99] 'Simplex' compared the lot of male servants in Britain to that of American slaves, especially in the practice of refusing them permission to marry or to see their families regularly: 'Our aristocracy and upper class so far live in glass house [sic] that they should not throw stones at Americans.'[100] However inappropriate the comparisons, these letters show a strong sense that the aristocracy should put its own house in order with regard to the poor, before venturing to reform the social relations of other societies. The gender of the anti-slavery protesters was of little importance compared to their public representation of their class. Karl Marx made use of a similar critique in an article for the *People's Paper* in the following year. Pointing to the clearances of the Highland estates of the Sutherlands and the Atholes, the enforced

[97] *The Times*, 2 Dec. 1852, p. 6 col. c.
[98] *The Times*, 1 Dec. 1852, p. 8 cols. b–c: letters from 'Academicus' and 'An Englishwoman'.
[99] Ibid.   [100] *The Times*, 3 Dec. 1852, p. 8 col. a.

emigration of the Highland population, and the replacement of people by sheep and eventually by game for the entertainment of the aristocracy, Marx concluded that 'The enemy of British Wages Slavery has a right to condemn Negro-Slavery; a Duchess of Sutherland, a Duke of Athol [sic], a Manchester Cotton-lord—never!'[101]

Thomas Carlyle also poured scorn on the duchess's anti-slavery activities, conjoining his loathing for organized philanthropy and his extreme racial prejudice to a mocking contempt for those whose views were different from his own. He wrote to Arthur Clough of 'a big foolish meeting' at 'Aunt Harriet's Cabin,—so they now call the Duchess's grand palace', concluding that 'only the weak-minded and strong-lunged are concerned in the phenomenon'.[102] Carlyle's opposition was to the entire abolitionist movement, but the involvement of 'quality people' such as Harriet Sutherland, whom he construed as 'irrational', fuelled his dislike.[103]

Middle-class and American anti-slavery activists took advantage of the duchess's support of their cause, but they too remained aloof from it. J. B. Estlin's comment on the Stafford House address sums up the amused contempt of the 'professional' campaigner for the enthusiastic, socially elevated amateur, while revealing the benefits of such a prominent supporter:

The Duchess of Sutherland's Address amuses me: it is useful for exciting discussion; it is too very satisfactory to see people of the Established Church condescending to think & speak, if not very sensibly, on Am[erican] AntiSlavery[.] Another memorial & subscription for Mrs Stowe is on foot. Of course we *oppose* none of these harmless amusements.[104]

According to this view, the activities of the socially prominent could thus serve useful purposes, but they could not rise above the character of 'harmless amusements'.

Middle-class philanthropists found it difficult to treat the charitable activities of aristocratic women with due seriousness—as have historians—because they worked within such an unfamiliar set of rules and expectations. They were irregular, personal, and paternalist at a time when regularity and organization were at a premium, and when the middle classes were seeking to usurp their position as the natural patrons of the poor. Moreover, their

[101] Karl Marx, 'Sutherland and Slavery; or, The Duchess at Home', *People's Paper*, 12 Mar. 1853, p. 5 cols. a–b.

[102] Thomas Carlyle to Arthur H. Clough, 12 May 1853, Bod., MS. Eng. lett. d. 177, fos. 176–7.

[103] With his emphasis on the cult of the hero, it is likely that Carlyle regarded the protection and championing of slaves by women as further proof of their unfitness for freedom or equality.

[104] J. B. Estlin to Maria Weston Chapman, Dec. 1852, in Taylor, *British and American Abolitionists*, 392.

charitable activities often took the form of apparently frivolous social occasions, giving pleasure to the benefactors in the course of raising money for the poor or disadvantaged. The combination of pleasure and duty was alien to the nonconformist conscience which motivated so much Victorian charitable work, and denied the accumulation of moral capital to the aristocratic patron. Charity, however, was an important part of the culture of aristocratic patronage, which continued to operate in Victorian society, and in which women continued to operate effectively and often independently. This culture was not restricted to relations with the poor. For aristocratic women, it remained fundamental to their continued activity in the political life of the nation.

4

'Aristocratical and Female Influence': Elections and Electioneering

The management of estates and local communities was directed towards maintaining and enhancing the prestige and authority of the aristocracy; one test of its success was the parliamentary election. Patronage and deference were not restricted to relations with the poor, and the return of the landowner's candidate remained a sound indication of the influence of the aristocratic landowner. Despite changes to the franchise carried in 1832 and 1867, and an increasingly vociferous debate on the nature and scope of 'legitimate influence', before the radical extension of the county franchise in 1884–5, the aristocracy continued to play a significant part in the return of members to the lower house.[1]

The nature of the 'influence' which aristocrats, in common with a more widely defined landed interest, possessed or sought to exercise is particularly problematic, especially after the Reform Acts had done away with many of the pocket and nomination boroughs which were explicitly in the gift of a landowner. Thompson has pointed out that the influence which remained could, in theory and sometimes in practice, be ignored by the electorate, but more usually 'could be expected to prevail, given reasonable tact in the management of the constituency and a certain amount of care in avoiding offence to the susceptibilities of the electors'.[2] The Reform Act of 1832 did not remove influence, and indeed had not attempted to do so, because, within limits, influence was construed as both legitimate and beneficial. Conflicts arose when the boundaries of those limits were disputed; by the end of the period under consideration here, the landowners' 'legitimate interests' were considerably restricted by comparison with their late eighteenth-century heyday, but had not been eliminated.

LEGITIMATE INFLUENCE

The exercise of such influence was more subtle than the label of 'corruption' suggests. Although 'treating', bribing, and bullying were not uncommon,

[1] See e.g. Heesom, ' "Legitimate" *versus* "illegitimate" influences'; Cannadine, *Decline and Fall*, esp. ch. 4; and Thompson, *English Landed Society*, esp. ch. 10.

[2] Thompson, *English Landed Society*, 46. See also R. J. Olney, 'The Politics of Land', in G. E. Mingay (ed.), *The Victorian Countryside* (2 vols., Routledge & Kegan Paul, 1981), i. 58–70.

influential electors, who were, after all, property owners with at least aspirations to gentility, had to be approached with greater finesse: in 1843, James Stuart Wortley wrote after a visit to his constituency during which he had attended a ball, that 'I flatter myself that I shall go away having established the popularity of Lord Bute's member for the County'.[3] Likewise, in 1852, the factor of the Sutherland estates, James Loch, wrote to advise the landowning Lady Stafford that

I have always thought that what a Landlord should do, on such occasions, is simply to express his own opinions and wishes; and in most instances, where a good feeling exists between him and his tenants, the bulk of them will adopt the course most agreeable to him. If any of them should take a different line it is the landlord's duty and it is his interest to regard their conduct as proceeding from honest and conscientious motives.[4]

Many landlords did not show this degree of respect for the opinions and political consciences of their tenants; but direct evidence of female landowners seeking to impose their political opinions on their tenants through the use of sanctions is scarce.

Female influence in this arena was, by definition, indirect: candidates and electors alike were male, as were election officials. Nevertheless, aristocratic women could exert considerable influence over the polls, as owners of property and as the friends and relatives of candidates. In some instances, their very femininity could be enlisted in support of a candidate. The conjunction of feminine and aristocratic patronage was as considerable in political affairs as in charitable matters. Palmerston wrote to Lady Sandwich, canvassing her support, that 'There is no Influence like that of fair Ladies and in that Capacity you will I trust protect my cause but you have double means of assisting me by your aristocratical as well as by your Female influence'.[5]

From an early age, aristocratic women were brought up to expect to participate in the elections of fathers, brothers, and friends. It was, of course, illegal for peers of the realm to intervene directly in elections to the House of Commons; but their wives and daughters, like their brothers and sons, appear to have been deemed sufficiently removed from the lords to be exempt from charges of legal interference. Lady Dorothy Nevill recalled that as a child, she and her sister rode their ponies at the head of the

[3] James Stuart Wortley to Caroline Wharncliffe, 22 Oct. 1843, quoted in Grosvenor and Beilby (eds.), *The First Lady Wharncliffe*, ii. 332.

[4] James Loch to Anne Stafford, 16 Mar. 1852, Sutherland MSS (Staffs.) D593 P/28/10. See also, Olney, 'Politics of Land', 61, and O'Gorman, *Voters, Patrons and Parties*, 7.

[5] Palmerston to Louisa Sandwich, 25 Dec. 1825, Sandwich Papers, Cambridgeshire County Record Office (Huntingdon) (hereafter Sandwich MSS (Cambs.)), Hinch/8/233.

procession of Orford tenants to the poll, while during her father's campaign for Cheshire in 1832, the third daughter of Elizabeth Belgrave 'has got a large blue and yellow bow [her father's colours] which she has worn every day and fastens on the top of her nightcap when she goes to bed'.[6] Elections have been characterized by Frank O'Gorman as inclusive of wider sections of the community than the narrow franchises would suggest. Through ceremony and ritual, he has argued, all sections of the community engaged in a reaffirm-ation of local hierarchies.[7] The inclusion of aristocratic women and children in such community events tends to support this view; although aristocratic women seldom appeared publicly during the poll, their arrival in the town and public knowledge of their presence lent glamour to the occasion, and affirmed the legitimacy of their interest in the outcome.

Perhaps the most famous intervention by an aristocratic woman in polit-ics in the modern period was the kiss bestowed by the 'beautiful duchess' Georgiana Devonshire on a Westminster butcher to purchase six votes for Charles James Fox in the notorious election of 1784.[8] The actions of the duchess in the Whig cause, which led to sensationalist publicity and her pub-lic vilification by Fox's Tory opponents, were never repeated in the Vic-torian period, despite the continued presence of aristocratic women at elections, partly as a result of the removal of the more obviously corrupt electoral practices. But the nature of their involvement changed, or at least did not follow the path suggested by the duchess of Devonshire's actions. Although aristocratic women continued to interest themselves in elections, they confined their activities to their local county and borough constituen-cies, where they had a personal or patronage connection with the electors; the duchess of Devonshire's actions in the metropolitan Westminster seat were unusual, and hence reprehensible, because neither she nor her family had any direct interest in the seat being contested, and her canvassing was not among dependants but among strangers. Criticisms of the French aris-tocracy, and the women in particular for involving themselves in politics, which ended on the guillotine, also had an impact on the cosmopolitan and Francophile British aristocracy, encouraging women to return to the less

---

[6] R. Nevill (ed.), *Life of Lady Dorothy Nevill*, 7; Gervase Huxley, *Lady Elizabeth and the Grosvenors: Life in a Whig family, 1822–1839* (Oxford: Oxford University Press, 1965), 105.

[7] Frank O'Gorman, 'Campaign Rituals and Ceremonies: The Social Meaning of Elections in England, 1780–1860', *Past and Present*, 135 (May 1992), 79–115.

[8] Gower, *Face without a Frown*, chs. 7 and 8, esp. pp. 110–13. See also the analysis by Linda Colley, *Britons: Forging the Nation, 1707–1837* (New Haven: Yale University Press, 1992), 242–50. The duchess's wider political career is examined in Amanda Foreman, 'A Politician's Politician: Georgiana, Duchess of Devonshire and the Whig Party', in Hannah Barker and Elaine Chalus (eds.), *Gender in Eighteenth-Century England: Roles, Representations and Responsibilities* (Longman, 1997), 170–204.

prominent role in elections which they had had before Georgiana Devon-shire's experiments.[9] Further, the broad revolution in taste, manners, and sensibility which took place in this period, from which derived Victorian notions of woman's role, had its influence. Although I argue that this revolution affected aristocratic women less than women of other classes, they could not remain entirely immune to it, particularly in the kinds of behaviour that were expected on public occasions. Thus, although the aristocratic woman continued to exert influence in elections throughout the period, it was impossible for them to follow the example of the duchess of Devonshire in the manner in which they chose to exert that influence. One of the critics of Georgiana Devonshire commented that 'when people of rank descend below themselves and mingle with the vulgar for mean and dirty purposes, they give up their claim to respect, forfeit their privileges and become fair game for censors'.[10] It is significant that this criticism was made in terms of class, not gender. After the French Revolution, the aristocracy was more cautious about the risking its position, and aristocratic women conducted themselves differently as a consequence.

MANAGING UNREFORMED ELECTIONS

The redoubtable Louisa, Lady Sandwich, is an interesting example of a woman deeply involved in the electoral process, both before and after the first Reform Act. Daughter of the first earl of Belmore, Lady Louisa Corry married Viscount Hinchinbrooke, heir to the earldom of Sandwich, in 1804. The Sandwich family and the dukes of Manchester carved up the represen-tation of the county of Huntingdon, in a coalition which 'derived its force from mutual fear of the expense of a contested election rather than from cor-dial agreement', while the borough of Huntingdon was effectively in the gift of Sandwich, the result of the judicious exercise of patronage.[11] The first records of Louisa Sandwich's (or Hinchinbrooke as she was known before 1814) involvement in elections are from 1806, the year, incidentally, that Georgiana Devonshire died. Hinchinbrooke, who supported the ministry, was standing for re-election to the Commons as one of the Huntingdonshire county members. Lady Hinchinbrooke set about drumming up support for her husband, writing to those possessed of votes to encourage them to

[9] Margaret H. Darrow, 'French Noblewomen and the New Domesticity, 1750–1850', *Feminist Studies*, 1 (Spring 1979), 41–65   [10] Gower, *Face without a Frown*, 112.
[11] R. G. Thorne (ed.), *The House of Commons 1790–1820* (4 vols., The History of Parliament Trust, Secker & Warburg, 1986), ii. Huntingdonshire entry, 209–13, and Huntingdon entry, 213. See this work for a discussion of the detailed negotiations concerning the representation of the borough and the county.

pledge themselves and their connections to Hinchinbrooke's cause.[12] Thus a Mr Cockerell wrote to her that he hoped the election would fall on a date convenient for him to attend the poll himself, and saying that he had 'already written to my friends in the County', encouraging them to 'promote Lord Hinchinbrook's [sic] success'.[13] Similarly, Lord Frederick Montagu, son of the fourth duke of Manchester, the other great Tory family in the county, and himself retiring as a member for Huntingdonshire, wrote to Louisa Hinchinbrooke from London with information about the election, and offering his services: 'Perhaps I can be of use to Hinch and Fellowes in forwarding communications to the Freeholders in London,' he wrote. '[I]f so, I beg they will employ me.'[14] Lady Hinchinbrooke was not the only aristocratic woman interested in her husband's success in Huntingdonshire: the widowed Lady Olivia Sparrow, an influential landowner related to the Manchester interest, gave her agent permission to state publicly that 'she begs that her Tenants and all others who are under obligation to her, will give their Votes and Interest to Lord Hinchinbrooke and Lord Proby'.[15] Lord Frederick Montagu reported that Lord Aboyne's support was certain, as 'my Mother [the duchess of Manchester] canvassed him some time ago, and he promised it'.[16] The duchess of Manchester was also active in correspondence, receiving the assurances of Henry Cipriani, an army officer at the Woolwich barracks, that he had enquired in his regiment as to those who held the franchise in the Huntingdonshire election. He reported that 'Sergt. Fox I believe is the only freeholder in the Corps besides myself, & as every dependence may be placed on him, I have given him a Furlough with directions to call on Capt. Dobyns on his arrival at Huntingdon'.[17] The duchess's energies were occasionally misdirected, as, for example, in her bid for the support of one gentleman, who expressed his willingness to be of service, but regretted that 'in the present instance I cannot do it, as I possess no interest whatever in Huntingdonshire'.[18]

[12] This was of course the more necessary under the old franchise, when many freeholders did not reside on the property which gave them their votes.

[13] S. P. Cockerell to Louisa Hinchinbrooke, [May 1807], Sandwich MSS (Cambs.), Hinch/8/129.

[14] Lord Frederick Montagu to Louisa Hinchinbrooke, [8 May 1807], Sandwich MSS (Cambs.), Hinch/8/133/21.

[15] Benjamin Whitney to Messrs. Maule and Sweeting, 5 Nov. 1806, Sandwich MSS (Cambs.), Hinch/8/129.

[16] Lord Frederick Montagu to Louisa Hinchinbrooke, [8 May 1807], Sandwich MSS (Cambs.), Hinch/8/133/21.

[17] Henry Cipriani to Elizabeth Manchester, 7 May 1807, Sandwich MSS (Cambs.), Hinch/8/144/1.

[18] Sackville to Elizabeth Manchester, [May 1807], Sandwich MSS (Cambs.), Hinch/8/144/2.

This brief consideration of the first decade of the century provides a glimpse of the kinds of actions involved in pre-reform electioneering by aristocratic women, and also some notion of the 'mental world' of pre-reform politics, in which interests and personal obligations took precedence over political ideologies, and in which it was acceptable to use all available means to increase the poll for one's candidate: had Sergeant Fox been a Whig, or merely less politically dependable, it is unlikely that his leave of absence for the election would have been granted.

Hinchinbrooke succeeded to the Sandwich earldom in 1814, three years after the birth of an heir; the succession of course involved a move to the House of Lords, and there is no further evidence of interest in elections in the papers until the mid-1820s. (Equally, neither the borough nor the county seats were contested at elections in this period, all the seats being filled by unopposed Tories.) Lord Sandwich died in 1818, leaving a 7-year-old to inherit the title and the estates; Louisa Sandwich was appointed one of the trustees for the estate and guardian of the children until the son came of age in 1832. She took this trust to involve a continued presence in the electoral business of the county, agreeing to support Palmerston in the 1825 election. He thanked her, saying that 'Four or Five votes would be a great acquisition as every vote must be of Consequence in a Contest that must necessarily be very hard run'.[19] In 1826, she entered into an acrimonious dispute with the agent George Frederick Maule over the election expenses incurred the previous year. Lady Sandwich had agreed to bear part of the costs—'with some difficulty'—but refused to pay all the items on the bill, including £70 interest which had been charged owing to delay in payment. She maintained that she had asked for the bill six months previously; moreover, when the bill finally arrived, she found it to be 'drawn up in a very loose and unsatisfactory manner . . . which I cannot think proper'.[20] Maule responded in kind, considering that the charges he made were reasonable in light of the time he had spent on the election, the anxiety and fatigue caused to him, and 'the serious neglect of other business' which it had occasioned. Further, he was offended by the abuse of his method of drawing up a bill, and sent a copy of the absolute expenditure on the election. He concluded that 'I do not know when my feelings have been so much hurt, but at the same time allow me to add that it shall not cause me to relax in my exertions to promote the interests of the House of Hinchingbrook [sic] so long as I have the honour to be employed'.[21]

[19] Palmerston to Louisa Sandwich, 25 and 31 Dec. 1825, Sandwich MSS (Cambs.), Hinch/8/233, 235.

[20] G. F. Maule to Louisa Sandwich, 8 Jan. 1826, and Louisa Sandwich to G. F. Maule, 10 Jan. 1826, Sandwich MSS (Cambs.), Hinch/8/214/1 and 214/2.

[21] G. F. Maule to Louisa Sandwich, 14 Jan. 1826, Sandwich MSS (Cambs.), Hinch/8/214/3.

Maule put aside his injured feelings (which must have been salved by the income which agents derived from their work), for in 1831 he was again acting as electoral agent for the county. The elections of 1831–2, in the midst of the Reform Bill crisis, were fought particularly bitterly, and Lady Sandwich's opposition to the bill led her again to be deeply involved in the elections in Huntingdon. The strength of her feelings on the subject may be gauged by her declaration that 'I am ready to subscribe £1,000 towards the return of any member who will honestly oppose the overthrow of all existing rights & endanger a Constitution under which England has been the wonder and admiration of the world [sic].'[22]

The campaign began on a hostile note, in a correspondence with the mayor of the city of Huntingdon, Mr Rowley, who had agreed to permit a reform meeting to be held, as the request was 'signed by many respectable folk'. He defended his decision, as refusal would not have prevented the meeting, whilst so doing would have 'attacked the influence of the Sandwich family in the area'.[23] Louisa Sandwich did not agree. The connection of the family with the town had been of benefit to Huntingdon; moreover,

Has the nomination of the Members for the town ever been converted to profligate purposes? Have they ever acted against the wishes of the nominators? . . . Your letter has decided a determination on which I have been deliberating for some time, that of taking no further concern in any thing connected with Huntingdon as a Boro'.[24]

There is no further correspondence revealing involvement in the borough, although the agent, Maule, kept Louisa Sandwich informed of events in that constituency.[25] If Lady Sandwich kept her resolution with respect to the borough of Huntingdon—a resolution the more easy to keep as there was no heir or other son of age to hold down the seat—the county remained a matter of great concern. Three candidates stood in May 1831: Viscount Mandeville, J. B. Rooper, a county landowner, and Lord Strathavon, heir to the earl of Aboyne who also owned land in the county. Aboyne had attempted and failed to run his son as a candidate in 1814, in an attempt to break the Montagu monopoly, believing that 'Lord Sandwich and the Montagu interest assume more than their property entitles them to'.[26] This

[22] Louisa Sandwich to Lord Strathavon, 2 May 1831, Sandwich Papers, Mapperton House, Dorset (hereafter Sandwich MSS (Mapperton)), Box 288.

[23] Mr Rowley to Louisa Sandwich, 18 Feb. 1831, Sandwich MSS (Cambs.), Hinch/8/274.

[24] Louisa Sandwich to Mr Rowley, 21 Feb. 1831, Sandwich MSS (Cambs.), Hinch/8/275.

[25] G. F. Maule to Louisa Sandwich, 1 and 3 May 1831, Sandwich MSS (Cambs.), Hinch/8/149/2 and 149/5.

[26] Quoted in Thorne (ed.), *House of Commons 1790–1820*, ii. 211.

background is of importance in understanding the events of 1831. Also of importance is the reminder that the Montagu dukes of Manchester and the Montagu earls of Sandwich were rivals for the political leadership of the county, a rivalry which was kept submerged for much of the time in order to avoid contested elections. In 1831, Viscount Mandeville, the Manchester heir, was standing for election, and his support for the Sandwich candidate, Strathavon, as the second member, was not certain.

Lady Sandwich had invoked her interest on behalf of Strathavon on the understanding that he would oppose the Reform Bill. By the end of April, however, there was evidence to suggest that his resolve was weakening. W. H. Fellowes, an important figure in county politics, wrote to Louisa that he had been dissatisfied with the extent of Strathavon's commitment, but that on receiving assurances from both Strathavon and Louisa Sandwich that his opposition was sufficiently rigorous, he had instructed his agent to give him all assistance at Romsey.[27] Information reached Lady Sandwich at the beginning of May that Strathavon had had 'an offer of the *Blue Flags* in his procession' (blue being the colour of the reformers), and Maule expressed some doubt as to his refusal.[28] Louisa immediately sent a demand to Strathavon that he either stick to his opposition or forfeit the support, financial and political, of his sponsors, including the £1,000 she was herself providing. The annoyance caused to her by the rumoured defection was great, and she was aware of displaying no feminine reticence in her challenge to him: 'I am so deeply pledged *for you and by you*, that I dare not allow of any misconstruction to arise from what in this instance of vital importance, would be a weak and mistaken delicacy.'[29] Once more, this predicating of class interests over gendered behaviour suggests that the strictures of 'correct feminine behaviour' were not the infrastructure on which the lives of aristocratic women were built, but rather an outer covering, which could be cast off when their position in the hierarchy was challenged.

Strathavon clearly returned the required reply, and Fellowes wrote to Lady Sandwich of his reassurance.[30] However, his troubles were not over, as the Mandeville camp refused to support him with the second votes of those electors who had promised their first votes to Mandeville, causing Maule to fear that it would cost Strathavon his election. He therefore entreated Lady Sandwich to urge the duke of Manchester and Lord Westmorland to lend

[27] W. H. Fellowes to Louisa Sandwich, 30 Apr. 1831, Sandwich MSS (Cambs.), Hinch/8/149/1.

[28] G. F. Maule to Louisa Sandwich, 1 May 1831, Sandwich MSS (Cambs.), Hinch/8/149/2.

[29] Louisa Sandwich to Strathavon, 2 May 1831, Sandwich MSS (Mapperton), Box 288.

[30] W. H. Fellowes to Louisa Sandwich, 2 May 1831, Sandwich MSS (Cambs.), Hinch/8/149/4.

Strathavon their support.[31] The day after writing this letter, Maule went to Lord Mandeville's committee 'to communicate your Ladyship's liberality', which was greeted with 'perfect indifference' and a 'decided determination to use that Interest *solely* for Lord M.'; he therefore recommended that Strathavon's supporters reciprocate by 'securing our Votes solely for Lord S.'.[32] On the second day of polling, 6 May, it was clear that the tactics of the Kimbolton faction had succeeded in keeping out Lord Strathavon, the results standing at Mandeville 610, Strathavon 442, and Rooper, the reform candidate, heading the poll at 626. Maule attributed this unsatisfactory result to 'the conduct of Lord Mandeville's friends', as did the young Lord Sandwich, who wrote to his mother the next day that

by this time the poll is closed and Lord Strathavon thrown out thanks to our friends Lds Mandeville and Manchester who had they chosen to act with any consistency . . . or any wish to keep up the Montagu interest with respect to us there is no doubt that Rooper must have given up . . . for myself, I will never support either the Duke or Lord Mandeville either in the County or out of the County for the Shabby and almost rascally way they have treated us.[33]

The Sandwich faction took a small revenge in retiring their candidate from the election on 10 May, thereby preventing Mandeville from heading the poll, at which he was 'greatly mortified'. The final result was thus Rooper 841, Mandeville 812, Strathavon 573.[34]

The elections over and the county lost, Maule returned to the subject of the borough, despite Louisa's assertion that she would have nothing more to do with it, having in mind only 'the promotion of Lord Sandwichs [sic] Interest'. The mayoralty of Huntingdon was vacant, and difficulties were experienced in filling the position; Maule had volunteered to fill it, but it had been deemed politically inexpedient for him to take office. There remained the option of Captain Edwards, who was reluctant on financial grounds, but was 'so attached to the Interest that if your Ladyship were to ask him to take the Mayoralty this year I think he would do so', particularly if Lady Sandwich extended to him the offer of £150 a year made to Maule. There is no record of Louisa Sandwich's reply, but it is unlikely that she could have withstood the argument that even if the proposed reform of parliament were effected, 'his Lordship's Influence and property, with I trust

[31] G. F. Maule to Louisa Sandwich, 3 May 1831, Sandwich MSS (Cambs.), Hinch/8/149/5.

[32] G. F. Maule to Louisa Sandwich, 4 May 1831, Sandwich MSS (Cambs.), Hinch/8/149/6.

[33] Maule to Louisa Sandwich, 6 May 1831, and Sandwich to Louisa Sandwich, 7 May 1831, Sandwich MSS (Cambs.), Hinch/8/149/9 and 149/10.

[34] Maule to Louisa Sandwich, 9 May 1831, Sandwich MSS (Cambs.), Hinch/8/149/11.

some sparks of gratitude still left, will always secure the return of the member for the Borough'.[35]

Lord Sandwich came of age in 1832, apparently ending the dominance of his mother in the electoral affairs of the county. However, the election caused by the death of William IV in 1837 occurred while Sandwich was visiting Paris, and once more, Louisa took the centre stage, directing the use of the Sandwich political interest. Writing to his mother from France, Sandwich demonstrated that the Sandwich interest in the borough of Huntingdon had not been given up, reassuring her that a radical opposition would be 'fruitless, and I think as long as the present Members stand there is nothing to fear', a belief which was borne out by the return of two Conservatives unopposed in every election until 1868.[36] Lady Sandwich had expressed reservations about the possible success for the Conservatives in a contested election; her son made rejoinder that 'in the County you say justly that petty jealousies amonst [sic] the Tory party will prevent any successful contest, but I say successful or not the contest must be tried if ever now, when the mind of the young Queen will naturally be biased towards the majority'.[37]

The reservations were evidently the long-term result of the election of 1831, the 'petty jealousies' being between the Sandwich and Manchester families. Mandeville was still sitting for the constituency, although it was widely expected that he would retire before this contest,[38] and much of the correspondence in which Louisa engaged was devoted to persuading suitable alternative candidates to come forward to represent the Conservatives and oppose the Whig, J. B. Rooper. If the letter from W. H. Fellowes is sincere, it was the arguments of Lady Sandwich which persuaded him that he 'might perhaps be considered wanting in zeal for our cause' if he prevented his son's candidature, while Veasey, the Huntingdon agent, reported with alacrity the candidature of Mr Thornhill, saying 'the two gentlemen coalesce'.[39] Veasey had previously reported on the meeting of the Huntingdon Conservative Association which had agreed to support these two candidates, at which he had encouraged their adoption by saying that 'two Ladies of the highest rank in the County' would subscribe a generous sum if they came forward 'in a manner wh. was satisfactory to the County'.[40] Both ladies

[35]   Maule to Louisa Sandwich, 25 July 1831, Sandwich MSS (Cambs.), Hinch/11/71.

[36]   Sandwich to Louisa Sandwich, 23 June [1837], Sandwich MSS (Mapperton), Box 290. Electoral details for the period after 1832 are confirmed in F. W. S. Craig, *British Parliamentary Election Results 1832–1885* (Aldershot: Parliamentary Research Services, 1989; 1st pub. 1977).

[37]   Sandwich to Louisa Sandwich, 23 June [1837], Sandwich MSS (Mapperton), Box 290.

[38]   James Rust to Louisa Sandwich, n.d., Sandwich MSS (Mapperton), Box 290.

[39]   W. H. Fellowes to Louisa Sandwich, [27 June 1837]; D. Veasey to Louisa Sandwich, n.d., Sandwich MSS (Mapperton), Box 290.

[40]   D. Veasey to Louisa Sandwich, 2 July 1837, Sandwich MSS (Mapperton), Box 290.

(the other was Lady Olivia Sparrow) had promised to subscribe £300; as both candidates had strictly limited budgets, this subscription was of great importance. When the subscription reached £3,070, Louisa was informed that there was 'nothing yet I believe from Kimbolton', the seat of the Manchesters, who were apparently still pursuing their opposition to the Sandwich candidates.[41]

The extent of Lady Sandwich's continued interest in the election is revealed in the detailed breakdown of the likely voters in the county which Veasey provided, listing the major landowners by their political preferences. The result was more open than previously, as this was the first contest since the passage of the Chandos amendment to allow £50 tenants-at-will the franchise, which in Huntingdonshire 'lets in an immense number of tenants who had before no votes'; much of Veasey's assessment was of these new voters.[42] But the expectation continued that tenants would vote to oblige their landlords. In the same letter, Veasey remarked that he had questioned 'young Peppercorn' about 'my Lord's tenants at St. Neots & he assured me that they wd. all be ready'. Peppercorn himself informed Lady Sandwich that he had accompanied the candidates on their canvass, and that they had 'each met with the support of Lord Sandwich's friends here, to the utmost of my expectation'.[43]

I have dwelt at some length on the experience of Lady Sandwich as an example of the roles available to aristocratic women in elections in the era of the first Reform Act. Her activity was to some extent conditioned by the early death of her husband and the long minority of her son, but the ease with which she stepped into the role of political manipulator, and the ready acceptance of her role by political agents and county society alike, point to the predominance of her class interests over the behavioural requirements of her gender. Despite the gradual waning of the aristocratic hegemony during Victoria's reign, the 'aristocratical' influence of the 'fair Ladies' did not end with the Reform Act, and they continued to be active in the elections of their family and political friends throughout this period. Electoral influence was in part, at least, a function of the paternalist ethic subscribed to by most aristocrats in their guise as landowners, as part of the triumvirate of duties which David Roberts has analysed in paternal thought, of 'ruling, guiding, and helping' their neighbours, tenants, and labourers.[44]

---

[41] James Rust to Louisa Sandwich, n.d., Sandwich MSS (Mapperton), Box 290. There were rumours that the Manchesters were planning to field their own candidate, a Col. Scole, but they came to nothing. See Veasey to Louisa Sandwich, 4 July 1837, Box 290.

[42] D. Veasey to Louisa Sandwich, 2 July 1837, Sandwich MSS (Mapperton), Box 290.

[43] G. Peppercorn to Louisa Sandwich, 18 July 1837, Sandwich MSS (Mapperton), Box 290.

[44] Roberts, *Paternalism in Early Victorian England*, 5–6.

WOMEN AND THE REFORMED ELECTORAL SYSTEM

Of course, participation in elections was not altruistic; the aristocratic woman sought to further the interests of her family, her class, and her political party by her activity. There were a number of ways in which she might pursue these ends. She could follow, without intervening in, the election of a particular candidate, husband, son, or friend, in any constituency. In an area where she was known to have influence, her interest could be sought for a candidate by third parties. Alternatively, she could take a position of ostentatious non-intervention. Finally, there was direct intervention in a constituency. Probably the most frequent was the first, connecting once again the domestic and political, the public and private imperatives in the lives of the aristocratic woman.

At a time when the aristocracy dominated membership of the House of Commons as well as the House of Lords, there were few aristocratic women who had no son, brother, or husband involved in electoral contests at some point in their lives.[45] Consequently, few avoided electoral politics entirely, even if, for many, participation was limited to a concern never expressed beyond the family circle. Such, for example, was the case of Lady John Russell, who, herself intensely devoted to certain liberal causes, such as the unification of Italy and the extension of the franchise, was nevertheless deeply resistant to her husband holding office, and who was believed to be a major obstacle to his later career. Her papers contain few references to Lord John's personal elections, and she does not appear to have been involved in the process at all. On the other hand, when her eldest son, John, viscount Amberley, sought election for Nottingham in 1866, the subject filled her letters to her youngest son; she heaped abuse on the other candidates, amongst whom were three other Liberals—Bernal Osborne, having stood for the seat without invitation, was described as 'by way of be[in]g a Radical but not by [way] of be[in]g a gentleman', and she deemed the seat unsuitable, and the electors 'a bad set, accustomed to bribes and riots'. When the seat was won a few days later, the complaints were forgotten in her delight at her son's success.[46] Mr Bouverie reported to Lady Minto on the progress of her son's canvass at Folkestone in 1837, while, when viscount Chelsea stood for Bath in 1873, his wife remained in London and received reports on his activities from her brother-in-law who was assisting in the campaign.[47]

[45] Cannadine, *Decline and Fall*, 184; Thompson, *English Landed Society*, 276–7.

[46] Lady John Russell to Rollo Russell, 3 and 17 May 1866, Bod., MS. Eng. lett. e. 111, fos. 86–7, 88–9.

[47] Mr Bouverie to Mary Minto, 7 July 1837, Minto MSS, MS11906, fos. 211–12; Cecil Cadogan to Beatrix Chelsea, 29 Apr. [1873], Cadogan MSS, CAD/143.

The correspondence of James Stuart Wortley with his mother, Caroline, Lady Wharncliffe, in the late 1830s and 1840s contains full reports of his electoral activity, from his unsuccessful attempt at re-election in Halifax in 1837 and his subsequent election for Buteshire under the nomination of his relative the marquess of Bute in 1842.[48]

To seek the influence of a woman in the election of a particular candidate was a public acknowledgement that aristocratic women had duties which arose from landownership as well as men. We have already seen how Lady Sandwich's influence was sought by candidates, for the financial support which she was able to offer, because of the specific votes she could command, and because of the more intangible benefits of such influence in persuading electors to cast their votes. Also in the 1830s, the marquess of Douro solicited the aid of Sarah Sophia Jersey in his election for Aldborough, saying, 'I understand you have great influence over Mr Bainbridge who possesses some votes in this Division. If you approve of my principles I wish you would persuade him to assist me which I fear, without your intervention, he will not do.'[49]

Frances Anne Londonderry, who treated her local political interests in much the same way as she did her estates and industrial concerns, will be discussed further below. Here it is enough to note that any Conservative, and sometimes Liberals also, wishing to stand for any of the county and borough seats in Durham would ritually seek her approval before continuing in his endeavour. For example, W. Lindsay, a Liberal, standing for Tynemouth and North Shields wrote:

When I consider your great influence in this quarter, & the high esteem in which your Ladyship is deservedly held by all whom you employ & those who really know you, I consider it my duty to advise your Ladyship of the step I have taken. I think my return is certain but if I could be favoured with any support from you, it would be placed beyond all doubt.[50]

Similarly, in 1864, Lord Loughborough wrote to Lady Londonderry to enquire whether she would wish him to stand for a Durham seat recently vacated by the death of the incumbent, or if 'your wishes & intentions have

---

[48] See e.g. James Stuart Wortley to Caroline Wharncliffe, 12 and 31 July 1837, Wharncliffe Muniments, WhM 583/23 and 24; see also letters of 9 Aug. 1839, WhM 485/12, and 30 Nov. 1842, WhM 587/27. See further Carnarvon to Eveline Portsmouth, 31 May and 29 June 1868, Wallop MSS, 15M84, Box 30.

[49] Douro to Sarah Jersey, 29 Oct. [1830?], Jersey MSS, Acc 1128/186.

[50] W. Lindsay to Frances Anne Londonderry, 18 Apr. [n.y.], Londonderry MSS, D/Lo/C 182 (14). See also James Farrer to Frances Anne Londonderry, 8 Apr. [n.y.] and 16 Mar. [n.y.], D/Lo/C 183 (1) and (2); Mr Mowbray to Frances Anne Londonderry, 14 Mar. 1857, D/Lo/C 183 (4); and Arthur Pakenham to Frances Anne Londonderry, 12 Apr. 1859, D/Lo/C 182 (6).

undergone any change since you were good enough to select me as a proper candidate and to furnish me with letters to several of the principal electors'.[51]

A further benefit to be reaped from connections with aristocratic women was the use of their extensive family networks: thus in 1865 W. E. Gladstone sought the assistance of his close friend, Harriet Sutherland, in the acquisition of a suitable seat for his eldest son (who later married her granddaughter). She contacted her daughter, who was the wife of the heir to the marquessate of Westminster, and reported back that 'Grosvenor & his Father would be delighted that Willy should stand but that his Father has little to do with the second member'.[52] None the less, William Gladstone received the support of the Westminster family, particularly of Lord Grosvenor who accompanied him during the election, and was returned for Chester, a city dominated by the Westminster interest.

If knowledge of the landowner and employer's political preferences could be a significant factor in the voting practices of electors, in the decades after the Reform Act an increasing number of aristocrats took a position of nonintervention in the votes of their tenants and dependants. In part, this was because the advent of the secret ballot in 1872 meant that their traditional influence was negated, although Disraeli believed in 1873 that 'It is clear that the personal influence of candidates *and their wives* will be considerable under the [secret] ballot'.[53] In the late 1880s, Anne Athole was invited to lend her support for the Conservative candidate for the eastern division of Perthshire, but replied: 'I have been much amused at Mr Reginald MacLeod's idea that I should send forth the fiery Cross to secure a good audience for Mr Boase—I have never interfered with the Political opinions of any one, & think it rather [Illeg.] late in my day to begin.'[54] Before the changes of 1872, in particular, such determinations were not always supported by candidates, who persisted in seeking the influence of landowners: in 1852 Lord Milton stood for County Wicklow, and sought the support of the eponymous earl. Lady Milton reported to her father-in-law earl Fitzwilliam that 'Ld. W. says he wishes Tom [Lord Milton] well but will not interfere—Tom thinks if he wd really support him it might stop the contest & wd at all events make his (Tom's) election safe. If you were to write to him it . . . wd have much effect.'[55]

[51] Loughborough to Frances Anne Londonderry, 24 Jan. 1864, Londonderry MSS, D/Lo/C 182 (21).

[52] Harriet Sutherland to W. E. Gladstone, n.d. [1865], BL Add. MS 44,328, fos. 219–20.

[53] Disraeli to Anne Chesterfield, 16 Oct. 1873, in Zetland (ed.), *Letters to Lady Bradford and Lady Chesterfield*, i. 33, my emphasis.

[54] Anne Athole to T. G. Murray, n.d. [Feb. 1889], Atholl MSS, Bundle 1664.

[55] Frances Milton to Fitzwilliam, [28 Apr. 1852], Wentworth Woodhouse Muniments, WWM G75/14.

In an undated letter to Lady Jersey, the second marquess of Hertford confessed that 'I did not interfere in last year's elections', but clearly regretted the action, and

Luckily, I enquired how my tenants voted—I had only 52 registered—48 voted with us 4 agt.—since, many more have registered, & as I made a voluntary ten per cent abatement, I feel sure I can bring about 65 to 75 to the Post. I can only say further that I will make such executions as you may command, & only *when* you command.[56]

These two examples might lead us to believe that it was the women who were most interested in the maintenance of the systems of informal patronage and control. The novelist Anthony Trollope certainly shared this view, crediting his central character, the duke of Omnium, with the effort to give up his nomination of the member for the borough of Silverbridge, while it was his wife, Lady Glencora, who sought to maintain the influence of the family, rejecting the duke's arguments by saying: ' "You know I think that instead of killing an evil, you have murdered an excellent institution." '[57] It is not possible in the confines of this chapter to discuss the relative merits of the positions of this fictional duke and his wife, or, from the evidence presented, to assert with confidence that Trollope's fiction was matched by a version of reality. None the less, it seems permissible to speculate that the aristocratic woman, outside the formal constitution and without a vote or a seat in the House of Lords, had more to lose by the widening of the franchise and the weakening of the aristocratic hegemony than her male counterparts.

Anne Hay Mackenzie married the heir to the duke of Sutherland, Lord Stafford, in 1849, and succeeded to her father's vast property in Ross-shire less than a month later.[58] During the election of 1852, this combination of factors was a cause of some political difficulty for Lady Stafford, who had married out of a strongly Conservative family into an equally strongly Whig one. The tenantry had been encouraged in the past to vote in accordance with her father's political creed, and for the most part, they did so. In 1852 she received a request from Sir James Matheson, who was standing as a Liberal, that she allow Mr Scott, her agent, to canvass on his behalf, and she supported his political position (whether from her own beliefs or because she had adopted those of her husband, it is impossible to say). She referred the matter to the factor, James Loch. He admitted that on this occasion there

[56] Hertford to Sarah Jersey, [n.d.], Jersey MSS, Acc 510/563.

[57] Anthony Trollope, *The Prime Minister* (2 vols., Oxford: World's Classics, 1983; 1st pub. 1876), i. 300.

[58] According to Bateman, in 1883 the Sutherlands owned 149,999 acres in Ross-shire, bringing in an annual rental of £12,002, 'most' of which belonged to the duchess. Bateman, *Great Landowners*, 431.

were circumstances 'of a very delicate nature' complicating the usual relationship between landlord and tenants during an election, arising from 'your father's [Protectionist] opinions of the subject of free trade, and those opinions being held by many of the tenants', and the duchess's inclination to depart 'from the line of conduct pursued by him, on the first occasion of the sort, that has happened since your accession'. Loch's advice was that, as her opinion was in fact different from that of her father, 'there could be nothing wrong in such being disclosed', provided that the tenants should not be urged to change their minds also. Scott was to reveal her opinion to anyone who asked, and was to be instructed 'not to take an active part, against Sir James Matheson, if that should be his inclination and that he should abstain from voting unless his disposition would lead him to vote for Sir James'.[59] Further, Loch suggested that it would not be inappropriate for Lord Stafford to express his opinion to the tenants: not himself the owner of the land, his political opinions would not represent a volte-face on previous practice, while making it perfectly plain to the tenants what the views of the landlords now were. The following day, Loch amended his advice, counselling Stafford to ask that the tenants merely abstain from voting rather than asking for their support for a particular candidate, as '[t]his would have the advantage also of being less opposed to the course originally & formerly followed—It would also enable them to comply with his wishes more easily— as it would not be opposed to what they did before.'[60] Sir James was elected in 1852 by 288 votes to 218, out of a total electorate of 832. It is not clear whether the 326 (39.2 per cent) electors who cast no vote were influenced by this recommendation; however, in the previous contested election in 1837, an identical percentage of the electorate cast no vote.[61]

This kind of influence, which is the most difficult to assess and quantify, was probably the most widespread, not merely among aristocratic women. Others took more direct action. During the election of 1847, the duke of Sutherland was abroad, and management of the electoral affairs of Staffordshire was left to his wife. The complications which ensued were not a result of this absence, although the duchess clearly felt that the presence of the duke would have smoothed matters over. The incident is nevertheless illustrative of the responsibility for elections which could fall on an aristocratic woman under certain circumstances: it is significant that the duchess was considered the natural alternative to the duke in the management of the election, rather than a male relative or proxy. The correspondence concern-

[59] James Loch to Anne Stafford, 16 Mar. 1852, Sutherland MSS (Staffs.), D593 P/28/10.
[60] James Loch to Anne Stafford, 17 Mar. 1852, Sutherland MSS (Staffs.), D593 P/28/10.
[61] Craig, *British Parliamentary Election Results*.

ing the election which remains is between Harriet Sutherland and Lord John Russell. The close relationships in the 'Whig Cousinhood' meant that women's actions in a constituency would be scrutinized by the party leadership, not minor officials: a duchess could not be instructed or reprimanded by the party whip.

The circumstances of the 1847 North Staffordshire election as explained by Harriet Sutherland to Lord John Russell were these: Edward Buller had sat for the county as a Whig between 1832 and 1841. In this latter year, two Conservatives, C. B. Adderley and J. D. W. Russell, had taken the seats unopposed. In 1847, the earl of Ellesmere's son, Lord Brackley (who was also the nephew of the duke), proposed standing for the seat, as did Buller, who received a letter of support from the duke. Buller called on the duchess, proposing that Brackley should be his running mate, not least because Brackley had been staying with the Sutherlands, and had used Trentham as his residence in his address to the electors, and that 'no neutrality would be believed'. The duchess responded that Brackley was 'the Duke's nephew & . . . that he was at Trentham as a Guest & that no such influence should be gathered'. Buller then attempted to persuade Brackley to join him, and failed. The duchess wrote to Ellesmere, trusting 'the Duke's position & absence to him', but received in the afternoon the distressing intelligence that Brackley was running with Mr Adderley, the Peelite candidate. The duchess exonerated herself with the comment: 'Why Mr Adderley has appeared to him a preferable person to coalesce with to Mr Buller I could not anticipate *nor* that there would be that touch of Protection in his address.'[62]

Russell, who believed that Brackley could be brought in as a Whig, and was concerned that the duchess's actions might provoke him into joining the Tories, must have criticized the duchess's handling of the affair, as she sent him a disclaimer, refusing to 'acknowledge any mistake & [I] think I did exactly as you would have had me do'.[63] The land steward was sent a letter instructing that as Buller was standing, and that as Brackley appeared to be standing as a Conservative, the duke's interest was to be given for Buller. Further, if there was a contest, Brackley would not continue as a guest at Trentham, and the steward was ordered to tell those who wished to know that 'as a matter of political Feeling, his [the duke's] wishes must be with the

---

[62] Harriet Sutherland to Lord John Russell, 3 Aug. [1847], Russell MSS, PRO 30/22/6E, fos. 39–40.

[63] Harriet Sutherland to Lord John Russell, 7 Aug. 1847, Russell MSS, PRO 30/22/6E, fos. 51–2. Russell, in fact, gained Brackley's allegiance for the Whigs in the House of Lords after 1857.

Government Member, though his nephew is in the Field'.[64] Perhaps because of the confusion, or because of the unpopularity of the anti-protectionist Whigs, or perhaps because the weight of aristocratic influence was decreasing, Buller failed to win a seat. The important point for the purposes of this study, however, is not whether aristocratic influence in elections was or was not increasing: rather, it is that aristocratic women continued to behave as if that influence was undiminished.

The kinds of activities in which they took part were varied, and indeed, a tentative pattern of change can be charted over the period. This pattern is, broadly, a generational one: those women who came to prominence before the 1830s—Ladies Jersey, Palmerston, Londonderry, the duchess of Sutherland, and Lady Charlotte Guest, for example—took an unequivocally public stance in the electoral process, which continued until their deaths in the 1860s.[65] There was then a lull, the younger generation taking a lower profile in elections: Lady Milton and Lady John Russell are perhaps not untypical. Then in the late 1870s and 1880s, there appears to have been a resurgence of activity by aristocratic women such as Lady Derby, Lady Salisbury, Lady Randolph Churchill, and Louisa Athole. It is not simple to account for this generational difference; it is possible to speculate that the domestic model of womanhood made a greater impact on aristocratic women with respect to direct public electioneering in the period between 1840 and 1870 than in other areas of their self-construction, and that the general discussion of the 'woman question' from the 1860s onwards restored confidence in the exercise of their former influence.

Lady Sandwich clearly belonged to the early generation, while Lady Jersey made no apology for canvassing the support of her influential friends (especially the duke of Wellington) on behalf of her son in the 1830s.[66] Similarly, she supported Lord Mahon's efforts to return to parliament after his election in 1833 was overturned on petition, offering 'to mention [his] name to Lord B. as a person who is much annoyed at being excluded from Parlt. & very desirous of re-entering it'.[67] Lady Palmerston concentrated her political energies at the Westminster centre, but after Palmerston's death, had sufficient interest in the electoral affairs on her Derbyshire estates to write to her agent, Fox, whom she considered 'a little shaky himself' in his support of the two Liberal candidates, to exert all the influence he could muster in their

[64] Harriet Sutherland to the Trentham land steward, 5 Aug. 1847, Russell MSS, PRO 30/22/6E, fo. 45.

[65] The first four died respectively in 1867, 1869, 1865, and 1868. Lady Charlotte Guest lived until 1895, but her second marriage in 1855 effectively removed her from the political scene.

[66] Wellington and others to Sarah Jersey, Nov.–Dec. 1835, Jersey MSS, Acc 510/490–4.

[67] Mahon to Sarah Jersey, Monday afternoon, [n.d. 1833], Jersey MSS, Acc 1128/291.

favour, reinforcing her own opinion with that of her brother and husband by adding 'the certainty I felt that Ld Melb[our]ne and Ld Palmerston would have supported the Liberal party now, against such a bad Govern[men]t as the present one and such a Minister as Disraeli'.[68]

Lady Londonderry treated elections in Durham as her personal preserve, at least in so far as they related to the Conservative candidates and her family. The 1837 election was a particular triumph, with the return of a Conservative candidate for both the northern division of the county—the first in twenty years—and the borough of Durham, in the face of the opposition of the other great aristocratic family in the county, the radical earl of Durham. Frances Anne reported to her great ally and correspondent Disraeli that '[w]e have won a glorious victory and I hear the Earl is fit to be tied. Liddell headed the poll till the last hour.'[69] Celebrating the return of a Conservative at the head of the poll for the borough of Durham at the same election, Lady Londonderry visited the city, where the victors 'dragged my carriage in and all the respectable people in the Co[unty] followed in cavalcade'. The following day, she gave a dinner for fifty people, this providing the most convenient method 'to see and thank all our agents and people'. A few days later, there was to be 'a more civilized party of the same number—the gentlemen'.[70]

The extent of Frances Anne's authority in Conservative politics in County Durham, derived in part from her financial contributions to the electoral process and in part from the numbers of her tenants and employees, may be gauged from her correspondence with Disraeli in 1861 and again in 1863, when there were efforts to impose candidates without her consent. In 1861, amid rumours of an impending dissolution, there was a movement to run a Conservative candidate other than Lady Londonderry's son, Lord Adolphus Vane; Disraeli was informed, and he responded that he had

written to Taylor to say, that if he, or any one connected with the party, either directly or indirectly, interfere with the county, or the City of Durham, you will withdraw your influence from the party . . . without you, the Conservatives can do nothing, either in County or City, and, therefore, it is no use kicking against the pricks.[71]

Frances Anne commented that the local agitators could scarcely fail to know that 'only my son could sit as a Conservative for this Liberal Division', and

---

[68] Emily Palmerston to William Cowper, [Sept. –Oct. 1868], quoted in Lever, *Letters of Lady Palmerston*, 367.

[69] Frances Anne Londonderry to Benjamin Disraeli, [8 Aug. 1837], Londonderry MSS, D/Lo/C 530 (5).

[70] Frances Anne Londonderry to Disraeli, n.d. [Aug. 1837], Londonderry MSS, D/Lo/C 530 (7).

[71] Disraeli to Frances Anne Londonderry, 14 Dec. 1861, Londonderry MSS, D/Lo/C 530 (202).

that this was possible largely because she was 'so largely embark'd in trade and commerce'.[72] It is noteworthy that after Vane's death in 1864, the county did indeed return to electing two Liberal members. Again, in 1863, Frances Anne appealed to Disraeli, informing him that 'the Carlton Club are at their old tricks meddling here', and were attempting to get up a contest which 'can only end in complete failure'. Mr Spofforth, the offender, persisted in his attempts, even after being reminded by all whom he consulted that 'all must depend on me [Frances Anne]', who was astonished by his 'impudence and folly', and hinted threateningly to Disraeli of the withdrawal of her considerable financial support for the Conservative cause in the county: 'I write you this line because if they go on meddling they will repent it and I will not be answerable for results.'[73] There was no contest in Durham in 1863.

Lady Londonderry's paternalist approach to electoral management contrasted, as did so many aspects of their lives, with that of Lady Charlotte Guest. Lady Charlotte's biography makes plain that her role in getting her husband re-elected for the Merthyr Tydfil constituency had more in common with the roles of the later nineteenth-century election committees than with the strictly aristocratic approach of Lady Londonderry. She worked as secretary to her husband's campaigns, handled his publicity, and canvassed the constituency, declaring that 'I never failed to exert myself when I have it in my power to do anything that would be advantageous to my party'.[74]

This generation of politically active women was followed by a more constrained one; Lady John Russell's dislike for 'lady politicians' was probably not uncommon, and for a time, younger women did not intervene in the return of members of parliament. Unfortunately, few if any commented on their reasons for withdrawing from this kind of activity, so the withdrawal must be inferred from the decline of comment on elections in the sources, and any reasons must be speculative. Lady Milton, who kept her father-in-law informed about the progress of her husband's election campaign in County Wicklow in 1852, wrote to the earl Fitzwilliam that 'You will think I dream of the Wicklow election as I have never written about anything else, but I wish to save Tom [Lord Milton] all the writing I can—*and there are not many people I can write to for him*'.[75] This was not an inhibition from which Lady Jersey or Lady Londonderry would have suffered, and suggests a

---

[72] Frances Anne Londonderry to Disraeli, [17 Dec. 1861], Londonderry MSS, D/Lo/C 530 (204).

[73] Frances Anne Londonderry to Disraeli, [3, 12, and 16 Aug. 1863], Londonderry MSS, D/Lo/C 530 (212), (213), and (214).   [74] Guest and John, *Lady Charlotte*, 48.

[75] Frances Milton to Fitzwilliam, [4 May 1852], Wentworth Woodhouse Muniments, WWM MF67 G75/15, my emphasis.

greater susceptibility to changing notions of decorum and feminine behaviour on the part of this generation. It is also worth noting that, until considered generationally, this shift is not immediately apparent, as the active generation's lives coincided in great measure with those of the inactive, and, just as they died, they were replaced by a younger generation of politically active women.

WOOING THE WIDER ELECTORATE

To complete the picture, it is necessary to consider briefly this resurgence of activity in the 1870s and 1880s by aristocratic women in elections, both as individuals and, for the first time, as members of organizations.[76] Mary, Lady Derby, was as active in politics in her way as Lady Palmerston had been, although her husband, despite being foreign and colonial secretary, lacked Palmerston's dominion of the political scene, vacillating a great deal in his political allegiances, moving from the Conservative to the Liberal cabinet between 1878 and 1880, and on to the Unionist party. During the local and general elections of 1879–80, Mary Derby was in regular contact with William Vernon Harcourt, soon to be home secretary in Gladstone's second ministry, thereby keeping the Liberal party informed of her husband's actions and intentions.[77] Derby claimed to take a neutral position in the election of 1880, supporting neither Liberal nor Conservative candidate.[78] However, Lady Derby's correspondence reveals that this neutrality had in fact much in common with the old-fashioned exercise of influence, permitting the agent of the Liberal candidate to say that Derby *was personally interested in the success of Ld Ramsay*', while she suggested to Harcourt that a notice be put in the Liverpool newspapers advertising the visit of Lord Ramsay and his wife to Knowsley.[79] It is difficult to perceive much difference between this 'neutrality' and the partisanship of former days, beyond an awareness that such partisanship was no longer considered a natural and acceptable form of influence.

A bridge between this kind of activity and that of the women's political organizations was the canvassing work undertaken by women such as Lady

---

[76] This generation has been much better served by historians, particularly those seeking the origins of the suffrage movement. See e.g. Pugh, *Tories and the People*; Jalland, *Women, Marriage and Politics*; Esther Shkolnik, *Leading Ladies: A Study of Eight Late Victorian and Edwardian Political Wives* (New York: Garland, 1987); Brian Harrison, *Separate Spheres: The Opposition to Women's Suffrage in Britain* (Croom Helm, 1978); Linda Walker, 'Party Political Women; A Comparative Study of Liberal Women and the Primrose League, 1890–1914', in Jane Rendall (ed.), *Equal or Different: Women's Politics 1800–1914* (Oxford: Blackwell, 1987), 165–275.

[77] Mary Derby to William Vernon Harcourt, 4 Nov. 1879, MS. Harcourt, dep. 208, fos. 145–6.

[78] Mary Derby to Robert Morier, 16 Feb. 1880, Morier MSS, Box 6.

[79] Mary Derby to William Vernon Harcourt, 20 Jan. [1880], MS. Harcourt, dep. 209 fos. 6–7.

Randolph Churchill and the future Lady Battersea. Lady Randolph and her sister-in-law, Lady Georgiana Curzon, undertook to canvass the borough of Woodstock on behalf of Lord Randolph, and in his absence in 1885; their efforts met with success (hardly surprising given the dominating presence of the Churchill family home, Blenheim Palace, in the vicinity). Lady Randolph, after her husband was returned at the head of the poll, commented that 'I certainly experienced all the pleasure and gratification of being a successful candidate', and repeated the exercise on several future occasions.[80] Similarly, Lady Battersea, then Mrs Flower, accompanied her husband to canvass Brecon in South Wales, visiting the important women in the town to elicit their support, and addressed a few words to the crowd of their supporters when he was returned for the borough.[81]

A completely different kind of activity was the involvement of aristocratic women in the new women's party organizations which arose in the 1880s to meet the need for unpaid canvassers after the passage of the Corrupt Practices Act. These organizations rose to prominence only after the close of the period with which this book is primarily concerned, but it is worth indicating the direction in which aristocratic women's involvement in elections was to go in the future. The organization with the most aristocratic involvement was the Conservative Primrose League; from its earliest days, it had a women's branch, the duchess of Marlborough serving as president of the Ladies' Grand Council.[82] The Women's Liberal Federation also had aristocratic patronage, in the persons of Catherine Gladstone and Rosalind, Lady Carlisle, but the split in the Liberal party over home rule for Ireland had swept away the majority of female aristocratic supporters of the party.[83] The organizations were to provide a new forum for aristocratic women to play a role in electoral politics, but it was an attenuated role, controlled to an extent by the parallel male organizations and dominated by women of other classes. However, it did provide opportunities for women who otherwise stayed outside the electoral process to take a public role, as, for example, in the case of Louisa Athole, who headed the Athole Habitation of the Primrose League, and made a speech to that organization in 1887, despite her 'great dislike of doing those sort of public things'.[84] Lady Salisbury explained

---

[80] Mrs George Cornwallis West (Lady Randolph Churchill), *The Reminiscences of Lady Randolph Churchill* (Edward Arnold, 1908), 126.

[81] Battersea, *Reminiscences*, 181–6. Catherine Gladstone was regularly given a place on the platform next to her husband during his Midlothian campaigns, the first woman to be thus formally recognized, although, of course, she did not speak.

[82] West, *Reminiscences of Lady Randolph Churchill*, 98–9.

[83] Walker, 'Party Political Women'; Claire Hirschfield, 'A Fractured Faith: Liberal Party Women and the Suffrage Issue in Britain, 1892–1914', *Gender and History*, 2 (1980), 173–97.

[84] Louisa Athole to Anne Athole, 12 Dec. 1887, Atholl MSS, Bundle 1657.

to Anne Sutherland the way in which the League could be utilized to have the same effect as the old practices of influence: in Hatfield, she reported, virtually all the working men and their wives were members, the radical candidate not even finding it worth his while to have a committee room in the town. 'And yet all our tenants were told to vote freely as they pleased—I am sure all that is needed is to see as much of the people as we can & to continue the work of the League.'[85]

In formalizing the role of aristocratic women in politics in accordance with the increasingly democratic and structured electoral system, that role was diminished into a largely ceremonial one, prefiguring the future part to be played by aristocratic males in the constitution. In her reminiscences, Lady Randolph Churchill wrote of the League, of which she was a founder-member, that 'politics, like charity, is a great leveller':[86] such a view would have been completely alien to the earlier generation of Lady Londonderry and Lady Palmerston, for whom politics, like the rest of society, was governed by a series of strict hierarchies.

The specific part assigned to gender and the exploitation of femininity, suggested by Palmerston's reference to 'fair Ladies', had also shifted by the end of the century. In the 1850s, Emily Eden wrote to Richard Monckton Milnes about the electoral tactics in his Pontefract constituency:

I think it is artful of Preston to arm himself with such a face as Georgie's to help his canvassing. . . . If you see the slightest danger of defeat . . . fight Preston with his own weapon. Meet him with your wife on your arm—& your general incomprehensible independence principle on your tongue.[87]

By contrast to this approving exploitation of feminine charms at the hustings, in 1888, Gathorne Hardy condemned both the activity of women at the polls and the breakdown of political exclusivity, noting in his diary that 'Public house work by Irish MPs told & they were very plausible. Lady Sandhurst canvasses hard with other females. In short Electioneering has become a work of all sorts & conditions of men, women & plans, not pleasing. . . .'[88] For the generation of Lady Palmerston, electioneering was a normal activity, part of the duties and rights associated with aristocratic privilege. The generation which followed retreated from the task, while their successors returned to the fray—albeit in a less powerful position, given the new

[85] Georgina Salisbury to Anne Sutherland, 11 Dec. [n.y.], Sutherland MSS (Staffs.), D593 P/28/8/18.

[86] West, Reminiscences of Lady Randolph Churchill, 99.

[87] Emily Eden to Richard Monckton Milnes, n.d. [1852], Houghton MSS, 7/200.

[88] Nancy E. Johnson (ed.), The Diary of Gathorne Hardy, Later Lord Cranbrook, 1866–1892: Political Selections (Oxford: Clarendon Press, 1981), 23 June 1888, p. 709.

political conditions—via the women's political organizations. There was thus less novelty in women's political activity at the end of the century than is commonly assumed. Ironically, the criticisms levelled against the new breed of female canvassers were little removed from those aimed at the duchess of Devonshire in the previous century: women were going among strangers to seek support for political ideas, not among personal connections to seek support for family. Thus the political activity of the intervening generations of aristocratic women can be seen to have been accepted as normative, in terms of both feminine behaviour and of aristocratic rights and duties. For a restricted group of aristocratic women, the same understanding of the nature of political society made their intervention in national politics both possible and material to the conduct of the political game.

5

'Party' Politics: Metropolitan Political Society

In an article on what he deemed the 'irresponsible and illegitimate' influence of the 'petticoat in politics', Justin McCarthy observed that 'Social influence is a tremendous power in English politics. The drawing-room often settles the fate of the division in the House of Commons. The smile or the salute of the peeress has already bought the votes which are necessary to secure her husband's triumph.'[1] Despite the conviction of contemporaries that aristocratic women exercised influence in British political life in the nineteenth century, historians until recently have not recognized their significance. Informative interpretations of the activities of political hostesses have been presented in recent years by Pat Jalland, Brian Harrison, and Martin Pugh, but for all three authors the activities of the political hostess have been incidental to their main projects.[2] Moreover, each is concerned, from a different point of view, to discover the origins of female political action, a retrospective perspective which leads them to view the political hostesses as the precursors of the female suffragists, and consequently as (however unwilling) proto-feminists. The effect of this approach is to place the political hostess rather uncomfortably at the beginning of a tradition of civic feminism. If this chronology is abandoned, the early and mid-Victorian political hostess can be viewed in her own context, not at the origin of modern female political action, but at the end of a long tradition of aristocratic government. Emily Palmerston, Sarah Jersey, and Frances Waldegrave had more in common with the court politics of Sarah Marlborough and Abigail Masham and the Grand Whiggery of Georgiana Devonshire than with the suffragist, parliamentary, and socialist politics of Millicent Garrett Fawcett, Nancy Astor, and Ellen Wilkinson.[3]

[1] Justin McCarthy, 'The Petticoat in the Politics of England', *Lady's Own Paper*, 9 July 1870, p. 20. It is ironic that McCarthy himself was not averse to utilizing such petticoat influence, as his letter of 30 Aug. 1889 to Mary Gladstone Drew thanking her for her 'kindly intervention' with her father, reveals. In author's possession.

[2] Jalland, *Women, Marriage and Politics*, 190–5; Harrison, *Separate Spheres*, 81–3; Pugh, *Tories and the People*, 43–7.

[3] See e.g. Frances Harris, *A Passion for Government: The Life of Sarah, Duchess of Marlborough*

Unlike middle-class feminists, aristocratic women did not perceive the political system as a closed world from which they were excluded and into which they demanded admittance. Despite the increasing encroachments of bureaucracy, meritocratic practices, and the broadening franchise, political and social life in this period remained inextricably intertwined for the aristocracy of both genders. In the working of an aristocratic polity, a separation of spheres between 'politics' and 'society' was not only unnecessary but undesirable. Patronage and family connections remained important paths to professional advancement, while political allegiances were often a matter of family tradition and personal obligation rather than of ideological conviction and party loyalty. Politics, interpreted by those empowered by the political structure, were seen as the legitimate preserve of the aristocracy; social events could thus be endowed with political significance, for it was in the social context that much political activity took place. It is at this interface between the social and the political that the aristocratic woman found a role which, while having a limited impact on the content of political discourse, was of immense importance in defining its context.

The nature of aristocratic women's involvement in the political process was such that we should not expect to find—as they did not expect to have—involvement in the details of executive policy making. It is very rare to find examples of the direct influence of aristocratic women on the development of policy or ideology: without formal education, even the most intelligent were unlikely to be original political thinkers.[4] Moreover, the influence which they wielded was usually personal and conversational, hence little written evidence survives. This is a problem which occurs whatever aspect of the political hostesses' careers is in question. The influence of 'a smile or a salute' is difficult to define, even as it occurs, and leaves no documentary record. Few politicians recorded specific instances of female influence, although some, like Disraeli, recorded their obligations in general terms. One exception is provided in the memoirs of Sir William Gregory, who recorded that he was dissuaded by Lady Waldegrave from his intention to move an amendment to the bill disestablishing the Irish Church.[5] But this is exceptional: where evidence of influence exists, it is generally in matters of

(Oxford: Clarendon Press, 1991); Stella Tillyard, *Aristocrats: Caroline, Emily, Louisa and Sarah Lennox, 1740–1832* (Chatto & Windus, 1994); Colley, *Britons*, 242–8. See also Elaine Chalus, ' "That Epidemical Madness": Women and Electoral Politics in the Late Eighteenth Century', in Barker and Chalus (eds.), *Gender in Eighteenth-Century England*, 151–78.

[4] Recent work on the eighteenth century suggests that this represents a significant shift in the practices and expectations of aristocratic women in politics. See Chalus, ' "That Epidemical Madness"', and Foreman, 'A Politician's Politician'.

[5] Sir William Gregory, *An Autobiography* (John Murray,1894), 255.

appointments and positions rather than policy. The decline of the Namierite school of eighteenth-century history, with its emphasis on patronage and personal advancement, in favour of a more ideologically based history, has meant that personal advancement and the continued importance of patronage networks have been rather neglected in the nineteenth century.[6] Peel's supposed preference for 'measures, not men' has been absorbed into the historiography, thus further marginalizing the activities of aristocratic women, whose primary concerns reversed his priorities.

To few circumstances can the concept of separate spheres have been more inappropriately applied than that of Victorian political society. A dividing line between politics (public) and society (private) can only be arbitrary, and has the effect of misleading the reader about the nature of aristocratic political culture. Politics and policies were discussed in social and domestic settings, and social events took on political significance as a result of the close-knit, socially cohesive nature of the governing classes. In consequence, any attempt to apply the notion of separate spheres along gendered lines in this context is doomed to failure: the 'female sphere' is partially occupied by men, and the apparently domestic concerns of the aristocratic family had public consequences. The absence of separation between politics and social life, between home and work, had physical consequences for the practice of politics. Far from being confined to the palace of Westminster, the 'theatre of politics' frequently found its stage in the drawing-rooms and salons of the political hostesses.[7]

The concept of the 'incorporated wife', to describe women implicated in, yet excluded from, the organizational structure of their husbands' careers, is of particular value in discussing the political hostess.[8] Discussion of political hostesses is impossible without a framework which allows us to talk about women-as-wives without dismissively removing their autonomy and reducing them to passive compliance in a male-ordered society. The idea of incorporation permits an unapologetic examination of the significance of a subordinate role, accepted and even enjoyed by its players, whose priorities were different from those of late-twentieth-century women.[9] Aristocratic women engaged in politics because it was the occupation of their husbands,

---

[6] But see Rubinstein, 'End of "Old Corruption" '. See also Arno J. Mayer, *The Persistence of the Old Regime: Europe to the Great War* (Croom Helm, 1981).

[7] David Cannadine and Simon Price (eds.), *Rituals of Royalty: Power and Ceremonial in Traditional Societies* (Cambridge: Cambridge University Press, 1987), 1–2.

[8] Ardener (ed.), *Perceiving Women*, esp. Hilary Callan, 'The Premiss of Dedication: Notes towards an Ethnography of Diplomats' Wives', 87–104; Ardener and Callan (eds.), *Incorporated Wife*.

[9] See Alison Wall, 'Elizabethan Precept and Feminine Practice: The Thynne Family of Longleat', *History*, 75 (Feb. 1990), 23–38, for an account reaching similar conclusions through a different framework and for an earlier period.

brothers, and sons, and because politics provided the *raison d'être* of their class; they did not, on the whole, engage in them on their own behalf. Yet the part which they took in political society was significant for the smooth running of that society, providing venues for informal political meetings and discussions between both supporters and opponents, and keeping together political parties at a time when a formal structure was lacking. The intangible influence of the hostess in making her gatherings both pleasant and useful was recognized everywhere. One of most revealing assessments of the role of the hostess is given in Greville's account of the relative failure of the notorious Lady Blessington at Gore House:

> There is no end to the men of consequence and distinction in the world who go there occasionally . . . Her house is furnished with a luxury and splendour not to be sur-passed; her dinners are frequent and good . . . but all this does not make society in the real sense of the term. . . . The reason of this is that the woman herself, who must give the tone to her own society, and influence its character, is ignorant, vulgar, and commonplace.[10]

This chapter will examine the activities of the political hostesses, demonstrating their importance for Victorian political culture. It will then discuss other ways in which aristocratic women engaged with national politics, to substantiate the thesis that political hostesses were exceptional only in their degree of engagement. Lacking the political chronology and official documentation of the activities of male politicians, the evidence for female involvement in national politics is at best fragmentary and episodic; the argument thus proceeds from the accumulation of telling examples.

POLITICAL HOSTESSES

Virtually all aristocratic women were engaged to some degree in activities—such as entertaining political connections, exercising patronage, guarding political confidences, and offering advice—which were the particular speciality of the political hostess. This poses a problem if we wish to distinguish between the political hostess and the aristocratic political wife—or, in more concrete terms, if we wish to highlight the differences which the Victorians themselves recognized between the parties held by say, Harriet, duchess of Sutherland, the leading female member of the Grand Whiggery in the 1840s and 1850s, and Emily Palmerston, the foremost political hostess of the same period. Jalland evades the problem by conflating the political hostess with the political wife (although admitting to differing degrees of success and competence), and arguing that the work of political entertaining was

---

[10] Charles C. F. Greville, *The Greville Memoirs (Second Part): A Journal of the Reign of Queen Victoria 1837–1852* (3 vols., Longmans, Green & Co., 1885), i. 167–8.

essentially an activity which could be designated as belonging to the private sphere.[11] By contrast, Pugh sets out a series of intrinsic requirements for a woman who aspired to be a political hostess: a wealthy husband, houses for entertaining, both in the country and near Westminster, and personal characteristics such as beauty, charm, and intelligence.[12] Necessary such features undoubtedly were; they were not, however, sufficient. What Pugh cites as the defining characteristics of the political hostess could, with a little imaginative effort (particularly in the areas of beauty and intelligence), be applied to most of the aristocratic female population. But very few of them either aspired to be, or succeeded in becoming, political hostesses. For example, Frances Anne Londonderry met all Pugh's requirements, being additionally the friend, correspondent, and patron of Benjamin Disraeli; but she was not, at least in this period, a political hostess.

Ultimately, it is probably impossible to point to any characteristic of political hostesses not shared to some degree by the more general group of political wives. Both groups entertained political colleagues, aspirants, and enemies, received political confidences from husbands and friends, and engaged in political discussion and manœuvring. Likewise, as we have seen in previous chapters, both groups of women were subject to requests for patronage, and sought patronage for others; both were liable to be called into service as go-betweens; both regulated the access of aspiring members of political society to the centres of power. All were engaged in the daily business of issuing invitations, scrutinizing guest lists, organizing the arrangement of their houses, directing their servants, and timetabling their own and their husbands' engagements elsewhere. The skill, effort, and time required for successful political entertaining must not be underestimated, especially in the present day, when such functions are generally allocated to specialist professionals. The Victorian political hostess or wife could not call in a catering company or a team of public relations experts, delegate the tedious administration to secretarial help, and hold a press conference to advertise her success.[13]

With this much in common, it may seem perverse to attempt to distinguish between the ordinary activities of aristocratic wives and the salons of women described as political hostesses. Yet contemporaries did so. Of course, not all contemporaries agreed on who exactly was a political hostess at any given moment, indicating a measure of uncertainty of definition.

[11] Jalland, *Women, Marriage and Politics*, esp. 198–204.

[12] Pugh, *Tories and the People*, 44.

[13] The first professional party organizer in London Society was Percy Armytage, who managed his first event in 1885. See Percy Armytage, *By the Clock of St James's* (John Murray, 1927).

For example, in 1870, the *Lady's Own Paper* quoted an American newspaper's view that the 'three notable women of the time' were the Ladies Waldegrave, Salisbury, and Molesworth.[14] Five years later, the *World* maintained that only two women entertained 'in an avowedly political capacity', Lady Waldegrave and Lady Granville.[15] The woman against whose success all others were constantly measured was Lady Palmerston, wife of the foreign secretary and prime minister and doyenne of Cambridge House, herself the successor to Lady Holland of Holland House and the Whig tradition of political entertaining. The distinguishing feature of these political hostesses, of which group Ladies Palmerston, Holland, Jersey, and Waldegrave were leading examples, was probably the degree of enthusiasm and perceived success which marked their endeavours, and the centrality of politics in their lives, which lifted their activities from the general category of the political wife into the more publicly recognized role of political hostess.

The one characteristic that the successful Victorian political hostesses seem to have shared was unorthodox social position. The Canningite Palmerston, it has been noted, 'had never been really liked or accepted by the Whigs: he was not one of themselves',[16] while his wife belonged to a family new to the peerage, with distinctly impeachable moral credentials. Lady Jersey's money came from banking; Lady Holland had been divorced; Lady Molesworth took care to disguise her antecedents, but had been a professional singer for a number of seasons.[17] Lady Waldegrave had bourgeois, theatrical, Jewish parents, and four husbands. With uniformly eccentric social and/or moral backgrounds, the career of political hostess gave these women the opportunity to establish themselves and their families in the highest ranks of society, from which they might otherwise have been excluded. Brazening out indiscretion had always been an option, as Lady Blessington demonstrated at Gore House, and as Jane Austen has Mary Crawford suggest in the case of the adulterous Mrs Rushworth: 'In some circles, we know, she would never be admitted, but with good dinners, and large parties, there will always be those who will be glad of her acquaintance.'[18]

Political hostesses operated in three related arenas, each of which had different problems and opportunities: extended house parties during the parliamentary recess, held in country houses often far distant from the

---

[14] *Lady's Own Paper*, 7 May 1870, p. 281 col. c.

[15] 'Stateswomen', *World*, 31 Mar. 1875, p. 283.

[16] Airlie, *Lady Palmerston and her Times*, ii. 121.

[17] Alison Adburgham, *A Radical Aristocrat: Sir William Molesworth of Pencarrow and his Wife Andalusia* (Padstow: Tabb House, 1990), 97–106.

[18] Jane Austen, *Mansfield Park* (1814), ch. 47.

metropolis; house parties at weekends in a suburban or home counties retreat; and entertaining during the sessions of parliament, with 'good dinners and large parties' in London. The annual migration in August from London to the country and the return to Town for the opening of parliament in January provided the basic structure of life for the political classes. (The timetable could vary, especially if extra sittings of parliament were called. It was also common to go back to the country after the opening of parliament, returning to London in April for the season.) The country-house party, that paradigm of Victorian high society, familiar to the readers of Trollope and recalled nostalgically in many a volume of aristocratic memoirs, was thus, for a large part of the year, the site of political activity.[19] At such parties, politics, sport, and socializing intermingled. Because the participants took their culture for granted, and seldom recorded it in a systematic fashion, it is, perhaps, most satisfactory to turn to fiction for an example of the political uses of the country-house visit. Phineas Finn is invited to Loughlinter to meet political magnates by his patron, Lady Laura Kennedy, for 'at least a semi-political, or perhaps rather a semi-official gathering'. Trollope's description of subsequent events, including Finn's integration into the society of his hosts and their colleagues, amply demonstrates the conjunction of politics and society:

He had killed a stag in company with Mr Palliser, and had stopped beneath a crag to discuss with him a question as to the duty on Irish malt. He had played chess with Mr Gresham, and had been told that gentleman's opinion on the trial of Mr Jefferson Davis. Lord Brentford had—at last—called him Finn, and had proved to him that nothing was known in Ireland about sheep.[20]

Of course, there were many country-house parties at which politics took no part: many such events were convened for families to meet, socialize, flirt, marry, hunt foxes or deer, and shoot at grouse, pheasants, and other game. It has been convincingly argued that these events, particularly sporting parties, none the less served the political purpose of binding together county society.[21] By virtue of the presence of political society, which existed wherever its members met, the country houses themselves acquired a national importance: more than the rural homes of their owners and centres of local political authority, they were also part of the structure of the national

---

[19] See e.g. D. Nevill, *My Own Times*, esp. ch. 9; Lady Tweedsmuir (Susan Buchan), *The Lilac and the Rose* (Gerald Duckworth, 1952), 63–77; Frances, countess of Warwick, *Afterthoughts* (Cassell, 1931), esp. ch. 4 and 19; Aberdeen, 'We Twa', esp. i. ch. 16; Cardigan and Lancastre, *My Recollections*, esp. ch. 5.

[20] Anthony Trollope, *Phineas Finn* (1869), i. 163–5.

[21] Thompson, *English Landed Society*, 144–50.

political society. The annual peregrinations of the governing classes throughout the three kingdoms served a similar purpose to the royal progresses of previous centuries, moving the centre of government around the country and, arguably, symbolically unifying the realm by so doing.[22] The unwillingness of English aristocrats to hold house parties on their Irish estates, while doing so on those in Scotland, highlighted Irish distinctiveness. At the same time, the political heart of the country remained in London, and political hostesses made their reputations in the metropolis.

In basic format, London entertainments remained essentially similar throughout the period. They usually took place in a town house, close to the political centre of Westminster. Lady Palmerston entertained at Carlton House Terrace, and later at Cambridge House, Piccadilly; Lady Waldegrave's house was in Carlton Gardens, Lady Jersey's in Berkeley Square, Lady Molesworth's in Eaton Place. Only Holland House was removed from this centre, in Kensington, but it ceased to be important after Holland's death in 1840. As rail transport improved, the weekend retreat on the outskirts of London became a viable alternative, as by the 1850s many of the great houses in the home counties were brought within an hour or so's journey of London. Harriet Sutherland's weekend parties at Cliveden, near Maidenhead, were among the earliest;[23] Frances Waldegrave's Twickenham house, Strawberry Hill, and the Aberdeens' retreat at Dollis Hill, also fell into this category, as did the country house of the Salisburys, Hatfield House, and those of the Cowpers at Panshanger, the Clarendons, The Grove (which were all in Hertfordshire), and, to her increasing chagrin, that of the queen, Windsor Castle.

The hostesses tended to specialize in slightly different forms of party, with different constituencies of guests. Ladies Holland and Jersey usually gave small dinner parties, with allegiance to political party providing the unifying factor among their guests. Lady Palmerston took the evening reception or 'drum' as her principal forum, and invited a broad spectrum of political opinion, while Lady Molesworth was renowned for her dinner parties for a wide range of guests. Lady Waldegrave also gave evening parties in Carlton Gardens, and introduced the idea of the 'Saturday to Monday' party at Strawberry Hill, to which 'people seem quite wild to come'.[24] Her guests were of a far broader social and professional mix than those of any of her predecessors.

[22] Clifford Geertz, 'Centers, Kings and Charisma: Reflections on the Symbolics of Power', in his Local Knowledge: Further Essays in Interpretative Anthropology (Fontana, 1993; 1st pub. 1983), 121–46.

[23] For the Cliveden weekends, see Matthew, Gladstone, 1809–1874, 149–50. A study of the Royal Blue Book and Court Guide for the period demonstrates vividly the proximity in which the political classes lived to each other.

[24] Frances Waldegrave to Constance Braham, Lady Strachey, 6 June 1874, Strachey MSS,

These differences reflected changes in the structure of politics and the altering status of political parties. While Lady Holland and Lady Jersey were in their heyday, between 1810 and 1845, political allegiances were relatively well defined, with opinion polarizing around specific issues—reform, Catholic Emancipation, the Corn Laws—with the social implication of separate-party entertaining. Thus in 1821, Emily Cowper wrote to her brother, Frederick Lamb, that a recent dinner for Lady Holland 'was uncommonly agreeable because she begged to have a mixed dinner—"*some of the company not her daily bread*", meaning the big Whigs'. She went on to observe that 'The same political set at dinner every day must be tiresome in the long run', a tedium to which Lady Cowper was careful not to expose herself.[25] Elizabeth Holland had established her position at Holland House shortly after her divorce and re-marriage in 1797; by the period under discussion here, her reign as principal Whig hostess was drawing to an end. She was never received in all sections of Society, however. Lord Leicester, for example, was prepared to be her guest, and to invite her husband to Holkham, but he would not allow her under his roof.[26] Despite a reputation for tyranny over her guests, and the fierce Whiggery of her salon, Greville noted on her death that while 'her society was naturally and inevitably of a particular political colour', she had sought to make it possible for a person of 'any party, opinion, profession, or persuasion' to frequent Holland House.[27] But the 'particular political colour', that of the Whigs, inevitably dominated her circle.

Sarah Sophia, countess of Jersey, whom the duke of Bedford described as 'the warmest female politician I know',[28] also entertained, in a deeply partisan spirit, for the Tories. Earlier in the century she certainly saw herself as a Whig; an undated and unaddressed letter in her hand outlines her understanding of Whiggery in favourable terms—'the Whigs have been for all rational improvement, & the Tories for keeping things as they are. This is the grand distinction'[29]—but by the 1830s, her social colours at least were nailed to the Tory mast. She claimed to be in the confidence of the duke of Wellington, and hence to have access to the latest political information,

DD/SH C1189 D17. For contemporary assessments of Ladies Waldegrave's and Molesworth's parties, see Ralph Nevill (ed.), *The Reminiscences of Lady Dorothy Nevill* (Edward Arnold, 1906), 145, and Frederick Leveson Gower, *Bygone Years: Recollections* (John Murray, 1905), 275–6.

[25] Emily Cowper to Frederick Lamb, 16 Mar. 1821, in Airlie, *Lady Palmerston and her Times*, i. 87.

[26] Sir Herbert Maxwell (ed.), *The Creevey Papers* (John Murray, 1923), 674–5.

[27] Greville, *Greville Memoirs (Second Part)*, ii. 308. See also Sonia Keppel, *The Sovereign Lady: A Life of Elizabeth Vassall, Third Lady Holland, with her Family* (Hamish Hamilton, 1974).

[28] Bedford to Lady William Russell, 31 Oct. 1833, quoted in Georgiana Blakiston, *Lord William Russell and his Wife 1815–1846* (John Murray, 1972), 286.

[29] Sarah Jersey to ?, n.d., Jersey MSS, Acc 510/566.

which provided her salons with appeal to those who sought such knowledge. Sceptics such as Greville doubted the extent and accuracy of her information, while Disraeli (one of her protégés) satirized her in his novels as the self-important but ineffectual Lady St Julians.[30] Known ironically as 'Silence' and given to violent emotional displays, she was an unlikely choice of confidante. Emily Palmerston and Dorothea Lieven, admittedly hostile witnesses, recorded the vagaries of her relationship with Wellington in their correspondence, and commented more generally that 'you know her well enough not to put much faith in what she says'.[31] Her ties with the Tories were deepened by the marriage of her eldest son to Sir Robert Peel's daughter, and although she retained connections with some of those who became Whigs, notably the Palmerstons, her allegiances were firmly with the Tories, under whom her husband held a court appointment.[32] The services of such exclusive entertaining were summed up by Lady Palmerston after the death of Lord Holland in 1840. She wrote that 'he is a great loss privately and publickly, for his House kept the Party together, and was of much use as a place of meeting, and had great effect upon literary people, and the second class of politicians'.[33]

Peter Mandler has observed that, contrary to this model of exclusive entertaining, in the 1820s Lady Cowper (who by her second marriage in 1839 became Lady Palmerston) entertained across party lines, maintaining 'an atmosphere in which people of fashion could mingle without letting politics come between them'.[34] This was to prove invaluable in the unstable years from 1846 until Palmerston's death in 1865, during which time Lady Palmerston's parties reflected the shifting coalitions that made up the governments of the day. Still socially exclusive, the reception allowed a much broader spectrum of political opinion to be invited, solicited, cajoled, and rewarded than the more intimate dinner parties of the earlier years. For example, a party was held at Carlton Gardens (the move to Cambridge House took place in 1854) on Saturday, 28 February 1852, following the collapse of Russell's ministry as a result of Palmerston's manœuvrings. Present were a large proportion of the diplomatic corps and some 270 other named guests, including three members of Derby's newly formed cabinet

[30] Greville is quoted in Jersey, *Records of the Family of Villiers*, 52; Disraeli, *Sybil*, ch. 4. She has also been identified as the Zenobia of the same author's *Endymion* (1880).

[31] Emily Cowper to Dorothea Lieven, 13 Nov. 1837, in Lord Sudley (trans. and ed.), *The Lieven–Palmerston Correspondence 1828–1856* (John Murray, 1943), 140. See also ibid. 35, 65–6, and 117.

[32] The most surprising of her Whig friends was Brougham, a reminder of her support in 1820–1 for Queen Caroline, for whom Brougham acted during her trial.

[33] Lady Palmerston to Frederick Lamb, 23 Oct. 1840, in Lever, *Letters of Lady Palmerston*, 237.

[34] Mandler, *Aristocratic Government*, 54.

and/or their wives (Lady Malmesbury, Lord and Lady John Manners, and Benjamin and Mrs Disraeli); the Clanricardes and Lords Granville and Campbell represented the outgoing Russell administration (the Russells, with the exception of the duchess of Bedford, were conspicuous by their absence); and three members of the cabinet which Aberdeen was to form in December 1852 were also present—Earl Granville, Sir James Graham, and W. E. Gladstone. This range of political opinion and allegiance was reflected in the back-bench MPs attending, some forty-two in number, who came from all shades of the political spectrum.[35] The variety of political opinion encompassed by Lady Palmerston's parties reflected the party-political instability of the 1850s and 1860s, whilst the continuation of the dominance of the aristocracy was reinforced by the social exclusivity which limited entry to Cambridge House. Within three months of her marriage, Lady Palmerston had developed the formula which was to work with such success for the next twenty-five years: 'my parties are very popular, and their success is chiefly due to the fact that all political factions are to be found there.'[36]

Lady Waldegrave's parties in the later 1860s and 1870s embody a further change in the social structure of politics. The passing of the second Reform Act had broadened the political base, and the authority of aristocratic political culture was diminished by the concurrent redistribution of power. Arno J. Mayer's comment that the function of the hostesses was 'to serve as catalysts for the ongoing fusion of the old nobility . . . with the new magnates . . . on terms favourable to the aristocratic element'[37] holds particularly true under the inexorably changing political circumstances of the post-reform decade. Frances Waldegrave's background and connections ideally suited her for this more inclusive entertaining. Her credentials with the traditional aristocracy were enhanced by her connections through her third husband, George Granville Harcourt, to the Whig grandees, and by her status as the preferred hostess of the deposed French Orleanist royal family. At the same time, her theatrical family background—her father was the celebrated tenor John Braham—gave her connections with the cultural and artistic worlds, whom she introduced into high political society for the first time.[38]

According to Lady Jeune, Frances Waldegrave's 'reception rooms were open to Whigs, Tories, and Radicals, as well as to representatives of art, science, and literature. She broke away the last barriers of exclusiveness, and

[35] *Morning Post*, 1 Mar. 1852, p. 5 col. e.

[36] Emily Palmerston to Dorothea Lieven, [Feb. 1840], in Sudley (ed.), *Lieven–Palmerston Correspondence*, 183.

[37] Mayer, *Persistence of the Old Regime*, 91–2.   [38] Davidoff, *Best Circles*, 78.

socially helped more than anyone to destroy the lines of cleavage.'[39] Aristocratic women had presided over literary and artistic salons for generations, but their guests were not admitted to 'Society', to general acceptance as anything other than the talented clients of aristocratic patrons. When Harriet Sutherland consulted her sister Georgiana, Lady Dover, about inviting the actor Charles Kemble to a social event, she received the dampening reply that 'it is always objectionable to introduce theatricals into Society, and you can never know where or how it will stop', and the reminder that her husband, the duke, 'disliked that sort of society'.[40]

If the forms of hospitality offered by the hostesses varied, from the dinner party for ten to the 'drum' for 600, from the weekend party to the dinners specifically for MPs which Frances Waldegrave made a feature of her entertainment, the organization and preparation required scarcely changed over time. It was to this end that much of the household organization, discussed in Chapter 1, was directed: hospitality served the fundamentally political purpose of displaying 'the power and status of herself and her family . . . through the food and drink that she offered, the entertainment she provided, and the splendour and magnificence of her setting'.[41] At least a part of Lady Holland's influence was attributed to the excellence of her chef, as was Lady Molesworth's, while the Palmerstons' move from Carlton Terrace to Cambridge House on Piccadilly was dictated by its superior facilities for entertaining.[42] Frances Waldegrave virtually rebuilt Strawberry Hill, which had become derelict through neglect, in part as an escape from her querulous third husband, but also because she recognized its potential for entertaining.[43]

It is remarkable that, despite the huge numbers who attended the gatherings in these houses, detailed accounts of what went on at them are extremely scarce. Many letters and memoirs record the bare facts of attendance at Cambridge House or Strawberry Hill; some record the names of guests, others fragments of conversations. Lord Granville reported on an evening's entertainment to Lord Canning, who was in India. After a dinner at Frances Waldegrave's, he went to a drum at Lady Palmerston's, which 'appeared to differ in no respect from those which you were wont to frequent'.[44] None that

---

[39] Mary, Lady Jeune, 'Political Great Ladies', *Realm*, 5 Apr. 1895, p. 785 col. a.

[40] Georgiana Dover to Harriet Sutherland, n.d. [Mar. 1840?], Sutherland MSS (NLS), Dep. 313/903.

[41] Ward, *English Noblewomen*, 75. In this respect, little had changed in 500 years.

[42] Keppel, *Sovereign Lady*, 250–1; Adburgham, *Radical Aristocrat*, 198; Airlie, *Lady Palmerston and her Times*, ii. 169. [43] Hewett, *Strawberry Fair*, ch. 10.

[44] Granville to Canning, 10 Feb. 1856, in Fitzmaurice, *Life of Lord Granville*, i. 163. See also e.g. Sir Horace Rumbold, *Recollections of a Diplomatist* (2 vols., Edward Arnold, 1902), i. 152–3, ii. 65–7 and 85; and Greville, *Greville Memoirs (Second Part)*, i. 314–15 and 330, ii. 105.

I have been able to trace gives any account of what might be termed the 'choreography' of the occasion.[45] Taken entirely for granted by aristocratic society, we have again to turn to literature and to the occasional descriptions left by foreign visitors for the accounts which are missing from the letters and papers of the native participants. Trollope's duchess of Omnium displays many of the characteristics of Ladies Palmerston and Waldegrave, although she can scarcely be regarded as a portrait of either, and his accounts of her parties, especially in The Prime Minister—held in Carlton Terrace and Richmond, a clear reference to Lady Waldegrave's house in neighbouring Twickenham—are drawn from Trollope's own experiences of attending the parties given by Lady Stanley of Alderley.[46] The description of the party at Mrs Gresham's in Phineas Finn admirably captures the crush of the large party and the struggle to ascend the grand staircase, at the top of which, usually within a small antechamber, the hostess would receive the most favoured of her guests.[47] Cambridge House, noted for its two gates (to allow for the flow of carriages arriving at the door), was bedecked in yellow satin and gold Empire furniture. Lady Airlie recounted that although the rooms were large, they were not numerous, and noted that Lady Palmerston had been unable to accommodate her son-in-law, because the room which he might have occupied was 'the only room I can use for a tea-room' at her parties.[48] The tea-room was her inner sanctum, penetrated only by the most persistent guests, by the most needed allies, and the closest relations.[49]

Mary King Waddington, the American-born wife of the French ambassador in London (1883–93) described the large evening parties of that period as 'the most frightful species of entertainment that the human mind has ever devised'.[50] Trollope's most succinct account of the evening party sums up both the nature of the event and its most profound mystery:

Lady Baldock had evenings. People went to her house, and stood about the room and on the stairs, talked to each other for half an hour, and went away. . . . Why

[45] C. Northcote Parkinson's humorous analysis of a cocktail party, which, despite its comic purposes, rests on acute observation, suggests the uses to which such a choreography might be put; Parkinson's Law, or The Pursuit of Progress (John Murray, 1961; 1st pub. 1957), 60–8. The highly formalized structure of the court of Louis XIV has lent itself more readily to the kind of sociological and anthropological analysis which is possible only in a most rudimentary form for the Victorian hostesses. See e.g. Elias, Court Society, 41–65.

[46] Trollope, Prime Minister, see esp. i. chs. 9, 18–21, 37. See also Halperin, Trollope and Politics, 83, 219–21.

[47] Trollope, Phineas Finn, ch. 70.   [48] Airlie, Lady Palmerston and her Times, ii. 171.

[49] Lord Redesdale, Memories (2 vols., Hutchinson, 1915), i. 124.

[50] Mary King Waddington to G. K. S. (Mrs Eugene Schuyler), 23 Feb. 1885, in Mary King Waddington, Letters of a Diplomat's Wife (Smith, Elder, 1903), 199.

people should have gone to Lady Baldock's I cannot explain;—but there are houses to which people go without any reason.[51]

Mrs Waddington supplied the reason—politics—along with one of the fullest descriptions of the course of such an evening, albeit from a slightly later period. To her sister in America she described a 'typical London *Season* evening'. They dined with one hostess, Lady Vivian, who found all her guests 'in a hurry to get away', as they were all moving on to two further parties, at Lady Derby's in St James's Place and Lady Salisbury's in Arlington Street. Piccadilly was crowded with carriages, making progress to the former slow. On arrival at Lady Derby's, she continued,

The staircase was a mass of people struggling to get in, an orchestra playing, and about 1,200 people in rooms that would hold comfortably about half. Of course on such occasions one doesn't talk. We spoke to our host and hostess, were carried on by the crowd, made the tour of the rooms and got down again with much waiting and jostling.

They then struggled back into their carriage, and repeated the process at Lady Salisbury's party, where the crowd was even larger—'I should think the whole Conservative party'—before collapsing at home.[52]

Invitations to all varieties of Victorian social events were the province of the woman in whose name the invitations were issued. This gave her tremendous social authority, which could be wielded inclusively, as Mayer suggests, or exclusively, as Davidoff has argued.[53] Access to certain social circles was a prerequisite for admittance into the informal political world, and hence for political success. The argument that political society remained impervious to outsiders should not be overstated: as Mayer suggests, new (i.e. non-aristocratic) men clearly did enter the political realm. But the point is that successful assimilation into the dominant culture was of the greatest possible value for aspiring politicians, and the hostesses were often in a position to facilitate or hinder that assimilation. An outstanding example is W. E. Gladstone, who through his patroness Harriet Sutherland made important connections with the Whigs, notably Argyll, Granville, and the Cavendishes, at a time when, as a Peelite, he was seeking a new political home.[54] Lady Waldegrave's independence in issuing her invitations was virtually complete. Her third husband, George Granville Harcourt, frequently objected to many of her guests (not least because he suspected

[51] Trollope, *Phineas Finn*, 233–4.

[52] Mary King Waddington to G. K. S., 6 May 1885, in Waddington, *Letters of a Diplomat's Wife*, 210–11.

[53] Mayer, *Persistence of the Old Regime*, 91–2; Davidoff, *Best Circles*, ch. 3.

[54] Matthew, *Gladstone, 1809–1874*, 149–50.

their motives), but was unable to prevent her from inviting whom she pleased, especially to the parties which she held in her own house at Strawberry Hill and in Dudbrook House in Essex. The large collection of lists of names for parties, visits, and balls which remain among her papers are all in her own (unfortunately illegible) handwriting.[55] Emily Palmerston's entertaining was carried out for her husband's benefit, and she also had charge of the guest lists. It is clear, however, that Palmerston frequently assisted in the process, as in 1857 she wrote that 'It is very perplexing to have to make up a party [at Broadlands] without you and I feel it a great worry . . . we must fish for company and if you have the opportunity of asking any good person pray don't fail to do so.'[56] The Palmerstons' dislike for being apart means that their correspondence is relatively sparse, but it shows that political entertaining, although predominantly supervised by women, was not an exclusive 'sphere'. Naturally, since Palmerston was constantly in office, and had a reputation for zeal about his work, most of the work involved in entertaining fell to his wife. Invitations were written and addressed by hand, sometimes with the assistance of her two daughters, Ladies Shaftesbury and Jocelyn; for their delivery it is possible that she took advantage of one of the schemes such as that offered by the publishers of the *Royal Blue Book and Court Guide*, which undertook to deliver 300 cards for £1 'with promptitude and exactness'.[57] Lady Waldegrave relied increasingly on her niece, Constance Braham (later Lady Strachie) for administrative assistance with her parties, sometimes delegating to her the task of finding 'some men to dine & sleep here on Monday—L. Napier or any other young man' to make up a party.[58]

Still more important were decisions about the timing of parties. Avoiding clashes with other events ensured good attendance, and averted hostility between hostesses. Lady Palmerston's right to Saturday evenings during the season was rapidly established: through her connections with the Foreign Office, she could be sure of the attendance of foreign ambassadors and visiting dignitaries, and as Palmerston's power increased, so did the attraction of her parties. Aware of the dominance of her own parties, Emily Palmerston would inform other hostesses of the days on which she did not expect to receive guests, 'as you like sometimes to have Saturday Parties that do not interfere with me'.[59] A clash with one of Lady John Russell's rare dinners brought the apology that 'I was sorry our dinner was settled before

[55] 'Guest Lists', Strachey MSS, DD/SH C1189 G318.

[56] Emily Palmerston to Palmerston, 20 Oct. 1857, Broadlands MSS, BR30.

[57] Airlie, *Lady Palmerston and her Times*, ii. 43; *The Royal Blue Book and Court Guide* (1872), p. xi.

[58] Frances Waldegrave to Constance Braham, 6 June 1878, Strachey MSS, DD/SH C1189 D17.

[59] Emily Palmerston to Frances Waldegrave, Thursday 21 [no month or year], Strachey MSS, DD/SH C1189 G277.

yours, & that we carried away St Aulaire from you. After Easter I will leave
you all the Saturdays you like to take.'[60] This negotiation was the more
necessary as the hostesses were all aiming at the same constituency of
guests, supporters of the Palmerstonian and Liberal coalitions. It must be
remembered that these parties were viewed not simply as social occasions,
but as significant contributions to the popularity of men and political parties.
Lady Palmerston's purpose was to garner support for her husband, a
purpose shared by Frances Waldegrave after her fourth marriage, to
Chichester Fortescue. Lady Waldegrave had already established herself as a
hostess before her marriage, and considered her work to be on behalf of the
Liberal party as much as for her husband's benefit. Along with the success of
politicians without successful hostesses as wives, Fortescue's failure to make
the front rank of politicians has been regarded as a sign of his wife's failure
and of the weakness of hostesses in general; this conclusion disregards the
importance of her work for the Liberal party as a whole, and derives from
the view that political hostesses were indeed merely playing a supportive,
subordinate role to their husbands.[61]

The salons had several important functions, beyond the promotion of the
careers of the men of the family. In the first instance, they provided a physical location for extra-parliamentary political activity. Such provision was
necessitated not only by the personal preferences of members of the aristocratic élite, but by the inadequacy of the buildings of the houses of parliament for social and informal contact between members. Both the Old Palace
of Westminster, destroyed by fire in 1834, and the Barry palace which was
used by both houses for the first time in 1852 suffered from severe pressure
on space, making alternative venues both desirable and necessary. During
the almost twenty-year rebuilding programme, the difficulties were exacerbated. John Wilson Croker had described the Old Palace in 1833 as 'notoriously imperfect, very crazy as buildings, and extremely incommodious in
their local distribution'.[62] Sir Charles Barry's replacement building met the
original specification for a House of Commons dining-room to seat thirty,
illustrating in bricks and mortar the expectation that the majority of members would either own town houses or be in receipt of sufficient invitations
to dine as to render a larger facility in Westminster redundant. However, the
historian of the buildings, Michael Port, reveals that in the opening session
of 1867, some 6,412 dinners were served, with more than 200 members

[60] Emily Palmerston to Lord John Russell, 25 [May 1847], Russell MSS, PRO 30/22/6C.

[61] Pugh, Tories and the People, 44; Jalland, Women, Marriage and Politics, 195.

[62] Quoted in Michael Port (ed.), The Houses of Parliament (New Haven: Yale University
Press, 1976), 5.

dining on some evenings.[63] Under such circumstances, the close proximity of a number of hostesses offering invitations to dine, or to spend the evening in the company of other political persons (without the embargo on politics which mixed company, outside the understood conventions of a political hostess's dinner, often entailed), and the possibility of access to men with powers of patronage and political advancement, was of more than mere gastronomic or social benefit. Disraeli, it is true, claimed to dislike the constant sociability of politics, writing to Lady Chesterfield that 'I don't think dining together a very good way of transacting business', but he acknowledged its necessity.[64] By contrast, the diplomat Sir George Hamilton Seymour told a select committee on official salaries: 'Certainly I consider giving dinners is an essential part of diplomacy . . . I have no idea of a man being a good diplomat who does not give good dinners.'[65] The eagerness with which invitations were sought, and the bitterness with which exclusion could be greeted, are further indications, if such are needed, of the importance which contemporaries attached to spending an evening in the hot, crowded salons of the political hostesses.[66]

The parties served to integrate some of the new men into aristocratic political culture: an appearance at a Cambridge House evening or at Strawberry Hill on a Sunday afternoon served as credentials for further invitations to other houses. Hostesses were more likely to invite a man of unknown (to them) origins, and possibly his wife and daughters, to a party for several hundred than to invite the unknown quantity to a select dinner. Still less were they likely to invite them to a country-house party, where unfamiliarity with the habits and manners of the aristocracy could expose both guest and host to embarrassment. The large parties thus served as a kind of filter, selecting those who were prepared to adapt to the dominant culture, and eliminating those who either could not, or would not, adapt. Through the diaries of W. E. Gladstone it is possible to trace the contacts between one such politician and the London hostesses.[67] As a young Conservative in the 1830s without pronounced aristocratic connections, he waited upon the great ladies of his

[63] Ibid. 184–5.

[64] Disraeli to Anne Chesterfield, 31 Dec. 1874, in Zetland (ed.), *Letters to Lady Bradford and Lady Chesterfield*, i. 187.

[65] Parliamentary Papers, xv (1850), 426. I am grateful to Professor Muriel E. Chamberlain for this reference.

[66] Lord Chelsea to Emily Palmerston, 13 [Mar. 1857], Strachey MSS, DD/SH C1189 G246. Chelsea, along with other opponents of Palmerston's policy, had not been invited to Cambridge House following the motion of censure over the *Arrow* incident, and had written in protest to Lady Palmerston. See also Jasper Ridley, *Lord Palmerston* (Panther, 1972; 1st pub. 1970), 631.

[67] Foot and Matthew (eds.), *Gladstone Diaries, passim.*

party, including Sarah Jersey and Frances Salisbury two or three times a year. (He was to continue visiting Lady Jersey on this basis until 1859.) During the 1840s, he attended very few social occasions in the London houses of aristocratic women, a pattern which was to change dramatically in the 1850s, following the development of his friendship with Harriet Sutherland, whom he visited at least once a month when they were both in London. Throughout the 1850s and 1860s, he frequently attended Lady Palmerston's gatherings (ten times in 1852, seven times in 1864), continuing to visit her after Palmerston's death until her own in 1869. He was also a regular guest of Lady Waldegrave, recording visits to her at least twice a year between 1858 and 1878. As he aged and as his political eminence increased, his attendance at such gatherings decreased, confirming, unsurprisingly, that the salons of the hostesses were of greatest importance to those men who were still making their careers.

Dinners given specifically for back-bench MPs were another method incorporating and encouraging newcomers and those on the fringes of aristocratic culture. For example, Lady Palmerston's papers include a list of thirty-one Irish MPs, annotated with their constituencies and headed 'to be invited to dinner 1862'.[68] The list included prominent men, such as Sir John Acton, Chichester Fortescue, and Isaac Butt, and more obscure members such as John Ennis, Lawrence Waldron, and Michael Dunne. Frances Waldegrave gave a series of MP dinners in the 1870s, which became so well known that the prince of Wales indicated his wish to attend one.[69] During the short-lived Conservative ministry in 1852, MP dinners were given in St James's Square for both ministers and back-benchers; it is significant to note that, while the Morning Post invariably referred to Lady Palmerston's dinners and receptions, these events were reported with Lord Derby as the host.[70] Although a valuable confidante and assistant to her husband, Emma Derby was notoriously unsuccessful as a hostess: Lord Redesdale's comment on her parties, 'of a dulness as depressing as a London fog', contrasted them with the corruscating brilliance of the events held by Ladies Palmerston, Clarendon, and Granville.[71] Although Lady Derby's soirées were reported in her name, the explicitly political gatherings for members of the government were attributed solely to her husband. Successful entertaining of the political variety seems to have been a predominantly Whig and Liberal

[68] Broadlands MSS, 22(11)/19.
[69] Francis Knollys to Frances Waldegrave, 24 Feb. and 15 May 1877, Strachey MSS, DD/SH C1189 G300. See also Hewett, Strawberry Fair, 233.
[70] Morning Post, 2, 5, 9 Feb. 1852.
[71] Redesdale, Memories, i. 534. See also Wilbur Devereux Jones, Lord Derby and Victorian Conservatism (Oxford: Blackwell, 1956), 10.

feature of the London scene. Lady Derby at least made the effort to entertain her husband's political friends; by the 1870s, Disraeli was bemoaning the lack of willing hostesses in his party: 'With forty years of political experience, I never knew a party so deserted by all social influences as ours. I wonder how they are kept together—not a solitary dinner or a single drum! . . . It seems to me we have not a woman with the slightest ambition.'[72]

The widening of Society entailed by such inclusive entertaining was by no means universally approved: by the end of the century, Lady Dorothy Nevill was one of many who recorded her disdain for the rise of the 'railway kings' and the importation of the 'bustle of the Stock Exchange into the drawing-rooms of Mayfair', a tendency enhanced by the well-known predilection of the prince of Wales for 'plutocrats', for the super-rich businessmen, often with colonial, Jewish, or American antecedents, who were prominent in the Marlborough House set.[73] None the less, for the public beyond political circles, the lines of carriages arriving at Cambridge House stood as a symbol for the unity of the political classes.

The political situation itself created a need for political hostesses. In the absence of any highly structured party organizations, either within or outside parliament, there was no formal method of communication between members, between front and back benches, or between opponents; still fewer were the means of communicating with supporters outside parliament.[74] Moreover, for much of this period the political parties themselves were in a state of turmoil, with members changing party affiliation and a rapid turnover of ideological positions. When members voted in parliament on the basis of personal conviction or personal advancement, not in accordance with a party whip, much was to be gained by extra-parliamentary persuasion. Lady Palmerston commented on the value of her twice-weekly 'At homes': 'my house is a very convenient meeting place for these gentlemen, and, moreover, helpful also to Lord Palmerston, because very often a little word on the quiet is more successful than a long interview.'[75] These conditions altered noticeably during the 1880s, both in terms of the widening of society itself, and hence the diminishing hegemony of the aristocracy, and in terms of the emergence of more effective parliamentary

[72] Disraeli to Selina Bradford, 26 Apr. 1876, in Zetland (ed.), *Letters to Lady Bradford and Lady Chesterfield*, ii. 41.

[73] R. Nevill (ed.), *Reminiscences*, 102.

[74] For attendance at Lady Palmerston's as a means of gathering political information, see e.g. Robert Eadon Leader (ed.), *The Life and Letters of John Arthur Roebuck* (Edward Arnold, 1897), 251–2.

[75] Emily Palmerston to Dorothea Lieven, 13 Nov. [1840], in Sudley (ed.), *Lieven–Palmerston Correspondence*, 197.

and constituency party organizations.[76] Thus it is reasonable to assert, as Lady Jeune did in 1895, that Frances Waldegrave was the last of the political hostesses, because after her death the political culture had altered to such an extent that the influence of the aristocratic political hostess was essentially redundant.[77]

'Influence' is a particularly difficult feature of the political scene to trace. In the first instance, it was seldom exercised in writing, leaving few quantifiable traces for the historian.[78] There is no study which examines the political effect of an invitation to dine, or of the opportunity to be present at a grand reception of potential supporters or opponents of governments and measures, and it is doubtful that such a study could be written for the Victorian period.[79] None the less, the fact remains that contemporaries certainly believed that such methods were efficacious, as their recorded comments show, and as their eager attendance at such events appears to confirm. Emily Palmerston is quoted as greeting the need for votes to support her husband's ministry with the rallying cry, ' "Stay! we will have a party." '[80] One commentator on her influence suggests that her utility to Palmerston was that 'she cemented his friendships, attracted the waverers, and disarmed many of his political opponents',[81] while another noted that 'No political hostess in England ever held the same sway as Lady Palmerston at Cambridge House. . . . It was always said that an invitation to her parties had determined many a wavering vote.'[82]

In attempting to elucidate the actions of Victorian political hostesses, and to explain their contribution to political culture, it is not necessary to quantify or 'prove' that political hostesses in fact exercised political influence: it is enough to show that they believed they did, and that the political culture in which they operated also acted in accordance with that belief.

[76] Nancy W. Ellenberger, 'The Transformation of London "Society" at the End of Victoria's Reign: Evidence from the Court Presentation Records', *Albion*, 22 (Winter 1990), 633–53. More generally, see Cannadine, *Decline and Fall*, ch. 8; H. J. Hanham, *Elections and Party Management: Politics in the Time of Disraeli and Gladstone* (Longmans, 1959); John Vincent, *The Formation of the Liberal Party, 1857–1868* (Constable, 1966), esp. 82–96.

[77] Jeune, 'Political Great Ladies'. Vincent, *Formation of the Liberal Party*, 22–3, suggests, by contrast, that the demise of Palmerston and the Whigs and the emergence of a new, apolitical 'high society' around the Prince and Princess of Wales at Marlborough House marked the end of the power of the hostesses.

[78] Roberts, *Paternalism in early Victorian England*, has a similar difficulty.

[79] Sophisticated studies of the operation of patronage exist for other countries and periods. See e.g. Elias, *Court Society*; Mettam, *Power and Faction*, esp. ch. 2; Ward, *English Noblewomen*, esp. ch. 7.

[80] Airlie, *Lady Palmerston and her Times*, ii. 42–3.

[81] R. C. Lucas, sculptor, 'Continuation of the Enquiries of Artist, Clericus, Scalpel and Baggs', May-Day 1878, Broadlands MSS, BR/28/10.

[82] Jeune, 'Political Great Ladies'.

Thus, one of the reasons for the declining possibilities for political hostesses after the death of Lady Waldegrave was the result of a declining belief in the influence of the hostesses. This can perhaps be linked to the increasing dominance of the domestic ideology (but not, of course, its reality), which certainly had an impact on sections of the aristocracy, and in accordance with which political activity by women, regardless of class, was thought to demonstrate unwomanliness. As early as 1842, Anne, Lady Cowper (daughter-in-law to Lady Palmerston) commented that 'the less a woman has to do with eager, ardent, virulent politics, the better', while Lady John Russell inveighed against the 'regular hardened lady politicians'.[83] Frances Waldegrave's jubilant note of 1875 after Hartington had fought off Forster's challenge and become leader of the Liberals in the Commons—'Do you remember the *Times* saying the *Salons* had *no* influence now? That *put my back up* & I am *very* glad we came to town in time to be of use'[84] —indicates both her perception of the influence she wielded and the contrary view.

While Lady Waldegrave lived, her firm conviction of her influence and the large circle of her admirers kept the influence of the hostesses (or at least of this particular hostess) going. She had no successor. It is important to note that there is really only one Whig/Liberal hostess at a time, although Lady Holland and Lady Palmerston overlapped for a few years, as did Ladies Palmerston and Waldegrave, each entertaining a slightly different genera-tion of the party. This is because these women were the 'official' hostesses not so much for their husbands but for their political party. There was no room, or any need, for more than one such hostess at a time, because the pri-mary function of the entertainments was to enable the members of the party to gather for the transfer of information, for the bestowal and seeking of patronage, and the drumming up of support for measures and men. If more than one hostess entertained for the party, these functions would be diluted and less efficiently carried out. There was also the danger of internal factions meeting at different houses, as to some extent occurred in the 1870s, when Frances Waldegrave increasingly supported the anti-Gladstonian sections of the Liberal party, leaving Gladstone to the tender mercies of his female relatives' entertaining (although, as has already been seen, he made some effort to continue to attend Lady Waldegrave's parties). After Frances Waldegrave's death in 1879, entertaining the Liberals fell back on Gladstone and Granville; the latter attempted to work in tandem with his leader, writing that 'If we give dinners [to MPs], it might be a good thing for Mrs Gladstone and Lady Granville to give parties. Everybody would go to each,

[83]   Quoted in Jalland, *Women, Marriage and Politics*, 196.
[84]   Frances Waldegrave to Lady Strachey, Feb. 1874, quoted in Hewett, *Strawberry Fair*, 244.

& it would enable both of us to ask a larger number.'[85] The necessity for a single and agreed place where men of differing views could meet was particularly acute in the 1840s and 1850s, as Lady Palmerston recognized: 'The wonderful political events of the last few months have made everybody glad to have some talks, and this has answered particularly now, since all parties meet willingly in our House.'[86] The political hostesses recognized their activities for what they were—service to the party—and they carried out their self-imposed tasks from a sense of duty as much as from any pleasure in the activity. Such constant, public entertaining could be a strain, as may be detected in Emily Palmerston's acceptance of the Whig defeat in 1841, with the prospect of a future ministry beginning again 'like a Giant refreshed', and in Frances Waldegrave's occasional outbursts against her self-imposed tasks.[87] Shortly after her marriage to Palmerston, Lady Palmerston listed the benefits of her new house, which she considered 'so suited to reception', which were to be able to 'gratify' the diplomatic corps (Palmerston was, of course, foreign minister at this time), to 'give our party advantage in many ways', and finally, as something of an afterthought, to 'amuse Fanny', her younger, unmarried daughter.[88] Emily Palmerston clearly did not regard her entertaining primarily in the light suggested by Leonore Davidoff, as a mechanism for regulating Society and the marriage market,[89] but rather as a tool of party politics. In 1849, confronted with the contentious repeal of the Navigation Acts in parliament, Emily Palmerston wrote to ask her husband: 'When is the Navigation in the Lords? If the 28th is coming on to that time perhaps *I had better have* a party on the 28th. It tends to give a Spirit and to keep the party together & induces our people to meet.'[90] This is as clear a statement of the self-perceived functions of the entertainments given by political hostesses as one could hope to find. Similarly, Frances Waldegrave, in an undated letter concerning a 'hateful' bill in parliament, mentioned that 'I am very busy sending out cards for a Party tomorrow night. I had not intended to receive, but but [sic] I think it as well to try to get people together before Thursday.'[91] More important are her comments on the

---

[85] Granville to Gladstone, 1 Oct. 1884, in Agatha Ramm (ed.), *The Political Correspondence of Mr Gladstone and Lord Granville, 1876–1886* (2 vols., Oxford: Clarendon Press, 1962), ii. 272.

[86] Emily Palmerston to Mrs Huskisson, 19 Mar. 1846, in Lever, *Letters of Lady Palmerston*, 273.

[87] Emily Palmerston to Palmerston, [Aug. 1841], in Lever, *Letters of Lady Palmerston*, 257; Frances Waldegrave to Chichester Fortescue, [12 Sept. 1859], Strachey MSS, DD/SH C1189 G336; Frances Waldegrave to Josephine Bolton, [n.d.], in Hewett, *Strawberry Fair*, 226.

[88] Emily Palmerston to Margaret de Flahault, 15 Mar. 1840, in Lever, *Letters of Lady Palmerston*, 225. [89] Davidoff, *Best Circles*, 49–58.

[90] Emily Palmerston to Palmerston, 17 Apr. 1849, Broadlands MSS, BR30, my emphasis.

[91] Frances Waldegrave to William Vernon Harcourt, Tuesday, n.d., MS. Harcourt, dep. 93, fos. 41–2.

suggestion that Fortescue might be returned to Ireland as chief secretary in 1870:

I never said that I would not go to Ireland *at all*, but that I could only be there during the times it was absolutely necessary for Chichester to carry out his work, & that I should not be such a fool again, as to put my whole heart and soul in the business of making the Govt popular there et cta as I had done last year with as you must know from O Hagan & others great success.[92]

It was not Fortescue whom she had sought to make popular, but the government: party interest had taken precedence over personal wishes. Of course, this same letter implies that, as the party had not rewarded Fortescue in a suitable manner, Frances would in future place her family interests before those of the party, going to Ireland to support her husband, but not actively to enhance the image of the Liberal government there. This was a significant threat, and did not overestimate her achievements during Fortescue's earlier term of office.

With all the complexities of Irish political life, a capacity to extend hospitality and integrate potentially hostile MPs into the political system was perhaps even more important in Dublin than in London. In 1861, one of the main recommendations for Sir Robert Peel as chief secretary was that 'he wd make highly spiced speeches, and he could entertain to any amount in Dublin with Lady Emily'.[93] Still more telling is the advice of Edward Hamilton to the secretary of a subsequent lord-lieutenant, Lord Spencer:

If Lady Spencer gives any more parties, I would venture to suggest . . . that some of the Irishmen who have recently deserted Parnell's ranks and joined the supporters of the Government should be thought of. . . Also, perhaps you might go through a Division List like that of last night and see what names are not on Lady Spencer's list. No people are more alive to a little civility especially from a house like Spencer House than some of the more extreme members of the party.[94]

Frances Waldegrave was fully aware of the value of 'a little civility', both for the popularity of the ministry and for the success of Fortescue, whom she had married in 1863. Fortescue's appointment as chief secretary owed something to his wife's campaigning on his behalf, and not a little to her reputation as a hostess. Despite the Peels' capacity for entertaining, their term of

---

[92] Frances Waldegrave to William Vernon Harcourt, 2 Oct. 1870, MS. Harcourt, dep. 93, fos. 43–8.

[93] Chichester Fortescue to Frances Waldegrave, 22 July 1861, Strachey MSS, DD/SH C1189 G336.

[94] E. W. Hamilton to J. R. Dasent, 10 Mar. 1882, in Peter Gordon (ed.), *The Red Earl: The Papers of the Fifth Earl Spencer 1835–1910* (2 vols., Northampton: Northamptonshire Record Society, 1981), i. 19.

office had not been a success, and Clarendon wrote to J. T. Delane, the editor of *The Times*, that 'Lady Waldegrave however will do better in Ireland, and if so minded, she may be of great use'.[95] For four years, she was indeed so minded: Bernal Osborne described her as 'incessant in her entertainments', a view which found its way into *The Times*, which reported on the brilliance of the 1866 season in Dublin, ascribing it to the influence of Lady Waldegrave, who 'has reminded the older citizens of Dublin of what the Viceregal Court once was. She has shown them what it should be.'[96] Frances Waldegrave gave an account of one week's entertaining to William Vernon Harcourt, which included four dinners for between fourteen and thirty guests and a ball.[97] Bernal Osborne went on to describe the explicitly political nature of her Dublin entertainments (incidentally highlighting the difference from her London parties):

I took a *Turkish bath* with *seven hundred* other persons here [Phoenix Park] on Friday last, the rooms being qualified to contain *three hundred and fifty*! Probably with a view to conciliate the future constituency of Dublin, a great part of the company was made up of *six-pound* householders, not calculated on their rating, but rental.[98]

Obviously, invitations to parties and dinners with celebrated peeresses could not resolve the difficulties of the Irish political system, if only because it assumed the existence of a similar aristocratic political culture in Ireland as in England. Lady Waldegrave (and Lady Spencer after her) attempted to integrate Irish MPs into the culture of Westminster—many of those whom she met in Ireland were subsequently invited to Strawberry Hill; but in this instance at least, society and politics had moved so far apart as to be irreconcilable. That the attempt was none the less viewed as important is witnessed by its continuation after Lady Waldegrave's departure.

Management of government relations with the press was another arena in which the activities of political hostesses had some significance. Lord Granville commented that of the three ways in which 'public men' could communicate with 'writers in the press', the first was 'showing them social civilities', and acknowledged that, despite some 'personal inconvenience from the impression which it creates', John Thadeus Delane and Henry Reeves of *The Times* 'have frequently dined with me and have come to Lady Granville's parties'.[99] Both Lady Palmerston and Lady Waldegrave

[95] Clarendon to John T. Delane, 19 Jan. 1865, in Arthur Irwin Dasent, *John Thadeus Delane, Editor of 'The Times': His Life and Correspondence* (2 vols., John Murray, 1908), ii. 159.

[96] Quoted in Hewett, *Strawberry Fair*, 189–90.

[97] Frances Waldegrave to William Vernon Harcourt, 3 Jan. 1866, MS. Harcourt, dep. 93, fos. 21–6.

[98] Bernal Osborne to John T. Delane, 4 Jan. 1866, in Dasent, *Delane*, 162.

[99] 'Memorandum by Lord Granville', 25 Jan. 1855, in Fitzmaurice, *Life of Lord Granville*, i. 91–2.

recognized the importance of the press for demonstrating the success of their endeavours and as a vital tool in the cultivation of political and popular opinion. In 1844, J. C. Hobhouse dined with Sir John Easthope of the *Chronicle* and his wife, and with patrician condescension observed that 'Lady Easthope, a very handsome person, performed the honours very well, and so did her husband . . . The gay, good-natured Lady Palmerston went through the ceremonies of the visit very well, and was as civil as if the hostess had been her fashionable friend of thirty years.'[100] The Palmerstons' recognition of the importance of press support led them actively to woo the most important political editor of the day, Delane of *The Times*, who maintained a strongly anti-Palmerstonian line in his paper during the 1840s and early 1850s. Unsuccessful in their first attempts in 1850–1, by 1857 they had won him over as a recognized member of the Palmerstons' circle. Confided in by Palmerston, Delane was regularly included in many of Lady Palmerston's London parties, and invited to Broadlands to shoot.[101] The historian of *The Times*, describing the acceptance by Henry Reeve (its leader-writer) of invitations to Cambridge House and his subsequent adoption of the Palmerstonian line, magisterially declared that 'such trivial considerations cannot have influenced the editorial conduct' of the newspaper.[102] The evidence, however, is entirely to the contrary. Emily Palmerston's grasp of press affairs is demonstrated in her advice to Palmerston in 1849, recommending him to leak a piece of information to the *Morning Herald* rather than the *Globe*, as it was 'not known to have intelligence from the Foreign Office & then a Morning paper has more effect'.[103] Lady Waldegrave improved on Lady Palmerston's contacts with the press, early acquiring as friends and allies Delane; Abraham Hayward, who wrote for the *Morning Chronicle* and the reviews; and J. D. Cook of the *Saturday Review*.[104] She enlisted Cook in 1857, specifically to promote the cause of the Orleanist pretenders to the French throne, who were among her most frequent guests and most fervent admirers, and engaged any number of her friends and relations to write on that subject for the journal. Cook also managed the *Continental Review*, set up by the duc d'Aumale, who used Frances Waldegrave as a go-between to preserve his anonymity.[105] The deliberation with which Lady Waldegrave

[100] Diary, 5 June 1844, in Lady Dorchester (ed.), *Lord Broughton (J. C. Hobhouse): Recollections of a Long Life* (6 vols., John Murray, 1909–11), vi. 110.

[101] Ridley, *Lord Palmerston*, 707–9; Dasent, *Delane*, i. 250–7; Palmerston to Emily Palmerston, 29 Aug. 1860, Broadlands MSS, BR23 AA/1.

[102] *The History of 'The Times'*: ii: *The Tradition Established 1841–1884* (*The Times*, 1939), 247.

[103] Emily Palmerston to Palmerston, 19 Apr. 1849, Broadlands MSS, BR30.

[104] Dasent, *Delane*, ii. 68, 139.

[105] John D. Cook to Frances Waldegrave, 12 Mar. 1859, and Frances Waldegrave to John D. Cook, 12 Mar. 1859, Strachey MSS, DD/SH C1189 G336.

treated her conquest of the press is reflected in a comment made to Lady Clarendon in the same year, that 'Lady Palmerston and I are two Delilahs. She has cut the hair of the *Times* and I of the *Saturday*'.[106]

The political hostesses thus served an important purpose in integrating newspaper editors into political society, apropos of which Lord Derby observed in 1871 that 'from Delane downwards every editor reckons on invitations to great houses as part of the perquisites of his office: the result is that they cannot write honestly about men and things'. Quoting Robert Lowe, he went on to record that Chichester Fortescue was 'a man whose position had been entirely made for him by the newspapers. He, or rather Ly Waldegrave, invited & courted all the journalists, so that whatever Fortescue might do, not one of them would write against him.'[107] Enraged by what she perceived as the interference of the *The Times* in foreign policy, Queen Victoria wrote to Palmerston demanding that the editors be excluded from society. Her argument provides a concise summing up of the influence of the salons, not merely for newspaper men, but more generally:

> Their introduction into our higher society and political 'Reunions' to the extent to which it is now carried and the attention which is publicly shown to them there, is, the most direct encouragement they could receive, adding both to their importance and power for mischief.[108]

THE CULTURE OF POLITICS

Although large-scale entertaining was the most publicly recognized political role for aristocratic women, and provided the defining activity of the political hostess, it was by no means the only arena in which women of this class contributed to the culture of politics. Restricted in numbers, political hostesses and their explicitly political entertainments were not aberrations from a norm of female disengagement from national politics, but rather an extension of usual practice to its extreme. In this light, notwithstanding the argument that the parties of the hostesses had importance beyond the mere promotion of their husbands' careers, the political hostesses were prime examples of 'incorporated wives'. It is the intention here to consider three areas in which aristocratic women more generally influenced the politics of the nation: as wielders of patronage, as confidantes, and as go-betweens. The majority of these women, it will be shown, were willing participants in the political careers of husbands, sons, and friends, and accepted both the

[106] Hewett, *Strawberry Fair*, 132.

[107] John Vincent (ed.), *A Selection from the Diaries of Edward Henry Stanley, 15th Earl of Derby (1826–93), between September 1869 and March 1878*, Camden 5th ser. iv (1994), 200.

[108] Queen Victoria to Palmerston, 6 Oct. 1855, in *History of 'The Times'*, ii. 202.

scope and the limitations placed on their capacity to act by their gender and class. Not all women were adept at the political game. Some, like Emma Derby, undertook the public duties imposed by their husbands' positions without conspicuous success; others, notably Catherine Gladstone, were simply uninterested in the role of hostess, and either neglected it or handed it over to other members of the family. A few were actively hostile to the demands of the political culture, and rejected the incorporation into their husbands' careers which provided the boundaries of legitimate and acceptable female political participation.

The case of Lady John Russell is instructive for defining the expectations surrounding a political wife, and for mapping the accepted limits on female political activity. Despite an intelligent interest in politics and commitment to the success and welfare of her husband, Lady John exemplified to her contemporaries how a political wife should not behave.[109] In the first instance, she profoundly disliked London, preferring their grace-and-favour residence, Pembroke Lodge, in Richmond Park.[110] Further, she disliked the entire structure and tone of London entertaining, writing to Lord John of her ambition 'to establish some more popular and rational kind of society than is usual in London'.[111] Her preference for meeting people 'in twos & threes, better than in hundreds & thousands' did not fit her for enjoyment of the prevailing patterns of London entertaining, which, as has been shown, tended to be on the latter scale.[112] But perhaps her biggest objection was to precisely the role which was available to aristocratic women in the political system, in the politics of personality. There was little room in mid-Victorian political culture for women interested in ideological issues, especially if those issues were separated from the management of practical politics. Lady John was such a woman. 'I care very much for the [political] questions themselves,' she wrote in 1848, 'but grow wearied to death of all the details and personalities belonging to them, and consequently of the conversation of lady politicians, made up as it is of those details and personalities.'[113] A resolute Whig, Lady John is one of the few women whose papers contain the regular expression of apparently independent political ideas, maintaining a

[109]   Prest, *Lord John Russell*, p. xvi.

[110]   Lady John Russell to [?] George William Gilbert Russell, 4 Feb. [1863?], Bod., MS. Eng. lett. e. 111, fos. 20–3.

[111]   Lady John Russell to Lord John Russell, 27 Feb. 1846, in Desmond MacCarthy and Agatha Russell (eds.), *Lady John Russell: A Memoir* (Longmans, Green & Co., 1926; 1st pub. 1910), 84. See also Lady John Russell to Mary Dunfermline, 23 Feb. 1870, ibid. 224.

[112]   Lady John Russell to Rollo Russell, 25 May 1871, Bod., MS. Eng. lett. e. 112, fos. 35–6.

[113]   Lady John Russell to Lady Mary Abercrombie, 3 Aug. 1848, in McCarthy and Russell (eds.), *Lady John Russell*, 101–2.

strong line on Italian unification and, after her husband's death, on home rule for Ireland, of which she was a fervent supporter.[114]

In spite of all her apparent qualifications as a political hostess—political interests and a well-placed husband who had been the most important of the *habitués* of Lady Holland's salon—Lady John not only did not become a political hostess, but was frequently held responsible for her husband's failings, abused for misuse of her position, and generally derided for her alienation from the prevailing political culture. Undoubtedly, she was filled with dread at the prospect of her husband taking office, both on her own account and on account of the toll on his health, and her relief in 1868, knowing that he would never again accept office, is palpable.[115] Such reluctance aside, Lady John was regularly credited as a negative influence on her husband's career: her frequent illnesses were unfavourably cited as the reason for his failure to form a government in the winter of 1845–6.[116] Russell's vacillations in the 1850s were unfairly attributed to her influence: in 1854, when Aberdeen was forming his ministry, Gladstone wrote that he doubted if anyone but Lord Aberdeen 'could have borne what he [Aberdeen] has had to bear during the last seventeen months from *Lady John*'.[117] Whatever her thoughts about the politics of personality, personal feeling certainly inspired Lady John's antagonisms. She was clearly hostile to Aberdeen, and more so to the idea of her husband, who had been prime minister, serving under another leader; her dislike of Aberdeen, whom she described as 'the poor old stumbling-block', included his most fervent admirer, Gladstone.[118] In 1852 she had written of her dream of Russell heading a ministry of 'old Whigs, young Whigs, the cream of the Radicals & the cream of the Peelites, leaving Gladstone & others as skimmed Milk to the Tories'.[119] Although she might have contributed to Russell's difficulties, she was certainly not their cause: Russell was quite capable of vacillation on his own account. Indeed, Lady John sometimes even advised her husband against the courses of action for which she was subsequently blamed, as, for example, over the mode of his resignation in 1855.[120] Ill feeling between Gladstone and Russell has been

[114] See e.g. Lady John Russell to Rollo Russell, 9 July [1895?], Bod., MS. Eng. lett. e. 113, fos. 88–9.
[115] Lady John Russell to [?] Rollo Russell, 18 Feb. 1868, Bod., MS. Eng. lett. e. 111, fos. 187–9. See also Lady John Russell to Lord Minto, 9 Dec. 1845, Minto MSS, MS11774, fos. 86–7; Lady Mary Abercrombie to Lady John Russell, 10 Jan. 1846, Russell MSS, PRO 30/22/5A, fos. 58–61.
[116] See e.g. Airlie, *Lady Palmerston and her Times*, ii. 100, Lord Beauvale to Lady Palmerston, 1 Jan. 1846: 'The Queen attributes much of John's want of resolution to his wife's state of health, and this is the only excuse found for him at Windsor.'
[117] Quoted in Muriel E. Chamberlain, *Lord Aberdeen: A Political Biography* (Longman, 1983), 510.
[118] Lady John Russell to Minto, 21 Feb. 1854, Minto MSS, MS11775, fos. 1–2.
[119] Lady John Russell to Lady Mary Abercrombie, 7 Jan. 1852, Minto MSS, MS11904, fos. 122–3.
[120] See Lady John Russell to Minto, 29 Jan. 1855, Minto MSS, MS11775, fo. 73.

attributed in great measure to the so-called Kennedy affair of 1854–5, which looked set to precipitate the fall of the ministry, had not the Crimean War intervened.[121] The widespread feeling that behind Lord John's actions was the meddling and political jobbery of his wife is reflected in Henry Grenfell's comment that 'Mrs Kennedy is a Romilly and a Romilly married an Elliot, & in short Lady John [an Elliot by birth] ought to be placed in safe *keeping* somewhere'.[122]

This kind of negative recognition of the wife's role in her husband's career, coming to light only in instances of failure, is, according to Soraya Tremayne, typical of the incorporated wife who does not meet the expectations of the professional organization or culture to which she and her husband belong. It is in this sort of contested area, where roles are unclear, and when the actions and inactions of a wife put the interests and reputation of her husband at risk, that the 'assumed but unspoken role that a woman should play in her husband's professional life is articulated'.[123] The trouble with Lady John was neither that she influenced her husband, nor that she used his position to gain positions or influence for members of her family, although she undoubtedly did (as did many other political wives).[124] Her problem was that, uncomfortable with the prevailing political culture, she lacked the discretion to keep her views to herself. She wrote to her father that 'If this kind of thing goes on I shall not behave like an angel any more but say what I think everywhere & to every-body & do a great deal of mischief & break up the ministry'.[125] While such comments within the family were perhaps excusable, the frame of mind that lay behind them became public knowledge. As Russell himself ruefully admitted, she lacked the political sense of a Lady Palmerston, who was known for her calculated indiscretion, and Lady John's indiscretions could be damaging both to his and to her own reputation.[126] While a politically acute wife was by no means a prerequisite for a successful career, a wife without such acumen could limit her husband's career (or perhaps provide an excuse for his own inadequacies).[127]

Most aristocratic women, however, fell somewhere between the two examples of Lady John and Emily Palmerston. The majority supported their

---

[121] For details of the affair, see J. B. Conacher, *The Aberdeen Coalition 1852–1855: A Study in Mid-Nineteenth-Century Party Politics* (Cambridge: Cambridge University Press, 1968), 377–82. See also John Prest, 'Gladstone and Russell', *Transactions of the Royal Historical Society*, 5th ser. 16 (1966), 43–63.

[122] Henry Grenfell to Frances Waldegrave, 22 Jan. 1854, Strachey MSS, DD / SH C1189 G254.

[123] Soraya Tremayne, 'Shell Wives in Limbo', in Ardener and Callan (eds.), *Incorporated Wife*, 123.

[124] See e.g. Lady John Russell to Minto, 27 Jan. 1853, Minto MSS, MS11775, fos. 1–2.

[125] Lady John Russell to Minto, 20 Feb. 1851, Minto MSS, MS11774, fos. 198–9.

[126] Hewett, *Strawberry Fair*, 111.

[127] The duke of Richmond told Lord Salisbury that ' "If Lady S. were the Duchess of Richmond you never wd. have been leader" ': Johnson (ed.), *Diary of Gathorne Hardy*, 10 May 1881, p. 476.

husbands and friends indirectly, through reciprocal entertaining, and, most importantly, by acting as their confidantes. The value of an intelligent, sympathetic, private audience is difficult to estimate, although the frequency with which such relationships occurred, and their persistence throughout the century, imply that they served a useful psychological function for politicians.[128] Such relationships were often within marriages, and, where husband and wife spent most of their time together, are difficult to document. A number of published collections of letters between spouses, such as the Wharncliffes and Westmorlands, show husband and wife corresponding extensively on political as well as family affairs, indicating that politics were as much a part of the common currency of aristocratic female life as of that of their male relations.[129] Such correspondences were by no means confined to spouses: mothers corresponded with their sons on politics, as has been seen in the case of Lady John Russell, and sisters with their brothers—Emily Palmerston's chief correspondent was her brother, Frederick Lamb, Lord Beauvale.[130]

More unusual were the men who sought confidantes outside their families. In such relationships, the politician had the benefit of a sounding-board who could be distanced from personal and political loyalties, without the dangers inherent in exposing himself to another man who might take political advantage of any knowledge gained by this route. Disraeli's predilection for women correspondents and his succession of female patrons are well known; to Lady Bradford in particular he confided political secrets, ambitions, and dilemmas.[131] The duke of Newcastle (who was also an unsuccessful suitor) made Frances Waldegrave his confidante. During the 1850s, one of Gladstone's chief confidantes was, as already noted, Harriet, duchess of Sutherland; Clarendon, surprisingly, corresponded regularly with the Tory duchess of Manchester, who was herself the mistress and confidante of, and ambition behind, the Whig Lord Hartington.[132] The latter relationship was a cause of constant concern to his colleagues, who attributed his political recalcitrance to having 'taken in poison at

---

[128] The persistence of this form of relationship can be seen in the cases of Frances Horner and H. H. Asquith and of A. J. Balfour and Mary Elcho. See H. C. G. Matthew, 'Asquith's Political Journalism', *Bulletin of the Institute of Historical Research*, 49 (May 1976), 147, and Ridley and Percy (eds.), *Letters of Arthur Balfour and Lady Elcho*.

[129] Weigall (ed.), *Correspondence of Priscilla Westmorland*; Grosvenor and Beilby (eds.), *First Lady Wharncliffe*.

[130] He is the principal recipient of the letters in Lever, *Letters of Lady Palmerston*.

[131] Zetland (ed.), *Letters to Lady Bradford and Lady Chesterfield*; Londonderry, *Letters from Disraeli to Frances Anne . . . Londonderry*.

[132] A. L. Kennedy (ed.), *'My Dear Duchess': Social and Political Letters to the Duchess of Manchester 1858–1869* (John Murray, 1956).

K[imbolton, the duchess's house] as usual', and considered that 'his "antient Egeria" [the duchess], loyal to himself, is perpetually working against his colleagues'.[133] The duke of Wellington was notorious for his succession of female correspondents and admirers (who in many respects served to fill the political vacuum created by his thoroughly unincorporated wife, Catherine). Harriet Arbuthnot was the first, and most important, of his female friends, but after her death in 1834, his circle widened, to include Sarah Jersey, Frances Salisbury, Priscilla Burghersh (later Westmorland), Mary Wilton, and Mary Salisbury (later Derby).[134] Unlike, for example, the Clarendon–Manchester correspondence, which appears to have remained more or less secret, Wellington's confidantes were a matter of public knowledge and speculation: 'Lady Jersey is greatly neglected, and I do not think there is at present any reigning beauty. Lady Burghersh enjoys his confidence more than anyone else, although Lady Salisbury [Frances] likes to think that she is the favourite,' Emily Cowper remarked in 1836.[135]

These correspondences could also serve the wider purpose of transferring information, at a time when news, political or otherwise, could move very slowly, and when much political activity simply never made it into the press. Private correspondence was an invaluable method of gathering intelligence from around the country and, more particularly, from abroad. The cosmopolitan nature of the British aristocracy and of London society is often neglected, but connections with continental aristocracies, courts, and politicians were close, and not exclusively confined to members of the diplomatic corps. The connection of Frances Waldegrave with the French Orleanist family has already been noted, while Dorothea Lieven provided a link with Russian, Austrian, and French courts. Even casual visits to the Continent could be turned to purpose, as, for example, when Anne Stafford returned from a visit to Hungary in 1861, and was asked by Palmerston for her 'Impressions as to the state of that Country and as to the Points of Difference between the Austrian Government and the Hungarian'.[136] Charlotte Canning, who had accompanied her husband on his appointment as governor-general of India, was a frequent source of information on Indian

---

[133] Gladstone to Granville, 11 Sept. 1885, in Ramm (ed.), *Correspondence of Gladstone and Granville*, ii. 394, and Granville to Gladstone, 19 Dec. 1883, ibid. ii. 131.

[134] Francis Bamford and the duke of Wellington (eds.), *The Journal of Mrs Arbuthnot, 1820–1832* (2 vols., Macmillan, 1950); 7th duke of Wellington (ed.), *Wellington and his Friends: Letters of the First Duke of Wellington* (Macmillan, 1965); Oman, *Gascoyne Heiress*; Lady Burghclere (Winifred Gardner) (ed.), *A Great Man's Friendship: Letters of the Duke of Wellington to Mary, Marchioness of Salisbury, 1850–1852* (John Murray, 1927).

[135] Emily Cowper to Dorothea Lieven, 11 Mar. 1836, in Sudley (ed.), *Lieven–Palmerston Correspondence*, 117.

[136] Palmerston to Anne Stafford, 25 Sept. 1861, Sutherland MSS (Staffs.), D593 P/28/8/17.

affairs for both the court and the government, particularly during the Rebellion of 1857.[137]

More consistent correspondence about international relations naturally took place between members of the diplomatic corps and their wives and their correspondents in England. One of the most notable of correspondents on foreign affairs was Mary Derby (previously Lady Salisbury), whose extensive range of foreign correspondents included Queen Sophie of the Netherlands; Lord Cowley, sometime ambassador to France; Sir Robert Morier, eventual ambassador to St Petersburg; and the veteran of the German embassies, Lady William Russell.[138] As wife of the foreign secretary in Disraeli's cabinet (1874–8) and the colonial secretary under Gladstone (1882–5), she was in a position to pass information between her correspondents and her husband both on foreign affairs and on the state of politics in England. (She had been a close friend and confidante of her second husband for some years prior to their marriage, during which time he had served as Lord Stanley as foreign secretary in the Derby/Disraeli cabinets. By her first marriage she was stepmother to Lord Salisbury, who was at the India Office under Disraeli's first ministry until Derby's resignation, when he became foreign secretary. He was, of course, subsequently both foreign secretary and prime minister.) As with Lady John Russell, Mary Derby's sharing of information was sometimes considered indiscreet, and she was much criticized during the Eastern Crisis of the 1870s for her links with the Russian diplomatic mission, and particularly with Count Schouvaloff, and was widely held to have been leaking information from Disraeli's cabinet to both the Russians and the Liberal opposition. Sir William Harcourt was a friend of Schouvaloff, and 'The Count saw much of Lady Derby, . . . and from this source Harcourt, and through him the Opposition leaders, were kept informed of the progress of events within the Cabinet.'[139] More usually, these informal channels of communication were welcomed, and Morier at least placed great reliance on Lady Derby's discretion and political acumen. Aware that a cabinet minister was unlikely to relish additional reports from Germany, and aware that his own opinion might not carry great weight, Morier directed his extensive disquisitions on foreign policy to Mary Derby (or Salisbury as she then was), 'with the hope that some evening at Hatfield

---

[137] See e.g. various letters to Granville, in Fitzmaurice, *Life of Lord Granville*, i. 270–2, 283–6, and to the queen, in Virginia Surtees, *Charlotte Canning: Lady-in-Waiting to Queen Victoria and Wife of the First Viceroy of India, 1817–1861* (John Murray, 1975), chs. 20–2.

[138] See Burghclere (ed.), *A Great Lady's Friendships*; Morier MSS, *passim*; and Blakiston, *Lord William Russell and his Wife*.

[139] A. G. Gardiner, *The Life of Sir William Harcourt* (2 vols., Constable, 1923), i. 311. Johnson (ed.), *Diary of Gathorne Hardy*, 9 Dec. 1877 and 3 Jan. 1878.

you might make the suggestion for me to the Foreign Secretary [Stanley] and so peradventure it might receive a moment's attention from his Lordship between tea and seltzer water time'.[140]

As in all other areas of aristocratic life, the manipulation of patronage was an important part of the aristocratic woman's contact with the machinery of national government, as the discussion of political hostesses has shown. The promotion of aspiring politicians could be assisted by letters of encouragement from female friends, as, for example, in 1873, when Frances Waldegrave passed on to both Gladstone and Hartington the information that William Harcourt was willing to accept the position of solicitor-general.[141] The diplomatic service stands as a good example of the important role which female correspondents could play in acquiring patronage, positions, and promotions for those who were often necessarily removed from direct contact with Westminster and Whitehall. It was to Mary Salisbury that Morier turned when he wanted influence in the foreign office in 1865 after a mix-up over his next posting. She 'contrived to get behind the scenes at the F.O. for a glimpse into your affairs', and sent a conciliatory report to Morier's wife.[142] At this level, however, the principle functions of patronage were carried out by introducing aspiring politicians and diplomats into the sort of society where they could make their own impression on the people with power.

A final example of the engagement of aristocratic women in politics, which also serves to demonstrate their integration into their husbands' careers, is the way in which they could, on occasion, represent their husbands for political purposes, and speak for them in decisions affecting their careers. Built into the political system was a requirement that the foreign office have a woman who could play hostess to the *corps diplomatique*, to receive the wives of ambassadors and other foreign guests and present them at court. Lady Granville, the foreign secretary's wife, was away when Mary Waddington had to be presented to the queen, so Lady Harcourt, as wife of the home secretary, was detailed to present the French ambassador's wife.[143] Similar functions were expected of the wife of the lord-lieutenant of Ireland (who could be superceded by the wife of the chief secretary, as has been seen in the 1860s). When it was proposed to send Hartington in the former position to Ireland, the queen was categorical that his mistress, the duchess

---

[140] Robert Morier to Mary Salisbury, 5 Nov. 1867, Morier MSS, Box 33.

[141] William Vernon Harcourt to Frances Waldegrave, n.d., Strachey MSS, DD/SH C1189 G261; Hartington to Frances Waldegrave, 7 Nov. 1873, Strachey MSS, DD/SH C1189 G263; Frances Waldegrave to Gladstone, 4 Nov. 1873, BL Add. MS 44,441, fos. 13–14.

[142] Mary Salisbury to Alice Morier, 14 Sept. 1865, Morier MSS, Box 54.

[143] Mary King Waddington to Henrietta L. King, 1 Dec. 1883, in Waddington, *Letters of a Diplomat's Wife*, 174.

of Manchester, 'must not do the honours'. Gladstone reassured the queen that one of the ladies of the unmarried marquess's family would be prevailed upon to 'discharge the duties of Vice-reine'.[144] These duties could include meeting people on behalf of the lord-lieutenant and reporting back to the prime minister, as Katherine Clarendon found in 1847, for example, when she held and noted a conversation with an agricultural lecturer in the absence of Clarendon and sent a record of the meeting to Lord John Russell.[145]

Instances of consulting wives about their husbands' intentions are relatively common, as was the practice of using female correspondence to find out intentions or opinions in an informal manner which could be disregarded if the outcome was unfavourable. Lady Westmorland was sounded out by Palmerston as to the likelihood of her husband consenting to remain in Berlin on the change of ministry in 1846, largely as a matter of convenience: relying on her knowledge of Westmorland's wishes, it was quicker to seek a response from Lady Westmorland in London than from her husband in Berlin.[146] Likewise, in 1851 Lord Stanley made an approach to Lord Lyndhurst through Georgiana Lyndhurst about the presidency of the council (in the event of the collapse of the Russell ministry), because of his concern about Lyndhurst's health.[147] The use of the correspondence between wives for the conveyance of sensitive information is illustrated by the letters exchanged between Catherine Gladstone and Henrietta Ripon over the conversion of Lord Ripon to the Roman Catholic Church in 1874, which have been described as 'written (through a wifely medium) by one ex-minister to another'.[148] Perhaps the best-documented case of such use of the 'wifely medium' was the switch of the fifteenth earl of Derby from the Conservative to the Liberal party in 1882, in which Mary Derby played a major part. From shortly after his resignation from the Disraeli cabinet in 1878, Derby was wooed by the Liberals, with the apparent connivance of his wife. Her co-operation with William Harcourt was instrumental in arranging for Hartington to visit Derby at Knowsley in October 1879, a visit which was central in the effort to align Derby with the Liberals: in announcing the visit to the press, Harcourt added: 'You may comment as you please on this.

---

[144] Foot and Matthew (eds.), *Gladstone Diaries*, v, 6 Dec. 1868. In the event, Hartington declined to go to Ireland.

[145] Katherine Clarendon to Lord John Russell, 26 Dec. 1847, Russell MSS, PRO 30/22/6H, fos. 228–9.

[146] Palmerston to Priscilla Westmorland, 8 July 1846, in Weigall (ed.), *Correspondence of Priscilla Westmorland*, 81.

[147] Stanley to Georgiana Lyndhurst, 5 May 1851, Lyndhurst MSS, Trinity College Library, Cambridge, fos. 129–30.

[148] Josef L. Altholz and John Powell, 'Gladstone, Lord Ripon and the Vatican decrees, 1874', *Albion*, 22 (Fall 1990), 450–1.

It means what it seems to mean.[149] Lady Derby was anxious to see her husband come in from the political wilderness into which his resignation had cast him, and, after a couple of false starts, it was through her that the approach was made in May 1882 for Derby to join the cabinet. Indeed, the tactic of communication through wives was used to the full, with both Gladstone and Catherine Gladstone visiting Mary Derby for confidential discussions about Derby's future, in which the principal took no part.[150] Moreover, after Derby declined to enter the cabinet, Gladstone again wrote to Lady Derby, expressing his regrets and clearly attempting to keep open the channels for future negotiations.[151] Further discussions did indeed take place through Mary Derby, who wrote the final letter of rejection.[152] The fact that the correspondence all passed through Lady Derby's hands, and that the rejection came, laced with regret, from her, rather than her husband, left the door open for his admission to the cabinet as secretary for the colonies in December of the same year (having raised the objection that Lady Derby's deteriorating eyesight would 'prevent his being of social use'[153]).

To conclude, aristocratic women had a considerable voice in the political affairs of the nation, in part through their engagement with the political careers of the men in their families, and in part because of the nature of the aristocratic culture which blended politics and society inextricably. While politics was in essence an aristocratic pursuit, and the political world remained small enough to be encompassed by a season's entertaining, aristocratic women were incorporated into the political culture. The broadening of the franchise and the rise of a more plutocratic society both served to marginalize aristocratic women in politics. At mid-century, national politics still had a domestic character, and the family interests of aristocratic women had political importance. At court, this situation was reversed, as the Victorian monarchy strove to put a domestic face on public, political institution.

[149] Mary Derby to William Vernon Harcourt, Oct. 1879, MS. Harcourt, dep. 208, fos. 122–33, *passim*; William Vernon Harcourt to Frank Hill, 15 Oct. 1879, MS. Harcourt, dep. 727, fo. 240. See also Mary Derby to Gladstone, 26 Oct. 1879, BL Add. MS 44,461, fos. 86–9.

[150] John Brooke and Mary Sorensen (eds.), *W. E. Gladstone*, iv: *Autobiographical Memoranda 1868–1894* (HMSO, The Prime Ministers' Papers Series, 1981), 60–2, memoranda of conversations with Lady Derby, 18 and 24 May 1882. See also Ramm (ed.), *Correspondence of Gladstone and Granville*, ii. 313–15, 370–2.

[151] Gladstone to Mary Derby, 17 May 1882, BL Add. MS 44,475, fo. 156.

[152] Mary Derby to Gladstone, 29 May 1882, BL Add. MS 44,475, fos. 205–6.

[153] Granville to Gladstone, 29 Nov. 1882, in Ramm (ed.), *Correspondence of Gladstone and Granville*, ii. 460–1.

6

'A Busy and Suspicious "Cabal" ' or 'Head Housemaids'? The Ladies of Queen Victoria's Household

In the hierarchical society of Victorian Britain, the queen represented the apex. While Victoria herself has been the subject of frequent biographical studies, both scholarly and popular, and while the institution of the monarchy itself has come under increasing scrutiny, little attention has as yet been focused on the organization which surrounded and supported the queen, the court.[1] And yet the court was of vital significance for the monarchy, for it provided the context in which the sovereign was displayed to her subjects, the channels of information (and disinformation) both to and from the monarch, and her closest personal links beyond her family. The court, in previous reigns, had an explicitly political function, and in 1837 there was small reason to assume that the new court would be any different in this respect. The changing circumstances of nineteenth-century politics, and of Victoria herself, however, meant that by the end of the reign, the political nature of the court had altered. Victoria's cultivation of a public façade of disengagement from party politics disguised her continuing active participation in government; and, in consequence, the political nature of the court was less publicly recognized, beyond the continued practice of certain officers of the household changing with the ministries.[2]

---

[1] For biographies, see Longford, *Victoria R. I.*; Cecil Woodham Smith, *Queen Victoria, Her Life and Times 1819–1861* (Hamish Hamilton, 1972); Weintraub, *Victoria*; Monica Charlot, *Victoria: The Young Queen* (Oxford: Blackwell, 1991). For works on particular aspects of Victoria's career and the monarchy, see Dorothy Thompson, *Queen Victoria: Gender and Power* (Virago, 1990); Jeffrey L. Lant, *Insubstantial Pageant: Ceremony and Confusion at Queen Victoria's Court* (Hamish Hamilton, 1979); Frank Hardie, *The Political Influence of Queen Victoria, 1861–1901* (Oxford: Oxford University Press, 1938; 1st pub. 1935); David Cannadine, 'The Context, Performance and Meaning of Ritual: The British Monarchy and the "Invention of Tradition", *c*.1820–1977', in Eric Hobsbawm and Terence Ranger (eds.), *The Invention of Tradition* (Cambridge: Cambridge University Press, 1983), 101–64; William M. Kuhn, 'Ceremony and Politics: The British Monarchy, 1871–1872', *Journal of British Studies*, 26 (Apr. 1987), 133–62, and William M. Kuhn, *Democratic Royalism: The Transformation of the British Monarchy, 1861–1914* (Macmillan, 1996).

[2] Compare, for example, the account of Victoria's daily life given in her *Leaves from a Journal of our Life in the Highlands* (Smith, Elder, 1868) which she published together with the record

Victoria herself is necessarily beyond the scope of this book; as her private secretary's son, Arthur Ponsonby, wrote: 'She bore no resemblance to an aristocratic English lady, she bore no resemblance to a wealthy middle-class Englishwoman, not to any typical princess of a German court. . . . she was simply without prefix or suffix "The Queen".'[3] She must, however, dominate any discussion of the court. With a queen regnant for the first time for more than a century, the scale of female membership of the royal household and the proximity to the sovereign assured by their sex constituted an unfamiliar situation in 1837, and one which caused considerable misgivings. The accommodation made between the gender and the rank of the sovereign had also to be made with the ladies of her household. For Victoria, the accommodation was facilitated by her preference for the role of submissive wife, which, during Albert's lifetime, handed much effective power to him. After his death, it seems plausible that the role of grieving widow which she played with such notorious enthusiasm for the next forty years provided a sufficient cloak of femininity for the political role which she was obliged to play. Much more than any of the aristocratic women discussed elsewhere in this book, Victoria shared the ideal of the private, domestic woman and the public, political man; her popularity with the middle and lower-middle classes has been attributed in great measure to this perceived identity of values.[4] At the same time, the queen's consistent shows of reluctance to appear in public and to be seen to be an active, political sovereign came in time to be viewed by her public as suitably womanly, and her eventual appearances as courageous acts. Unlike aristocratic women, then, Victoria disguised a legitimate public, political role with a show of 'feminine weakness'. To a still greater extent was her behind-the-scenes use of the royal prerogative disguised, an intriguing reversal of the usual dichotomies of public and private, domestic and political. Likewise, although her houses apparently had more in common with the aristocratic palaces discussed in Chapter 1 than with the private retreats of the bourgeoisie, within those houses the queen maintained a rigid division between her private rooms, where she spent most of her time, and the rooms in which she was a 'public person'. On first going into waiting in 1853, one of her maids of honour, Mary Bulteel, hoped to acquire a personal knowledge of the queen, but was rapidly disillusioned. Although she 'rather longed to . . . see what her tastes and occupations were,

---

of her dealings with her ministers in the same period, in *LQV*, 1st ser. See also Matthew, *Gladstone, 1809–1874*, 207–10, and Foot and Matthew, introduction to *Gladstone Diaries*, x and xi, esp. pp. clxiii–clxv.

[3] Arthur Ponsonby, *Sir Henry Ponsonby: His Life from his Letters* (Macmillan, 1942) 70.

[4] But see D. Thompson, *Queen Victoria*, 123–5.

and to get to know her opinions', she 'became accustomed to see the door leading to the Queen's rooms shut silently behind the page who came backwards and forwards for orders'.[5] The division between public and private, which had so little meaning for aristocratic women, and which, in reality, could have little meaning for the queen, was enthusiastically embraced by Victoria. Particularly after Albert's death, her rejection of Buckingham Palace for all but the most formal public occasions, her dislike of Windsor, where she was easily accessible to both politicians and visiting dignitaries (and which she once referred to as 'the Old State Prison'[6]), and her preference for Osborne and Balmoral, cut off by the sea and the distance from London, and both on a scale too small to accommodate many visitors comfortably, all pointed to her attempts to establish a physical barrier between her public and domestic personas. It also accounts for her greater ease with her domestic servants than with her courtiers: the former were the adjunct of any propertied household, while the latter were a constant reminder of her national and political role.

The court and royal household provided a few aristocratic women with paid, public employment, which was in some instances directly connected to the political administration. Here, if nowhere else, aristocratic women could explicitly and with impunity disregard the restrictions on female participation in public events and in the world of work apparently demanded by both their gender and their class. However, it will become apparent that maintaining the appearances of a separation between the queen's personal household and the political functions of the court early became an important part of the Victorian agenda, which was reinforced over time by the personal characteristics of the women appointed to the court.

In the absence of any systematic study of the Victorian court, this chapter will begin with a discussion of the structure of the queen's female household, its office-holders, and the nature of their service, before considering the changing significance of female court appointments.

STRUCTURE OF THE FEMALE HOUSEHOLD

The basic structure of the queen's female household was established shortly after the accession on 20 June 1837, and changed very little in the next sixty years. Belonging to the lord chamberlain's department, there were, from the beginning, eight ladies of the bedchamber (usually referred to as ladies-in-waiting), eight women of the bedchamber, eight maids of honour, and one mistress of the robes. The ladies were paid £500 per year, and took three

---

[5] M. Ponsonby, *Mary Ponsonby*, 2.
[6] Victoria to Anne Athole, 3 Nov. 1886, Atholl MSS, Bundle 1647.

waitings a year of a fortnight each. The maids received £300, and, waiting in pairs, spent three months a year at court. The bedchamber women also received £300 annually, and initially took their turns in residing with the queen. On Victoria's marriage in 1840, this latter position ceased to be residential, 'as I do not then require the attendance of so many ladies', and its duties were confined to ceremonial occasions.[7] This basic structure remained constant throughout the reign, although there were occasional variations: on the accession, one of the ladies-in-waiting, Lady Lansdowne, was designated 'principal lady', a post which lapsed on her resignation in 1838. At two points in the reign, 1837–9 and 1861–5, a 'resident woman of the bedchamber' was appointed; more frequently, the queen would appoint her ladies as 'extras' on their resignation.[8]

The single event which did most to determine the future form of Victoria's court was the Bedchamber Crisis of 1839, in which Peel's attempt to form a ministry to replace that of Melbourne foundered on the issue of the queen's refusal to part with any of the ladies of her household.[9] On the accession, Melbourne, as the prime minister, was charged with forming a household for the new queen. In accordance with general expectations and previous practice, he proposed members of his own party and their wives and daughters to surround the queen. Notwithstanding these expectations,[10] there was disquiet over the close connections between the court and the ministry, which came to a head in 1839. The Times pronounced that 'The household has been rigorously and emphatically, not ceremonial, but political—not an appendage to the Palace, but to the Treasury—not to the Queen's person, but to the Ministers—a plastic image of the Cabinet; not a court, but a busy and suspicious "cabal".'[11] The female household comprised not merely Whigs, but the close relations of members of the cabinet, including two wives of ministers, two sisters, two sisters-in-law, and a daughter.

[7] At the same time, the ladies of the bedchamber were informed that they would not be required to reside with the queen while she was in London, although they would still be expected for dinner. Victoria to Harriet Sutherland, 4 Dec. 1839, Royal Archives, Windsor Castle (hereafter RA), Add. A24/204. See also RA Add. A24/106 and A24/144, which suggest that during the first three years of the reign, all the ladies waited for a month at a time.

[8] Of most use in determining the structure of the court is W. A. Lindsay, The Royal Household, 1837–1897 (Kegan Paul, Trench, Trubner & Co., 1898). Lindsay gives a complete record of the appointments to the household and their dates until 1897, and biographical information on the office-holders.

[9] For a more detailed examination of the Bedchamber Crisis and female political appointments in the royal household, see K. D. Reynolds, ' "A Sharp Thorn in the Side": Queen Victoria's Mistresses of the Robes' (unpublished paper, 1993). The essential sources for the crisis are printed in LQV, 1st ser. i. 153–75 and 268–312.

[10] See e.g. Quarterly Review (June 1839), 233. [11] The Times, 13 May 1839, p. 4 col. b.

On the fall of the ministry in May 1839, Peel sought to make changes in the household, including the ladies, to end its exclusively Whig character, and to prevent the possibility of his ministry being undermined by the court. When Victoria declined to make the changes, Peel declined to pursue his attempt to form a ministry, and Melbourne was returned to power by default. By 1841, the situation had changed somewhat: the exclusively Whig character of the female household had been broken by the appointment of Mary Sandwich in July 1839, and the queen had married, and was in the process of transferring her dependence from Melbourne to her husband. More experienced in her role, through the mediation of Albert's private secretary, George Anson, Victoria arranged that the matter of the female household would not again be raised between herself and Peel, by letting it be known that the three ladies most closely connected with the Whig ministry would tender their resignations. Despite the reluctance of the duke of Bedford, his wife resigned alongside Lady Normanby as ladies-in-waiting, while Harriet Sutherland tendered her resignation as mistress of the robes.[12] From this time onwards, only the mistress of the robes was considered a political appointment, made by the sovereign and after a recommendation from the prime minister and resigning with the government. (This was to cause considerable difficulties for Gladstone in his third and fourth ministries, when no woman of suitable rank could be prevailed upon to hold the office under his home rule governments.[13])

The long-term effect of the crisis on the household was to depoliticize the female appointments; the queen insisted that they served her in a purely domestic manner, providing her with company, not political opinions, and that she 'never talked politics with them'.[14] Whatever the truth of this statement (and it will be seen that, certainly by the 1880s, it was not true in any but the most narrow understanding of the term), the outcome was the separation of the appointment of the mistress of the robes from the other female appointments and a lowering of the political temperature of the female household.[15]

---

[12] Duke of Bedford to duchess of Bedford, 11 June 1841, Royal Archives (Microfilms) (hereafter RA(M)), 'Changes of Government, Cabinet Reconstructions and Political Crises 1837–1901', C21/53; Bedford to Melbourne, 18 Aug. 1841, C21/70; Victoria to Melbourne, 31 Aug. 1841, C4/35; Harriet Sutherland to Victoria, n.d. [Sept. 1841], C21/71; Maria Normanby to Victoria, 14 Aug. 1841, C21/68.

[13] 'The Flight of the Duchesses', *Saturday Review*, 61 (1886), 601–2.

[14] Queen Victoria's journal, 9 May 1839, *LQV*, 1st ser. i. 165.

[15] It is worth bearing in mind that the male household continued to change with the ministries, with the exception of a tiny number of permanent positions, such as the keeper of the privy purse and the private secretaries.

After the initial confusion caused by the Bedchamber Crisis, the procedure by which the female household was appointed remained stable throughout the reign. With the single exception of the mistress of the robes, all the appointments were made at the queen's pleasure. By the terms of the accommodation reached with Peel in 1841, the queen would inform the prime minister of her intentions in regard to the ladies-in-waiting, 'to leave him room for objection in case he should deem their appointment injudicious to his Govt., when the Queen wd probably not appoint the Lady'.[16] In practice, this kind of consultation does not appear to have survived the Peel ministry: determined to avoid a repetition of the events of 1839 and averse to frequent changes in her household, from 1841, Victoria sought to 'choose moderate people who wd not have scruples to resign in case another Administration should come in, as changing was disagreeable to her'.[17] By 'moderate people' the queen meant women whose husbands took no prominent party-political positions, either in the House of Lords or in the cabinet. In 1841, she decided against inviting Charlotte Canning to join her household on account of her husband being under-secretary for foreign affairs, although in the following year she changed her mind.[18] But thereafter, with the exception of the mistress of the robes, the household positions were filled by women whose male relatives played no major role in the political life of the country.

Who were the women of the court? There were strikingly few of them: in the course of the sixty-three years of the reign, thirty-six women served as ladies-in-waiting, fifty-four as maids of honour, and twenty-four as women of the bedchamber.[19] In addition, two women (Mary Anne Davys and Lady Augusta Bruce) held appointments as resident women of the bedchamber, and ten women held the office of mistress of the robes. The different offices were open to women of different ranks: thus ladies of the bedchamber were wives (and increasingly, widows) of peers of the realm, while maids of honour were the unmarried daughters or granddaughters of peers. The bedchamber women were usually within the same degrees of the peerage, and were usually married women, although towards the 1880s, the queen began appointing long-serving maids of honour as women of the bedchamber, removing them from the rota of waitings which limited their attendance at court. There were, inevitably, exceptions. Harriet Lister, appointed on the accession, was the only maid of honour not to meet the criterion of rank: she

[16] Victoria to Peel, 11 May 1841, RA(M) C21/19.
[17] Victoria to Melbourne, 30 Aug. 1841, RA(M) C4/34.
[18] Victoria to Melbourne, 2 Sept. 1841, RA(M) C4/39.
[19] Lady Mount Edgecumbe and Mrs Anson both served twice, while a fifty-fifth maid of honour, Adelaide Cavendish, was never in waiting, and is hence excluded from these figures.

was, however, the sister of Lord John Russell's first wife. Similarly, Victoria's admiration for Frances Jocelyn, wife of the heir to the Roden earldom and daughter of Emily Palmerston, led her to appoint her as lady-in-waiting in 1841, commenting to Lord Melbourne (the lady's uncle) that 'She is such a delightful person & one the Queen wd so much like to have about her, & Ld Roden is sure to live 30 or 40 years longer, so that the Queen might have to wait eternally before she cd make Fanny a lady.'[20]

Court appointments were likely to be long-term commitments: of the thirty-six ladies-in-waiting, twenty held office for more than ten years, and for these twenty the average length of service was around twenty-two years. Only eight held office for less than three years, and of these, five were appointed during the initial Whig ministry. The longest-serving of the ladies were Lady Churchill (forty-six years) and the duchess of Athole (forty-three years). Only five of the women of the bedchamber resigned their appointments within five years, the remaining nineteen remaining in their posts for an average of twenty-five years. The maids of honour were most likely to serve for a short period of time: they were required to retire on marriage. The average appointment lasted nine years, rising to thirteen years if they remained at court for more than three years. For the seventeen who held their appointments for more than a decade, the average appointment lasted for twenty years.[21]

Across the reign, there was a fairly regular flow of appointments (see Table 6.1), but the general trend was towards an ageing household of long-standing courtiers. Although the new appointments, particularly as maids of

TABLE 6.1. Annual appointments to the royal household

Date	Ladies	Women	Maids
1837–50	19	9	19
1851–60	5	6	5
1861–70	5	1	8
1871–80	3	5	4
1881–90	4	2	10
1891–1900	1	2	6
Totals	37	25	52

Note: Based on information taken from W. A. Lindsay, *The Royal Household, 1837–1897* (Kegan Paul, Trench, Trubner & Co., 1898).

[20] Victoria to Melbourne, 4 Sept. 1841, RA(M) C4/42.

[21] These calculations do not take into account the six women who served as both women of the bedchamber and maids of honour—their lengths of service are included in each separate total. Horatia Stopford served from 1857 to 1901 and Harriet Phipps from 1862 to 1901 in both capacities.

honour, were generally of younger women, even a rough calculation demonstrates that, not surprisingly, the court aged with its queen (see Table 6.2).

TABLE 6.2. Average ages of Victoria's female household

Date	Ladies	Women	Maids	[Victoria]
1843	32	36	32	24
1873	51	*55	38	54
1893	*61	*60	37	74

Notes: Based on information taken from Lindsay, Royal Household. The dates of birth of two women, Viscountess Chewton and Mrs Ferguson, are unavailable: estimates have been used to complete the calculations marked with an asterisk.

At appointment, most maids of honour were aged between 21 and 25, the youngest being Sylvia Edwardes (17 at her appointment in 1897), and the oldest Amelia Murray (42 in 1837). At 21, Frances Jocelyn was the youngest woman to become a lady-in-waiting, Lady Charlemont, at 56, the oldest. Such averages, of course, disguise the great age of several of Victoria's attendants by the end of the reign: Elizabeth Waterpark retired at the age of 74, while the duchesses of Athole and of Roxburghe died in office at 83 and 81 respectively. This ageing court reflects Victoria's preference for widows— seven of her ladies-in-waiting were widowed during tenure of office, and a further nine were appointed after the deaths of their husbands. While those with living husbands outnumbered the widowed, it is significant that the latter group provided the queen's closest friends and longest-serving courtiers, including the duchesses of Athole and of Roxburghe, Jane Ely, and Jane Churchill. On the death of the duke of Athole in January 1864, the queen wrote to 'my *own* dearest duchess' as 'a *broken*-hearted Widow . . . to *one* who *now* belongs to that *saddest* of Sisterhoods'.[22] Women of the bedchamber were more likely to be widows: fourteen were widows on appointment, and a further five were widowed during their appointment. This was a result both of the queen's personal preferences and of her use of court appointments as patronage for the less fortunate among the aristocracy.

THE LADIES OF THE COURT

The Victorian court, by the end of the reign, had a reputation for strict etiquette, rigid morality, undying gloom, and unutterable tedium, which contrasted vividly with the brightly coloured social whirl of the Marlborough House set around the prince of Wales. At the beginning of the reign, this division between court and Society did not exist, and, indeed, the court had,

[22] Victoria to Anne Athole, 16 Jan. 1864, Atholl MSS, Box 61.

for some forty years, been celebrated as the pinnacle of aristocratic society and reprobated as a centre for immorality. Presentation at court was the *sine qua non* of admission to Society, and was, in the early years of the reign, essentially confined to the aristocracy, as Nancy Ellenberger's analysis of the court presentation records has shown.[23] By the end of the century, presentation had changed from being an acknowledgement of an existing personal relationship between sovereign and subject, in which the court represented merely the 'greatest house among very many great houses,'[24] to being the point at which such a relationship was established for the first time, and gave the seal of approval for the admission of the presentee to Society. Victoria's court was thus notable for the manner in which it detached itself from Society, and set itself apart from the social life of the aristocracy. None the less, large numbers of aristocrats remained willing to hold office at court, and the queen never had any difficulty in recruiting women to hold the non-political offices in her household.

At the beginning of the reign, no assumptions could be made about the tone of the court. The gender and youth of the monarch were equated iconographically with innocence and virtue, while after her marriage the predominant image became that of domestic family virtue.[25] At the same time, the queen was a Hanoverian, and perceived as the potential heir to the venality and licentiousness of her predecessors.[26] Victoria, however, fully supported attempts to claim for the court the moral high ground, instructing the mistress of the robes, Harriet Sutherland, to tell the lord chamberlain 'how *much* I rely on *him* that he will preserve the *dignity* and *morality* of my Court'.[27] Of particular concern were the maids of honour, unmarried young women, whose reputations were perceived as at risk when they were removed from parental control. In 1838 (before the unfortunate affair of Lady Flora Hastings, which led to even stricter enforcement of the regulations concerning the maids of honour[28]), Sarah Lyttelton wrote of 'the universal pursuit of keeping them [the maids] in order. Not that they are disorderly inclined, poor little things, but there is a painful recollection of doings in the last reign, which makes everybody *over*-careful now almost.'[29]

---

[23] Ellenberger, 'Transformation of London "Society" '. See also Davidoff, *Best Circles,* esp. 24–5.   [24] Davidoff, *Best Circles,* 24.

[25] See e.g. Christopher Lloyd, *The Royal Collection* (Sinclair Stevenson, 1992), esp. ch. 5.

[26] See D. Thompson, *Queen Victoria,* esp. ch. 3.

[27] Victoria to Harriet Sutherland, 10 July 1837, RA Add. A24 / 101.

[28] In which Lady Flora, one of the duchess of Kent's ladies, was accused of being pregnant, when she was in fact suffering from terminal cancer of the liver.

[29] Sarah Lyttelton to Caroline Lyttelton, 15 Oct. 1838, in Wyndham (ed.), *Correspondence of . . . Lady Lyttelton,* 283–4.

The potential dangers of court appointments were raised (only to be dismissed) in the attempt to persuade Lady Wenlock to allow her daughter to become a maid of honour in 1841:

I have heard Ly Lyttelton talk a great deal of the extreme care and surveillance that the Maids have, & I *know* that she thinks that if a girl is ever to be at Court in this capacity that she cannot be placed under better regulations or be less likely to suffer in any sense or way by her place than she would do at this Court now.[30]

In a note added to this letter, Lady Wenlock indicated that she declined the offer on her daughter's behalf, but offered assurances of her conviction of the 'happiness and complete security' of the young women at court.

Moral rectitude was thus early established as an essential qualification for women holding court appointments, as it became for their presentation at court. The prohibition of divorced women, even when they were the innocent parties, was inviolable: attempts by successive duchesses of Sutherland to get the restrictions relaxed (in favour of Mrs Caroline Norton and Mrs Effie Millais) were firmly rebuffed by the queen.[31] The only female member of the 'fast set' to hold office was Louise, duchess of Manchester, who was mistress of the robes (and hence non-resident) during Derby's short-lived ministry in 1858. However, although she was from her arrival in England (she was Hanoverian by birth) a prominent member of society, she had not by 1858 either begun her lifelong friendship with the prince of Wales or her long-standing liaison with the marquess of Hartington, whom she was to marry in 1892. The queen was initially delighted to have a German in her household, but rapidly became highly disapproving of the duchess, whom she considered had 'done more harm to Society from her *tone* . . . than almost anyone'.[32] The only other glimmer of scandal to approach the female household concerned Elizabeth Desart, whose irregular private life became a matter of such concern to the queen that she discussed with Prince Albert the possibility of bringing about her voluntary resignation (Lord Clarendon noted of her that 'she does not pretend to have been exclusively devoted to her husband'.[33]) This course of action being deemed unwise, the queen contented herself with '*not* taking her with me on any public occasion, like any journey abroad, or in the Country, & I shall certainly not pass over any thing

---

[30] Mary Lyttelton to Caroline Wenlock, 20 July 1841, Wharncliffe Muniments, WhM 486/29.

[31] Victoria to Harriet Sutherland, 19 May 1851, RA Add. A24/298 and Victoria to Anne Sutherland, 3 May 1874, Sutherland MSS (Staffs.), D593 P/28/1/30.

[32] Quoted in Philip Magnus, *King Edward the Seventh* (John Murray, 1964), 110.

[33] Kennedy (ed.), *'My Dear Duchess'*, 231.

wh. I may see, for the future—so that she may be aware of my feelings'.[34] Lady Desart resigned in 1864. Of course, a complete double standard was in operation with regard to the moral status of courtiers: the queen's permanent lord-in-waiting, Lord Torrington, conducted a long-standing affair with Andalusia Molesworth, which was well known in society and was recognized by the queen to the extent that she sent enquiries after Lady Molesworth through her lover.[35]

Moral rectitude was an inescapable requirement for the female household; but within the boundaries of Christian observance, the queen took a more latitudinarian line on religion. Preferring the Presbyterian worship of the Church of Scotland for herself, and disliking any obtrusive manifestations of religious fervour, whether high or low, her female attendants came from all branches of the established faith. Indeed, as we have seen (in Chapter 2), one of her mistresses of the robes, Charlotte Buccleuch, converted to the Roman Catholic Church in 1860 after many years of struggle. Despite Victoria's personal dislike for the high church element, both Harriet Sutherland and Charlotte Canning were devout adherents; Mary Bulteel, a maid of honour who subsequently married Sir Henry Ponsonby, the queen's private secretary, seriously considered joining an Anglican religious community.[36] The Presbyterian Ladies Erroll and Gainsborough and the duchess of Athole were more in tune with the queen's religious preferences, along with Lady Augusta Bruce, herself brought up in the Church of Scotland, but who, by her marriage to the dean of Westminster, A. P. Stanley, was aligned firmly with the broad church movement. In this respect, at least, the court was inclusive, although it can scarcely be considered representative of society at large. Piety came a long way behind morality as a prerequisite for court office.

Young women had to meet rigorous standards if they were to be considered for appointment as maids of honour at court.[37] Fluency, both written and spoken, in French and German, was essential for communication with the queen's visitors. Musical ability was required, as the maids were frequently called upon to accompany the queen, Albert, and, in later years, the princesses, on the piano. They also had to be able to ride, as they had to accompany members of the royal family. They had to have well-developed

[34] Victoria to Harriet Sutherland, 8 July 1861, RA Add. A24/75.

[35] Adburgham, Radical Aristocrat, 195, 201.

[36] Charlotte Canning to Mary Bulteel, 8 Mar. 1857, in Ponsonby, (ed.), Mary Ponsonby, 27–33.

[37] Victor Mallet (ed.), Life with Queen Victoria: Marie Mallet's Letters from Court 1887–1901 (John Murray, 1968), 4.

social skills, to enable them to converse with the queen's guests. Sir Thomas Biddulph, then master of the household, described the success of a new maid of honour, Florence Seymour, in 1864: 'She is not a bit too shy, nor the reverse, but appears at her ease, and talks nicely, quite as much as one expects from a young lady. The Queen expressed herself pleased at her manner.'[38] Most importantly, they had to be single, and likely to remain so for at least the foreseeable future, as they were obliged to resign on marriage. The queen's eventual hostility to any of her household marrying is well known: she violently objected when she learned that Lady Augusta Bruce had 'most unnecessarily, decided to *marry* (!!)', and in 1899, when her doctor and confidential adviser Sir James Reid told her of his engagement to one of her maids of honour, Susan Baring, she raged privately and refused to allow him to announce it publicly for a month.[39] The queen was particularly short-sighted about the comfort of her attendants, and rather considered service to herself to be preferable to matrimony. One observer noted that the queen gradually reconciled herself to Lady Augusta's marriage, having at first 'so "wondered that Augusta should like to give up her independence". An amusingly Royal idea. I was so thankful for poor Lady A that she was just about to acquire it.'[40] Before Albert's death, the queen was more understanding of the matrimonial ambitions of her courtiers, although she objected both to the potential subordination of her interests to those of the new spouse and family and to the inconvenience of change.[41] The queen was notoriously inconsiderate of the families of her courtiers, refusing the latter permission to visit their relatives while they were in waiting, and resenting the demands made by their children and by childbirth; in 1859 she observed that 'Lady MacDonald is to be confined I believe in the Spring—& then the *baby* will I fear be *in the way*, for 5 or 6 months'.[42]

A vacancy in the female household would often be followed by a flurry of applications for the post, to avoid which the queen developed the practice of not announcing a resignation until after the vacancy had been filled. The correspondence between the queen and her mistress of the robes, Harriet Sutherland, reveals the frequency of such applications, which required the

[38] Thomas Biddulph to Francis Seymour, 13 Aug. 1864, Seymour of Ragley MSS, CR114A/654/1.
[39] Victoria to Leopold I of the Belgians, 12 Nov. 1863, RA (M) Y110/22; Michaela Reid, *Ask Sir James* (Hodder & Stoughton, 1987), 178–89.
[40] Lady Fanny Howard to Lady Anna Maria Dawson, 23 Dec. [1863], Bod., MS. Eng. lett. c. 399, fos. 76–7.
[41] See e.g. Victoria to Harriet Sutherland, 4 Mar. 1847, RA Add. A24/244; 12 May 1857, RA Add. A24/62; and 28 Jan. 1861, RA Add. A24/364; Thomas Biddulph to Francis Seymour, Seymour of Ragley MSS, CR114A/654/2.
[42] Victoria to Harriet Sutherland, 16 Nov. 1859, RA Add. A24/70.

maintenance of lists of potential courtiers.[43] Most applications appear to have been made by parents wishing their daughters to be maids of honour, while few appear to have been made for ladies-in-waiting. The application of Lady Glenlyon (soon to become duchess of Athole) in 1845 to replace Lady Dunmore as lady-in-waiting was unsuccessful on that occasion, but was recalled in 1854, when she was appointed to succeed Lady Charlemont.[44] In 1840, Lady Charlotte Guest consulted Lady Lansdowne about court appointments, having developed 'rather a fancy to be about the Queen'; but finding that she was eligible only to be a woman of the bedchamber, and that 'that will under the present system bring me very rarely into contact with her', she pursued her enquiry no further.[45] Jane Ely's husband was keen that his wife should have a court appointment, and wrote to Francis Seymour, equerry to Prince Albert, to ascertain how best to make his approach. 'I am quite sure that nothing in this world is to be had without asking,' he commented, '& I am only anxious to know what is the proper channel through which such an application on my part should be made.'[46]

Having been brought up in isolation from aristocratic society, and maintaining that separation between court and society as queen, Victoria was in great measure reliant on persons applying for office and for the recommendations of her existing courtiers in selecting new recruits. Of very few did she have personal knowledge before the appointments were made. Fanny Jocelyn was an exception: she had been one of the queen's bridesmaids and a frequent visitor to the court under the patronage of her uncle, Lord Melbourne, and she owed her position as lady-in-waiting to the queen's personal preference.[47] Lady Lyttelton noted that 'The Queen looks upon it as a nice sugar-plum for herself to have her dear Fanny belonging to her quite.'[48]

Appointments were made after a series of informal enquiries on behalf of the queen, often by her mistress of the robes or lady-in-waiting, aimed at checking on the suitability of the candidates, and their likely response to an invitation. The queen herself took an active interest in the investigations, but did not herself correspond with candidates until she had been assured of

[43] See e.g. Victoria to Harriet Sutherland, 5 June 1853, RA Add. A24/40; 24 June 1854, RA Add. A24/44; and 3 Dec. 1856, RA Add. A24/336.

[44] Anne Glenlyon to Victoria, 31 Oct. 1845, and Victoria to Anne Glenlyon, 5 Nov. 1845, Atholl MSS, Box 61; Victoria to Anne Athole, 18 May 1854, Atholl MSS, Box 61.

[45] Bessborough (ed.), *Lady Charlotte Guest*, 110–11.

[46] Ely to Francis Seymour, n.d., Seymour of Ragley MSS, CR114A/654/3.

[47] Lady Jocelyn had in fact been hoping for an appointment for her husband, not herself: Frances Jocelyn to Melbourne, n.d. [Sept. 1841], RA(M) C22/29.

[48] Sarah Lyttelton to Caroline Lyttelton, 30 Sept. 1841, in Wyndham (ed.), *Correspondence of . . . Lady Lyttelton*, 318–19. See also Victoria to Charlotte Canning, 28 May 1842, Canning MSS, Photo Eur 321/1.

their acceptance. Intended to avoid the embarrassment which a refusal would cause to both queen and subject, the queen insisted on secrecy when approaches were declined, and became annoyed if any hint of the offer became public.[49] The queen, of course, was responsible for the selection of the replacement courtiers, deciding on their suitability and eligibility for the office in question. 'I am sorry to say that poor Miss Wemyss wd not I fear be eligible, from all what [sic] I hear,' Victoria commented in 1856, 'wh. I very much regret on acct of her poor Father's memory.'[50]

Once political considerations had ceased to play the major role in female court appointments, family connections became the single most important factor in their selection. In 1842 Victoria wrote to Susan Dalhousie that 'Tho' not personally acquainted with you, I have so high an opinion of your Family & of your Sister, Lady Douro, whom I have the pleasure of knowing, that I wish to offer you the situation of Lady of the Bedchamber'.[51] Georgiana Liddell owed her appointment as maid of honour in 1841 to her sister, Lady Normanby, whose resignation as lady-in-waiting had recently been required on the formation of Peel's ministry.[52] Horatia Stopford's parents were known to the queen, and her aunt, Lady Mary Stopford, was 'a great friend' of the queen.[53] The success of one member of a family at court could lead the queen to attempt to appoint their close relations. Charlotte Canning became a favourite of both the queen and Prince Albert after her appointment in 1842, and in 1851 the queen hoped, in vain, to engage her sister Louisa Waterford in a similar position.[54] As Victoria aged, her constitutional antipathy towards change of any kind became more pronounced, and as members of her household died or resigned, she replaced them with their relations. Louisa Antrim, lady-in-waiting from 1890, was the daughter of General Charles Grey, who had been the queen's private secretary until his death in 1870; Anne Roxburghe followed her mother-in-law Stephania Roxburghe by becoming a lady-in-waiting in 1897, having previously served as mistress of the robes. The extent to which the court became associated with particular families may be gauged by the fact that of fifty-four maids of honour, fourteen had fathers who held places in Victoria's household, four mothers, seventeen siblings, and six grandparents. If the degrees of relationship are extended to include aunts and uncles, a further twenty-seven connections can be made. To take a single example, Mary Bulteel (maid of

[49] See e.g. Victoria to Charlotte Canning, 13 July 1851, Canning MSS, Photo Eur 321/1.

[50] Victoria to Harriet Sutherland, 3 Dec. 1856, RA Add. A24/336.

[51] Victoria to Susan Dalhousie, 19 Jan. 1842, Dalhousie MSS, GD45/14/590.

[52] Bloomfield, Reminiscences, i. 119–20.

[53] Victoria to Harriet Sutherland, [12 May 1857], RA Add. A24/62.

[54] Surtees, Charlotte Canning, 184–5.

honour 1853–61) was the daughter of Lady Elizabeth Bulteel, *née* Grey, and through her mother was the niece of Lady Caroline Barrington, Louisa Durham, and General Charles Grey, all of whom held court appointments, as did General Grey's wife Caroline. Her aunt-by-marriage Theresa Grey was a bedchamber woman to the princess of Wales. Moreover, she married Henry Ponsonby, who was to become the queen's private secretary, and through him was connected to the Bessboroughs, who were also a prominent court family, and both of her sons held court appointments.

In distributing household offices, the queen had in mind her own comfort and dignity, but also a species of patronage which she could bestow on aristocratic women, in much the same way that aristocratic women would use patronage for the benefit of their own friends and dependants. No longer regarded as political patronage, the queen used her female household as, in part at least, a method of offering relief to needy aristocrats. Court appointments provided a regular and not insubstantial income, a place of residence for a significant part of the year, public dignity, and a form of employment which enhanced rather than diminished social standing. Explaining the requirements of rank in her household appointments, Victoria observed that 'the Office [maid of honour] is one wh. enables the Queen to be of use to those of the Aristocracy who are not in good circumstances'.[55]

Although the court was undoubtedly aristocratic, and although the female household was headed by a duchess, and often by a socially and politically prominent duchess, few of the appointments were held by members of the 'high' aristocracy. The embargo on political appointments naturally excluded the immediate families of aristocrats who had a high profile in the House of Lords and those who belonged to clearly defined political groupings, such as the Whig Cousinhood; while the moral standards of the court came to exclude families which took a prominent part in social leadership and the members of the Marlborough House set. The queen thus made something of a virtue of necessity in choosing members of the more obscure aristocratic families to form her female household. Among the ladies-in-waiting, prominent families were certainly represented—the duchess of Wellington (wife of the second duke) first took office as Lady Douro in 1843, and the wives of two subsequent governors-general of India, Charlotte Canning and Susan Dalhousie, held office in the 1840s. More typical were Ladies Charlemont, Dunmore, Mount Edgecumbe, and Waterpark, whose husbands made little, if any, impact on the politics of the day, and who themselves are rescued from obscurity solely on account of their offices. Of the maids of honour, only eighteen were daughters of peers or heirs to peerages, most of them obscure: Lords Lurgan, Hereford, and Strathallan, for example. The remainder were another generation removed from the peerage, and from the family wealth which descended through the eldest son.

Poverty was a reason for seeking court appointment: it lay at the root of the applications of both Lord and Lady Glenlyon (later the duke and duchess of Atholl) in 1845. Anne Glenlyon placed the income it would generate at the head of her congratulations to her husband on his appointment as a lord-in-waiting: 'I long to hear too how much you are to get for yr. services—Forgive my *mercenary* views, but I confess *they* have the greatest weight in my approbation! *Therefore* if Lord Exeter's place was a more lucrative one I should like you of course to have it.'[56] The salaries of maids of honour (£400 per year) served not only to give a degree of financial independence to young women otherwise dependent on their fathers and brothers, but also to relieve their male relatives of the provision of their board for a quarter of each year. The advice given by Lady Ravensworth to her daughter, Georgiana Liddell, when she took up her court appointment, included recommendations about the use of her salary which make clear that parental responsibility for her financial needs was being withdrawn in the face of an independent income:

The disbursement of money is rather more difficult, as you have a larger income, and of course heavier calls and responsibilities, but as a general rule I should advise you to lay out half your salary in dress; one quarter in journeys and charities, and the remaining hundred to lay out in the funds, to form a little nest egg for any future emergency.[57]

Moreover, on marriage, the queen gave her retiring maid of honour a dowry of £1,000, which could be a valuable addition to that provided by her family, at a time when financial settlements were still an important prelude to engagements.[58] In taking on financial responsibility for the maids of honour, as well as in surrounding them with the moral and social safeguards that might be expected in their family homes, the queen and the court acted as substitute families for these women. For those who did not marry and remained in royal service for many years, the court further served as their principal home. The problems of 'superfluous women' were not confined to

[56] Anne Glenlyon to Glenlyon, 3 Feb. 1846, Atholl MSS, Box 58.

[57] Lady Ravensworth to Georgiana Liddell, 2 Dec. 1841, in Bloomfield, *Reminiscences*, i. 25.

[58] Mrs Steuart Erskine (Beatrice Caroline) (ed.), *Twenty Years at Court: From the Correspondence of the Hon. Eleanor Stanley, Maid of Honour to Her Late Majesty Queen Victoria 1842–1862*, (Nisbet, 1916), 22; Joan Perkin, *Women and Marriage in Nineteenth-Century England* (Routledge, 1989), ch. 3.

the middle classes, and for a small number of less well-off aristocratic women, court appointments, and indeed court patronage, provided a measure of independence, useful employment, and a secure social status.[59] Indeed, it is arguable that, after 1861 at least, the court was one of those 'formal institutions' and 'woman-controlled spaces' which Martha Vicinus has discussed as 'alternatives to the nuclear family'.[60]

Victoria's personal empathy with the widowed and the bereaved made them the natural recipients of her patronage and appointments at court; the number of widows at court has already been remarked. Thirty-four of the fifty-four maids of honour had lost one or both of their parents (twenty-five of them fathers) before the date of their appointment, again supporting the view that court appointments were used as a means of supporting financially insecure aristocrats. However, the queen also used the appointments as a means of recognizing the widows and daughters of her own previous courtiers, and those who died on official business, and providing them with a pension. Thus the wives of Sir Charles Phipps, Sir Charles Grey, and Sir Henry Ponsonby were all appointed extra women of the bedchamber after their husbands' deaths, as was Magdalen Wellesley, the widow of the dean of Windsor. Emily Cathcart's father was killed in action at the battle of Inkerman, while Lady Chewton's husband died from wounds received at the battle of Alma. Lord Mayo, the governor-general of India, was assassinated in 1872; Lady Mayo was appointed a lady-in-waiting five months later, and was voted an annuity by parliament. Court appointments could thus also act as recognition for a male relative's services, if only after his death.

This analysis of the composition of Victoria's female household is a necessary prelude to a discussion of the nature of the services which they performed, an understanding of why aristocratic women should choose to place themselves in a subservient position, and an analysis of the relationship between gender and politics at court.

SERVICE IN THE ROYAL HOUSEHOLD

The willingness with which aristocratic women (and indeed men) accepted, and even sought, court appointments during Victoria's reign appears, at first sight, to be rather mysterious. The British aristocracy was proud of its status and lineage—indeed, many courtiers' families felt themselves to be of

[59] For the problems of single women, see Sheila Jeffreys, *The Spinster and her Enemies: Feminism and Sexuality 1890–1930* (Pandora, 1985), and Vicinus, *Independent Women*. The queen's patronage was not confined to the appointment of her courtiers. Of considerable value was her power of granting grace-and-favour residences, such as those at Hampton Court. See Vera Watson, *The Queen at Home: An Intimate Account of the Social and Domestic Life of Queen Victoria's Court* (W. H. Allen, 1952), 172–4.   [60] Vicinus, *Independent Women*, 7.

considerably more ancient and distinguished blood than the parvenu house of Saxe-Coburg-Gotha which they served. The Murray family was a case in point: 'I felt at first as if it were *infra dig of you* to be in waiting on *any body*, but upon reflection I daresay I am *wrong*,' Anne Glenlyon wrote to her husband in 1846.[61] Lord William Russell made the point still more clearly to his wife: 'I value & love the people & honour the monarchy, but I prefer my own class to either.'[62] The economic motivations discussed above go some way to accounting for the appointments of the maids of honour and of the bed-chamber women, but offer little in the way of explanation for the acceptance of office by the women who held the mistress-ship of the robes, or even by many of the ladies-in-waiting. The court was clearly diminishing in political power, and the explicit separation of the female household from govern-ment meant that after 1841 there was little obvious political advantage to be gained from court office. More importantly, Victoria's determination to be seen to stand aside from party politics, learned in the aftermath of the Bed-chamber Crisis, meant that her court, unlike that of her predecessors, did not compete with the houses of the great London hostesses to become the centre of any political party. Whigs, Tories, Liberals, and Conservatives were alike received at court, regardless of the ministry in power; and, despite the mythological nature of the queen's personal political impartiality, the Victorian court did not again acquire a popular reputation for political parti-sanship.[63] The amount of patronage wielded by the queen was increasingly circumscribed by the influence of the prime minister: the court was no longer a route to personal and family fortunes, although at the margins it could play a significant role. Likewise, while the court remained in theory the fount of honours—of garters, thistles, advances in the peerage, and new creations—in practice, these honours were generally conferred with the sanction of the government. But the queen did retain an effective power of veto in the matter of honours, which she frequently exercised, perhaps using her influence over honours as a way of balancing the decline of her preroga-tive in matters such as foreign policy. The routes to political power, wealth, and honour, which had in earlier centuries focused on the court and the sov-ereign at its centre, under Victoria were thus in the process of devolving on the cabinet and the prime minister, though much more slowly in fact than

---

[61] Anne Glenlyon to Glenlyon, 3 Feb. 1846, Atholl MSS, Box 58.

[62] Lord William Russell to Lady William Russell, 8 July 1839, in Blakiston, *Lord William Russell*, 424.

[63] Which is not, of course, to suggest that the late Victorian court was in fact anything but deeply partisan; knowledge of the depth of political feeling at court was confined to higher polit-ical circles.

Victorian constitutional historians and theorists, notably Walter Bagehot, believed.

What, then, was the attraction of court office for a woman such as Harriet, duchess of Sutherland, or Elizabeth, duchess of Wellington? Their social position was undisputed, their wealth immense, the political influence of their families considerable, their rank the highest possible, and none of these things could be enhanced by court office. Trollope has his duchess of Omnium ask her husband to make her mistress of the robes, and her husband is amazed that she 'should be so depressed by not being allowed to be the Queen's head servant'.[64] From Paris, Dorothea Lieven enquired after the impression made by Harriet Sutherland at court in 1840, saying, 'I hear that she is a little too humble, a little too much like a head-housemaid: can that be possible?'[65] The Atholes made much of their pride and dignity, but both took court office, the duchess remaining in the queen's service for forty-three years.[66] The explanation can only be based on the hierarchical nature of society in the nineteenth century. As previous chapters have sought to demonstrate, the aristocracy functioned (if only on an ideal level) within an understanding of society as a series of mutual obligations and dependencies: honour accrued to a family through its right performance of its obligations to its dependants. So far, aristocratic women have been seen at the top of the social pyramid, benevolence flowing downwards, respect flowing upwards. At court, this position was reversed. It seems likely that aristocrats were willing to burden themselves 'with the intricacies and subserviences, with the tedium and pomposities of Court life'[67] precisely because they viewed themselves as part of this ordered society: their honour and service to the queen justified their expectations of honour and service from their own dependants.[68]

The mistress of the robes had the most clearly defined set of duties, which corresponded to those of the other great offices of state. Although not a residential position, the mistress of the robes could expect a measure of personal acquaintance with the queen, which, in the case of Harriet Sutherland, her first and longest-serving mistress of the robes, translated into confidence

---

[64] Trollope, *Prime Minister*, i. 70.

[65] Dorothea Lieven to Emily Palmerston, 19 Jan. 1840, in Sudley (ed.), *Lieven–Palmerston Correspondence*, 180.

[66] See e.g. Glenlyon to Anne Glenlyon, 9 Feb. 1846, and Anne Athole to Athole, n.d. [Mar. 1848], Atholl MSS, Box 58.   [67] Trollope, *Prime Minister*, i. 58.

[68] It would require considerable research of a different kind to that undertaken here to pursue this idea further; it has also been suggested by Leonore Davidoff, 'Mastered for Life: Servant and Wife in Victorian and Edwardian England', *Journal of Social History*, 7 (Summer 1974), 411: 'Ruling groups perpetuated an image of society built on a hierarchy of service.... All had obligations to serve those above them, to show their loyalty and devotion through service.'

and friendship. Certainly until the 1880s, it was the mistress of the robes whom the queen used most frequently for her enquiries about potential courtiers, and whom she used as her intermediary in negotiating the acceptance of such offices.[69] It was also the mistress of the robes who drew up the rotas of the waitings for the ladies and maids, and who had to make contingency plans when one of the ladies could not, through illness, pregnancy, or some other reason, take her pre-arranged waitings.[70] The mistress of the robes would attend the queen on major ceremonial occasions and at levees and drawing-rooms, but most of her duties did not entail her presence at court. She was the head of the office of robes, which had a staff of four: the groom of the robes, the clerk of the robes, a messenger, and a furrier, of whom only the clerk and the messenger were in any sense permanent.[71] The original duty of the office was the purchase and maintenance of the sovereign's robes of state, which in Victoria's reign were acquired under the direction of Harriet Sutherland. In that reign, the more important duties of the office were the settlement of the queen's personal clothing bills, paying the salaries of her dressers, wardrobe maids, and hairdresser, and the issuing of the increasingly important warrants of appointment to tradespeople. While the daily administration of these tasks was the occupation of the clerk of the robes, the mistress of the robes was responsible for signing the quarterly accounts of the office and the warrants of appointment. Moreover, the letter-books of the office of robes reveal that the mistress of the robes was not infrequently drawn into the general management of the office, mediating in disputes between the clerk and the messenger in 1890, for example,[72] and making applications to the treasury for increased salaries and pensions for her staff.[73] The mistress of the robes was thus required to play both a ceremonial role in public and an active managerial role in the running of her department. By the 1880s, the drawing up of the rotas and much of the communication with the office of robes passed quietly into the hands of the queen's resident women of the bedchamber, her former maids of honour Horatia Stopford and Harriet Phipps, who were to serve unofficially as the queen's secretaries for the last twenty years of the reign.

[69] See Victoria to Harriet Sutherland, RA Add. A24, *passim*.

[70] See e.g. Victoria to Harriet Sutherland, 6 Nov. 1848, RA Add. A24/25; 30 Nov. 1853, RA Add. A24/41; and n.d. [1855?], RA Add. A24/45. See also Harriet Sutherland to Anne Atholl, 16 Mar. 1852, Atholl MSS, Box 61, and Victoria to Anne Sutherland, 23 Nov. 1873, Sutherland MSS (Staffs.), D593 P/28/1/28.

[71] The papers of the office of robes are a part of the Lord Chamberlain's Papers, PRO L.C. 13/2–5.   [72] PRO L.C. 13/5, fos. 119–20, and 125–8.

[73] Charlotte Buccleuch to the Treasury, 2 June 1846, and Anne Atholl to the Treasury, 24 June 1852, PRO L.C. 13/2.

The duties performed by the resident ladies of the court (the ladies-in-waiting and maids of honour) were seldom arduous.[74] The ladies commented more frequently on the dullness of their waitings than on the rigours, although a visit from a foreign monarch or a visit by the queen could be physically and emotionally taxing: Sarah Lyttelton commented in 1839 that 'I feel so sick of being beautifully dressed and talking French, and running up and down stairs and curtseying'.[75] The duties were essentially of attendance. The queen never went out without at least one of her female attendants, and usually two. They could be called upon to ride with her or accompany her in her carriage, or (in later years) to jog along beside her pony trap, to dine with her (although this was less frequently required during Albert's lifetime), to entertain with singing or playing the piano, or (at least in the 1840s) by joining in card-games. They would be in attendance on occasions of state, such as the opening of parliament, and at the drawing-rooms at which women were presented to the queen. They also had duties towards the queen's guests, whom they were to greet on arrival and entertain when not with the queen. During state visits by foreign monarchs, and during the queen's own visits abroad, the ladies were required to entertain the courtiers of the visitors. 'Waiting' often meant precisely that: standing in the Corridor (which was a large gallery, not a passageway) at Windsor while the queen drank coffee after dinner and made the rounds of her guests; remaining in their rooms at Windsor or Balmoral for the whole morning in case the queen should have orders for them; standing around the queen during her reception of guests. The prognostications of Lady Ravensworth were only too accurate, when she warned her daughter that 'you must accustom yourself . . . to sit or stand for hours without any amusement save the resources of your own thoughts', and that 'Your natural good sense will also show you that the least brusquerie or appearance of ennui is incompatible with high breeding and the respect due to the Sovereign'.[76] The waitings of the resident ladies were marked by their complete passivity on public occasions. For example, during the drawing-rooms, they neither spoke nor moved: they provided a backdrop for the queen, and one which became less decorative as the reign progressed; for, after Albert's death, the queen, her

[74] Courtiers were requested not to keep diaries, and were expected to be discreet in their communications with the outside world (see Erskine (ed.), *Twenty Years at Court*, 6). The main published sources for this section are Erskine (ed.), *Twenty Years at Court*; Mallet (ed.), *Life with Queen Victoria*; Surtees, *Charlotte Canning*; Wyndham (ed.), *Correspondence of . . . Lady Lyttelton*; Longford, *Louisa, Lady in Waiting*; M. Ponsonby (ed.), *Mary Ponsonby*.

[75] Sarah Lyttelton to Caroline Lyttelton, 12 Sept.1839, in Wyndham (ed.), *Correspondence of . . . Lady Lyttelton*, 291.

[76] Lady Ravensworth to Georgiana Liddell, 2 Dec. 1841, in Bloomfield, *Reminiscences*, i. 22.

ladies, and her servants never went out of mourning, although the unrelieved black of the early 1860s was relaxed to allow mauve, grey, and white. (Official court mourning, which applied to all visitors to the court, ended in 1863.) In the more private circumstances of the daily life of the royal family, the resident ladies played a more active role, participating in the entertainment of the queen and her family, accompanying them on their excursions, and performing the minor domestic services which in an ordinary aristocratic household would have been performed by a daughter, companion, or upper servant, such as picking up shawls, pinning on head-dresses, or sending messages to friends and well-wishers.[77]

In the performance of their paid duties, aristocratic women appeared to be fulfilling the 'feminine virtues' of decoration, passivity, domesticity, and silence. But the very existence of a female household, their appointments recorded in the *London Gazette*, their coming in and going out of waiting recorded daily in the court columns of the newspapers (then normally printed on the leader page), and their daily activities likewise reported for public consumption, undermined the notion of their conformity to any ideal of feminine exclusion from the public and political world. The very domesticity of Victoria's court disguised the active participation of the queen in the government of the country and, from 1880, her hostility towards Gladstone's Liberal administrations. It also disguised the role the female household played in reinforcing the queen's political prejudices.

INFLUENCE AT COURT

'Influence' at court has always been regarded as a significant factor in British politics in all eras except the modern one initiated by Victoria's reign. While effective authority remained in great degree in the hands of the sovereign, proximity to the person of the monarch, and the access to the king or queen's ear which it entailed, was sought as a necessity by all those seeking to influence events or to enhance their own standing. Courtiers, and, in particular, those with the constant access occasioned by membership of the royal household, were thus well placed either to accrue influence on their own behalf or to act as intermediaries and patrons for less favourably positioned friends and relatives.[78] The extent to which such influence was legitimate is a question that has exercised the minds of historians and political

---

[77] See e.g. Wyndham (ed.), *Correspondence of . . . Lady Lyttelton*, 286–8; Katharine Bruce to Anne Athole, 12 Jan. 1864, and Jane Ely to Anne Athole, 29 Apr. 1872, Atholl MSS, Box 61.

[78] In the French court of Louis XIV, the king used the court as an instrument for the direct rule of his nobles and the moderation of their political ambitions: see Elias, *Court Society*.

theorists from the Middle Ages onwards. Wherever the boundaries of legitimacy have been placed, the influence wielded by women at court—whether consorts, mistresses, mothers, or courtiers—has been regarded with almost uniform suspicion.

The immediate precedents at the time of Victoria's accession were not propitious for those who feared the influence of women over the sovereign. George IV's reign, and the regency which preceded it, had been increasingly dominated by his obsession with his current mistress: by the late 1820s, he could scarcely be prevailed upon to fulfil his most basic duties without the sanction of Elizabeth Conyngham.[79] William IV, having cast off his mistress of many years, kept his illegitimate family around him, and bestowed considerable patronage on them, while his wife, Adelaide, was suspected of influencing him against the Reform Bill.[80] The most recent precedent of a queen regnant was still less encouraging, for Anne's reign had been marked as much by the feuds between her female courtiers as by the disputes between her male ministers.[81] Whether for political manoeuvrings, sexual intrigue, or simple venality, female influence at the British court was regarded with deep suspicion, tinged with alarm born of the belief that it was the illegitimate influence of women at Louis XVI's court that had triggered the French Revolution in 1789.

Such was the background to Victoria's accession in 1837, and the source of the fears and alarms which exploded during the Bedchamber Crisis two years later. There was no necessity to prove that Ladies Normanby and Tavistock were seeking to influence the queen in favour of their husbands' policies: it was enough to know that they were in a position to do so. Peel made the ladies an indicator of the queen's personal and political confidence in his ministry, a confidence which did not exist in fact, and which, at this stage, the young queen was unwilling to feign.[82] The press seized on the issue of female influence, but took care to attribute all political motivations to the men behind them: Melbourne was criticized for his original formation of an exclusively Whig household for the queen. *The Times* fulminated that 'The appointments were one and all in such a manner that the Queen should see nothing, and hear nothing, have access to no intelligence, observation, complaint or warning,—that she should receive no impressions of any kind

[79] See e.g. Christopher Hibbert, *The Court at Windsor: A domestic History* (Longmans, 1964), 154–7.

[80] See e.g. Dorothea Lieven to Emily Cowper, 18 Sept. 1832, in Sudley (ed.), *Lieven–Palmerston Correspondence*, 35–6; Keppel, *Sovereign Lady*, 292.

[81] Harris, *A Passion for Government*; R. O. Bucholz, ' "Nothing but Ceremony": Queen Anne and the Limitations of Royal Power', *Journal of British Studies*, 30 (July 1991), 288–323.

[82] Peel to Victoria, 10 May 1839, *LQV*, 1st ser. i. 169.

with regard to persons, principles, character or facts, save only through such channels as were at the devotion of the Minister.'[83] It went on to describe Lady Normanby as 'locked, like an indissoluble nightmare, round Her Majesty, as the confidential instrument and devoted agent of the most reckless and licentious revolutionist within the British Empire [i.e. Lord Normanby]'.[84] Lord Morpeth's sisters, Lady Burlington and Harriet Sutherland, were likewise accused of being placed 'as *videttes* [spies]'in the court, to observe and undermine the policy of any Tory ministry. The greatest fear was that, through the ladies of the court, the Whigs would form 'a closet camarilla about the Queen, after the ostensible demise of the outward Cabinet'.[85] The retention of the ladies of leading opposition families about the queen would be read as a signal to parliament and the public that the ministry did not have the queen's confidence, 'whilst her *female advisers* at the Palace would, under directions from their husbands and brothers, have directed in the Palace boudoir all their attacks as an Opposition, *ostensibly* and *palpably* receiving the support of the Court'.[86]

Throughout the affair, the queen denied discussing politics with her ladies, and asked: 'Was Sir Robert so weak that *even* the Ladies must be of his opinion?'[87] She was alone in her assumption that the political complexion of the female household had no political significance. There is little to be gained here from discussing whether these particular ladies did aim to, or did succeed in influencing the politics of the new monarch, not least because the sway of Melbourne with the queen was so great that he had little need of support from outside sources, although his government was in a very weak position by 1839.[88] The important point was that it was widely believed that they could influence the queen, and that such influence could have a significant impact on the political affairs of the country. By the end of the reign, neither viewpoint was current beyond the political and court circles who had most invested in shrouding the involvement of the palace in politics in mystery.

The ending of the political affiliation of the female household with the ministry in 1841, coinciding with Victoria's marriage in the previous year, closed the public debate on female influence at court. Her regular pregnancies and increasing reliance on Albert's political judgement almost reduced Victoria to a cipher between 1840 and 1861, during which time the male

---

[83] *The Times*, 13 May 1839, p. 4 col. b.   [84] Ibid. col. c.

[85] *The Times*, 11 May 1839, p. 4 col. c; *The Times*, 13 May 1839, p. 4 cols. b–c.

[86] *The Standard*, 11 May 1839, quoted in *The Times*, 13 May 1839, p. 4 col.e.

[87] Queen Victoria's Journal, 9 May 1839, LQV, 1st ser. i. 166.

[88] Charlot, *Victoria*, chs. 6–8; Longford, *Victoria R. I.*, ch. 9.

household, particularly the keepers of the privy purse, General Charles Grey, Sir Thomas Biddulph, and Sir Charles Phipps, was firmly entrenched as the queen's political staff, to the exclusion of the ladies.[89] Moreover, Albert's early resolution to distance himself from the women of the court was rigorously implemented, thereby restricting the possibilities for gossip and political intrigue.[90] During these years the appointment of the mistress of the robes (the only one to retain a political character) was entirely without political acrimony: Harriet Sutherland served in all Whig and Liberal ministries until the death of her husband in 1861, with the duchesses of Buccleuch, Athole, and Manchester serving in the successive Conservative administrations.

The ladies of the household only became an issue again after Albert's death, when, during the queen's long seclusion, they almost alone had privileged access to the queen. It was during this period that Victoria developed the practice of using her ladies as go-betweens, to spare herself from low-level political interviews, and even to avoid direct contact with her male household.[91] Certain of the ladies in the household, most notably Jane, Lady Ely, and after her Horatia Stopford and Harriet Phipps, became recognized as agents of the queen. The extent to which they were privy to political secrets is difficult to ascertain: none of their papers have been traced, and it is known that Harriet Phipps at least had all hers destroyed on her death.[92] It is clear from other sources that these ladies, and also Jane, Lady Churchill, were used extensively by the queen in the regulation of the household, and by members of the household who wanted the queen's personal approval for a course of action.[93] Their involvement in the queen's political business is not to be doubted. One occasion on which the queen used Lady Ely was noted by Henry Ponsonby, the queen's private secretary, in 1877, during the resurgence of the eastern question. He told his wife that 'The Queen evidently distrusts me in that particular and shows me only parts of her discussions with Beaconsfield. This of course is quite right, but what I might be hurt about is that she employs Lady Ely to write to Monty Corry [Beaconsfield's secretary].'[94] After Gladstone's return to power in 1880, the queen wanted to maintain her contact with the sympathetic former prime minister, and proposed a circuitous route to Ponsonby: he was to use Lady Ely as

---

[89] Thompson, *Queen Victoria*, ch. 3.   [90] See Ponsonby (ed.), *Mary Ponsonby*, 4.

[91] She also used lower-ranking women to carry messages to members of the household, who often resented this manner of proceeding. Sir Thomas Biddulph was put out to be informed of Derby's resignation by the French governess: Ponsonby, *Henry Ponsonby*, 54.

[92] Mallet (ed.), *Life with Queen Victoria*, 2.

[93] See e.g. Ponsonby, *Henry Ponsonby*, 58; Weintraub, *Victoria*, 397–8, and Reid, *Ask Sir James*, 80.   [94] Ponsonby, *Henry Ponsonby*, 166. See also Weintraub, *Victoria*, 426–7.

his go-between, who would write to Corry, who would in turn pass on his information to Beaconsfield. Ponsonby refused, and the queen circumvented him entirely, by recommending that Corry correspond with Prince Leopold or Horatia Stopford, who were described as 'all quite safe'.[95] The examples of the queen's use of Lady Ely as a go-between could be multiplied, as could examples of the use made by politicians of Lady Ely as a source of information for the activities of the court.[96] But to do so would do little to explain why, forty years or so after the great outcries about female influence, this new generation of court women with unprecedented access to the queen and her confidence, were allowed to carry on unremarked.

One explanation is the divorce between parliamentary politics and the female court. The preponderance of widows among the queen's favoured ladies enhanced the feeling that these were women with no direct connections to any political party, who could therefore be assumed to be serving the queen in a spirit of personal, not party, loyalty. A second explanation lies in the characters and personalities of the women in whom the queen confided. Discretion was the byword of the court, and most courtiers were punctilious in its observance: the chances of knowledge of the roles played by female courtiers coming to the attention of those who might be expected to object to 'female influence' were slight.[97] Moreover, the queen's chosen agents were personally implausible as manipulators of the political world. Jane Ely, in particular, was shy, nervous, easily bullied, and completely intimidated by the queen, whom she served beyond the limits of her capacities and physical strength.[98] Even before she came to occupy such an important place in the household, Lady Ely's limitations were recognized by the maids of honour. Mary Bulteel wrote, on the occasion of a visit to the French court in 1855, that 'Lady E. is more utterly the reverse from what she ought to be on this occasion than anybody can possibly conceive. I mean, I see she is preparing to be foolishly cringing to all the little miseries of etiquette . . . I quite long for somebody as the Queen's first lady with more natural dignity.'[99] If her nervousness were insufficient evidence of her inadequacy as an intriguer, her habit of communicating in 'mysterious whisperings' which

---

[95] Victoria to Disraeli, 26 Apr. 1880, quoted in Longford, Victoria R. I., 436.

[96] See e.g. Longford, Victoria R. I., 470, 483, 490; Kennedy, 'My Dear Duchess', contains frequent references to Clarendon's conversations with Lady Ely, e.g. 72, 110–11, 136,152.

[97] Such objectors might include those committed to the restriction of the sovereign's political role and those seeking a more accountable political structure, as well as those who held the prevailing assumptions about femininity and female incapacity.

[98] Ponsonby, Henry Ponsonby, 57–8.

[99] Mary Bulteel to Lady Elizabeth Bulteel, Aug. 1855, quoted in Ponsonby, Mary Ponsonby, 18.

her listeners could not decipher must stand as proof. In 1875, Disraeli sat next to 'Dearest Jane' at dinner at Windsor, where 'She told me many secrets, but alas! had they been in the tongue of the dwellers at Suez, they could not be more unintelligible. It is provoking to be told, in confidence, something which she could only tell to me, and not catch a word.'[100] Lady Churchill does not appear to have had a role beyond the confines of the household, but she too stood in too much awe of the queen to have been useful for any political machinations; while Harriet Phipps belonged to a dynasty of courtiers, whose loyalties were to the queen and the court rather than to any political faction. The queen thus chose as her confidantes, whether deliberately or not cannot be determined, women who were attached to her personally, and who entirely subordinated themselves to the performance of her wishes.

Above all, there had been a sea change in the debate on the role of the court. By the time Victoria ended her long seclusion in the 1870s, the central question relating to the politics of the court was not who exercised influence over the queen, or the legitimacy and extent of that influence, but the degree to which the queen herself had a right to intervene in the political affairs of the nation at all. The widely divergent views of the queen and her ministers on this point were kept from the public with great success until after Victoria's death.[101] Only Gladstone and Granville knew the full extent of her partisan hostility to Liberal governments, and they, for their own political reasons, were careful to exclude radical members of Liberal cabinets from this knowledge. Under these circumstances, the queen herself was the essential political problem: her chosen agents might cause inconvenience or annoyance, but they were viewed as symptomatic, not the cause, of the difficulties engendered by an ageing, widowed queen who retained a view of her own political function which was less and less shared by her ministers.

None the less, it would be a mistake to discount entirely the influence of the court on the queen as a matter of political significance, even while acknowledging the difficulties inherent in attempting to chart such influence. There were two moments during this later phase of the reign when the actions and opinions of the female household may be seen as having had an impact on the actions of the queen, and hence of having been of political sig-

[100] Disraeli to Lady Bradford, 26 Nov. 1875, in Zetland (ed.), *Letters to Ladies Bradford and Chesterfield*, i. 307. See also Ponsonby, *Henry Ponsonby*, 57.

[101] Walter Bagehot's view of her role in *The English Constitution* (1867) was widely taken as a reflection of the real situation until the publication of her letters between 1907 and 1932. The extent of her interventionism then revealed was a source of surprise and indignation. See e.g. Hardie, *Political Influence of Queen Victoria*, and Kingsley Martin, '*Imperium et libertas*', *Edinburgh Review*, 247 (Jan. 1928), 178–201.

nificance. The first was during the seclusion, the second in her fraught relationship with Gladstone and the Liberals in the last twenty years of the reign.

The decade of the queen's seclusion was vital in establishing some, at least, of the ladies of the household as the queen's agents. What in the early months of her bereavement had been a natural preference for those who had been with her at Albert's deathbed hardened into an active withdrawal from those who had not been there.[102] Lady Augusta Bruce and Anne Athol were in attendance, and Harriet Sutherland, whose own husband had died in the previous February, was sent for the following day.[103] The marriage of Princess Alice in 1862 removed the queen's only daughter of an age to be confided in, and upon whom much of the burden of the queen's incapacity had fallen.[104] Lady Augusta, resident woman of the bedchamber since the death of her previous mistress, the duchess of Kent, was to be the first of the queen's ladies to take on secretarial duties.[105] Although she ceased to be resident on her marriage in 1863, she retained a position in the household, and continued to correspond with the queen, offering a channel of information between the queen and the broad church, in the person of her husband, A. P. Stanley.[106] In 1868, on a visit to Ireland, she took the opportunity of urging the queen to visit that country, for the advantages to be gained by creating for Ireland the same sort of popularity as the queen's patronage had created in Scotland and the personal popularity of the royal family; the subtext seems to suggest that Lady Augusta was encouraging not merely a visit to Ireland, but a public visit anywhere to restore the queen's fading popularity. (She was, of course, unsuccessful. [107]) Princess Louise's marriage in 1871 was the immediate cause of the queen's invitation to Jane Ely 'to live as much with me as she can,—as without some one Lady whom I know long & intimately being a gt. deal with me I do not know what I shd. do'.[108]

Harriet Sutherland's role during the seclusion (the end of which she did not live to see) was more explicitly concerned with attempts to encourage

---

[102] This preference encompassed those who had also been present at the death of her mother, the duchess of Kent, in April 1861, who included Jane Ely and Augusta Bruce. See A. V. Baillie and Hector Bolitho (eds.), *Letters of Lady Augusta Stanley: A Young Lady at Court 1849–1863* (Gerald Howe, 1927), 196.

[103] Harriet Sutherland to Gladstone, 17 Dec. 1861, BL Add. MS 44,325, fos. 266–73.

[104] See e.g. Kennedy, *'My Dear Duchess'*, 196–7.

[105] 'We both watched & wept thro' that dreadful night & morning [of the duchess of Kent's death], & this is a powerful tie between us': Victoria to Harriet Sutherland, 8 Apr. 1861, RA Add. A24/74.

[106] See e.g. Lady Augusta Stanley to Victoria, n.d. [1870], Augusta Stanley MSS, vol. 2 (not foliated). On Lady Augusta's death, the queen wrote in her journal, 2 Mar. 1876, 'She used to write such interesting letters and knew so many interesting people': *LQV*, 2nd ser. ii. 449.

[107] Lady Augusta Stanley to Victoria, 3 Oct. 1868, Augusta Stanley MSS, vol. 2.

[108] Victoria to Anne Sutherland, 10 Nov. 1870, Sutherland MSS (Staffs.), D593 P/28/1/15a.

the queen's return to an active public role, and is evident in her correspondence with Gladstone at this time. The duchess had long enjoyed a confidential friendship with the queen, boosted by her immense respect for Prince Albert. One of the original Whig household, she retained her sense of the political importance of the Crown. On her first attempt to resign in February 1861, she wrote to Gladstone of the 'importance of being near the Queen & The Prince—& in the privilege of place & intimacy— & the power of saying what one feels to be right'.[109] It is impossible to gauge the influence of the duchess on the queen from the extant correspondence, although it is clear that the duchess was unable to persuade the queen of the merits of either Garibaldi or Gladstone, both of whom the duchess fêted. The queen considered the former a revolutionary of suspect motives, and Harriet Sutherland 'half-crazed' for her reception of him at Stafford House.[110] As for Gladstone, Clarendon recorded that 'The Queen mimicked her [Harriet Sutherland] when she talked of her adoration of Gladstone.'[111]

In the months after Albert's death, Gladstone and the duchess corresponded frequently on the subject of the queen and her response to her bereavement. In February, Gladstone wrote: 'We cannot afford to create an intense degree of pity for the Woman at the cost of her character as a Queen.'[112] The duchess's reply sought to allay his fears that the queen was in danger of being seen to want 'balance and measure': that is, that the prince's death had brought out the family tendency towards insanity, by treating the queen as a national, universal symbol of mourning womanhood: 'It is *The* Widow speaking to Her Children.'[113] But by March, the duchess was beginning to share his concerns, and after an outpouring from the queen wrote: 'This is discouraging—it will remind you of what you heard of the first—& we cannot see improvement.'[114] It is impossible to document how far the duchess articulated her concerns to the queen, but it seems unlikely that she would fail to 'say what was right', and to encourage the queen to resume her public duties.

A similar problem of documentation exists in regard to Anne Athole, as Frank Hardie noted when recording the *Quarterly Review*'s opinion that 'the influence of the Duchess of Atholl upon the Queen was unique. No one, perhaps, ever charmed her Royal Mistress so completely.'[115] The duchess is a

[109] Harriet Sutherland to Gladstone, [13 Feb. 1861], BL Add. MS 44,325, fos. 80–3.
[110] Longford, *Victoria R. I.*, 363–4; Victoria to Harriet Sutherland, 18 Apr. 1864, RA Add. A24/78.
[111] Kennedy, 'My Dear Duchess', 67.
[112] Gladstone to Harriet Sutherland, 24 Feb. 1862, BL Add. MS 44,326, fos. 44–5.
[113] Harriet Sutherland to Gladstone, 26 Feb. 1862, BL Add. MS 44,326, fos. 46–51.
[114] Harriet Sutherland to Gladstone, 3 Mar. 1862, BL Add. MS 44,326, fos. 68–71.
[115] Hardie, *Political Influence of Queen Victoria*, 227.

shadowy figure in all the biographies of the queen, and is never given the prominence of Jane Ely or Jane Churchill. Yet she was one of the longest-serving of the courtiers, whom the queen refused to allow to resign,[116] and on whose house in Dunkeld the queen conferred the unusual distinction of several personal visits. Indeed, before Albert took that office on himself, the queen had asked the duchess to be chief mourner at the funeral of the duchess of Kent.[117] The existing correspondence between the queen and the duchess reveals a great measure of confidence, but little explicitly political material. The one letter which survives in which the duchess offers advice to the queen is a carefully drafted document, expressing reservations about the wisdom of the marriage of the Princess Louise to a commoner (the heir to the dukedom of Argyll). The revealing point is less the subject of the letter than the duchess's comment that 'as Your Majesty has always graciously allowed me to say what I really think, I should not feel myself honest, if on this momentous occasion, I entirely abstained from so doing'.[118] The substance of Anne Athole's advice on other subjects will probably never be known. A comment made by Mary Ponsonby, however, suggests that she was skilful in her management of the queen:

Had a long talk with the Duchess of Atholl; she understands everything, and nothing can be truer than all her views about things. The complete folly of opposition if started at once, without any care, and the ease with which advice may be given and received if you don't begin in antagonism.[119]

The avoidance of antagonism was impossible for the Liberal governments of the 1880s and 1890s. The queen's hostility to Gladstone was intense, and attributable not merely to their incompatible personalities but to profound political differences. The court, and the female household in particular, can scarcely be held responsible for this incompatibility, although it is undeniably true that the permanent household had taken on a predominantly Conservative aspect during the 1870s, notwithstanding the presence of her Whiggish private secretary and his radical wife.[120] Although the ladies of the household had no explicit connections with political parties, it would be a mistake to assume that they were so far removed from aristocratic society as to be without political opinions. As with the political hostesses, those opinions bore more on personalities than on policies. In 1839, Lady Louisa

---

[116] Victoria to Anne Athole, 13 Dec. 1890, Atholl MSS, Bundle 1648.
[117] Anne Athole to Athole, 18 Mar. 1861, Atholl MSS, Box 61.
[118] Anne Athole to Victoria, 14 Oct. 1870, Atholl MSS, Box 61.
[119] Mary Ponsonby's diary, 8 Feb. 1868, in Ponsonby (ed.), *Mary Ponsonby*, 62–3.
[120] Longford, *Victoria R. I.*, 346–7.

Stuart had written a letter of advice to her niece, Lady Anna Maria Dawson, then going into waiting on the duchess of Kent, cautioning her

> never to say a careless word that can injure another, or throw ridicule of any sort on their neighbours . . . if once a prejudice gets into a Royal head, it can never be got out again to the end of time. Princes form a class apart; they do not, like us, mingle with the world and hear different opinions, nor does anybody venture to contradict theirs; so impressions upon them, once made, are indelible.[121]

The awe and veneration with which most of the female household regarded the queen in the last twenty years of her reign—so different from the familiar, mocking references to 'Eliza and Joseph' of the 1850s[122]—were certainly not conducive to the encouragement of political debate or difference. The home rule crisis and the consequent split in the Liberal party reduced still further the possibility of pro-Liberal views being expressed at court, even when the Liberals were in power, owing to the virtual desertion of the party by the aristocracy. This was the cause of considerable difficulties for Gladstone, even in filling some of the offices around the queen, most particularly that of mistress of the robes, which went into abeyance during his 1886 and 1892–4 ministries. Gladstone himself called the queen's attention to the absence of Liberal opinion 'in the powerful social circles with which Your Majesty has ordinary personal intercourse', and the danger this caused to the future of the monarchy.[123] Sir Henry Ponsonby had noted in the previous decade that

> not a day passes without some crime being attributed to the Government—some sneer uttered about them or some *denigréing* remark, most of which go to the Queen and set her against the Ministers. Perhaps now it does not really matter whether the Queen dislikes them or not, but I think Sir R. Peel was right in insisting that the ladies of the bedchamber should change with the Government. Incessant sneers or conversation against a policy always damages. I must say the Queen says as little as possible, but one can't help seeing that she is impressed by it.[124]

The ladies of the court ended the reign, then, by doing precisely what was feared of them at its beginning: acting as a 'closet camarilla', a party at court opposed to the ostensible government. That they did so without design and without the impetus of husbands and brothers with political careers to make, and that they lacked any particular purpose, made little difference to

---

[121] Lady Louisa Stuart to Lady Anna Maria Dawson, 25 Sept. 1835, in Erskine (ed.), *Twenty Years at Court*, 23–4.
[122] Kennedy, *'My Dear Duchess'*, *passim*.
[123] Quoted in Matthew, *Gladstone Diaries*, introduction to vols. 12 and 13, p. lxxiv.
[124] Henry Ponsonby to Mary Ponsonby, 23 Apr. 1873, in Ponsonby, *Henry Ponsonby*, 154.

the effects of their interventions. The lack of explicit party ties among the ladies of the court—or the equation between the Conservative/Unionist interest and a supposedly 'non-political' national interest which emerged in this period—served only to enhance their personal loyalty to the queen and, during the later part of her reign, their constant reinforcement of the prejudices of the sovereign.

Service in the royal household thus offers an intriguing and revealing counterpoint to the other activities of aristocratic women. Again, their situation derived from their peculiar combination of class and gender. Their social status was important for maintaining the prestige of the monarchy— the obeisances of the lowly could be taken for granted, but those of people of rank served both to inflate the honour of the monarchy and to remind the aristocracy of their inferiority to the throne. When Sarah Lyttelton described the female household as 'we menials',[125] she highlighted the apparent contradiction between her status within the royal household and her status in the rest of society. In terms of gender, service in the royal household embodied a breakdown in the concepts of 'public' and 'private': as in their own homes, the private had public significance, while the public (in this case, the fact of their salaried employment, their position as the confidential servants of the monarch, and the public attention which their position entailed) was manifested in a private, domestic setting.

[125] Sarah Lyttelton to Caroline Lyttelton, 3 June 1844, in Wyndham (ed.), *Correspondence of Lady Lyttelton*, 345.

Conclusion

What I most desire, is to see married women of the *middle classes* stand on the same terms of equality as prevail in the working classes and the highest aristocracy. A *great lady* or a *factory woman* are independent persons—personages—the women of the middle classes are nobodies, and if they act for themselves they lose caste!

Lydia Becker, in Lewis, *Women in England 1870–1950*

This book has sought, through an examination of the lives of aristocratic women during the first forty years of Victoria's reign, to propose a reading of aristocratic political society which does not rest on a notion of 'separate spheres', and in which women played an active part. Lydia Becker's statement about the independence and equality of women of the highest aristocracy is a rhetorical exaggeration. It has not been my intention to attempt to demonstrate that these women played the same roles as men in the life of the aristocracy, or that they were able to live their lives independently of male authority and power. Rather, I have tried to show that aristocratic women were actively engaged (or 'incorporated') in the pursuits of their families—whether on their estates, in local institutions, in national politics, or at the court—in partnership with the other members of their families. As women, the nature of their involvement differed from that of men of the same class, but as aristocrats, their interests were shared. Unlike other Victorian institutions, a working aristocracy required women as well as men to function fully, and not simply for the hereditary dimension.

Politics, whether national or local, was the motivating force of aristocratic society: it determined the timetable of social life, and provided the predominant occupation of the men of the class and the topics for conversation at dinners, parties, and country-house visits. The maintenance of the social and political dominance of the landed classes, and the enhancement of the status of particular families in the social hierarchy, underpinned aristocratic activity, and in these projects women played significant roles. Identifying primarily with their class rather than their gender, aristocratic women in the high Victorian years had little to gain from taking up any of the demands of the women's movement: as members of a politically effective, socially dominant, economically superior aristocracy, women had a series of roles and functions which gave content and meaning to their lives, and in which they appear to have found personal fulfilment. Any increase in the electorate, whether from women's votes or from working-class votes, diminished the political importance of the aristocracy, and muted the voice of the aristocratic woman.

Aristocratic women did not operate in a 'separate sphere'; nor were they rigidly defined by any notion of femininity. Their public and private lives intertwined to such a degree that it is not useful to seek to unravel them. It is more constructive to regard them as an integral part of an aristocratic culture in which they had some roles, such as those of wives and mothers, which were essentially defined by their gender, and other roles, which have been the subject of this book, which were the consequence of their membership of the aristocracy.

Biographical Appendix

Entries are listed under the title by which the subject appears most frequently in this book; other names and titles by which they are known are given in the entries.

LOUISA, COUNTESS OF ANTRIM

Born Louisa Grey in 1855, she was the daughter of the queen's private secretary, General Charles Grey, and Caroline Farquhar, who after Grey's death was appointed a woman of the bedchamber. Louisa married William McDonnell (1851–1918), sixth earl of Antrim in 1875; her own appointment, in the family tradition, as lady of the bedchamber in 1890, enabled her to spend a certain amount of time each year away from her erratic and hot-tempered husband. She served Queen Alexandra in a similar capacity, and died in 1949. Main residence: Glenarm Castle, Larne, Co. Antrim.

ELIZABETH, DUCHESS OF ARGYLL

Born Lady Elizabeth Leveson-Gower in 1824, the eldest daughter of George, second duke of Sutherland, and Lady Harriet Howard, she shared her mother's religious and philanthropic interests, and followed her as mistress of the robes (1868–70) in Gladstone's first administration. She married George Campbell (1823–1900), marquess of Lorne in 1844 (he became eighth duke of Argyll in 1847), and shared his liberal political interests. Having had twelve children, her health collapsed in 1870, and she died in 1878. Main residences: Argyll Lodge, Campden Hill, Kensington; Inverary Castle, Argyllshire; Roseneath, Dumbartonshire.

ANNE, DUCHESS OF ATHOLE

Born Anne Home Drummond in 1814, the daughter of Henry Home Drummond and Christian Moray, in 1839 she married George Murray (1814–64), baron Glenlyon, who in 1846 succeeded as sixth duke of Athole. Appointed mistress of the robes in Lord Derby's short-lived ministry of 1852, from 1854 until her death in 1897 she served as a lady of the bedchamber to the queen, and appears to have been one of her most trusted attendants and closest friends. Main residences: Blair Castle and Dunkeld House, Perthshire.

LOUISA, DUCHESS OF ATHOLE

Born Louisa Moncrieffe in about 1844, the eldest daughter of Sir Thomas Moncrieffe, seventh baronet, and Lady Louisa Hay. In 1864 she married John Murray (Stewart-Murray from 1865) (1840–1917), marquess of Tullibardine; Iain, as he was known to his family, became seventh duke of Athole the next year. Hers was a family-centred life, based on the family's Perthshire estates and the social round of the London season, especially in the 1880s and 1890s, when the futures of her three daughters were her prime concern. She died on a continental tour in 1902. Main residences: Blair Castle, Perthshire, and 84 Eaton Place, London.

CONSTANCE, LADY BATTERSEA

Born in 1843, elder daughter of Sir Anthony de Rothschild and Louisa Montefiore, in 1877 she married Cyril Flower (1843–1907), Liberal MP and party whip. He was created Baron Battersea in 1892. Lady Battersea was an active promoter of her husband's political career and an active philanthropist. She died in 1941. Main residences: 7 Hyde Park Place, London, and Aston Clinton, Buckinghamshire.

GEORGINA, LADY BLOOMFIELD

Born the hon. Georgina Liddell in 1822, she was the daughter of Thomas Liddell, first baron Ravensworth, and Maria Simpson. She was appointed a maid of honour to the queen in 1841, resigning on her marriage in 1845 to John Bloomfield (1802–79), who succeeded as second baron Bloomfield in 1846. She subsequently accompanied her husband on his diplomatic appointments to St Petersburg and Vienna, and in 1883 published *Reminiscences of Court and Diplomatic Life*. She died in 1905. Main residences: various European embassies; Ciamaltha, Newport, Co. Tipperary; Bramfield House, Hertfordshire.

CHARLOTTE, DUCHESS OF BUCCLEUCH

Born Lady Charlotte Thynne in 1811, daughter of Thomas Thynne, second marquess of Bath, and the hon. Isabella Byng. In 1829 she married Walter Montagu-Douglas-Scott (1806–84), fifth duke of Buccleuch and seventh duke of Queensberry. She served as mistress of the robes in Sir Robert Peel's conservative ministry (1841–6). Profoundly religious, after some twenty years of doubt she converted to the Roman Catholic Church in 1860. She died in 1895. Main residences: Dalkeith Palace, near Edinburgh; Drumlanrig Castle, Dumfriesshire; Bowhill, Selkirkshire; Boughton House, near Kettering, Northamptonshire; Montagu House, Whitehall Gardens, London.

BEATRIX, COUNTESS CADOGAN

Born Lady Beatrix Craven in 1844, she was the daughter of William, second earl of Craven, and Lady Emily Grimston. In 1865 she married George Cadogan (1840–1915), who became viscount Chelsea the next year, and succeeded as fifth earl Cadogan in 1873. Her husband was somewhat wayward, a conservative politician, and a member of the circle surrounding the prince of Wales. Lady Cadogan interested herself in household management, which was complicated by the absence of a regular country estate, and in charitable activities. She had seven sons and two daughters, and died in 1907. Main residences: Chelsea House, Cadogan Place, London, and Babraham Hall, Cambridge, rented from the Adeane family.

CHARLOTTE, COUNTESS CANNING

Born the hon. Charlotte Stuart in 1817, elder daughter of Charles Stuart, baron Stuart de Rothesay, and Lady Elizabeth York, she was noted for her beauty and devotion to religion. In 1836 she married Charles Canning (1812–62), viscount Canning, who was created earl Canning in 1859. She served as a lady of the bedchamber between 1842 and 1855, when her Peelite husband was sent to India as governor-general. A great admirer of the prince consort, she was one of the queen's favourite companions. She was in India throughout the great revolt of 1857, and was India's first vicereine. She died there in 1861, while planning her return to England. Main residences: 10 Grosvenor Square, London; Government House, Calcutta.

ADELINE, COUNTESS OF CARDIGAN AND LANCASTRE

Born Adeline de Horsey in 1824, she was the daughter of Spencer de Horsey and Lady Louisa Rous. Her father belonged to a 'fast' set, and his daughter followed his example. She early became notorious for her affair with James Bruce (1797–1868), seventh earl of Cardigan: rumours circulated that she had borne his child. She married him two months after the death of his first wife in 1858. Never received by the more morally upright sections of society, she was none the less a well-known member of the racing and hunting set, and kept great state at Deene Park in Northamptonshire. In 1873 she married Antonio, count de Lancastre (d. 1898), but this marriage failed, and she spent most of her time at Deene. She died in 1915, having scandalized society one last time by publishing a scurrilous volume, *My Recollections*, in 1909. Main residences: Deene Park, near Wansford, Northamptonshire; 36 Portman Square, London; Cardigan Lodge, Newmarket.

KATHARINE, COUNTESS OF CLARENDON

Born Lady Katharine Grimston in 1810, daughter of James Grimston, first earl of Verulam, and Lady Charlotte Jenkinson. Her first husband was John Foster Barham, but he died in 1838 after only four years of marriage. She married again in 1839, the Whig George Villiers, fourth earl of Clarendon (1800–70). She accompanied him to Ireland, where he was lord-lieutenant (1847–52); as wife to the foreign secretary, she was a well-known hostess in the 1850s and 1860s. She died in 1874; her daughters became Ladies Derby, Lathom, and Ampthill. Main residences: The Grove, near Watford; 1 Grosvenor Crescent, London.

SUSAN, COUNTESS OF DALHOUSIE

Born Lady Susan Hay in 1817, the daughter of George Hay, eighth marquess of Tweeddale, and Lady Susan Montagu, whose selfish attention to their own interests was a family byword. In 1836 she married James Ramsay (1812–60), Lord Ramsay, tenth earl of Dalhousie, who was created marquess of Dalhousie in 1849. For some months in 1842 she joined her sister Elizabeth, then Lady Douro, as a lady of the bedchamber to the queen, but ill health forced her early resignation. She accompanied the marquess to India, where he was governor-general (1847–56), but died on a voyage home in 1853. Main residences: Dalhousie Castle, near Edinburgh; Colstoun House, near Haddington; Government House, Calcutta.

LADY ANNA MARIA DAWSON

Born in 1784/5, she was the daughter of John Dawson, first earl of Portarlington, and

Lady Caroline Stuart. Youngest of four daughters, she never married, but found occupation as lady-in-waiting to the queen's mother, the duchess of Kent, which position she held until 1858. She remained in close contact with court circles until her death in 1866 at the age of 71. Main residences: Clarence House, St James's; Frogmore House, Berkshire.

MARY, COUNTESS OF DERBY

Born Lady Mary West in 1824, she was the daughter of George West, fifth earl De La Warr and Lady Elizabeth Sackville. In 1847 she married James Gascoyne-Cecil (1791–1868), second marquess of Salisbury, as his second wife, and inherited her predecessor's mantle as one of the confidantes of the duke of Wellington. For twenty years she was the doyenne of the conservative circle based at Hatfield House in Hertfordshire. Salisbury died in 1868, and two years later she married Edward Stanley (1826–93), fifteenth earl of Derby. In this new situation, she was an important political figure, less as a hostess than as a significant point of contact between individuals and parties. She died in 1900. Main residences: Hatfield House, Hertfordshire; 20 Arlington Street, London; then Knowsley Hall, Prescot, Lancashire; 23 St James's Square, London; Holwood, Beckenham, Kent.

LADY HARRIET ELLIOT

She was the youngest of the five daughters of Gilbert Elliot, second earl of Minto, and Mary Brydone. Lady John Russell was her elder sister, and it was under her auspices that she appeared in London society. She died, unmarried, at an early age, in 1855. Main residences: Minto House, Hawick, and Melgund, near Jedburgh, both in Roxburghshire.

JANE, MARCHIONESS OF ELY

Born Jane Hope-Vere in 1821, she was the daughter of James Hope-Vere of Craigie. In 1844 she married John Loftus (1814–57), viscount Loftus, who in the following year succeeded as third marquess of Ely. In 1851 she was appointed lady of the bedchamber to the queen, and remained in the household until her death. After both she and the queen were widowed, she spent much of her time at court, where she was the queen's favoured go-between, a position for which she was temperamentally unsuited. Her death in 1890 was much lamented by the queen. Main residences: Ely Lodge, near Enniskillen, Co. Fermanagh; Loftus Hall, Co. Wexford; 9 Prince's Gate, Knightsbridge.

HARRIET, COUNTESS GRANVILLE

Born Lady Harriet Cavendish in 1785, she was the daughter of the fifth duke of Devonshire and Lady Georgiana Spencer. Brought up amid the notorious Devonshire House set, she belonged to the second generation of the Whig Cousinhood. In 1809 she married Lord Granville Leveson-Gower (1773–1846), who became successively viscount and earl Granville, and inherited the family produced by his liaison with her aunt, Lady Bessborough. She had a distinguished career as his ambassadress during his terms of office in Paris from 1827 to 1841; following his death she became noted for her evangelical piety. She died in 1862. Her eldest son was one of the leaders of the Gladstonian Liberal party, while one of her daughters was well known as a Catholic convert and novelist. Main residences: Embassy, Paris; Stone Park, Staffordshire; 13 Hereford Street, London.

LADY CHARLOTTE GUEST

Born in 1812, she was the daughter of General Albemarle Bertie, ninth earl of Lindsey, and his wife Charlotte Layard. Following her father's early death, her mother married the tutor of her children; to escape the social ignominy of this new relationship, in 1833 she married the Welsh ironmaster John Josiah Guest (1785–1852), who was created a baronet in 1838. Lady Charlotte, who was a noted scholar and published a well-regarded translation of the *Mabinogion*, took an increasing role in the management of the Dowlais ironworks, and, following her husband's death, took control. In 1855 she married her children's tutor, Charles Schreiber (1826–84), and gave up the works. She became a celebrated collector of porcelain, and a benefactor of the Victoria and Albert Museum. She died in 1895. Main residences: Dowlais, South Wales; Canford Manor, Dorset; 11 Upper Belgrave Street, London; Exeter House, Roehampton.

ELIZABETH, LADY HOLLAND

Born Elizabeth Vassall, probably in 1781, she was the daughter of Richard Vassall, who owned sugar plantations in Jamaica, and his American wife, Mary Clarke. In 1786 she married Sir Godfrey Webster, fourth baronet (1747–1800), of Battle Abbey, Sussex; they had five children. In 1794 she met Henry Fox, third baron Holland (1773–1840), in Naples; their first child was born in November. Webster divorced her in July 1797, and two days later she married Holland. Despite her social notoriety, Lady Holland ran the most brilliant salon in London, at Holland House, Kensington, which became a renowned political and literary centre. Whiggery was the creed of Holland House, and in turn, it formed a new generation of Whig politicians, most notably Lord John Russell. Imperious, querulous, and ambitious, Lady Holland dominated Whig society for a generation, until Holland's death in 1840, after which she could not bear to live at Holland House. Her own death followed in 1845. Main residences: Holland House, Kensington; then 33 South Street; 9 Great Stanhope Street.

SARAH SOPHIA, COUNTESS OF JERSEY

Born Lady Sarah Fane in 1785, she was the daughter of John Fane, tenth earl of Westmorland, and Sarah Anne Child. She was the heir to the banking fortune of her grandfather, Robert Child, of Child's Bank, and to his Middlesex estate, Osterley Park. She was to take an active interest in the management of the bank. In 1804 she married George Villiers (1773–1859), viscount Villiers, who in the following year succeeded as fifth earl of Jersey. Lady Jersey was a keen politician and conduit of political information; the Whiggery of her early years (she was a prominent supporter of Queen Caroline during the divorce case) bent under the weight of family connections with leading Tories in the 1820s and 1830s, principally the duke of Wellington and Sir Robert Peel. A patroness of the exclusive balls at Almack's, the fact that her own fortune came from banking was a hindrance to the marriage of her daughter to the Austrian Prince Esterhazy. Lady Jersey died in 1867. Main residences: Middleton Park, near Bicester, Oxfordshire; Osterley Park, Middlesex; 38 Berkeley Square, London.

FRANCES, VISCOUNTESS JOCELYN

Born Lady Frances Cowper in 1820, ostensibly the daughter of Peter Cowper, fifth earl Cowper, and his wife, Emily Lamb, her father was in fact probably her mother's lover and eventual second husband, Lord Palmerston. A celebrated beauty, she was expected to make a 'great match'; she married Robert Jocelyn (1816–54), viscount Jocelyn and heir to the earldom of Roden in 1841. The contrast between the sternly religious Ulster family of the Rodens, who were notorious Orangemen, and the secular, worldly Cowpers and Palmerstons was marked. Fanny Jocelyn, who had been a bridesmaid at Victoria and Albert's wedding, became a lady of the bedchamber in 1841, an office she retained until 1867. Her husband, with whom she had an unsettled relationship, and who was a serving army officer, died dramatically from cholera in his mother-in-law's drawing-room in 1854. Blaming herself for the failure of their marriage, she virtually isolated herself after his death, devoting herself to her children and, from 1867, to the motherless children of her elder daughter. Tragedy continued to mar her life: of her six children, five died before her, from tuberculosis. Lady Jocelyn died in 1880. Main residence: Hertford Street, London.

FRANCES ANNE, MARCHIONESS OF LONDONDERRY

Born Frances Anne Vane in 1800, daughter of Sir Henry Vane and Anne Catherine Macdonnell, countess of Antrim in her own right. She was heiress to the vast estates of her family, principally in Co. Durham. In 1819 she married, as his second wife, Charles Stewart, baron Stewart (1778–1854), who changed his name to Vane, and in 1822 succeeded his brother as third marquess of Londonderry. Lady Londonderry had a varied career, as ambassadress in Vienna, as a leading Tory hostess in London, and, especially after her husband's death, as the manager and director of the huge industrial and agricultural concerns of the family in England and Ireland. An early patron of Disraeli, she also directed the political interests of her family after 1854, and was a dominant voice in the politics of Co. Durham. She died in 1865. Main residences: Wynyard Park, Stockton-on-Tees; Seaham Hall, Sunderland; Mount Stewart, Co. Down; Garron Tower, Co. Antrim; Holdernesse House, Park Lane, London.

CECIL, MARCHIONESS OF LOTHIAN

Born Lady Cecil Chetwynd Talbot in 1808, she was the daughter of Charles Talbot, second earl Talbot, and Frances Lambart. Brought up in a religious family, in 1831 she married John Kerr, seventh marquess of Lothian (1794–1841). When he died in 1841, she was left with seven children under 10 years old. Lady Lothian devoted herself to charitable and religious works; a correspondent of Henry Manning, she tied her religious future to his, and joined the Roman Catholic Church, a move which imperilled her guardianship of her own children. Having been a benefactor of high Anglican churches, her patronage was redirected to the Catholic Church, and her funeral sermon after her death in Rome in 1877 was preached by the Jesuit Peter Gallwey. Main residences: Newbattle Abbey, near Dalkeith; Blickling Hall, Norfolk.

SARAH, LADY LYTTELTON

Born Lady Sarah Spencer in 1787, she was the daughter of George Spencer, second earl Spencer, and Lady Lavinia Bingham. Georgiana, duchess of Devonshire, was her aunt; her grandmother, the pious dowager Lady Spencer, was an important influence in her early years. In 1815 she married William Lyttelton, third baron Lyttelton (1782–1837), and a year after his death accepted the position of lady of the bedchamber to the queen. In 1842 she was appointed governess to the royal children, in which post she supervised and administered the royal nursery until her resignation at the end of 1850. The death of one of her daughters in that year called her back to family duties, which were multiplied by the death of her daughter-in-law, Mary, Lady Lyttelton, in 1857, leaving twelve children. Lady Lyttelton died in 1870. Main residences: Hagley Hall, Worcestershire; 12 Stratton Street, London.

LOUISE, DUCHESS OF MANCHESTER

Born Countess Louise von Alten in 1832, she was the daughter of Karl, Count von Alten of Hanover. In 1852 she married William Drogo Montagu, viscount Mandeville (1823–90), who in 1855 succeeded as seventh duke of Manchester. She rapidly became established as a member of the prince of Wales's Marlborough House set, despite which she was appointed mistress of the robes under Lord Derby in 1858. A staunch conservative, she soon acquired the Whig Spencer Cavendish, Lord Hartington (1833–1908), as her lover; his liberal colleagues considered her a baleful influence. The relationship continued for more than thirty years, tacitly condoned by society (if not by the queen, who disapproved). Manchester died in 1890, and the regulation two years later, his widow married her lover, who in the meantime had both become a unionist and succeeded as eighth duke of Devonshire. Stalwart supporters of the race-track and the card-table, echoes of the Devonshire House set of a century before were heard once more among the now ageing conservative aristocrats. The 'Double Duchess' died in 1911. Main residences: Kimbolton Castle, Huntingdonshire; 1 Great Stanhope Street, London; after 1892, Chatsworth and Hardwick Hall, Derbyshire; Devonshire House, Piccadilly, London.

FRANCES, VISCOUNTESS MILTON

Born Lady Frances Douglas in 1819, she was the daughter of Sholto Douglas, seventeenth earl of Morton, and Frances Rose. In 1838 she married (having declined W. E. Gladstone) William Thomas Fitzwilliam, viscount Milton (1815–1902). Lady Milton and her husband, whom she called Tom, spent a considerable amount of time in the 1840s and 1850s managing the family's Irish estates at Coollattin Park, Co. Wicklow;

in the same period they produced twelve surviving children, seven sons and five daughters. In 1857 Milton's father died, and he succeeded as sixth earl Fitzwilliam and inherited the estates which included much industrial land in Yorkshire. Lady Fitzwilliam died in 1895. Main residences: Wentworth House, Rotherham, Yorkshire; Coollattin Park, Co. Wicklow; 4 Grosvenor Square, London.

MARY, COUNTESS OF MINTO

Born Mary Brydone in 1786, the daughter of Patrick Brydone of Lemuel House, Berwickshire, and Mary Robertson, in 1806 she married Gilbert Elliot (1782–1859), who in 1813 became viscount Melgund, and the following year succeeded his father as the second earl of Minto. She periodically felt inadequate to deal with the responsibilities of her social position, but was a conscientious patron of the poor on her estates. The Mintos were perennially financially embarrassed; in the 1850s they closed their Scottish house, and lived abroad for some time to retrench. Shaky finances contributed to their reputation for being 'political jobbers' (nepotistic seekers after office), not helped by the marriage of one of Lady Minto's daughters, Fanny, to the Liberal leader Lord John Russell. Lady Minto, who had been ill for some time, died in 1853. Main residences: Minto House, Hawick, Roxburghshire; Melgund, Jedburgh; 48 Eaton Square, London.

HARRIET, COUNTESS OF MORLEY

Born Harriet Parker in 1809/10, the only daughter of Montagu Parker of Whiteway, Devon, and Harriet Newcombe of Starcross, she first married William Coryton of Pentillie Castle, Cornwall. Following his death, in 1842 she married her second cousin, Edmund Parker, second earl of Morley (1810–64). Tangentially connected to the court (her husband was a lord-in-waiting 1846–52), she took great pride in her only son's career at court and in Liberal politics. She survived her husband by more than thirty years, and concerned herself with her Devonshire farms and estates and their inhabitants. Lady Morley died in 1897. Main residences: Saltram House, Plympton, Devon; Whiteway, Devon.

LADY DOROTHY NEVILL

Born Lady Dorothy Walpole in 1826, she was the daughter of Horatio Walpole, third earl of Orford, and Mary Fawkener. She and her sister Rachel were considered 'flighty' or 'fast', and in order to prevent further damage to her reputation, in 1847 she was married off to Reginald Nevill (1807–78), a cousin some years her senior, and a connection of the marquess of Abergavenny. Lady Dorothy settled into her role as chatelain of Dangstein in Hampshire, where she developed a great interest in horticulture, corresponding with naturalists including Darwin and Hooker; there is, however, some doubt as to the paternity of some of her children. As a hostess in London, her parties had a cross-section of guests from the worlds of politics, science, literature, and the arts; Disraeli was one of her favourites, and she and her daughter Meresia were active members of the Primrose League. In her old age, Lady Dorothy wrote a series of volumes of recollections, bemoaning the declining standards of social life. She died in 1913. Main residences: Dangstein, near Petersfield, Hampshire; 45 Charles Street, London.

EMILY, VISCOUNTESS PALMERSTON

Born Emily Lamb in 1787, she was the daughter of Peniston Lamb, first viscount Melbourne, and Elizabeth Milbanke. The dominant influence of her youth was her socially ambitious mother, whose close friend was Georgiana, duchess of Devonshire, and whose lovers were legion. Her brothers were Frederick (later Lord Beauvale), who became a diplomat, and William, who after years of ignominy (the notorious Lady Caroline Lamb was his wife), became prime minister in 1834. In 1805 she married Peter Leopold Cowper, fifth earl Cowper (1778–1837), a rather dull man, whom her brilliance dimmed still further. She was a leader of society, one of the lady patronesses of Almack's, and, in the later 1820s, the hostess of the Canningite faction, to which her most consistent lover, Henry Temple, third viscount Palmerston (1784–1865), belonged. In 1839, two years after her husband's death, Lady Cowper married Palmerston, and began a second career as the most influential and successful political hostess of her generation, a career which coincided with and helped to maintain the 'Age of Palmerston'. She survived Palmerston by four years, dying in 1869. Main residences: Panshanger, Hertfordshire; after 1839, Broadlands, Hampshire; 5 Carlton House Terrace, London; then Cambridge House, Piccadilly, London; after 1865, 21 Park Lane, London.

MARY, LADY PONSONBY

Born in 1832, the daughter of John Crocker Bulteel and Lady Elizabeth Grey, she became a maid of honour to Queen Victoria in 1853. Having broken off an engagement to William Vernon Harcourt, in 1861 she married an equerry, (Sir) Henry Frederick Ponsonby, who subsequently became Victoria's private secretary. The couple were frequently separated by the demands of the private secretary's job, but they wrote to each other daily. A woman of strong intellect, she published articles on philosophy, and, despite a high church youth, was suspected of agnosticism in later life. More radical in politics than even her Liberal husband, Lady Ponsonby was a suspect figure at Victoria's increasingly conservative court, accused of exercising political influence over her husband. She died in 1916. Main residences: Norman Tower, Windsor Castle; Osborne Cottage, Isle of Wight.

EVELINE, COUNTESS OF PORTSMOUTH

Born Lady Eveline Herbert in 1834, she was the daughter of Henry Herbert, third earl of Carnarvon, and Henrietta Howard-Molyneux-Howard. In 1855 she married Isaac Wallop, viscount Lymington (1825–91), who in 1855 succeeded as fifth earl of Portsmouth. Their family of six sons and six daughters placed a considerable strain on the family fortune; Lady Portsmouth regularly recorded in her diary her fears that she was again pregnant. She died in 1906, having successfully launched her younger sons on careers, and having found husbands for all her daughters. Main residences: Hurstbourne Park, Whitchurch, Hampshire; Eggesford House, Wembworthy, Devon.

LADY JOHN RUSSELL

Born Lady Frances Elliot in 1815, she was the second daughter of Gilbert Elliot, second earl of Minto, and Mary Brydone. After initially rejecting him, in 1841 she married the Whig leader, Lord John Russell (1792–1878). She was his second wife, and she inherited the responsibility for the two daughters of his first marriage, as well as her own three sons and a daughter. Intellectually interested in the issues of political liberalism, Lady John was constitutionally unsuited to the role of political wife. A poor manager, with uncertain health, she detested London and entertaining; worse still, the aspirations of her relatives were a political burden for Russell, while her capacity for saying the wrong thing earned her, probably unfairly, the reputation of hindering her husband's career. She was openly relieved on his retirement and removal to the House of Lords in 1861 as earl Russell. Her last years were spent bringing up the orphaned children of her eldest son, Lord Amberley, the younger of whom was the philosopher Bertrand Russell. Lady Russell died in 1898. Main residences: Pembroke Lodge, Richmond Park, Surrey; 31 Chesham Place, London.

FRANCES, MARCHIONESS OF SALISBURY

Born Frances Gascoyne, in 1802, she was the daughter of Bamber Gascoyne and Fanny Price, and heiress to a considerable fortune. In 1821 she married James Brownlow Cecil, viscount Cranborne (1791–1868), who became second marquess of Salisbury in 1823; a condition of their marriage and his acquisition of her fortune was that he take the additional surname Gascoyne. A confidante of the duke of Wellington, she had five children and died from dropsy in 1839. Her widower remarried Lady Mary West, later Lady Derby. Main residences: Hatfield House, Hertfordshire; 20 Arlington Street, London.

LOUISA, COUNTESS OF SANDWICH

Born Lady Louisa Lowry-Corry in 1781, she was the daughter of Armar Lowry-Corry, first earl of Belmore, and his second wife, Lady Harriet Hobart. In 1804 she married George Montagu, viscount Hinchinbrooke (1773–1818), an active Tory politician, who in 1814 succeeded as sixth earl of Sandwich. The early death from consumption of her husband in 1818 left Lady Sandwich the effective head of her family until her only son came of age in 1832: she was active in promoting Tory interests in Huntingdonshire. The elder of her two daughters became Lady Harriet Baring (later Lady Ashburton), a noted wit, hostess, and friend of Thomas Carlyle; the other married Count Walewski, later French ambassador in London, but died young. Lady Sandwich, who spent many of her later years in Paris, died in 1862. Main residences: Hinchinbrooke House, Huntingdonshire; 46 Grosvenor Square, London.

GEORGIANA, DUCHESS OF SOMERSET

Born Georgiana Sheridan in 1809, she was a granddaughter of the playwright and politician Richard Brinsley Sheridan. Georgiana Sheridan and her sisters, later Caroline Norton and Helen, Lady Dufferin, were known for their beauty as 'the three graces'. In 1830 she married Edward Seymour, Lord Seymour (1804–85), who succeeded as twelfth duke of Somerset in 1855. In 1839, she took the part of the 'Queen of Beauty' at the Eglinton Tournament. As her husband frequently held political office, she took a great deal of responsibility for the management of their widespread Somerset estates. Her later years were marred by the tragic deaths of both her sons in the 1860s. She died in 1884, a year before her husband. Main residences: Bulstrode Park, near Gerrards Cross, Buckinghamshire; Maiden Bradley House, Wiltshire; Stover Lodge, Devon; Wimbledon Park, Surrey; 30 Grosvenor Gardens, London.

LADY AUGUSTA STANLEY

Born in 1822, a daughter of Thomas Bruce, seventh earl of Elgin (of 'Marbles' fame), and his second wife, Elizabeth Oswald, the impoverishment of her family led her to seek employment at court. She was lady-in-waiting to the duchess of Kent for many years, and, after the death of the duchess in 1861, was appointed resident woman of the bedchamber to the queen. Victoria became particularly dependent on Lady Augusta Bruce, who lived permanently at court, and was outraged by her decision in 1863 to marry A. P. Stanley (1815–81), the dean of Westminster. Lady Augusta became an important hostess for the broad church party, and a channel through which the queen consented to be drawn, in small degree, back into society after Albert's death. Lady Augusta died after suffering horribly for some time, in 1876. Main residences: Frogmore, Berkshire; The Deanery, Westminster.

LADY CONSTANCE STANLEY

Born Lady Constance Villiers in 1840, she was the eldest of the three daughters of George Villiers, fourth earl of Clarendon, and his second wife, Lady Katherine Grimston. Brought up in an impeccably Whig household, her parents were surprised to find themselves connected with the equally impeccably conservative Stanley family, when she married in 1864 the hon. Frederick Stanley (1841–1908). Stanley was heir presumptive to his brother, the fifteenth earl of Derby, and succeeded him in 1893. Political and personal differences made her relationship with her brother- and sister-in-law somewhat fraught. She lived until 1922. Main residence: Witherslack Hall, Grange-over-Sands, Lancashire.

THE HON. ELEANOR STANLEY

Born in 1821, she was the daughter of Edward Stanley (of a cadet branch of the family of the earls of Derby) and Lady Mary Maitland. She was appointed a maid of honour to the queen in 1841, and remained at court until 1862. Her letters describing court life were published as *Twenty Years at Court*. She resigned in 1862 to marry her cousin, Charles Maitland (later Lord Lauderdale), but the marriage did not come off. In 1866 she married Lieutenant-Colonel Samuel Long (1799–1881) of Bromley Hill, Kent, as his fourth wife. She brought up his two daughters, and, following his death, settled in Bryanston Square, London. She died in 1903.

ANNE, DUCHESS OF SUTHERLAND

Born in 1829, she was the daughter and heiress of John Hay Mackenzie of Newhall and Cromartie and his wife Anne Gibson-Craig. She was married to the youthful

George Sutherland-Leveson-Gower, marquess of Stafford (1828–92) in 1849; the marriage failed in later years, and her husband took up with a Mrs Blair, whom he married after Anne's death. Having inherited considerable estates in her own right, she was created by Palmerston countess of Cromartie in her own right in 1861. She was mistress of the robes to the queen in Gladstone's first ministry, after the resignation of her sister-in-law, Elizabeth Argyll, from ill health in 1870. She died in 1888 at Torquay. Main residences: Trentham Hall, Staffordshire; Dunrobin, near Golspie, Sutherland; Lilleshall, Newport, Shropshire; Stafford House, London.

HARRIET, DUCHESS OF SUTHERLAND

Born Lady Harriet Howard in 1806, she was the daughter of the sixth earl of Carlisle and his wife Lady Georgiana Cavendish. A granddaughter of the celebrated Georgiana, duchess of Devonshire, she was at the centre of the Whig Cousinhood. In 1823 she married George Granville Leveson-Gower (1786–1861), who was then earl Gower; in January 1833 he became marquess of Stafford, and, following his father's death six months later, succeeded as second duke of Sutherland. A close friend of the queen, Harriet Sutherland served as mistress of the robes in every Whig administration from the accession of Victoria until their husbands' deaths in 1861. A devout high churchwoman, she was an energetic philanthropist, promoting the abolition of slavery. Her enthusiasm for both the unification of Italy (she entertained Garibaldi at Stafford House) and for her friend and confidante, W. E. Gladstone, found less favour in the queen's sight. She died in 1868. Main residences: Dunrobin, near Golspie, Sutherland; Trentham Hall, Staffordshire; Cliveden House, near Maidenhead, Berkshire; Stafford House, London.

FRANCES, COUNTESS WALDEGRAVE

Born Frances Braham in 1821, she was the daughter of John Braham, the famous operatic tenor, and his bourgeois wife Frances Bolton. Her mother had high social aspirations, and was delighted to marry Frances to John Waldegrave, the wild, illegitimate son of the sixth earl Waldegrave, in 1839. A heavy drinker, he was dead within the year. Having been convinced that it was not forbidden by scripture, she proceeded to marry his younger, but legitimate, brother, George, seventh earl Waldegrave in September 1840. The earl also died young, in 1846. Both brothers left their widow all they possessed. Her third husband, George Granville Harcourt (d. 1861) was a widower of 61; from him she acquired social respectability and connections with the old Whig aristocracy. During the 1850s she first blossomed as a hostess, the role in which she was to flourish until her death, entertaining for the Whig/Liberal party. Wooed by all manner of suitors, from the duke of Newcastle to the duc d'Aumale, her fourth marriage, to Chichester Fortescue in 1863, was one of great affection: he had been a devoted admirer for many years. She worked tirelessly to promote his career; his failure to achieve the front rank was his alone. Her death in 1879 devastated Lord Carlingford (as he had become in 1874). Main residences: Strawberry Hill, Twickenham; 7 Carlton Gardens, London; Dudbrook House, Essex; Chewton Priory, near Bath; Nuneham Park, Oxfordshire.

LOUISA, MARCHIONESS OF WATERFORD

Born in Paris in 1818, Louisa Stuart was the daughter of Lord Stuart de Rothesay and Lady Elizabeth Yorke. Her sister Charlotte became countess Canning. A pious, gentle, and artistic girl, her marriage in 1842 to the dissolute Henry de la Poer Beresford, third marquess of Waterford (1811–59), who was more familiar with the police courts and the race-track than the inside of a church, surprised many. But the marriage reformed her husband, who abandoned the uncontrolled friends of his youth, and became a reforming landlord on his Irish estates. Louisa Waterford lived mainly in Ireland, attempting to relieve some of the worst consequences of the Famine, until Waterford's death in a hunting accident in 1859. Thereafter she retired to Ford Castle in Northumberland, where she devoted herself to art: she was one of the most gifted amateurs of her time. She died in 1891. Main residences: Curraghmore, Portlaw, Co. Waterford; Ford Castle, Cornhill, Northumberland.

ELIZABETH, DUCHESS OF WELLINGTON

Born Lady Elizabeth Hay in 1820, she was the daughter of George Hay, eighth marquess of Tweeddale, and Lady Susan Montagu. She left an unhappy childhood for an unhappy marriage in 1839 to Arthur Wellesley, marquess of Douro (1807–84), the eldest son of the great duke of Wellington. Fortunately, her father-in-law doted upon her, and she escaped from the miseries of her marriage into a career as a courtier. She was a lady of the bedchamber from 1843 until 1858, and mistress of the robes from 1861 to 1868, and again from 1874 to 1880. She survived her husband by twenty years, dying in 1904. Main residences: Stratfieldsaye, Hampshire; Apsley House, Piccadilly, London.

ELIZABETH, MARCHIONESS OF WESTMINSTER

Born in 1797, Lady Elizabeth Leveson-Gower was the daughter of the marquess of Stafford (later first duke of Sutherland) and his wife Elizabeth Gordon, who was in her own right countess of Sutherland. In 1819 she married Richard Grosvenor, viscount Belgrave (1795–1869), who in 1831 became earl Grosvenor, and in 1845 second marquess of Westminster. Immense wealth and Grand Whiggery characterized her family. In 1879 she published an account of a yachting tour of Norway, Sweden, and Russia which she had made with her husband in 1827. She died at the age of 94 in 1891. Main residences: Eaton Hall, Chester; Fonthill Gifford, Wiltshire; 33 Upper Grosvenor Street, London; Motcombe House, Dorset.

PRISCILLA, COUNTESS OF WESTMORLAND

Born Lady Priscilla Wellesley-Pole in 1793, she was the daughter of the third earl of Mornington and Katherine Forbes. The marquess Wellesley and the first duke of Wellington were her uncles. In 1811 she married John Fane, Lord Burghersh (1784–1859), who in 1841 succeeded as eleventh earl of Westmorland. Her husband was a professional diplomat, and Lady Burghersh spent many years in Berlin and Vienna, which reinforced her political conservatism; she did not find it easy to settle back into British life after her husband was recalled. The Burghershes were patrons of music, being among the founders of the Royal Academy of Music. Lady West-morland was one of the confidantes of her uncle, the duke of Wellington. Three of her four sons predeceased her. She died in 1879. Main residences: Berlin; Vienna; Apethorpe, near Wansford, Northamptonshire; 16 Cavendish Square, London.

CAROLINE, LADY WHARNCLIFFE

Born Lady Caroline Crichton in 1779, she was the daughter of John Crichton, first earl of Erne, and Lady Mary Hervey. In 1799 she married James Stuart-Wortley-Mackenzie (1776–1845), a descendant of the prime minister Lord Bute, who in 1826 was created baron Wharncliffe. Her correspondence, particularly that with her son, James, reveals her to have been an active Tory, and an associate of Queen Adelaide. She died in 1856. Main residences: Wortley Hall, near Sheffield, Yorkshire; Wharn-cliffe House, Curzon Street, London.

SUSAN, COUNTESS OF WHARNCLIFFE

The second daughter of Henry Lascelles, third earl of Harewood, and Lady Louisa Thynne, Lady Susan Lascelles was born in 1834. She married Edward Stuart-Wortley-Mackenzie (1827–99) in 1855, just months before he succeeded as third baron Wharncliffe. A conservative and a sportsman, he was created earl of Wharn-cliffe by Disraeli in 1876. If her diary is an accurate reflection, Lady Wharncliffe's life, which revolved around her husband's shooting engagements, was largely devoted to her husband and household; her only child died in 1857. She lived until 1927. Main residences: Wortley Hall, near Sheffield, Yorkshire; Belmont Castle, Perthshire; Simonston, near York; Wharncliffe House, Curzon Street, London.

Bibliography

MANUSCRIPT SOURCES

Abercairny Papers, Scottish Record Office
Atholl Papers, Blair Castle, Blair Atholl, Perthshire
Broadlands Papers, Southampton University Library
Bulstrode Papers, Buckinghamshire Record Office
Buxton Papers, Rhodes House Library, Oxford
Cadogan Papers, House of Lords Record Office
Canning Papers, Oriental and India Office Collections, British Library
Census Records, Public Record Office
Dalhousie Muniments, Scottish Record Office
Gladstone Papers, British Library
Harcourt Papers, Bodleian Library, Oxford
Hobbs (Derby / Gathorne Hardy) Papers, Corpus Christi College Library, Cambridge
Houghton Papers, Trinity College Library, Cambridge
Jersey Papers, Corporation of London: London Metropolitan Archives
Londonderry Estate Archives, Durham Record Office
Lord Chamberlain's Papers, Public Record Office
Lyndhurst Papers, Trinity College Library, Cambridge
Mildmay (Dogmersfield) Papers, Hampshire Record Office
Minto Papers, National Library of Scotland
Morier Papers, Balliol College Library, Oxford
MS. Eng. lett., Bodleian Library, Oxford
Parker of Saltram Papers, West Devon Record Office
Peel Papers, British Library
Royal Archives, Windsor Castle
Russell Papers, Public Record Office, Kew
Sandwich Papers, Cambridgeshire Archives Service, County Record Office (Huntingdon)
Sandwich Papers, Mapperton House, Dorset
Seymour of Ragley Papers, Warwickshire County Record Office
Lady Augusta Stanley Papers, Westminster Abbey Archives
Strachey Papers, Somerset Archives and Record Service
Sutherland Papers, National Library of Scotland
Sutherland Papers, Staffordshire Record Office
Wallop Papers, Hampshire Record Office
Wentworth Woodhouse Muniments, Sheffield City Libraries
Wharncliffe Muniments, Sheffield City Libraries

Wilberforce Papers, Bodleian Library, Oxford
Yester Papers, National Library of Scotland

PRINTED SOURCES

Place of publication is London unless otherwise stated.

Autobiographies, Published Diaries, Letters, Memoirs, and Novels

ABERDEEN, earl and countess of (John and Ishbel Gordon), *'We Twa': Reminiscences of Lord and Lady Aberdeen* (2 vols., W. Collins, 1925).

AIRLIE, countess of (Mabell Ogilvie), *In Whig Society 1775–1818: The Correspondence of Elizabeth, Viscountess Melbourne, and Emily Lamb, Countess Cowper and afterwards Viscountess Palmerston* (Hodder & Stoughton, 1921).

—— *Thatched with Gold: The Memoirs of Mabell, Countess of Airlie* (Hutchinson, 1962).

ARMYTAGE, PERCY, *By the Clock of St James's* (John Murray, 1927).

AUSTEN, JANE, *Emma* (1816).

—— *Mansfield Park* (1814).

—— *Pride and Prejudice* (1813).

BAILEY, JOHN (ed.), *The Diary of Lady Frederick Cavendish* (2 vols., John Murray, 1927).

BAILLIE, A. V., and BOLITHO, HECTOR (eds.), *Letters of Lady Augusta Stanley: A Young Lady at Court 1849–1863* (Gerald Howe, 1927).

—— —— (eds.), *Later Letters of Lady Augusta Stanley 1864–1876* (Jonathan Cape, 1929).

BALSAN, CONSUELO VANDERBILT, *The Glitter and the Gold* (Maidstone, Kent: George Mann, 1973; first published 1953).

BAMFORD, FRANCIS, and WELLINGTON, duke of (eds.), *The Journal of Mrs Arbuthnot, 1820–1832* (2 vols., Macmillan, 1950).

BATTERSEA, LADY (Constance Flower), *Reminiscences* (Macmillan, 1922).

—— *Waifs and Strays* (A. L. Humphreys, 1921).

BENSON, A. C., and ESHER, VISCOUNT, *The Letters of Queen Victoria: A Selection from Her Majesty's Correspondence, 1837–1861* 1st ser. (3 vols., John Murray, 1907).

BESSBOROUGH, earl of (ed.), *Lady Charlotte Guest: Extracts from her Journal 1833–1852* (John Murray, 1950).

BLOOMFIELD, GEORGIANA, LADY, *Reminiscences of Court and Diplomatic Life* (2 vols., Kegan Paul, Trench & Co., 1883).

BOYKIN, EDWARD (ed.), *Victoria, Albert, and Mrs Stevenson* (New York: Rinehart & Co., 1957).

BROOKE, JOHN, and SORENSEN, MARY (eds.), *W. E. Gladstone, iv: Autobiographical Memoranda 1868–1894* (HMSO, The Prime Ministers' Papers Series, 1981).

BUCKLE, G. E., *The Letters of Queen Victoria, 1862–1885: A Selection from Her Majesty's Correspondence and Journal*, 2nd ser. (3 vols., John Murray, 1926).

—— *The Letters of Queen Victoria, 1886–1901: A Selection from Her Majesty's Correspondence and Journals*, 3rd ser. (3 vols., John Murray, 1930).

BURGHCLERE, Lady (Winifred Gardner) (ed.), *A Great Lady's Friendships: Letters to Mary, Marchioness of Salisbury, Countess of Derby, 1862–1890* (Macmillan, 1933).

—— (ed.), *A Great Man's Friendship: Letters of the Duke of Wellington to Mary, Marchioness of Salisbury, 1850–1852* (John Murray, 1927).

CARDIGAN and LANCASTRE, countess of (Adeline Lancastre Saldanha), *My Recollections* (Eveleigh Nash, 1909).

DISRAELI, BENJAMIN, *Endymion* (1880).

—— *Sybil; or, The Two Nations* (1845).

DORCHESTER, Lady (Charlotte Carleton) (ed.), *Lord Broughton (J. C. Hobhouse): Recollections of a Long Life* (6 vols., John Murray, 1909–11).

ERSKINE, Mrs Steuart (Beatrice Caroline) (ed.), *Twenty Years at Court: From the Correspondence of the Hon. Eleanor Stanley, Maid of Honour to Her Late Majesty Queen Victoria 1842–1862* (Nisbet, 1916).

FOOT, M. R. D., and MATTHEW, H. C. G. (eds.), *The Gladstone Diaries* (14 vols., Oxford: Oxford University Press, 1968–94).

GALLWEY, PETER, 'Cecil, Marchioness of Lothian', in *Salvage from the Wreck: A Few Memories of Friends Departed, Preserved in Funeral Discourses* (Burns & Oates, 1889), 125–63.

GOOCH, G. P. (ed.), *The Later Correspondence of Lord John Russell 1840–1878* (2 vols., Longmans, Green & Co., 1925).

GORDON, PETER (ed.), *The Red Earl: The Papers of the Fifth Earl Spencer 1835–1910* (2 vols., Northampton: Northamptonshire Record Society, 1981).

GOWER, FREDERICK LEVESON, *Bygone Years: Recollections* (John Murray, 1905).

—— *Letters of Harriet Countess Granville 1810–1845* (2 vols., Longmans, 1894).

GOWER, SIR GEORGE LEVESON, and PALMER, IRIS, *Hary-O: The Letters of Lady Harriet Cavendish 1796–1809* (John Murray, 1940).

GREGORY, SIR WILLIAM, *An Autobiography* (John Murray, 1894).

GREVILLE, CHARLES C. F., *The Greville Memoirs (Second Part): A Journal of the Reign of Queen Victoria 1837–1852* (3 vols., Longmans, Green & Co., 1885).

GROSVENOR, CAROLINE, and BEILBY, CHARLES, LORD STUART OF WORTLEY, (eds.), *The First Lady Wharncliffe and her Family, 1779–1856* (2 vols., Heinemann, 1927).

GUEDALLA, PHILIP, *The Queen and Mr Gladstone* (2 vols., Hodder & Stoughton, 1993).

In Memoriam: Harriet, Duchess of Sutherland (Newcastle, Staffs.: no publisher, 1872).

JERSEY, countess of (Margaret E. Child-Villiers), *Fifty-one Years of Victorian Life* (John Murray, 1922).

—— *Records of the Family of Villiers, Earls of Jersey* (Morton, Burt & Sons, 1924).

JOHNSON, NANCY E. (ed.), *The Diary of Gathorne Hardy, Later Lord Cranbrook, 1866–1892: Political Selections* (Oxford: Clarendon Press, 1981).

KENNEDY, A. L. (ed.), *'My Dear Duchess': Social and Political Letters to the Duchess of Manchester 1858–1869* (John Murray, 1956).

LEVER, TRESHAM, *The Letters of Lady Palmerston* (John Murray, 1957).

LONDONDERRY, Lady (Edith Vane-Tempest-Stewart) (ed.), *Letters from Benjamin Disraeli to Frances Anne, Marchioness of Londonderry, 1837–1861* (Macmillan, 1938).

LONGFORD, ELIZABETH (ed.), *Louisa, Lady in Waiting: The Personal Diaries and Albums of Louisa, Lady in Waiting to Queen Victoria and Queen Alexandra* (Jonathan Cape, 1979).

MALLET, VICTOR (ed.), *Life with Queen Victoria: Marie Mallet's Letters from Court 1887–1901* (John Murray, 1968).

MALMESBURY, earl of, *Memoirs of an Ex-Minister: An Autobiography* (2 vols., Longmans, Green & Co., 1884).

MASTERMAN, LUCY (ed.), *Mary Gladstone (Mrs Drew): Her Diaries and Letters* (Methuen, 1930).

MAXWELL, SIR HERBERT (ed.), *The Creevey Papers* (John Murray, 1923).

MITFORD, NANCY (ed.), *The Ladies of Alderley* (Chapman and Hall, 1938).

MURRAY, HON. AMELIA, *Recollections from 1803–1837 with a Conclusion in 1868* (Longmans, Green & Co., 1868).

NEVILL, BARRY ST. JOHN (ed.), *Life at the Court of Queen Victoria 1861–1901* (Exeter: Webb & Bower, 1984).

NEVILL, LADY DOROTHY, *My Own Times* (Methuen, 1912).

NEVILL, RALPH (ed.), *The Life and Letters of Lady Dorothy Nevill* (Methuen, 1919).

—— (ed.), *The Reminiscences of Lady Dorothy Nevill* (Edward Arnold, 1906).

PARKER, CHARLES STUART, *Sir Robert Peel: From his Private Papers*, 2nd edn. (3 vols., John Murray, 1899).

PEEL, GEORGE (ed.), *The Private Letters of Sir Robert Peel* (John Murray, 1920).

PONSONBY, ARTHUR, *Sir Henry Ponsonby: His Life from his Letters* (Macmillan, 1942).

PONSONBY, SIR FREDERICK, *Sidelights on Queen Victoria* (Macmillan, 1930).

PONSONBY, MAGDALEN (ed.), *Mary Ponsonby: A Memoir, Some Letters and a Journal* (John Murray, 1927).

RAMM, AGATHA (ed.), *The Political Correspondence of Mr Gladstone and Lord Granville, 1876–1886* (2 vols., Oxford: Clarendon Press, 1962).

REDESDALE, LORD, *Memories* (2 vols., Hutchinson, 1915).

RIDLEY, JANE, and PERCY, CLAYRE (eds.), *The Letters of Arthur Balfour and Lady Elcho 1885–1917* (Hamish Hamilton, 1992).

RUMBOLD, SIR HORACE, *Recollections of a Diplomatist* (2 vols., Edward Arnold, 1902).

ST HELIER, LADY (Susan Mary Elizabeth Jeune), *Memories of Fifty Years* (Edward Arnold, 1910).

STONEY, BENITA, and WELTZEN, HEINRICH C. (eds.), *My Mistress the Queen: The Letters of Frieda Arnold, Dresser to Queen Victoria* (Weidenfeld & Nicolson, 1994).

SUDLEY, LORD (trans. and ed.), *The Lieven–Palmerston Correspondence 1828–1856* (John Murray, 1943).

THOMPSON, FLORA, *Lark Rise* (Oxford: Oxford University Press, 1939).

TOLLEMACHE, HON. LIONEL A., *Old and Odd Memories* (Edward Arnold, 1908).

TROLLOPE, ANTHONY, *Can You Forgive Her?* (originally pub. 1864–5) (Penguin Classics, 1986).

—— *Castle Richmond* (originally pub. 1860) (Oxford: World's Classics, 1989).

—— *Phineas Finn* (originally pub. 1869) (Penguin Classics, 1985).

TROLLOPE, ANTHONY, *Phineas Redux* (originally pub. 1874) (Oxford: World's Classics, 1983).

—— *The Prime Minister* (originally pub. 1876) (2 vols., Oxford: World's Classics, 1983).

TWEEDSMUIR, LADY (Susan Buchan), *The Lilac and the Rose* (Gerald Duckworth, 1952).

VAUGHAN, ELLEN TWISLETON (ed.), *Letters of the Hon. Mrs Edward Twisleton Written to her Family 1852–1862* (John Murray, 1928).

VICTORIA, QUEEN, *Leaves from the Journal of our Life in the Highlands* (Smith, Elder, 1868).

—— *More Leaves from the Journal of a Life in the Highlands* (Smith, Elder, 1884).

VINCENT, JOHN (ed.), *A Selection from the Diaries of Edward Henry Stanley, 15th Earl of Derby (1826–93), between September 1869 and March 1878*, Camden 5th ser., iv (Royal Historical Society, 1994).

WADDINGTON, MARY KING, *Letters of a Diplomat's Wife* (Smith, Elder, 1903).

WARWICK, FRANCES, countess of, *Afterthoughts* (Cassell, 1931).

WEIGALL, LADY ROSE (ed.), *The Correspondence of Priscilla, Countess of Westmorland* (John Murray, 1909).

WELLINGTON, 7th duke of (ed.), *Wellington and his Friends: Letters of the First Duke of Wellington* (Macmillan, 1965).

WEST, MRS GEORGE CORNWALLIS (Lady Randolph Churchill), *The Reminiscences of Lady Randolph Churchill* (Edward Arnold, 1908).

WYNDHAM, HON. MRS HUGH (ed.), *The Correspondence of Sarah Spencer, Lady Lyttelton 1787–1870* (John Murray, 1912).

ZETLAND, marquess of (ed.), *The Letters of Disraeli to Lady Bradford and Lady Chesterfield* (2 vols., Ernest Benn, 1929).

Secondary Works

ADBURGHAM, ALISON, *A Radical Aristocrat: Sir William Molesworth of Pencarrow and his Wife Andalusia* (Padstow: Tabb House, 1990).

AIRLIE, countess of (Mabell Ogilvie), *Lady Palmerston and her Times* (2 vols., Hodder & Stoughton, 1922).

ALLSOBROOK, DAVID, *Schools for the Shires: The Reform of Middle-Class Education in Mid-Victorian Britain* (Manchester: Manchester University Press, 1986).

ALTHOLZ, JOSEF L., and POWELL, JOHN, 'Gladstone, Lord Ripon and the Vatican Decrees, 1874', *Albion*, 22 (Fall 1990), 449–59.

ANSTRUTHER, IAN, *The Knight and the Umbrella: An Account of the Eglinton Tournament, 1839* (Geoffrey Bles, 1963).

ARDENER, SHIRLEY (ed.), *Perceiving Women* (Croom Helm, 1975).

—— and CALLAN, HILARY (eds.), *The Incorporated Wife* (Croom Helm, 1984).

ARNSTEIN, WALTER L., *Protestant versus Catholic in Mid-Victorian England: Mr Newdegate and the Nuns* (Columbia, Mo.: University of Missouri Press, 1982).

—— 'Queen Victoria and Religion', in Malmgreen (ed.), *Religion in the Lives of English Women*, 88–128.

—— 'Queen Victoria Opens Parliament: The Disinvention of Tradition', *Historical Research*, 63 (June 1990), 178–94.

—— 'The Survival of the Victorian Aristocracy', in Frederic Cople Jaher (ed.), *The Rich, the Well Born, and the Powerful: Elites and Upper Classes in History* (Chicago: University of Illinois Press, 1973).

ASKWITH, BETTY, *The Lytteltons: A Family Chronicle of the Nineteenth Century* (Chatto & Windus, 1975).

—— *Piety and Wit: A Biography of Harriet, Countess Granville 1785–1862* (Collins, 1982).

BAILY, FRANCIS E., *The Love Story of Lady Palmerston* (Hutchinson, 1938).

BARKER, HANNAH, and CHALUS, ELAINE (eds.), *Gender in Eighteenth-Century England: Roles, Representations and Responsibilities* (Longman, 1997).

BATEMAN, JOHN, *The Great Landowners of Great Britain and Ireland*, 4th edn. (Harrison, 1883).

BATTISCOMBE, GEORGINA, *The Spencers of Althorp* (Constable, 1984).

BECKETT, J. V., *The Aristocracy in England, 1660–1914* (Oxford: Blackwell, 1989; first published 1986).

BEIK, WILLIAM, *Absolutism and Society in Seventeenth-Century France: State Power and Provincial Aristocracy in Languedoc* (Cambridge: Cambridge University Press, 1985).

BENCE-JONES, MARK, *The Twilight of the Ascendancy* (Constable, 1987).

BLAKE, ROBERT, *Disraeli* (Eyre & Spottiswoode, 1966).

BLAKISTON, GEORGIANA, *Lord William Russell and his Wife 1815–1846* (John Murray, 1972).

BOURNE, J. M., *Patronage and Society in Nineteenth-Century England* (Edward Arnold, 1986).

BRANCA, PATRICIA, *Silent Sisterhood: Middle-Class Women in the Victorian Home* (Croom Helm, 1975).

BUCHOLZ, R. O., ' "Nothing but Ceremony": Queen Anne and the Limitations of Royal Power', *Journal of British Studies*, 30 (July 1991), 288–323.

BURDETT-COUTTS, BARONESS ANGELA (ed.), *Woman's Mission: Papers on the Philanthropic Work of Women* (Sampson Low, Marston and Co., 1893).

BUSH, M. L., *The English Aristocracy: A Comparative Synthesis* (Manchester: Manchester University Press, 1984).

CALLAN, HILARY, 'The Premiss of Dedication: Notes towards an Ethnography of Diplomats' Wives', in Ardener (ed.), *Perceiving Women*, 87–104.

CANNADINE, DAVID, *The Decline and Fall of the British Aristocracy* (New Haven: Yale University Press, 1990).

—— and PRICE, SIMON (eds.), *Rituals of Royalty: Power and Ceremonial in Traditional Societies* (Cambridge: Cambridge University Press, 1987).

CANNON, JOHN, *Aristocratic Century: The Peerage of Eighteenth-Century England* (Cambridge: Cambridge University Press, 1984).

—— 'The Survival of the British Monarchy', *Transactions of the Royal Historical Society*, 5th ser., 36 (1986), 143–64.

CARLYLE, THOMAS, *Past and Present*, ed. Richard D. Altick (New York: New York University Press, 1965; first published 1843).

CASTERAS, SUSAN P., 'Virgin Vows: The Early Victorian Artists' Portrayal of Nuns and Novices', in Malmgreen (ed.), *Religion in the Lives of English Women*, 129–60.

CHALUS, ELAINE, ' "That Epidemical Madness": Women and Electoral Politics in the Late Eighteenth Century', in Barker and Chalus (eds.), *Gender in Eighteenth-Century England*, 151–78.

CHAMBERLAIN, MURIEL E., *Lord Aberdeen: A Political Biography* (Longman, 1983).

CHARLOT, MONICA, *Victoria: The Young Queen* (Oxford: Blackwell, 1991).

'Child & Co.: Three Hundred Years at No. 1 Fleet Street', *Three Banks Review*, 98 (June 1973), 40–8.

CLINTON, CATHERINE, *The Other Civil War: American Women in the Nineteenth Century* (New York: Hill & Wang, 1984).

COLLEY, LINDA, *Britons: Forging the Nation, 1707–1837* (New Haven: Yale University Press, 1992).

CONACHER, J. B., *The Aberdeen Coalition 1852–1855: A Study in Mid-Nineteenth-Century Party Politics* (Cambridge: Cambridge University Press, 1968).

COOTER, R. J., 'Lady Londonderry and the Irish Catholics of Seaham Harbour: "No Popery" out of Context', *Recusant History*, 13 / 4 (1976), 288–98.

COTT, NANCY F., *The Bonds of Womanhood: 'Woman's Sphere' in New England, 1780–1835* (New Haven: Yale University Press, 1977).

CRAGOE, MATTHEW, *An Anglican Aristocracy: The Moral Economy of the Landed Estate in Carmarthenshire* (Oxford: Oxford University Press, 1996).

CRAIG, F. W. S., *British Parliamentary Election Results 1832–1885* (Aldershot: Parliamentary Research Services, 1989; first published 1977).

DARROW, MARGARET H., 'French Noblewomen and the New Domesticity, 1750–1850', *Feminist Studies*, 1 (Spring 1979), 41–65.

DASENT, ARTHUR IRWIN, *John Thadeus Delane, Editor of 'The Times': His Life and Correspondence* (2 vols., John Murray, 1908).

DAVIDOFF, LEONORE, *The Best Circles: Society, Etiquette and the Season* (The Cresset Library, 1986; first published 1973).

—— 'Mastered for Life: Servant and Wife in Victorian and Edwardian England', *Journal of Social History*, 7 (Summer 1974), 406–28.

—— and HALL, CATHERINE, *Family Fortunes: Men and Women of the English Middle Class, 1780–1850* (Hutchinson, 1987).

DAVIES, JOHN, *Cardiff and the Marquesses of Bute* (Cardiff: University of Wales Press, 1981).

DREW, MARY, *Catherine Gladstone* (Nisbet, 1919).

DRUMMOND, ANDREW L., and BULLOCH, JAMES, *The Churches in Victorian Scotland 1843–1874* (Edinburgh: St Andrew's Press, 1975).

DYHOUSE, CAROL, *Feminism and the Family in England 1880–1939* (Oxford: Blackwell, 1989).

—— *Girls Growing Up in Late Victorian and Edwardian England* (Routledge & Kegan Paul, 1981).

EASTWOOD, DAVID, *Governing Rural England: Tradition and Transformation in Local Government 1780–1840* (Oxford: Oxford University Press, 1994).

ELIAS, NORBERT, *The Court Society*, trans. Edmund Jephcott (Oxford: Blackwell, 1983; first published 1969).

ELLENBERGER, NANCY W., 'The Souls and London "Society" at the End of the Nineteenth Century', *Victorian Studies*, 25 (Winter 1982), 133–60.

—— 'The Transformation of London "Society" at the End of Victoria's Reign: Evidence from the Court Presentation Records', *Albion*, 22 (Winter 1990), 633–53.

ELLIOTT, BERNARD, 'Laura Phillips de Lisle: A Nineteenth-Century Catholic Lady', *Recusant History*, 20 (May 1991), 371–9.

EMDEN, PAUL H., *Behind the Throne* (Hodder & Stoughton, 1934).

FANE, SPENCER PONSONBY, *Memoranda of Procedure at Her Majesty's Drawing Rooms and Other Ceremonials* (privately printed, 1895).

FITZMAURICE, LORD EDMOND, *The Life of Lord Granville, 1815–1891* (2 vols., Longmans, Green & Co., 1905).

FOSTER, JOSEPH, *The Peerage, Baronetage and Knightage of the British Empire for 1881* (2 vols., Nichols & Sons, 1881).

FOSTER, R. F., *Paddy and Mr Punch: Connections in Irish and English History* (Allen Lane, 1993).

FRANKLIN, JILL, 'Troops of Servants: Labour and Planning in the Country House 1840–1914', *Victorian Studies*, 19 (Dec. 1975), 211–39.

GARDINER, A. G., *The Life of Sir William Harcourt* (2 vols., Constable, 1923).

GEERTZ, CLIFFORD, *The Interpretation of Cultures: Selected Essays* (Hutchinson, 1975).

—— *Local Knowledge: Further Essays in Interpretative Anthropology* (Fontana, 1993; first published 1983).

GERARD, JESSICA, *Country House Life: Family and Servants, 1814–1914* (Oxford: Blackwell, 1994).

—— 'Lady Bountiful: Women of the Landed Classes and Rural Philanthropy', *Victorian Studies*, 30 (Winter 1987), 183–210.

GIROUARD, MARK, *Life in the English Country House: A Social and Architectural History* (New Haven: Yale University Press, 1980; 1st pub. 1978).

—— *The Return to Camelot: Chivalry and the English Gentleman* (New Haven: Yale University Press, 1981).

GORHAM, DEBORAH, *The Victorian Girl and the Feminine Ideal* (Croom Helm, 1982).

GOWER, IRIS LEVESON, *The Face without a Frown: Georgiana, Duchess of Devonshire* (Frederick Muller, 1944).

GRAY-FOW, MICHAEL J. A., 'Squire, Parson and Village School: Wragby 1830–1886', in Patrick Scott and Pauline Fletcher (eds.), *Culture and Education in Victorian England* (Lewisburg, Pa.: Bucknell University Press, 1990), 162–73.

GREELEY, DAWN M., 'Beyond Benevolence: Gender, Class and the Development of Scientific Charity in New York City, 1882–1935' (unpublished Ph.D. thesis, State University of New York at Stony Brook, 1994).

GUEST, REVEL, and JOHN, ANGELA V., *Lady Charlotte: A Biography of the Nineteenth Century* (Weidenfeld & Nicolson, 1989).

GUTTSMAN, W. L. (ed.), *The English Ruling Class* (Weidenfeld & Nicolson, 1969).

HAIG, ALAN, *The Victorian Clergy* (Croom Helm, 1984).

HALL, CATHERINE, *White, Male and Middle Class: Explorations in Feminism and History* (Cambridge: Polity Press, 1992).

HALPERIN, JOHN, *Trollope and Politics: A Study of the Pallisers and Others* (Macmillan, 1977).

HANHAM, H. J., *Elections and Party Management: Politics in the Time of Disraeli and Gladstone* (Longmans, 1959).

HARDIE, FRANK, *The Political Influence of Queen Victoria, 1861–1901* (Oxford: Oxford University Press, 1938; first published 1935).

HARE, AUGUSTUS J. C., *The Story of Two Noble Lives: Being Memorials of Charlotte, Countess Canning, and Louisa, Marchioness of Waterford* (3 vols., George Allen, 1893).

HARRIS, BARBARA J., 'Women and Politics in Early Tudor England', *Historical Journal*, 33 (June 1992), 259–81.

HARRIS, FRANCES, *A Passion for Government: The Life of Sarah, Duchess of Marlborough* (Oxford: Clarendon Press, 1991).

HARRIS, JOSE, *Private Lives, Public Spirit: Britain 1870–1914* (Oxford: Oxford University Press, 1993).

HARRISON, BRIAN, *Separate Spheres: The Opposition to Women's Suffrage in Britain* (Croom Helm, 1978).

HART, JENIFER, 'Religion and Social Control in Nineteenth-Century Britain', in A. P. Donajgrodzki (ed.), *Social Control in Nineteenth-Century Britain* (Croom Helm, 1977), 108–37.

HEALEY, EDNA, *Lady Unknown: The Life of Angela Burdett-Coutts* (Sidgwick & Jackson, 1978).

HEENEY, BRIAN, *The Women's Movement in the Church of England 1850–1930* (Oxford: Clarendon Press, 1988).

HEESOM, ALAN, ' "Legitimate" *versus* "Illegitimate" Influences: Aristocratic Electioneering in Mid-Victorian Britain', *Parliamentary History*, 7 (1988), 283–305.

HENLEY, DOROTHY, *Rosalind Howard, Countess of Carlisle* (Hogarth Press, 1958).

HEWETT, OSBERT WYNDHAM, *Strawberry Fair: A Biography of Frances, Countess Waldegrave 1821–1879* (John Murray, 1956).

HIBBERT, CHRISTOPHER, *The Court at Windsor: A Domestic History* (Longmans, 1964).

—— *Edward VII: A Portrait* (Allen Lane, 1976).

HILTON, BOYD, *The Age of Atonement: The Influence of Evangelicalism on Social and Economic Thought 1785–1865* (Oxford: Clarendon Press, 1988).

HIMMELFARB, GERTRUDE, *The Idea of Poverty: England in the Early Industrial Age* (Faber & Faber, 1984).

HIRSCHFIELD, CLAIRE, 'A Fractured Faith: Liberal Party Women and the Suffrage Issue in Britain, 1892–1914', *Gender and History*, 2 (1980), 173–97.

The History of 'The Times': ii: *The Tradition Established 1841–1884* (*The Times*, 1939).

HOBSBAWM, ERIC, and RANGER, TERENCE (eds.), *The Invention of Tradition* (Cambridge: Cambridge University Press, 1983).

HOFF, JOAN, 'Gender: A Postmodern Category of Paralysis?', *Women's History Review*, 3 (1994), 149–68.

HOLCOMBE, LEE, 'Victorian Wives and Property: Reform of the Married Women's Property Law, 1857–1882', in Vicinus (ed.), *A Widening Sphere*, 3–28.

—— *Wives and Property: Reform of the Married Women's Property Law in Nineteenth-Century England* (Oxford: Martin Robertson, 1983).

HORN, PAMELA, *Education in Rural England 1800–1914* (Dublin: Gill & Macmillan, 1978).

—— *Ladies of the Manor: Wives and Daughters in Country-House Society 1830–1918* (Stroud: Alan Sutton, 1991).

The Household: or, What Shall We Do with the Ladies? (J. Bain, 1839).

HOW, F. D., *Noble Women of our Time* (Ibister & Co., 1903).

HURT, J. S., *Elementary Schooling and the Working Classes 1860–1918* (Routledge & Kegan Paul, 1979).

HUXLEY, GERVASE, *Lady Elizabeth and the Grosvenors: Life in a Whig Family, 1822–1839* (Oxford: Oxford University Press, 1965).

ISRAEL, KALI A. K., 'Writing inside the Kaleidoscope: Re-Presenting Victorian Women Public Figures', *Gender and History*, 2 (Spring 1990), 40–8.

JALLAND, PAT, *Women, Marriage and Politics, 1860–1914* (Oxford: Oxford University Press, 1988; first published 1986).

JEFFREYS, SHEILA, *The Spinster and her Enemies: Feminism and Sexuality 1890–1930* (Pandora, 1985).

JONES, WILBUR DEVEREUX, *Lord Derby and Victorian Conservatism* (Oxford: Blackwell, 1956).

JUPP, P. J., 'The Landed Elite and Political Authority in Britain, c.1760–1850', *Journal of British Studies*, 29 (Jan. 1990), 53–79.

KEPPEL, SONIA, *The Sovereign Lady: A Life of Elizabeth Vassall, Third Lady Holland, with her Family* (Hamish Hamilton, 1974).

KERBER, LINDA K., 'Separate Spheres, Female Worlds, Woman's Place: The Rhetoric of Women's History', *Journal of American History*, 75 (1988–9), 9–39.

KERR, CECIL, *Cecil, Marchioness of Lothian: A Memoir* (Sands & Co., 1922).

KETTERING, SHARON, 'The Patronage Power of Early Modern French Noblewomen', *Historical Journal*, 32 (Dec. 1989), 817–41.

KUHN, WILLIAM M., 'Ceremonial and Politics: The British Monarchy, 1971–1872', *Journal of British Studies*, 26 (Apr. 1987), 133–62.

—— *Democratic Royalism: The Transformation of the British Monarchy, 1861–1914* (Macmillan, 1996).

LAMBERT, ANGELA, *Unquiet Souls: The Indian Summer of the British Aristocracy 1880–1918* (Macmillan, 1884).

LANT, JEFFREY L., *Insubstantial Pageant: Ceremony and Confusion at Queen Victoria's Court* (Hamish Hamilton, 1979).

LAQUEUR, THOMAS WALTER, *Religion and Respectability: Sunday Schools and Working-Class Culture 1780–1850* (New Haven: Yale University Press, 1976).

LASCH, CHRISTOPHER, *Haven in a Heartless World: The Family Besieged* (New York: Basic Books, 1977).

LEADER, ROBERT EADON (ed.), *The Life and Letters of John Arthur Roebuck* (Edward Arnold, 1897).

LEE, J. M., *Social Leaders and Public Persons: A Study of County Government in Cheshire since 1888* (Oxford: Clarendon Press, 1963).

LESLIE, ANITA, *Edwardians in Love* (Hutchinson, 1972).

LEWIS, JANE, *Women in England 1870–1950: Sexual Divisions and Social Change* (Brighton: Wheatsheaf Books, 1984).

LEWIS, JUDITH SCHNEID, *In the Family Way: Childbearing in the British Aristocracy 1760–1860* (New Brunswick, NJ: Rutgers University Press, 1986).

LIEVEN, D. C. B., *The Aristocracy in Europe 1815–1914* (Basingstoke: Macmillan, 1992).

LINDSAY, W. A., *The Royal Household, 1837–1897* (Kegan Paul, Trench, Trubner & Co., 1898).

LLOYD, CHRISTOPHER, *The Royal Collection* (Sinclair Stevenson, 1992).

LONDONDERRY, LADY (Edith Vane-Tempest-Stewart), *Frances Anne: The Life and Times of Frances Anne, Marchioness of Londonderry and her Husband Charles, Third Marquess of Londonderry* (Macmillan, 1958).

London Gazette

LONGFORD, ELIZABETH, *Victoria R. I.* (Weidenfeld & Nicolson, 1987; first published 1964).

LOW, SAMPSON, *The Charities of London* (1850).

LUMMIS, TREVOR, and MARSH, JAN, *The Woman's Domain: Women and the English Country House* (Viking, 1990).

McBRIDE, THERESA M., *The Domestic Revolution: The Modernization of Household Service in England and France, 1820–1920* (Croom Helm, 1976).

MACCARTHY, DESMOND, and RUSSELL, AGATHA (eds.), *Lady John Russell: A Memoir* (Longmans, Green & Co., 1926; first published 1910).

McCARTHY, JUSTIN, 'The Petticoat in the Politics of England', *Lady's Own Paper*, 9 July 1870.

MACDONAGH, OLIVER, *Jane Austen: Real and Imagined Worlds* (New Haven: Yale University Press, 1991).

McLEOD, HUGH, *Class and Religion in the Late Victorian City* (Croom Helm, 1974).

MACHIN, G. I. T., *Politics and the Churches in Great Britain, 1832 to 1868* (Oxford: Clarendon Press, 1977).

MAGNUS, PHILIP, *King Edward the Seventh* (John Murray, 1964).

MALET, HUGH, *Bridgewater, the Canal Duke, 1736–1803* (Manchester: Manchester University Press, 1977).

MALMGREEN, GAIL (ed.), *Religion in the Lives of English Women, 1760–1930* (Croom Helm, 1986).

MANDLER, PETER, *Aristocratic Government in the Age of Reform: Whigs and Liberals 1830–1852* (Oxford: Clarendon Press, 1990).

MANSEL, PHILIP, *The Court of France 1789–1830* (Cambridge: Cambridge University Press, 1988).

MARTINS, SUSANNA WADE, *A Great Estate at Work: The Holkham Estate and its Inhabitants in the Nineteenth Century* (Cambridge: Cambridge University Press, 1980).

MARX, KARL, 'Sutherland and Slavery; or, The Duchess at Home', *People's Paper*, 12 Mar. 1853, p. 5 cols. a–b.

MASON, PHILIP, *The English Gentleman: The Rise and Fall of an Ideal* (Deutsch, 1982).

MATTHEW, H. C. G., 'Asquith's Political Journalism', *Bulletin of the Institute of Historical Research*, 49 (May 1976), 146–51.

—— *Gladstone, 1809–1874* (Oxford: Oxford University Press, 1988).

—— *Gladstone, 1875–1898* (Oxford: Oxford University Press, 1995).

MAYER, ARNO J., *The Persistence of the Old Regime: Europe to the Great War* (Croom Helm, 1981).

MAYNE, ETHEL COLBURN, *The Life and Letters of Anne Isabella, Lady Noel Byron* (Constable, 1929).

MERTES, KATE, *The English Noble Household, 1250–1600: Good Governance and Politic Rule* (Oxford: Blackwell, 1988).

METTAM, ROGER, *Power and Faction in Louis XIV's France* (Oxford: Blackwell, 1988).

MIDGLEY, CLARE, *Women against Slavery: The British Campaigns, 1780–1870* (Routledge, 1992).

MONTGOMERY, MAUREEN E., *'Gilded Prostitution': Status, Money and Transatlantic Marriages, 1870–1914* (Routledge, 1989).

MOORE, D. C., 'The Landed Aristocracy', in G. E. Mingay (ed.), *The Victorian Countryside* (2 vols., Routledge & Kegan Paul, 1981), ii. 367–82.

—— *The Politics of Deference: A Study of the Mid-Nineteenth-Century English Political System* (Hassocks: Harvester, 1976).

Morning Post

NEAD, LYNDA, *Myths of Sexuality: Representations of Women in Victorian Britain* (Oxford: Basil Blackwell, 1988).

NEVILL, GUY, *Exotic Groves: A Portrait of Lady Dorothy Nevill* (Salisbury: Michael Russell, 1984).

OBELKEVICH, JAMES, *Religion and Society: South Lindsay 1825–1875* (Oxford: Clarendon Press, 1976).

O'GORMAN, FRANK, 'Campaign Rituals and Ceremonies: The Social Meaning of Elections in England, 1780–1860', *Past and Present*, 135 (May 1992), 79–115.

—— *Voters, Patrons and Parties: The Unreformed Electorate of Hanoverian England, 1734–1832* (Oxford: Clarendon Press, 1989).

OLNEY, R. J., 'The Politics of Land', in G. E. Mingay (ed.), *The Victorian Countryside* (2 vols., Routledge & Kegan Paul, 1981), i. 58–70.

OMAN, CAROLA, *The Gascoyne Heiress: The Life and Diaries of Frances Mary Gascoyne-Cecil, 1802–1839* (Hodder & Stoughton, 1968).

ONE OF HER MAJESTY'S SERVANTS, *The Private Life of Queen Victoria* (C. Arthur Pearson, 1897).

PARKER, ROSZIKA, *The Subversive Stitch: Embroidery and the Making of the Feminine* (Women's Press, 1984).

PARKINSON, C. NORTHCOTE, *Parkinson's Law, or The Pursuit of Progress* (John Murray, 1961; first published 1957).

PARRY, JONATHAN, *The Rise and Fall of Liberal Government in Victorian Britain* (New Haven: Yale University Press, 1993).

PECK, LINDA LEVY, *Court Patronage and Corruption in Early Stuart England* (Unwin Hyman, 1990).

PERKIN, JOAN, *Women and Marriage in Nineteenth-Century England* (Routledge, 1989).

PETERSON, M. JEANNE, *Family, Love and Work in the Lives of Victorian Gentlewomen* (Bloomington, Ind.: Indiana University Press, 1989).

—— 'No Angels in the House: The Victorian Myth and the Paget Women', *American Historical Review*, 89/3 (June 1984), 677–708.

—— 'The Victorian Governess: Status Incongruence in Family and Society', in Vicinus (ed.), *Suffer and be Still*, 3–19.

PIERSON, JOAN, *The Real Lady Byron* (Hale, 1992).

POOVEY, MARY, *Uneven Developments: The Ideological Work of Gender in Mid-Victorian England* (Chicago: University of Chicago Press, 1988).

POPE, BARBARA CORRADO, 'Angels in the Devil's Workshop: Leisured and Charitable Women in Nineteenth-Century England and France', in Renate Bridenthal and Claudia Koonz (eds.), *Becoming Visible: Women in European History* (Boston: Houghton Mifflin, 1977), 296–324.

PORT, MICHAEL (ed.), *The Houses of Parliament* (New Haven: Yale University Press, 1976).

POWIS, JONATHAN, *Aristocracy* (Oxford: Blackwell, 1984).

PREST, JOHN, 'Gladstone and Russell', *Transactions of the Royal Historical Society*, 5th ser. 16 (1966), 43–63.

—— *Lord John Russell* (Macmillan, 1972).

PRICE, RICHARD, 'Historiography, Narrative and the Nineteenth Century', *Journal of British Studies*, 35 (Apr. 1996), 220–56.

PROCHASKA, FRANK K., 'Charity Bazaars in Nineteenth-Century England', *Journal of British Studies*, 16 (Spring 1977), 62–84.

—— *Royal Bounty: The Making of a Welfare Monarchy* (New Haven: Yale University Press, 1995).

—— *Women and Philanthropy in Nineteenth-Century England* (Oxford: Clarendon Press, 1980).

—— 'Women in English Philanthropy, 1790–1830', *International Review of Social History*, 19 (1974), 426–45.

PUGH, MARTIN, *The Tories and the People 1880–1935* (Oxford: Blackwell, 1985).

PURVIS, JUNE (ed.), *Women's History: Britain 1850–1945* (UCL Press, 1995).

REID, MICHAELA, *Ask Sir James* (Hodder & Stoughton, 1987).

RENDALL, JANE, *The Origins of Modern Feminism: Women in Britain, France and the United States, 1780–1860* (Macmillan, 1985).

RICHARDS, ERIC, *The Leviathan of Wealth: The Sutherland Fortune in the Industrial Revolution* (Routledge & Kegan Paul, 1973).

RIDLEY, JASPER, *Lord Palmerston* (Panther, 1972; first published 1970).

RILEY, DENISE, *'Am I that Name?': Feminism and the Category of 'Women' in History* (Basingstoke: Macmillan, 1988).

RITCHIE, L. A., 'The Floating Church of Loch Sunart', *Records of the Scottish Church History Society*, 22 (1985), 159–73.

ROBERTS, DAVID, *Paternalism in Early Victorian England* (New Brunswick, NJ: Rutgers University Press, 1979).

ROBINSON, JOHN MARTIN, *The English Country Estate* (Century, 1988).

The Royal Blue Book and Court Guide

RUBINSTEIN, W. D., 'The End of "Old Corruption" in Britain, 1780–1860', *Past and Present*, 101 (Nov. 1983), 55–86.

—— (ed.), *Elites and the Wealthy in Modern British History: Essays in Social and Economic History* (Brighton: Harvester Press, 1987).

SCOTT, JOAN WALLACH, *Gender and the Politics of History* (New York: Columbia University Press, 1988).

SHKOLNIK, ESTHER, *Leading Ladies: A Study of Eight Late Victorian and Edwardian Political Wives* (New York: Garland, 1987).

SHORTER, EDWARD, *A History of Women's Bodies* (New York: Basic Books, 1982).

Sketches of Her Majesty's Household; Interspersed with Historical Notes, Political Comments, and Critical Remarks, etc. (William Strange, 1848).

SKLAR, KATHRYN KISH, *Catherine Beecher: A Study in American Domesticity* (New Haven: Yale University Press, 1973).

SMITH, CECIL WOODHAM, *Queen Victoria, Her Life and Times 1819–1861* (Hamish Hamilton, 1972).

SOMERSET, ANNE, *Ladies in Waiting: From the Tudors to the Present Day* (Weidenfeld & Nicolson, 1984).

SPRING, DAVID, *The English Landed Estate in the Nineteenth Century: Its Administration* (Baltimore: Johns Hopkins University Press, 1963).

—— *European Landed Elites in the Nineteenth Century* (Baltimore: Johns Hopkins University Press, 1977).

STEELE, E. D., *Palmerston and Liberalism, 1855–1865* (Cambridge: Cambridge University Press, 1991).

STONE, LAWRENCE, *The Family, Sex and Marriage in England 1500–1800* (Weidenfeld & Nicolson, 1977).

—— and STONE, JEANNE C. FAWTIER, *An Open Elite? England 1540–1880* (Oxford: Clarendon Press, 1984).

STUART, DENIS, *Dear Duchess: Millicent, Duchess of Sutherland, 1867–1955* (Victor Gollancz, 1982).

SUMMERS, ANNE, 'A Home from Home—Women's Philanthropic Work in the Nineteenth Century', in Sandra Burman (ed.), *Fit Work for Women* (Croom Helm, 1979), 33–63.

—— 'Pride and Prejudice: Ladies and Nurses in the Crimean War', *History Workshop*, 16 (Autumn 1983), 33–56.

SURTEES, VIRGINIA, *A Beckford Inheritance: The Lady Lincoln Scandal* (Salisbury: Michael Russell, 1977).

—— *Charlotte Canning: Lady-in-Waiting to Queen Victoria and Wife of the First Viceroy of India, 1817–1861* (John Murray, 1975).

—— *The Ludovisi Goddess: The Life of Louisa Lady Ashburton* (Salisbury: Michael Russell, 1984).

TAYLOR, CLARE, *British and American Abolitionists. An Episode in Transatlantic Understanding* (Edinburgh: Edinburgh University Press, 1974).

THOMAS, DONALD, *Cardigan: Hero of Balaclava* (Routledge & Kegan Paul, 1974).

THOMPSON, DOROTHY, *Queen Victoria: Gender and Power* (Virago, 1990).

THOMPSON, F. M. L., 'The End of a Great Estate', *Economic History Review*, 8 (1955), 36–52.

—— *English Landed Society in the Nineteenth Century* (Routledge & Kegan Paul, 1971; first published 1963).

—— 'English Landed Society in the Twentieth Century. I. Property: Collapse and Survival', *Transactions of the Royal Historical Society*, 5th ser. 40 (1990), 1–24.

—— *The Rise of Respectable Society: A Social History of Victorian Britain, 1830–1900* (Fontana, 1988).

THORNE, R. G. (ed.), *The House of Commons 1790–1820* (4 vols., The History of Parliament Trust, Secker & Warburg, 1986).

TILLY, LOUISE A., and SCOTT, JOAN W., *Women, Work, and Family* (New York: Holt, Rinehart & Winston, 1978).

TILLYARD, STELLA, *Aristocrats: Caroline, Emily, Louisa and Sarah Lennox, 1740–1832* (Chatto & Windus, 1994).

The Times

TOMKINS, ISAAC [pseud. Henry Brougham, Lord Brougham and Vaux], *Thoughts upon the Aristocracy of England* (no publisher, 1835).

TOSH, JOHN, 'Domesticity and Manliness in the Victorian Middle Class: The Family of Edward White Benson', in Michael Roper and John Tosh (eds.), *Manful Assertions: Masculinities in Britain since 1800* (Routledge, 1991), 44–73.

TRUMBACH, RANDOLPH, *The Rise of the Egalitarian Family: Aristocratic Kinship and Domestic Relations* (New York: Academic Press, 1978).

Truth

ULRICH, LAUREL THATCHER, *Good Wives: Image and Reality in the Lives of Women in Northern New England 1650–1750* (New York: Knopf, 1980).

Women's Work and the Dairy Industry c.1740–1840', *Past and Present*, 130 (Feb. 1991), 142–69.

VICINUS, MARTHA, *Independent Women: Work and Community for Single Women, 1850–1920* (Virago, 1985).

—— (ed.), *Suffer and be Still: Women in the Victorian Age* (Methuen, 1980; first published 1972).

—— (ed.), *A Widening Sphere: Changing Roles of Victorian Women* (Bloomington, Ind.: Indiana University Press, 1980; 1st pub. 1977).

VICKERY, AMANDA, 'Golden Age to Separate Spheres? A Review of the Categories and Chronology of English Women's History', *Historical Journal*, 36 (1993), 383–414.

VILLIERS, MARJORIE, *The Grand Whiggery* (John Murray, 1939).

VINCENT, JOHN, *The Formation of the Liberal Party 1857–1868* (Constable, 1966).

WALKER, LINDA, 'Party Political Women: A Comparative Study of Liberal Women and the Primrose League, 1890–1914', in Jane Rendall (ed.), *Equal or Different: Women's Politics 1800–1914* (Oxford: Blackwell, 1987), 165–275.

WALKOWITZ, JUDITH R., *City of Dreadful Delight: Narratives of Sexual Danger in Late-Victorian London* (Virago, 1992).

—— *Prostitution and Victorian Society: Women, Class and the State* (Cambridge: Cambridge University Press, 1980).

WALL, ALISON, 'Elizabethan Precept and Feminine Practice: The Thynne Family of Longleat', *History*, 75 (Feb. 1990), 23–38.

WARD, JENNIFER C., *English Noblewomen in the Later Middle Ages* (Harlow: Longman, 1992).

WASSON, E. A., 'The House of Commons, 1660–1945: Parliamentary Families and the Political Elite', *English Historical Review*, 106 (July 1991), 635–51.

WATSON, VERA, *The Queen at Home: An Intimate Account of the Social and Domestic Life of Queen Victoria's Court* (W. H. Allen, 1952).

WEIGALL, LADY ROSE, 'Our Friends in the Village', *Macmillan's Magazine*, 20 (Oct. 1869), 519–27.

WEINTRAUB, STANLEY, *Victoria: Biography of a Queen* (Unwin Hyman, 1987).

WELTER, BARBARA, 'The Cult of True Womanhood', *American Quarterly*, 18 (1966), 155–74.

WIENER, MARTIN J., *English Culture and the Decline of the Industrial Spirit, 1850–1980* (Cambridge: Cambridge University Press, 1981).

WILENTZ, SEAN (ed.), *Rites of Power: Symbolism, Ritual and Politics since the Middle Ages* (Philadelphia: University of Pennsylvania Press, 1985).

YATES, W. N., ' "Bells and Smells": London, Brighton and South Coast Religion Reconsidered', *Southern History*, 5 (1983), 122–53.

Index

Items marked * have an entry in the biographical appendix